WHITMAN COLLEGE LIBRARY

WITHDR

REBELLION
IN THE
BORDERLANDS

REBELLION IN THE BORDERLANDS

ANARCHISM AND THE PLAN OF SAN DIEGO, 1904–1923

BY JAMES A. SANDOS

University of Oklahoma Press : Norman and London

Text and jacket design by Bill Cason.

Sandos, James A.
　Rebellion in the borderlands : anarchism and the Plan of San
Diego, 1904–1923 / by James A. Sandos.—1st ed.
　　p.　cm.
　Includes bibliographical references and index.
　ISBN 0-8061-2433-4 (alk. paper)
　　1. Lower Rio Grande Valley (Tex.)—History. 2. San Diego Region
(Tex.)—History. 3. Flores Magón, Ricardo, 1873–1922—Influence.
4. Anarchism—Texas—History—20th century. 5. Mexico—History—
Revolution, 1910–1920.　I. Title.
F392.R5S26　1992
976.4'463—dc20　　　　　　　　　　　　　　　　　　　　　91-50870
　　　　　　　　　　　　　　　　　　　　　　　　　　　　　　　CIP

The paper in this book meets the guidelines for permanence and durability of the Committee on Production Guidelines for Book Longevity of the Council on Library Resources, Inc.

Copyright ©1992 by the University of Oklahoma Press, Norman, Publishing Division of the University. All rights reserved. Manufactured in the U.S.A. First edition.

For Eleanor Birkland Sandos,
who always encouraged my curiosity

CONTENTS

Illustrations List	ix
Acknowledgments	xi
A Note on Terminology	xiii
Introduction	xv
Abbreviations	2
Chapter 1. Becoming an Anarchist	3
Chapter 2. A Political Revolution	24
Chapter 3. A Contradiction in Terms	46
Chapter 4. South Texas	63
Chapter 5. The Plan of San Diego	79
Chapter 6. Assigning Blame	101
Chapter 7. The Plan of San Diego: Followers and Adherents	125
Chapter 8. The Plan of San Diego: International Connections and Confrontations	141
Chapter 9. Repressing Dissent and the Plan of San Diego	154
Chapter 10. Conclusion	172
Notes	178
Essay on Sources	205
Bibliography	211
Index	225

ILLUSTRATIONS

Figures

1. Poster of Anarchism	19
2. Poster of Liberation	53
3. Cartoon of U.S. relations with Mexican factions	54
4. Norias ranch house, 1915	90
5. Dead raiders at Norias, 1915	91
6. Plan of San Diego banner, 1915	93
7. Plan of San Diego handbill, 1915	95
8. Fresnos pump station, 1915	96
9. S. S. Dodds's burned Ford Roadster, 1915	97
10. Poster of Direct Action	99
11. Luis de la Rosa, 1914	102
12. Train wreck, Tandy's Station, 1915	104
13. U.S. Army troops entrenched along the Rio Grande, 1915–1916	105
14. U.S. Army troops, Rio Grande, 1915–1916	106
15. Mexicans and Americans on the Brownsville bridge, November 1915. Venustiano Carranza, center left, with glasses and full beard; behind his right shoulder, General Emiliano P. Nafarrate	123
16. Poster of U.S. government closure of anarchist newspapers, 1916	136
17. Ricardo and Enríque Flores Magón	139
18. Cartoon, "For the Love of Mike, Raid Us!"	158

Graph

Percentage of population by origin, Lower Rio Grande Valley, 1900–1920	65

Maps

1. Approximate location and extent of irrigated land, Lower Rio Grande Valley, 1900 and 1920	67
2. Growth of the railroad in South Texas, 1880–1920	68

Tables

1. *Regeneración* distribution by leading destination (subscribers and papers), November 22, 1915 — 59
2. American Socialist Press subscribing to *Regeneración*, 1915, by circulation — 60
3. Select Anarchist Press in America subscribing to *Regeneración*, 1914–1916 — 61
4. Total population and population by county, Lower Rio Grande Valley, 1900–1920 — 66
5. Increase in irrigated land, Lower Rio Grande Valley and Texas, 1909–1919 — 69
6. Value of farm property, Lower Rio Grande Valley, 1900–1920 — 70
7. Increase in capital invested in irrigation, Lower Rio Grande Valley and Texas, 1900–1920 — 70

ACKNOWLEDGMENTS

Thanking people for the help they have given me is a pleasure, but I have been with this project for so many years that knowing where to begin is difficult. I expressed my thoughts on the Plan of San Diego most recently in my 1978 doctoral dissertation; the present project, however, contains no more than a third of that material, almost all of which has been radically revised. With a few exceptions then, I want to acknowledge assistance received since 1978.

Past and present members of the History Department of the University of Redlands have been particularly helpful: Richard Gillam got me reading in U.S. labor history and David Tharp initiated me in anarchist thought. James Joll in London introduced me, through correspondence, to Dr. Haia Shpayer-Makov and Hermia Oliver, both of whom contributed to fleshing out my understanding of William C. Owen. Joll also urged me to write Paul Avrich, which resulted in an ongoing correspondence that has enriched my project. Avrich's scholarship suggested a way to tell the story of Mexican anarchists in the United States that sought to go beyond conventional stereotypes and to portray the complexity of their lives.

In addition to Avrich, Félix D. Almaráz, Jr., read and commented helpfully on an earlier draft of the manuscript, while David Weber offered thoughtful suggestions for strengthening the introduction. Satomi Kurosu translated the memoirs of a Japanese who participated in the Plan of San Diego; Adrienne Morgan drew the maps and composed the graph.

The personnel of the repositories in Mexico and the United States cited in my bibliography made possible my access to the wide range of sources that inform this study. Sandi Richey at the Armacost Library of the University of Redlands made Inter-Library Loan do the impossible in securing obscure, out-of-print works.

Financial support for this work has been hard to come by, but I thank Paul Avrich, Woodrow Borah, and John Womack, Jr., all of whom wrote on my behalf to various agencies without success. However, the University of Redlands Personnel Committee provided some summer research money in 1984 and 1985, including an award from the John Randolph Haynes and Dora Haynes Foundation.

There are those who deserve a special abrazo for their contribution to developing my insight in this project: Tony Zúñiga taught me the importance of standing up for myself in the fifth grade; José Cuello spent many a Friday afternoon in graduate school discussing borderlands history; Carlos and Ricardo Anzaldúa helped me understand South Texas; Tom Dublin showed me the relevance of the individual U.S. census schedules for this project; and José Limón kept faith in me. My wife Tish encouraged me more than she knows. I dedicate this book to my mother, for the reason given on the dedication page.

Finally, to those readers who have a project that has taken too long to bring to term, who have earned the public and/or private criticism of advisors and peers for delay, who have even begun to doubt themselves and their own ability to complete their work because it is easy to become discouraged and to give up when others say no, to you I say: persevere. Stay with it. *Por final, vale le pena.*

James A. Sandos

Redlands, California

A NOTE ON TERMINOLOGY

Although the cartographer Martin Waldseemüller in the sixteenth century named the lands of the whole hemisphere for the Italian navigator who coasted some of them,[1] we who live between the Great Lakes and the Rio Grande have taken to our exclusive use the term "American." The Spanish word *estadounidense* is more accurate since it refers to a citizen of the United States.[2] It is an exact and nonpejorative word, free of the implication that not being an American is to be unfortunate, if not inferior. But here in the "U.S.A.," the term American speaks culturally to Anglo-Saxon origins, to whiteness as opposed to other colors, to those whose accounts left in English constitute the bulk of the historical record. At some level in popular culture, American and Anglo are synonymous, the vast array of non-Anglo citizens and Americans notwithstanding. Such a culturally specific word then must be used with care.

The subject of my inquiry involves a study of people who were American in terms of their citizenship but not always in terms of Anglo culture or language. Anglos saw them and they saw themselves as "Mexicans," a hopelessly imprecise term that encompassed both native-born and naturalized citizens, itinerant Mexican nationals, and long-term resident aliens. In short, "Mexican" included all those of Mexican ancestry.

Place and time are also important to my study and affect my vocabulary. The primary area is South Texas and the border it shares with the Mexican state of Tamaulipas; the time is the period during the first two decades of the twentieth century. Since my language needs to be more precise without being unduly cumbersome, I have adopted some conventions. I use the term "American" essentially in its Anglo sense. When referring to the American dream I will make clear the distinction. I use "Mexican" to refer to Mexican nationals—where I can do so with precision—as well as to the non-Anglo cultural mix in which the Spanish language and Mexican customs predominated. I use "Tejano" to denote U.S. citizens of Mexican ancestry from Texas. Tejanos range from those who participated actively in the American political arrangements of their era to those who actively conspired to subvert that authority.

Followers of political factions I have designated in the Spanish manner, applying the appropriate *ista* ending to the proper noun. Thus, a follower of General Francisco "Pancho" Villa was a *Villista,* an adherent of the writings of Ricardo Flores Magón a *Floresmagonista,* and so forth. The economy of this construction in English is obvious. Residents of Los Angeles even today are called Angelenos. I have wrestled with using the term "Chicano" and have decided to use it only when referring to the community of Mexican ancestry from the 1960s forward. While some members of that community called themselves Chicanos as early as the turn of the century, the historical usefulness of the term has been undermined by changing usage over the past thirty years. For my inquiry, then, I shall employ less ambiguous terms.

Finally, while this study is informed by archival research in Mexico and the United States, I have tried, wherever possible, to cite generally accessible secondary titles in English and Spanish to facilitate further reading.

INTRODUCTION

This book explores a little known but significant episode in the history of the United States–Mexico borderlands during the epochal Mexican Revolution, 1910 to 1920. The focus of my inquiry is the well-known Mexican activist Ricardo Flores Magón, who lived in exile in the United States from 1904 until his death in 1922, and his followers, called *Floresmagonistas*.

Ricardo Flores Magón has had an important but unappreciated impact both within the United States and upon the events we now call the Mexican Revolution. Ricardo[1] gradually enlarged his political attacks to encompass economic exploitation and ethnic discrimination against Mexicans and Mexican Americans in the southwestern United States. His anarchist thinking lay behind the dramatic uprising of the downtrodden known as the Plan of San Diego, Texas. The Plan erupted in 1915, in the lower Rio Grande valley, and was suppressed two years later. Its influence, however, extended far beyond northern Mexico and South Texas and far beyond the immediate time period in which it occurred. It brought both countries to the brink of war in the summer of 1916, deciding U.S. policy at the time, and it continued to color official U.S. attitudes toward Mexico for seventy years.

The story of the Plan of San Diego involves questions such as why men and women rebel, who fights and who waits, what is risked and what sought when a segment of workers seeks redress of grievance. How does ideology help the worker to translate personal discontent into universal discontent and social consciousness? A closer look at the Plan reveals its varied supporters: domestic partisans included Mexicans, Mexican Americans, and African Americans; foreign participants included Mexican revolutionary factions, as well as German and Japanese freelances and operatives. American Bureau of Investigation agents saw Teutonic and Yellow Peril manipulation of the movement just as Anglo residents of the valley saw "bad Mexicans" versus "good Mexicans" as the real culprits. The focus on these exotic elements associated with the Plan blinded Americans to its roots in domestic discontent. A consideration of the extent of grass-roots versus external support for the movement is critical in analyzing the Plan. Answering the questions posed by the Plan involves discussion of the nature of the Mexican Revolution itself, not only in terms of its status as a foreign—versus domestic-made—phenomenon, but also in terms of what happened to radicalism in the Revolution.

The Plan of San Diego terrified Anglos in the valley that summer of 1915 because it sought to liberate Texas from American rule by exterminating all North American males over the age of sixteen.[2] The Plan, however, sought other goals as well. At the time, the U.S. Bureau of Investigation recognized in it elements of anarchist thought, which it traced back to Los Angeles, and to Flores Magón, his Mexican Liberal Party (PLM), and his newspaper, *Regeneración*.[3] Meanwhile, on rumor, a posse in South Texas attacked a ranch owned by Aniceto Pizaña. If, as they thought, *Regeneración* was the official newspaper of the Plan of San Diego,[4] then the discovery of Pizaña's subscription by local authorities signified to them ipso facto that he adhered to the Plan. Since they also found copies of a handbill—probably the anarchist PLM Manifesto of September 23, 1911—they simply regarded it as further proof of his involvement in a conspiracy.

But had Aniceto Pizaña's anger carried him to the extreme of waging war against a society in which he had succeeded? Was he, a Tejano, set upon without provocation by an Anglo posse that found him suspicious largely because of his ethnicity? Or had he, under the influence of the PLM, conspired to overthrow civil authority, and had the Anglo posse, as part of a reasonable police response, justifiably sought him out? Whatever Pizaña's personal truth, the Plan of San Diego must be understood in the context both of the Mexican Revolution and of the economic development of the lower Rio Grande valley. Following the posse's attack upon his ranch, Pizaña became a powerful leader of paramilitary forces that visited death and destruction upon valley residents to such an extent that he and his companion-in-arms, Luis de la Rosa, became the subjects of tense international dialogue between the Woodrow Wilson administration and the incipient government of Venustiano Carranza. Ultimately, the faction that emerged victorious from Mexico's civil war would be that which could secure the frontier, quell strife along the border, and deal effectively with Pizaña and De la Rosa. In short, the faction that could deliver to Wilson security on America's southern border would win Wilson's permission to govern Mexico.

The most radical ideology in the Mexican Revolution found much of its expression not there but in the United States. The Department of Justice found the links between Flores Magón and Pizaña and concluded those links revealed conspiracy between the Plan of San Diego and most of the suspected enemies of the United States, foreign and domestic. But what if the relationships were more complicated than that perception? Is it possible that Mexican anarchism, in exile in the United States, played perhaps its strongest hand during the Mexican Revolution not in Mexico but in South Texas? And why does the nagging doubt linger that the rebellion of Pizaña and all of its consequences could have been prevented?

A substantial body of literature suggests that radicalism was developing along similar lines in Western Europe and America at the turn of the twentieth century. American historians have portrayed radicalism as introduced and sustained by foreigners and concentrated in the urban centers and factories of the eastern United States.[5] Paul Avrich has qualified that picture by demonstrating interaction between European and American radicals and by revealing significant native-born adherents.[6] Here I want to explore Mexico's connection with frontier radicalism in America and relate it to the Mexican Revolution, 1910 to 1920. To study either subject on its own, as part of an individual national history, distorts to the point of loss the mutual past of both countries. Nonetheless, trying to recover historical memory in two cultures is a daunting task, especially since pertinent materials have been widely scattered.

The flexibility of the concept of Borderlands history, with its traditional concerns about culture contact and conflict along frontiers, opens possibilities for investigation into the history of both the United States and Mexico at multiple levels. I have done extensive research in local, regional, and national archives in both the United States and Mexico, focusing on political, economic, and social dimensions of this topic. I have combed the records of the special agents of the Departments of Justice and State, as well as the more conventional records, to establish the Wilson administration's perspective. To balance that perspective, I have delved into the politics of the Carranza faction in extenso to determine Carranza's actual relationship to the Plan and the relationship of his border commanders to the movement. Local police records help to reveal the nature of Plan adherents in northern Mexico.

I read widely in anarchist thought, as articulated both in Europe and the United States, before I turned to Ricardo Flores Magón's work. I have explored his relationship to American radicals to illuminate more fully the nature of his particular form of anarchism and to illustrate his changing political tactics. Using basic semiotic analysis, I have examined the handbills and circulars generated by the adherents of the Plan of San Diego and the poster and graphic art of *Regeneración* to illustrate how Mexican and Mexican American anarchists communicated with one another.

Through several sources, I have tried to recover a sense of who the individual Mexican and Mexican American anarchists were and how they lived. A subscriber list for *Regeneración*, the only one known to date, was obtained by the Post Office Department in 1915. It provided an opportunity for further inquiry. I collected the names of subscribers in Los Angeles and South Texas, including Brownsville, and then attempted to identify them through the 1910 individual census schedules. I succeeded in finding 27.0 percent of the Los Angeles subscribers, 27.9 percent of those in South Texas, and 38.9 percent of the Brownsville subscription takers. Through the census and through city directories, supplemented with other sources, I have been able to describe Mexican and Mexican American anarchists in a detail not previously possible. The picture that emerges is one that challenges prevailing stereotypes of conservatism or complacency in the community of Mexican ancestry in the United States.

As we shall see, the relationship between anarchists in the United States and Mexico is complex. If Floresmagonista thought and propaganda did in fact lie behind the Plan of San Diego, then we must determine how Ricardo Flores Magón came to be an anarchist. And to do that we must begin in Chicago in 1886, at the Haymarket.

REBELLION IN THE BORDERLANDS

ABBREVIATIONS

AGN	Archivo General de la Nación
AGNL	Archivo General del Estado de Nuevo León
AMG	Archivo de Manuel González
AREM	Archivo de la Secretaría de Relaciones Exteriores de México
AVC	Archivo de Venustiano Carranza
BL	Bancroft Library
DHRM	*Documentos Historicos de la Revolución Mexicana*
doc	Document, docket in Mexican Claims
FWFRC	Fort Worth Federal Records Center
Gray-Lane Files	Records of the United States Commissioners of the American and Mexican Joint Commission, 1916
INAH	Instituto Nacional de Antropología e Historia
INS	Immigration and Naturalization Service
LC	Library of Congress
LIRC	*Labor Internacional de la Revolución Constitucionalista*
LNFRC	Laguna Niguel Federal Records Center
M, Micr	Microfilm
Mexican Claims	Records of the Special Claims Commission, United States and Mexico, Created under the Claims Convention of September 10, 1923
MID	Military Intelligence Division
r	reel
RAGO	Records of the Adjutant General's Office
RG	Record Group
SNF	Straight Numerical File
STC	Silvestre Terrazas Collection
TSA	Texas State Archives
USNA	United States National Archives
UTA	University of Texas Archives, Austin
WNRC	Washington National Records Center

CHAPTER 1

BECOMING AN ANARCHIST

>Written rights, no more than jottings, are cruel jokes upon the people, mummified in constitutions.
>
>Praxedis Guerrero[1]

Ricardo Flores Magón, born of a mestiza mother and an Indian father in the Southern Mexican state of Oaxaca in 1873 or 1874, played the middle sibling role among three sons. His older brother Jesús became a lawyer and later found acceptance and success among the reform elements in Porfirio Díaz's Mexico. Enríque, three or four years younger than Ricardo, lionized Ricardo and joined with him in a life of rejection and opposition, first against Díaz and later against any form of tyranny.[2] The younger boys were approximately thirteen and ten respectively when the anarchist incident in Chicago impressed itself upon them. It would change their lives.

The struggle between labor and capital in Chicago in 1886 focused primarily on the issue of the eight-hour work day. Conflicts between police and strikers had become common, and, after some strikers had been shot, several prolabor groups came together at the Haymarket on the evening of May 4 to protest. The speakers were anarchists, and some of those in the crowd were foreign-born, responding to the call for the assembly printed in the newspaper *Arbeiter Zeitung*. Police augmented their reserves against possible calls to violence. Even the mayor, Carter H. Harrison, stopped at the Haymarket to listen, prepared to silence any speakers who advocated violence. Finding the proceedings innocuous, he left. At the police station he told Inspector John Bonfield that "nothing had occurred yet or was likely to occur to require interference."[3]

Nonetheless, Bonfield ignored the mayor's instructions and sent nearly two hundred police to disperse the crowd. At that point someone hurled a bomb into police ranks and the police responded with indiscriminate gunfire—killing and wounding civilians as well as some of their own. Officials blamed the result of what had been an unprovoked police riot on the orators exhorting the workers. Police quickly arrested eight anarchists and charged them with conspiracy to commit murder. Six of the accused had not been present when the bomb was thrown and three of them had not been at the Haymarket that night. But fear pervaded public sentiment, a fear of anarchist conspiracy that police and press exploited alike. Of the eight arrested, one committed suicide, four were executed in 1887, and three went to prison. In 1893, Governor John P. Altgeld reviewed the case, declared the trial a travesty, and unconditionally pardoned the survivors.[4]

The Haymarket tragedy became an important cause to anarchists worldwide, and the anniversary of the executions on November 11, 1887, became an international day of remembrance. In Mexico, those events captured the attention of the younger Flores Magón brothers. Although theirs was not an anarchist household, their father read the account to his wife; he thought that the men died for their principles and had been martyrs for the cause of the poor. A year or more later, at his mother's side and again listening to his father read something in memoriam to the Chicago anarchists, Enríque began thinking about them in terms of his own country. He wondered "how the bodies of the hanged men must have looked, dangling to and fro from the ends of ropes fastened to the branches of a tall, leafy oak, as men are hanged in Mexico." Enríque thought their ideals immortal and connected their sacrifice in the United States to the struggle in Mexico against Díaz.[5] By the time of Altgeld's pardon, the teenaged Ricardo had already been arrested and imprisoned for demonstrating against Díaz's fourth reelection in 1892.[6]

Although the younger Flores Magón brothers did not begin political life as radicals, they brought to their endeavors two valuable and intangible possessions: a sound education, including study of the law, and the courage of their convictions. They began by seeking political reform of Mexico's ills. Díaz had assumed power behind a slogan of no reelection, but he had come to violate that principle and had altered the constitution to get away with it. To the Flores Magón brothers, the original Constitution of 1857 needed to be restored. Rule by law, not individual whim, should prevail.

The Flores Magón brothers derived much of their initial impetus to political reform from the legacy of Benito Juárez and the Liberal movement. Juárez and his followers had produced the quintessential Liberal document, the 1857 Constitution. Liberalism, as defined in legislation and its constitution, sought abolition of special privileges—particularly those held by the Church and the Army—as well as creation of a class of freeholding agriculturalists, rule by law, and a decentralized, federal political structure. Ironically, the most efficient means to free individuals from the shackles that bound them to a Spanish past was through a strong, central government that epitomized that past. Thus, the struggle for personal freedom risked tyranny as its price. Díaz came to power as a Liberal, but, when in office, he began to behave like a Conservative. He slowly concentrated power in his personalist state, allowed land holdings to be consolidated under the power of the rich to promote modernization, repressed individual rights when they conflicted with his interests, and placed himself above the law by changing it to suit himself. Despite all this, he proved wily and popular.[7] By 1900 Díaz had held power for twenty-four years, and no end to his rule could be seen.

August 1900 proved propitious for Díaz's latent opponents. On August 7,

Ricardo and Jesús Flores Magón produced the first issue of *Regeneración*.[8] It began as a law review for Mexico City's School of Jurisprudence from which Jesús later secured a law degree. Ricardo and Enríque dropped out before graduating because of their increasing involvement in political opposition and the need to support their now widowed mother.[9] The journal was initially technical and seemed innocuous to Díaz's agents.

On August 30, in San Luis Potosí, Camilo Arriaga issued a manifesto, "Invitation to the Liberal Party," calling for the creation of Liberal clubs across the country. The clubs would in turn hold a national convention in San Luis Potosí in February 1901. Arriaga did not know it, but he had invited the opposition to go public in its struggle against the dictator. By the time of the convention, nearly fifty clubs or reading and discussion groups had emerged.[10] Ricardo Flores Magón responded, and on December 31, *Regeneración* became "An Independent Journal of Combat," marking its debut as a political organ.[11]

Arriaga, scion of a wealthy silver-mining family and convener of the First Liberal Congress, represented upper-class and upper-status intellectual elites dissatisfied with Díaz. Arriaga had been educated in Mexico's finest schools, had become an engineer, and had traveled to France. He combined the grace and erudition of a man whose education had been based upon the leisure that wealth made possible. A pale complexion, high forehead, and aquiline nose testified to the European exclusivity of his ancestry—a badge of elite honor signifying no discernible Indian blood in the line.

Arriaga, however, had made contact, at least by mail, with many low-status intellectuals whose origins lay in poor agricultural or working-class backgrounds. Arriaga read widely and voraciously, including socialist and anarchist tracts that he brought back from France as part of his remarkable personal library. He generously shared his collection with many of these people. Yet Arriaga's library was not the only source of radical literature in Díaz's Mexico. Such literature was published cheaply by the Spanish-owned Editorial Maucci; a market for it had developed because of the extensive growth of anarchism in Mexico in the late nineteenth century.[12] By 1900, Ricardo Flores Magón had read a great deal of it.

Arriaga called the Liberal convention to denounce Díaz's increasingly favorable treatment of the Roman Catholic Church. Liberals historically had stripped the church of privilege and land in the convulsive religious wars that had shaken the country from 1855–1867. Hence, Díaz's new amicability toward the church offended Arriaga and his associates. When Liberals gathered in San Luis Potosí in February 1901, however, Ricardo Flores Magón decided to try and convert them from priest baiters to anti-Díaz militants.[13] He wanted to go public with a political agenda.

Criticizing the Church was relatively safe; criticizing Díaz was not. As the delegates participated in their six-day convention, federal troops marched in the streets outside—an ominous show of force. Inside, Ricardo Flores Magón represented low-status intellectuals who had secured their education by their own work. His Indian features, strong voice, keen intelligence, and caustic, scathing wit impressed the assembly. In the midst of a fierce denunciation of the Church and its clerics, Ricardo boldly pronounced Díaz's administration "a den of thieves" three times. Delegates shrank from moving openly into the political arena, however, and passed resolutions no stronger than militantly anti-clerical. Ricardo, however, had met and won over for future action intellectuals of both high and low status. Even Camilo Arriaga, who later broke with him, had been deeply impressed and maintained his respect for Ricardo. At one respite between sessions, Ricardo and Camilo visited the celebrated library. Ricardo pointed to a copy of the Constitution of 1857, saying, "Look Camilo, what a beautiful thing! But it's a dead letter." Only arms would topple Díaz, according to Ricardo, but this was an opinion that few at the time shared. Camilo admired the clarity of Ricardo's insights but nonetheless thought him "a barbarian."[14]

The Liberal Congress demonstrated two things. First, opposition to the regime could assemble publicly if it chose another subject to discuss and cloaked its reform calls in Aesopian language. Second, it demonstrated that for some, including Ricardo Flores Magón, radicalism, not reform, had become the only logical alternative. Perhaps radicalism appealed precisely because reform could not be debated. In any case, Mexican reformers and radicals would inevitably be condemned to living a dual existence, feigning one character while pursuing another. It is this aspect of Mexican political life after 1900 that has made tracking Ricardo Flores Magón's journey to the Left very difficult. Ricardo posed as a classic Mexican Liberal while at the same time developing his radicalism through several phases toward anarchism. As a result, and despite the voluminous writings by and about him, he has appeared as a bundle of contradictions—an enigma.

Perhaps misunderstandings of Ricardo's behavior derive from misperceptions about the protean nature of anarchism. As a social philosophy anarchism seeks total individual liberty in a shared, nongovernmental society. Ideally, anarchists reject as unacceptable the concept of allowing the individual as much liberty as possible under the rule of law secured by government. Democracy is only tyranny disguised, the rights of the many prevailing over the few. In the act of selecting a representative individual, women and men surrender their personal liberty; for an anarchist, personal liberty, once obtained, must be kept at all cost.

Anarchists wanted freedom and individual liberty; they were prepared to abolish private property to achieve these goals. In this they shared a common ground with American socialists and with Karl Marx. Yet unlike the socialists, who were prepared to work "through the system" to reform it, anarchists rejected the system—any system—as inherently corrupt and impossible to reform. They viewed the "system" as corrupt because government supported stratification of society based on accumulation of land and capital by the few at the expense of the many. They viewed it as impossible to reform because government then subjugated the many to exploitation through law. Furthermore, unlike Marxists, who saw history progressing inexorably through contradictory dialectical stages until the workers seized power and imposed communism, anarchists saw no inevitable determinism in history—only the suppression of personal liberty; they thought the "dictatorship" of the proletariat accurately named and reprehensible.[15]

Ricardo Flores Magón explored a rich and convoluted pattern of European thought which challenged his initial Mexican Liberalism. While he had certainly read much anarchist literature before the First Liberal Congress, he still seemed at that time to be grappling with some of the same political issues confronting Marxists. What should be the role of the party? Would it be a free association of individuals who would voluntarily cooperate to propagandize the people, as the anarchists thought, or should be it an elite vanguard propagandizing and leading the people when it deemed necessary?

These questions could have been on his mind when Ricardo returned to Mexico City, where he continued to make *Regeneración* combative. He and Jesús were arrested on May 22, 1901, on charges of "insulting" Díaz; they were sentenced to twelve months at the notorious facility at Belén, and imprisoned. Within a month, their ailing mother died, and Díaz's authorities denied their request for a final visit to her.[16] Prison can be a powerful educator, but not necessarily of the lessons the jailer wants learned. Ricardo had time for further thinking and reading when not kept in a darkened cell. Another event in the United States gave him much to ponder.

On September 6, 1901, in Buffalo, New York, an unemployed blacksmith, Leon Czolgosz, shot the president of the United States in the abdomen twice. A week later, William McKinley died from those wounds. Meanwhile, Czolgosz revealed himself to be an "anarchist." This was the most startling anarchist episode in the United States since the Haymarket tragedy. A decade before McKinley's assassination, a Russian emigré anarchist, Alexander Berkman, had slightly wounded industrialist Henry Clay Frick, manager of Carnegie Steel, and been sentenced to twenty years. Americans thus associated anarchism with terrorism and with death by bomb, gun, and knife. In fact, most anarchists repudiated terrorism. Theoretically, anarchism included violence in the form of collective direct action as a means to change society once and for all. In this view, propaganda by the deed represented individual, erratic violence. But if terrorists called themselves anarchists and if some anarchists did commit acts of individual terror, how could the public determine what anarchism really meant? To identify with anarchism in America now was to seek ostracism.

Release from Belén on April 30, 1902, could have given Ricardo only limited joy. Jesús decided to quit their militant stance and to work at a quieter and more measured pace for reform. The Second Liberal Convention had never been held; it had been suppressed by Díaz's troops while the Flores Magón brothers sat in prison. Enríque joined Ricardo now, but *Regeneración* had been closed. They worked on another radical paper to continue the struggle while tempting the inevitable. Again it came, four months after Ricardo had been freed—the exact duration of the new sentence. The cycle was repeated in 1903, this time according to a different formula: two and a half months of freedom to propagandize earned the brothers six more months in Belén. They were released in October.[17]

Ricardo now decided that this was the end for them in Mexico under Díaz. Belén had been a hell, especially in the blackout cells where jailers placed difficult prisoners for varying lengths of time. Ricardo remembered it being "so dark that I could not see my own hands." He described the cell in detail:

> The dungeon was unpaved, and a layer of mud from three to four inches thick composed the floor, while the walls oozed a turbid fluid which prevented from drying up the expectorations countless, careless, former occupants had negligently flung upon them. From the ceiling enormous cobwebs overhung in which huge, black, horrid spiders lurked. In one corner, opening from the sewer, there was a hole. . . .[18]

Ricardo recognized that the dungeon was designed to break the prisoner's spirit, and he knew men who had been broken by it. Most horrifying of all for him was the absence of light. He needed light to read and write, to hope. Looking back in October 1903, Ricardo had spent twenty-two of the previous twenty-nine months in Belén Prison. It had to end. With Enríque he left Mexico City and made his way north, as had others, to the United States.

In January 1904, the Flores Magón brothers and a companion arrived in Laredo, Texas. Nearly destitute, they all took menial jobs to survive and to prepare for their journey to San Antonio where Arriaga had taken up his emigré residence. While in Laredo they met Aniceto Pizaña,[19] who would become a sustainer of their cause for more than a decade.

Their companion, Juan Sarabia, symbolized a type of bond they had made at the First Liberal Convention. Sarabia came from humble origins and had completed only primary education formally. He had worked with his hands at many tasks: as apprentice cobbler, as unskilled foundry worker, and as apprentice in a telegraph office. It was his training as a printer's assistant, however, that brought him sufficiently steady employment.

At one point, Arriaga helped Sarabia financially, enabling him to edit a newspaper, to educate himself in the writings of various radicals, and to write poetry. When Díaz's agents closed *Regeneración,* Ricardo and Enríque joined Juan in his opposition paper. Later, they all were sent to Belén, where Juan occupied the cell between Ricardo and Enríque.[20] In Texas, Arriaga helped the Flores Magón brothers financially through Sarabia.

In March, however—not long after Ricardo arrived in Texas—he and Arriaga quarreled over leadership of the exile movement against Díaz. Differences could have been based on ideology, on status, or on personal control. Because both men concealed the exact nature of the conflict, only speculation remains.[21]

Tactics may have been an issue. Mexican Liberalism in opposition had developed a loose strategy of forming small groups in as many communities as possible in preparation for the ultimate day of revolt. Floresmagonistas, in particular, favored small, fervent cells of supporters or *grupos* which could, when appropriate, mount paramilitary offensives or *focos*.[22]

Intellectually, Ricardo may have derived the idea of *grupos* from the legacy of Michael Bakunin and his follower, Sergei Nechaev. Both men were Russian emigrés; Bakunin made substantive contributions to anarchist thought that will be touched upon later. He also maintained a conspiratorial and secretive side, personally creating clandestine parties throughout Europe.[23]

Nechaev, a terrorist and fanatic, contributed only a theory, which took the notion of the revolutionary to an extreme point. The revolutionary must live solely for the revolution and must be willing to use terror against the state and all who support it.[24] The combination of decentralized, conspiratorial groups and the use of violence in the name of the people proved powerfully attractive to some. Ricardo Flores Magón's contemporary, the Russian emigré who used the pseudonym of N. Lenin, drew upon these ideas; the Floresmagonistas in Mexico and the United States did so as well.

Whatever the tactical or personal differences between Arriaga and Ricardo Flores Magón, Arriaga continued to help finance the resurrection of *Regeneración*, which issued its first number in exile on November 5 from San Antonio. Arriaga also contributed articles. One scholar locates the root of the difficulty between Flores Magón and Arriaga in the latter's relationship with other high-status intellectuals. One of these, Francisco Madero, son of a wealthy family of Jewish origin in Coahuilla, had advanced Arriaga $2,000 against properties in San Luis Potosí. Arriaga then used this sum to fund *Regeneración*.[25]

Madero, enticed by reform, thought that he could effect change within the system. He wrote to Ricardo in that vein, suggesting joint political action. Ricardo agreed, showing the mask of Liberalism behind which he concealed his anarchist leanings.

But Díaz would not be denied by a boundary and *Regeneración* fared little better in the United States than it had in Mexico. Díaz hired Furlong detectives, along with his own agents, to hound the Liberals in exile.[26] This pressure forced the Floresmagonistas to suspend *Regeneración* in January 1905, and to relocate to what they believed would be a safer climate. They chose Saint Louis, Missouri, a center of American labor organization with a significant anarchist contingent, mainly of European origin. American labor leaders such as Eugene V. Debs and Samuel Gompers, whether professed socialists or not, represented reform. To these men, Ricardo showed Liberalism. But, to those with stronger taste for more basic solutions of the social question, he showed his interest in anarchism. In Saint Louis, he made contact with and impressed one of the leading foreign-born orators of her day, Emma Goldman. He also established a strong working relationship with the Western Federation of Miners (WFM), whose radicalism complemented his own.

Arbitrary search and seizure did in fact continue, and the group resumed its flight, publishing *Regeneración* whenever possible. The newspaper became a sensation, supported by thousands and later tens of thousands of subscribers who would send what they could to sustain it. Ricardo's fiery editorials, vivid in depicting Díaz's evil and capitalism's exploitation, appealed especially to workers who were beginning to organize. Both incipient and relatively better developed trade unions found *Regeneración* a paper that spoke to them and addressed their needs. Subscriptions increased rapidly; by 1906, nearly 20,000 people paid for the newspaper, which was delivered by Mexican and American mail.[27] To avoid Mexican postal inspection, the paper was shipped inside hollowed-out Sears Roebuck catalogs.[28]

In late 1905, Ricardo as Liberal appealed through *Regeneración* for local Liberal clubs to write the newspaper with their ideas for what should be done in Mexico. Response overwhelmed *Regeneración*'s staff. Recording, sorting, and tabulating the results yielded a genuine expression of the Mexican people both in Mexico and America. Sarabia did much of the editing, but Ricardo, in flight, contributed program ideas. The final product, a democratically constructed document, became the "Program of the Mexican Liberal Party" (PLM), published in its now official newspaper, *Regeneración*, bearing the date July 1, 1906.

Beginning with a call to reduce the presidential term to four years without reelection, the document spoke to multiple facets of Mexican life. Henceforth, Mexican labor would work an eight-hour day at a minimum wage. Employment of children would end, and children would instead attend school until age fourteen. Churches would pay taxes. Indians would be protected and their former lands returned. Beneath the slogan "Reform, Liberty, and Justice" the Organizing Junta of the Mexican Liberal Party signed with Ricardo as president, Juan Sarabia as vice-president, and Enríque as treasurer. Four other officers also signed—showing that Ricardo had won over some of Arriaga's earlier supporters.[29]

Arriaga had been shunted out of the movement that he, more than anyone else, had begun. Ricardo had made the PLM his own, coopted some of Arriaga's adherents while damning him as a traitor in the process,[30] and issued a political program that would gain him short-term popularity at the expense of the truth.

Ricardo now had a platform which gave credibility to his Liberal mask. As a reformist and not a revolutionary program, the PLM manifesto of July 1, 1906, could be sent to conservatives of American labor to elicit their help. It also appealed to the broadening opposition to Díaz in Mexico. The PLM propagandized to widen its constituency, and by midsummer, 750,000 copies of the manifesto circulated in both countries.[31] To reformers, it promised change. Radicals could read it as a beginning. Even as the manifesto spread, however, a conflict between labor and capital in northern Mexico underscored Díaz's callousness toward workers, his American connections, and the conspiratorial nature of Ricardo's real PLM.

At Cananea, Sonora, home of Cananea Consolidated Copper Company, partially owned and managed by American William C. Greene, tension between workers and management had become critical by mid-1906. Greene followed the standard practice of paying Americans more than Mexicans, frequently for the same work. Eventually, this inequality began to rankle Mexicans. At Cananea, they represented 70 percent of a work force of 4,400; on any given day, the Americans earned two to four times as much as the Mexicans for doing the same job. Greene also provided superior housing and working conditions for the Americans. His company store, the only one available, encouraged worker indebtedness—borne more heavily by those who earned less. In this milieu, Floresmagonista propaganda found an audience.

In late 1905, in response to an appeal from the St. Louis junta for their support, Mexican workers at Cananea applied to the PLM to join. Once accepted, a group of fifteen met secretly on January 16, 1906, and organized what would be the first of two Liberal clubs there, the Unión Liberal Humanidad. They composed a written compact that formally recognized Ricardo's leadership. Originally a support group for the PLM in exile, the Unión began to see that *Regeneración*'s exhortations applied to their own condition. Following a Cinco de Mayo celebration and nationalist speeches, Lázaro Gutiérrez de Lara decided to appeal to the thousands of Cananeans not employed by the mine and established the Club Liberal de Cananea. Again, secret meetings and confidential compacts preceded inflammatory speeches and denunciation of the current situation.[32]

On May 31, handbills circulated, one of which, nailed to a fence, proclaimed, "Curse the thought that a Mexican is worth less than a Yankee; that a negro or Chinaman is to be compared to a Mexican. . . . Mexicans, Awaken! The Country and our dignity demand it!"[33] In the strain, strike talk became strike, and on June 1, 1906, Greene faced work stoppage.

Confrontations between company officials and strikers erupted in violence, claiming the lives of about seven men, Mexican and American. Greene and the U.S. consul wired in all directions for help, but the nearest police force was in Arizona. Ironically, Cananea was only accessible by railroad from the United States because of the mine. Arizona ranger Thomas Rynning, a former Rough Rider under Theodore Roosevelt, answered with a volunteer army of 270 from Bisbee and reached Cananea by train at midmorning on June 2. They made a display and then retired without gunfire. Mexican forces began to arrive that afternoon and evening, imposed martial law, and shot more Mexican strikers. By June 3, combined Mexican units from the rural police forces (*rurales*), gendarmes, and federal troops had grown to 1,500, and the strike stopped.

Greene and Díaz blamed the incident on the PLM and imprisoned local adherents. Administrative bungling, however, caused the release of Gutiérrez de Lara, founder of the Club Liberal de Cananea, who then fled to the United States. Díaz tried to minimize the significance of Americans invading Mexican territory to protect their investments and to break a Mexican strike, but his position was untenable. However he couched it, his opponents could see evidence that he did favor foreigners over Mexicans. Protection of the national patrimony came second to securing foreign-owned property.

Greene, convinced that the Western Federation of Miners (WFM) had supported the PLM in calling the strike, hired a spy to infiltrate WFM's inner circles in Denver. Greene found his suspicions partially confirmed. The WFM had supported the Cananea strike and directed funds and propaganda from Bisbee to "agitators" in Nacozari and Cananea.[34] The PLM and the WFM had cooperated in propagandizing the workers at Cananea, but the PLM had not called the strike, nor had it conspired to. The strike originated in real grievances and sprang spontaneously from the turbulent situation. Probably only lack of money, weapons, and organization prevented the PLM from doing what Greene and Díaz believed they had done.[35]

Regeneración, now an American newspaper, excoriated Díaz for Cananea. The editors were able to keep the issue visible because Díaz could not suppress the news as easily in the United States as he could in Mexico. Gutiérrez de Lara described the strikers as numbering ten thousand, a figure more than double the actual labor force, and claimed that hundreds of miners had been "massacred in cold blood upon the streets"—exaggerations that intensified resentment against Díaz and Greene.[36] Both men began to cooperate to find a way to suppress the threat to their interests the PLM posed. Their cooperation began to produce arrests of low-level Floresmagonistas.

The PLM now began to move. Ricardo Flores Magón and Juan Sarabia went to El Paso in early September, joining moderates such as Antonio Villarreal to coordinate activities for an uprising in Mexico. On September 26, a PLM band entered Jiménez, Coahuila, seized the town center, sacked its treasury, and cut the telegraph wires. Federal troops routed them next day, but the Floresmagonista uprisings had begun.[37] Other PLM *focos* initiated forays elsewhere in Coahuila and in diverse parts of Mexico; but they too failed. Deficiencies in logistics, communications, finances, and arms all contributed to the lack of success.

Díaz responded. On June 30, 1907, Manuel Sarabia, cousin of Juan, was arrested by an American detective in Douglas and later kidnapped and taken to Mexico. Passers-by in the United States heard his screams and reported them to American radicals who in turn, joined with PLM leaders to demand his return to the United States. American labor rallied to the call, forced publicity on the issue, and Díaz relented. Mexican authorities brought Sarabia back to Douglas, where U.S. officials released him. Sarabia's kidnap and near murder dramatized the plight of the PLM in exile and won widespread American support for its charges against Díaz's tyranny.[38]

Working with U.S. authorities, Díaz secured his real objective: the arrest of Ricardo Flores Magón and others in Los Angeles on August 23. This time Díaz's elaborate network of hired detectives and Mexican spies delivered enough circumstantial evidence to produce a long, legal tangle. Detention, rearrest, trial, and incarceration would eventually take Ricardo from Los Angeles to Arizona and prison for his alleged role in the Cananea strike. With a few brief periods of release, he would spend most of the next three years in jail or prison; the PLM would have to function with him removed from the center of its activity.

With Ricardo in jail, implementing PLM plans for revolution fell to Enríque and field commander Praxedis Guerrero. Born of wealthy landowners in Guanajuato in 1882, Guerrero completed his primary education in León and joined General Bernardo Reyes' Second Reserve Army, where he learned the military skills he would later turn against Díaz. A journalist by training and inclination, Guerrero also wrote poetry and read anarchist tracts. Anarchism appealed to his outrage at injustice in Mexico and prompted him to leave wealth and family for American exile to further the revolution against Díaz.

In Mexico, manual labor signified lower status, and all who would rise disdained it. In the United States, the former member of the Mexican elite worked as a miner and a wood cutter. Guerrero sacrificed materially for his beliefs. Moreover, he furthered those beliefs when he organized Spanish-speaking miners in Morenci, Arizona, for example, in 1906, and when he contributed to the perception of discontent that galvanized workers at Cananea.[39]

A committed anarchist and admirer of the writings of Prince Peter Kropotkin, Guerrero wrote vigorously and often beautifully in denouncing Díaz. Some of his finest constructions, called *Puntos Rojos*—literally "red dots" but figuratively "tracers"—were fired from his pen as illumination rounds exposing the dictatorship's hypocrisy. "According to *El Imparcial* [the official Díaz newspaper]," he wrote, "the causes of [Mexican] poverty are intoxication, sexual excess, absence of savings, subversive meetings, dice, and early marriage. Our aristocrats are drunk, intemperate wastrels, fond of immense carousals, eternal and quite juvenile merrymakers [who] have three or four women instead of one . . . and [who] nevertheless do not live in poverty."[40]

His "tracers" became familiar among workers and campesinos, passed from mouth to mouth as rallying cries and phrases of consolation. "Land! was the cry that saved Columbus. Land! is the cry that will free capital's slaves." He neatly encapsulated libertarian emphasis on personal liberty in "Live to be free or die to quit being a slave." Encouraging the timid, he wrote, "If you cannot be a sword, be lightning." Guerrero's perhaps most famous aphorism, "Better to die on your feet than to live on your knees," became so closely associated with Emiliano Zapata that it has been mistakenly attributed to him.[41]

Interpreting anarchism through his "tracers" gave Guerrero and his ideas popularity and allowed him to challenge, for example, the role of religion in Mexican life. "Behind religion is tyranny, behind atheism, liberty." He chided his countrymen, "Tyranny is not the crime of despots against the people: it is the crime of the people against themselves." And he defined their problem succinctly: "Monopoly of land by a few, monopoly of the articles of primary necessity, tyranny, ignorance, cowardliness, the vile exploitation of man by man, these are the mainstays of the rich middle class, these are the mainstays of proletarian misery."[42]

Guerrero's singular combination of intellectual and military prowess, harnessed to serve the ideal of liberating Mexicans from oppression, made him a romantic and popular leader in the PLM. He and Enríque worked tirelessly for the uprisings planned for the summer of 1908. More than thirty different PLM *focos* were to mount guerrilla operations throughout Mexico, demonstrating that the moment for people to seize their liberty had arrived. Weapons and ammunition had been purchased and stockpiled on both sides of the border; women had smuggled handguns and rifle parts to caches by hiding them in their long skirts.[43]

On the eve of paramilitary activity, Ricardo wrote revealingly to his brother and Guerrero, explaining their shared past and planned future. "If we had called ourselves anarchists from the start no one, or at best a few, would have listened to us. Without calling ourselves anarchists, we have been firing the people's minds with hatred against the owner class and governmental caste." He had been in contact with Spanish and Italian anarchists who had expressed support for his version of the PLM and the Mexican situation.

Few believed in the internationalism of worker solidarity more strongly than Ricardo, and he continued with fervid optimism: "It is quite possible that our revolution will upset Europe's equilibrium and that proletarians over there will do what ours are doing here. . . . I am certain that our brothers on the other side of the sea will not let us perish." He could not resist identifying those on the junta he would expel for their conservatism: Juan Sarabia was fine, but his cousin Manuel and the schoolteacher Villarreal would have to go.[44]

Before the assaults could begin, Mexican and American authorities moved against the PLM in a series of raids and arrests in both countries that ultimately frustrated the revolutionaries' plans. A police raid in El Paso uncovered 150 rifles, 3,000 rounds of ammunition, dynamite, and homemade bombs. Arrests ensued. Since El Paso was the base for the attack upon Ciudad Juárez, and, since that attack would have been the signal for the other assaults to begin, the PLM had been dealt a massive blow.

Federal arrests and seizures in Chihuahua further blunted PLM activities there. Even though some *focos* launched attacks in late summer and fall, the 1908 movement had been stymied. Despite extensive preparations, the Floresmagonistas had failed again, not just because of problems in logistics and finances, but also by compromised security. Somebody leaked information leading to arrests and confiscation of materials including smuggled letters.[45]

Given these problems, Praxedis Guerrero's field campaign in Chihuahua came to naught. Moreover, another serious internal problem surfaced in the PLM leadership there. Before an attack on Palomas, near the U.S. boundary, Guerrero thought that Enríque Flores Magón removed himself from the pending battle by deliberately shooting himself in the foot. Enríque, inexperienced with firearms and undoubtedly nervous, claimed the shooting had been an accident. Guerrero told at least two other people that Enríque had malingered, and this judgment may have set the foundation for future drift away from Ricardo.[46]

Despite the military reversals, PLM propaganda efforts received an important boost from Los Angeles Socialists. Job Harriman, a lawyer who represented Ricardo and other PLM junta members in many of their American legal battles, helped to broaden their popular support. Harriman had come to sympathize with the PLM through the work of junta member Anselmo L. Figueroa, who had helped organize the Spanish-speaking followers of the Los Angeles Socialists.[47]

Harriman arranged for a fellow Socialist party member, John Kenneth Turner, to meet Ricardo and the other prisoners and interview them for a local newspaper. Given Diaz's popularity in the United States, Turner wanted to know why these men opposed him, and why they were in jail. Hours of conversation convinced him that they were driven to violence against the Mexican government because of Diaz's horrible treatment of the common people and his ruthless suppression of any information about these actions. Turner was particularly struck by their accusation that Díaz permitted and encouraged chattel slavery. "Human beings bought and sold like mules in America! And in the twentieth century. Well," he decided, "if it's true, I'm going to see it."[48]

To do so, Turner needed an interpreter, and one of the prisoners, Gutiérrez de Lara, became his bilingual companion and guide. Six feet tall, movie-star handsome with a compelling personality, and a "genius as a 'mixer,' "[49] the interpreter had the right credentials to help with Turner's investigation. Gutiérrez de Lara had earned a law degree and practiced law, and had been a judge in Chihuahua when he, like some other members of the elite, turned against Díaz's system and embraced radicalism.[50] He committed himself to socialism, joined the PLM, and agitated at Cananea in 1906.

From his Sonoran experiences, Gutiérrez de Lara had learned of a nasty traffic in human beings. Yaqui Indians in Sonora had long resisted Mexican rule. Under Díaz, much of their land had been usurped to reward the dictator's supporters. Díaz countered Yaqui resistance with a military campaign to kill the obstreperous and capture the rest. Federales sent their Sonoran captives far to the south, where they were sold into slavery on henequen plantations in the Yucatan and on other estates in the Valle Nacional of Oaxaca. Posing as an investor considering henequen properties, and accompanied by Gutiérrez de Lara as his interpreter, Turner entered Mexico in September 1908.

Money for the trip came from Elizabeth Trowbridge, a young, wealthy, radical Bostonian who had become interested in the PLM because of the Manuel Sarabia kidnapping. While Turner and Gutiérrez de Lara travelled in Mexico, she bought a printing shop in Tucson; there she and Turner's wife, Ethel Duffy, and fellow Socialist John Murray published the *Border,* a magazine to defend Mexican refugees and to expose Díaz. She also funded Manuel Sarabia's *El Defensor del Pueblo,* printed in the same shop.[51]

Gutiérrez de Lara's contacts, educational background, and social skills enabled Turner to secure access to every aspect of the slave trade. Turner gathered data for nearly a dozen lengthy stories on all phases of the traffic. Upon returning to the United States, Turner joined his wife on the *Border*'s staff but left after a few weeks to sell his stories in New York. In his absence, someone forcibly entered the print shop at night and destroyed the press. Trowbridge and the others decided to abandon the publishing venture. She married Manuel Sarabia and they went to England.[52]

Turner sold his stories to *American Magazine,* a muckraking tabloid that had been growing progressively more conservative. The series, entitled *Barbarous Mexico,* began in October 1909. But *American Magazine* printed only three of the stories before dropping Turner, influenced, many contemporaries thought, by Díaz' displeasure. Turner sought another outlet, and one of the most powerful socialist papers of the day, *Appeal To Reason,* printed the stories.

For Eugene V. Debs, the prospect of publishing Turner's series offered an unmatched opportunity. He wrote to the managing editor of the paper, "Do not in the least doubt that it will be the most deadly material ever belched from the *Appeal*'s batteries . . . the fight will have its strongest element in its being international, wiping out the boundary line and making the fight a common one between the working class and the plutocracy. The dramatic element will not be lacking. . . . Exit *American,* degenerate betrayer of the people; enter *Appeal,* brave champion of their cause!"[53]

Turner's exposé achieved the desired effects. American public opinion against Díaz grew, the plight of Mexican refugees became a subject of popular concern, and Turner became famous. He found other publishers willing to bring out the series as a book, and *Barbarous Mexico* appeared simultaneously in England and America. Both the individual stories and the book received favorable reviews. *Barbarous Mexico* became as important in molding public opinion as Harriet Beecher Stowe's *Uncle Tom's Cabin* had been in its time.[54] Through Turner, the PLM had achieved an important victory over Díaz in the United States.

PLM leaders had also secured important support from mainstream U.S. labor. Largely through Gutiérrez de Lara's efforts, the conservative Samuel Gompers and his American Federation of Labor chose to protect Mexican refugees against deportation. Gompers claimed credit for American labor in persuading Presidents Theodore Roosevelt and William Howard Taft "to refuse to permit the United States government to hunt Mexican refugees."[55]

Socialist labor leader Debs had made the poor treatment of Ricardo Flores Magón an issue in his 1908 presidential campaign.[56] Ricardo used that support to broaden Debs' commitment to include the PLM. In early 1910, Ricardo smuggled a letter to Debs out of his Arizona prison, pleading that junta members would all be rearrested upon release if public attention were not focused on their plight. Debs internalized the fear and became convinced that men of integrity would again be wronged. Debs wrote an impassioned letter to editor Fred Warren of the *Appeal to Reason,* asking him to use the paper to save the PLM, even at the cost of omitting coverage of Warren's own trial! Ricardo's letter had "fired every drop of my blood. I have concluded that this is the case of supreme importance in the present moment," Debs wrote, "and that even your own does not begin to compare to it." For Debs, this was an issue of highest principle.

These heroes [PLM] have fought and suffered a thousand times more than any of us; they have been slugged, kidnapped, starved, beaten, and all but assassinated . . . I am ashamed of my paltry record when I think of these grand souls and their transcendent heroism rotting in our prisons . . . The very criminal [Rynning] who took the strike breakers across the Mexican line, armed, and broke the strike by murdering the strikers [at Cananea], trampling down the neutrality laws, and who ought to be in the penitentiary for life, is now, by the grace of [President] Taft, appointed prison keeper and has these heroes under his heel and their bodies under his lash. When I read of this I became almost wild.[57]

Debs and *Appeal to Reason* focused public opinion on Ricardo and the PLM's plight. In July, Debs suggested that a formal letter be sent to the president and the attorney general, demanding to know if the prisoners were "to be rearrested upon their release and if so *on what ground*. Tell them that a million and a half readers of the *Appeal to Reason* are interested in this matter and want to know."[58] Debs had committed himself deeply to protecting the PLM, but he saw only their reformist face. Ricardo had, during the same period, been showing his anarchism to more radical labor segments.

In 1905, William "Big Bill" Haywood, secretary of the WFM, hosted a convention designed to produce a new labor federation unfettered by ethnic or national differences—one in which racial prejudice would be abolished. He opened the first meeting by saying, "Fellow workers, this is the Continental Congress of the working class."[59] That congress produced the Industrial Workers of the World (IWW), which the WFM joined, thus creating the most radical American labor movement organization in U.S. history. Haywood and the IWW talked anarchism, especially the concept of "direct action" to effect change.

Ricardo's version of the PLM and the IWW were natural allies, and the IWW continued the old WFM tactic of recruiting Mexican workers. The IWW also created Spanish-speaking unions and cells. Debs remained chary but tolerant of the IWW, probably because, like the PLM, the anarchist commitment gradually emerged over time and did not become undeniably clear until after 1910.[60]

PLM success in winning support from American socialists, workers, and labor leaders meant that, upon release, Ricardo and the junta had maneuvering room. In that window of relative freedom, they intended to launch another series of uprisings against Díaz which, like those planned in 1906 and 1908, they believed would fell the tyrant. Ricardo had been smuggling missives out of prison, usually by his *compañera*, María Talavera, preparing for future action. He involved both IWW cells and individual socialists. To insure proper publicity, John Kenneth Turner met Ricardo and the others upon their release in Arizona and escorted them back to California.

In Los Angeles an enthusiastic crowd, mainly Mexican, greeted them with cheers, strewing flowers before them and carpeting the road. Ethel Turner remembered that "the men walked on a bed of flowers," and were carried on the shoulders of crowd members, taken to the speakers' platform, and greeted by socialists and Floresmagonistas.[61] Of course, they spoke; they were back in action.

They also sent out their most important voice; the official newspaper of the PLM, *Regeneración,* was issued anew. In Ricardo's absence, it had been renamed *Revolución,* and Guerrero had been a major contributor. It had regularly printed Kropotkin's anarchist writings on the last page; Ricardo, via the smuggler's route, contributed anarchist appeals to workers and campesinos.[62] In that incarnation, at least, the radical PLM message had been clear: Revolution constituted the end, anarchism the means. Reform was for others. Hence, when *Regeneración* reappeared in September 1910, all PLM supporters would look to it for direction.

On September 3, Ricardo unveiled a new and bizarre *Regeneración.* Its newness came from the English-language page, clearly designed, at this point, to appeal to the American socialists and conservative labor elements who had struggled on behalf of the PLM over the previous three years. Its bizarreness stemmed from the increased mixed messages *Regeneración* sent out. In English, it reprinted the reformist July 1, 1906, program. In Spanish, it announced a new era.

Opposite Villarreal's essay exhorting Mexicans that a rifle was their best friend, Ricardo proclaimed: "Here we are, the torch of Revolution in one hand and the Liberal Party Program in the other, declaring war . . . Let the cowards stand apart; we don't want them. For the Revolution only the valiant need enlist."[63] But which program: reform or revolution? Division on the subject existed within the PLM, and these messages failed to clarify the differences.

Guerrero contributed two stories for the front page—one of which addressed the ethnic exclusion of Mexicans by whites in Oklahoma, Arizona, and, in particular, Texas. Complaints about discrimination against Mexicans in the United States would become more frequent over the years, with greatest emphasis placed on Texas. In 1910, the new *Regeneración*'s emerging concern over ethnic discrimination in America foreshadowed the paper's growing role in agitating for fair treatment of Mexicans—which would be the cornerstone of the 1915 uprising against South Texas.

Regeneración had become genuinely binational in its concerns. *Regeneración*'s first page also called for financial help for Andrea Villarreal González, editor of *Mujer Moderna* in San Antonio, who had been harassed by Díaz's agents. Because liberation applied to all, equality between the sexes was important in anarchist thought. Front page coverage of *Mujer Moderna* testified to that anarchist ideal.

The most revealing and baffling part of that first issue, however, was a richly illustrated poster representing anarchism. The poster was printed on a separate page, beneath the *Regeneración* logo (see Figure 1). At the top, before a rising sun, are pictures of five men fanned across an open book. The side borders contain pillar-like, torch-bearing columns labeled Light (Lumen) and Truth (Veritas). Each base and capital also bears a man's picture. Within these borders, the central images are of three horsewomen

Fig. 1. Poster of Anarchism (*Regeneracíon*, September 3, 1910)

holding banners aloft, riding unfettered white steeds before a sun nearly full upon the horizon, galloping across the globe from Europe to America. On the right, the nearly nude rider holds an olive branch in one hand, and her banner exalts the "Ideal." The central rider, clothed, carries a torch, and her banner announces the "Advance of the Revolution." The third horsewoman, partially clothed, but with breasts exposed, wears a sombrero and a dagger in her sash. She is obviously Mexican. She holds aloft a broken shackle, and her banner proclaims "Land and Liberty"—the PLM slogan. Above this image of motion stand five select PLM leaders including Ricardo and Enríque Flores Magón; they are positioned just below the open book with the five faces upon it.

The rich imagery and use of detail permit analysis of the poster on at least two levels, that of communicator and that of observer. Consider first the communicator. In a single sign containing many symbols,[64] Ricardo reveals the anarchist influence on his thoughts—aptly, in the borders. Though the sign does not depend upon them for its message, examination of the four borders enhances appreciation of the sign. Kropotkin (1842–1921), the greatest anarchist thinker of the late nineteenth century,[65] stands in the center of the top five faces, in the same physical relationship to them that Ricardo, within the active part of the sign, has with the PLM. Kropotkin exerted the greatest single influence on Ricardo, and the title of Kropotkin's most famous work, *The Conquest of Bread* (*La conquista del pan*), can be read on the open book beneath him.

Kropotkin is flanked on his right by two anarchists, Charles Malato (1857–1938), French, and Errico Malatesta (1853–1932), Italian. Malato's *Philosophy of Anarchism* (*Filosofía del anarqismo*) and Malatesta's *Conversation between Two Workers* (*Entre campesinos*) are also visible in the book. On Kropotkin's left are Spanish anarchists Fernando Tarrida del Marmol (1861–1915) and Anselmo Lorenzo (1842–1914). Lorenzo, who was among the very first Spanish anarchists, found his new political faith in a four-hour meeting in Madrid in which Bakuninist Giuseppe Fanelli, who spoke no Spanish, persuaded the group in a mixture of Italian and French.[66] Lorenzo is represented by three titles in the book.[67]

An image of Bakunin (1814–1876) marks the capital of the left column. Bakunin and his disciples introduced anarchism to Italy and Spain; anarchists from those two countries stood with him in the split from Karl Marx that sundered the First International. The title of Bakunin's book, *God and the State* (*Dios y el estado*), can be read immediately below and is slightly obscured by Kropotkin's picture. This placement suggests Kropotkin's role in revising Bakunin's notions of anarchist communism; whereas Bakunin had emphasized worker production, Kropotkin shifted the basis of anarchist communism to worker need regardless of contribution.[68] The image at the right capital is that of Henrik Ibsen, whose plays inspired by Libertarian thought, *Ghosts* (*Los espectros*) and *Hedda Gabler,* are visible in the book.

The bases are Elisée Reclus, left, whose most famous pamphlet, *Evolution and Revolution* (*La evolución y revolución*), is in both the book and the bottom border.[69] Reclus's important argument is that revolution is a necessary part of human evolution toward liberty. Praxedis Guerrero (1882–1910), the only Mexican in the border, is the right column's base. He is depicted in uniform—the intellectual as warrior. While none of his works appear in the book, references to his writings can be found elsewhere in the sign.

The border represents both a history of anarchist thought and the elements within it that Ricardo admired. All but Bakunin were his contemporaries. They pursued various tasks. Ibsen and Reclus were, respectively, playwright and geographer. The Spanish anarchists were educators and newspapermen—the latter role also fulfilled by the Italian and French anarchists, by Kropotkin, and by the Floresmagonistas. Guerrero worked as a newspaperman and miner but also wrote fine poetry. Taken together, these men and their thoughts represented a world view in which individual liberty would be achieved imminently.

The borders frame the central image of Ricardo Flores Magón's interpretation of Kropotkin's anarchist communism. Ricardo and his colleagues translate European thought (the banner "Ideal") into a revolutionary movement (central banner) and apply it in Mexico ("Land and Liberty"). Women are important to this movement; they are active in spreading the word, smashing tyranny, and implementing the new order. The movement's propaganda vehicle *Regeneración*, the medium by which the downtrodden will be enlightened to empower themselves through Revolution, is the poster heading.

Observer response to the sign depends upon individual background. Those who cannot read the words can read the symbols. Important men, above the larger and recognizable faces of Ricardo's inner circle, influence that circle. Ricardo and his comrades inspire the magnificent horsewomen. These three women bring with them the olive branch, the torch, and the broken shackle, heralding a new day of freedom encompassing the globe. Female equality is shown by the image of the Mexican woman as warrior and emancipator. The Mexican horsewoman suggests Delacroix' celebrated *Liberty on the Barricades* (1830); both are bare-breasted, waving banners, and leading others forward. Delacroix' *Liberty* wears the Phrygian bonnet, the Mexican Liberty, a sombrero. These appealing and commanding images of women derive from the pre-1848 utopian-romantic era of anarchism, socialism, and European radicalism.[70] The detail of the sign is visually pleasing, and the message in the foreground is clear.

For the literate, a special appeal is found in the boxes on either side of the *Regeneración* logo. Inside are four English-language translations of Spanish quotations. Three of these are Guerrero's "tracers" designed to provoke response. "If you care to kneel down to a despot, do so. But lift a stone to send an honorable greeting." Another: "Afraid of the Revolution? Then renounce injustice and the fear will end." And: "For justice we do not beg nor do we ask; if it does not exist, we will make it."

The other quotation is by Francisco Ferrer (1859–1909), a Spanish anarchist. "Three thousand workers go to a victim's funeral. None to seek redress." Ferrer's passion was education. He created the first Modern

School (Escuela Moderna) in Barcelona in 1901, designed to educate both sexes in an environment free from the teachings of religion, monarchy, and sexism. He influenced Tarrida del Marmol and Lorenzo, among others, and the Modern School movement had some successes in the United States.[71]

These bilingual messages address American and Mexican workers directly, reinforcing the links between the PLM and the IWW. Those literate in Spanish would recognize many of the names and writings, connecting Ricardo and *Regeneración* with parallel developments in Europe. Kropotkin, at the center, represents anarchist communism as the most important message of *Regeneración*. Nonetheless, the presence of the Frenchman, Malato, and the Spaniard, Lorenzo, signify that anarchosyndicalism is also very important. Anarcho-syndicalism originated in France among the *syndicats,* or trade unions, and sought the general strike as the means to achieve the Revolution. Reflecting the importance of this branch of anarchism in Ricardo's thought is the title *The Great Strike* (*La gran huelga*) in the book in the top border.[72] Anarchosyndicalism bonded the IWW and the PLM.

The sign could be read with greater appreciation as the observer learned more about anarchism. Ricardo obviously thought the poster important and circulated thousands of copies of it. He reprinted it, for example, on January 1, 1913, and later that year included it in an English-language pamphlet.[73] By 1913, *Regeneración*'s message to its adherents would have been unmistakable. Yet the context of its original issue in September 1910, made understanding difficult. Conspicuously, neither Villarreal nor Juan Sarabia was included in the PLM leadership depicted.[74] Stories by or about them, however, appeared on the front page of that very first issue that included the poster.

Villarreal's and Ricardo's call to arms appealed to different sentiments. The former called for a revolution to reform Mexico; the latter demanded the Revolution to remake Mexican society and economy. Yet the English-language page reiterated only the old call for peaceful reform. Expediency alone should have dictated the least dishonesty possible to avoid confusion. But, Ricardo's personal struggle in becoming an anarchist seems to have been at issue.

In the United States, Ricardo maintained the two faces of reform and revolution he had adopted in Mexico. This tactic made him appear hypocritical and would later earn him enmity. In clarifying his relationship to anarchism, he entered another bind at which the poster hints. Malato had quarreled with a partisan that an anarchist group needed leadership and some minimal party control.[75] But, for more than twenty-five years, Kropotkin had argued vigorously against this view.

> . . . it is not secret societies nor even revolutionary organizations that can give the finishing blow to governments. Their function, their historic mission is to prepare men's minds for the revolution, and when men's minds are prepared and external circumstances are favorable, the final rush is made, *not by the group that initiated the movement*, but by the mass of the people altogether. . . .[76]

Ricardo's PLM in late 1910 contradicted Kropotkin's view.

Ricardo faced a dilemma. Would he, as the poster promised, translate Kropotkin into practice or would he take the tack pursued by Lenin? Failure to recognize the magnitude of this issue for Ricardo has led to subsequent confusion in interpreting his behavior during this period. The poster seems critical because it signifies both the depth of his knowledge and his basic commitment.

In 1840, the first man to call himself an anarchist and one of the movement's major theoreticians, Pierre-Joseph Proudhon, formulated the question and answer upon which all of Ricardo's subsequent anarchist thought rested. *What is Property?* he asked. "Property is theft." Ricardo inscribed the title in the book at the top of his poster. Although the future could only be more arduous than the past, publicly and privately there was no turning back.

CHAPTER 2

A POLITICAL REVOLUTION

> Those who do not believe in the goodness of paternal governments or in the impartiality of law fashioned by the bourgeoisie, those who know that the emancipation of the workers ought to be accomplished by the workers themselves, those convinced of DIRECT ACTION, those who deny the "sacred" right of property . . . these revolutionists are represented by the Organizing Junta of the Mexican Liberal Party.
>
> Ricardo Flores Magón[1]

While Ricardo Flores Magón and the PLM struggled for an anarchist revolution against Díaz, reform elements in Mexico strove to be heard. In a public ploy to enhance his reputation among foreigners for enlightened rule and to thwart incipient domestic criticism, Díaz told an American reporter in 1908 that he would retire at the end of his presidential term in 1910. Díaz claimed that by then he would be eighty, that the Mexican people, perhaps, would be ready for democracy, and that he would encourage the formation of political parties.

Francisco Madero, who had earlier contacted Camilo Arriaga and Ricardo Flores Magón to promote reform in Mexico, responded to Díaz's interview with a modest proposal. In *The Presidential Succession of 1910,* published early in 1909, Madero suggested that the new political parties be allowed to choose Díaz's next vice-president. Madero and other reformers—of high hopes and higher self-delusion—believed that the old man had meant what he said. He had not. Díaz replied to Madero's appeal for some degree of popular choice in selecting a running mate by choosing a man who was universally unpopular, even within Díaz's ruling cabal![2]

Reformers, angered but wishing to believe political change possible, moved to support Madero. The short, high-voiced, gentle, and emotional Coahuilan traveled the country speaking and gaining in popularity. Madero appealed to a central theme, a call for *justicia,* a term that loses much in literal translation as "justice." *Justicia,* a concept vivified by Juárez and the original Liberals, implied redress for past wrongs; it suggested a movement that would set things right and restore an intelligible social balance.

Justicia did not imply egalitarianism; it promised that the given social hierarchy, with its specific roles and rewards, would be returned to normal.

Excessive abuse was abnormal and, beyond a certain point, intolerable. The PLM also appealed to this sense in the slogan, "Reforma, Libertad y Justicia," accompanying its July 1, 1906, manifesto. Madero drew upon that sentiment in Mexican towns and villages, invoking *justicia* for everyone, campesino as well as miner, vaquero and hacendado, people and politicians.[3] Madero capitalized on the reform sentiment that had pervaded much of the earlier PLM coalition and moved to capture it for himself.

Madero arrived in Mexico City in April 1910, to receive the presidential endorsement of the Antireelectionist Party. Ironically, the issue of *his* vice-presidential candidate caused tension and controversy over the ensuing eighteen months. Madero's first running mate, Francisco Vásquez Gómez, Díaz's personal physician, at one point reminded Madero of the original goal. Citing Madero's call for reform in the selection of Díaz's vice-president, Vásquez Gómez asked Madero to nominate him to Díaz as a compromise to the dictator's unpopular choice, with Madero retiring altogether.[4] Thus, Madero's tentative political opposition began in ominous disunity—foreshadowing his political future.

Díaz, with thirty-five years of experience, knew how to handle his opposition: repression and jail. He had Madero arrested and imprisoned in San Luis Potosí. Madero missed the torments of Belén but he learned its most important lesson; only violence could unseat the tyrant. Free on bail, Madero watched helplessly as Díaz won the 1910 election with his usual fraud. Disguised as a railroad mechanic, Madero boarded a northbound train to Laredo on October 6, 1910, and escaped into American exile.[5]

A month later, at the Hutchins Hotel in San Antonio, Texas, Madero issued his Plan of San Luis Potosí, backdating it to the last day he had been in the latter city. He disavowed the elections, appointed himself provisional president able to declare war against Díaz, and called for a democratic presidential election to take place once half the states had been taken by insurgents. Upon victory, all laws enacted under Díaz would be reviewed and, if necessary, revised; public officials would become accountable for their conduct; and lands improperly taken would be subject to special judicial review. He invited the Mexican people to fight for him and for themselves.[6] An upper-class, high-status, exiled elite appealed for uprisings against the Mexican government. Madero had no network but he did spread the news, probably through sympathetic PLM cells.

Ricardo recognized the potential for confusion and rushed to meet it. On November 16, four days before the Maderista uprisings were to begin, Ricardo printed an appeal in a circular to his PLM adherents. Ricardo branded Madero's Antireelectionist Party a personalist movement and warned Floresmagonistas to prepare cautiously for their own, independently planned uprisings. If Madero's forces engaged the enemy then, in the ensuing confusion, all might rise.

The junta declared that it had made no deal with Madero or his followers and forbade *focos* to make common cause with the Maderistas. With pithy clarity Ricardo wrote, "the program of the Liberal Party [PLM] is distinct from the Antireelectionist program. The Liberal Party seeks political liberty, economic liberty by delivering to the people the lands illegally taken by the great landlords, an increase in wages and lessening of the hours of work, [and] nullification of the influence of clergy and government in the home. The Antireelectionist Party seeks only political liberty."[7]

Ricardo confounded this clarity in the conclusion, when he bound his followers to the July 1, 1906, PLM program and ended with the old slogan intoning *justicia*. The circular, coupled with the 1906 program, caused profound confusion in Mexico: how could the average person differentiate between Madero's goals and the PLM reforms? Moreover, if Madero's forces seemingly took the lead, why should not the PLM sympathizers follow suit?

Sporadic uprisings occurred. In the state of Chihuahua, Pascual Orozco, a muleteer, seized the town of Guerrero in late November, and Doroteo Arango, who went by his bandit name, Pancho Villa, took the hamlet of San Andrés. Both men acted independently but in response to Madero's appeal. These and other outbreaks were dispersed fairly easily, and amounted to little more than disturbances.[8]

Praxedis Guerrero, the most militarily skilled of the PLM leaders, left Los Angeles for Chihuahua in late November, more committed than ever to bringing about the revolution. Despite the aura of solidarity within the PLM junta, Guerrero left disgruntled. The recent double dealings of Ricardo left him dissatisfied: he had long yearned for an open unequivocal declaration of the PLM's anarchist leanings. His suspicion that Enríque had malingered before the battle of Palomas two and one-half years earlier finally prompted him to reveal those thoughts to Ethel Duffy Turner before he left. The warrior-poet, frustrated by Mexican and American police intrigues against the junta and by the lack of a clear anarchist message from the PLM, had grown tired of waiting and sought action with the *focos*.[9]

Guerrero planned operations in Chihuahua because of its critical location adjacent to the border. By engaging in "propaganda by the deed" in small villages and towns below Juárez, he could inspire the people to rise. With Juárez surrounded, its fall, crucial to all future success, would be assured. As the major port of entry in the north, Juárez constituted an entrepôt for arms and munitions as well as supplies. A rebel victory there would insure eventual success against Díaz. PLM forces had cooperated already with Orozco in Chihuahua, and the muleteer's interest in radical thinking was probably facilitated by contact with Guerrero.[10]

Guerrero began by attacking safely below Juárez and soon seized Casas Grandes, an important victory and site of a later Madero defeat. He continued operations, gathering and arming followers in his quest to achieve the PLM anarchist revolution. On December 30, 1910, while fighting for control of Janos, the unthinkable happened: Guerrero fell, killed by enemy fire.

Ricardo, unaware of Guerrero's disaffection, roared in disbelief upon hearing the news. Ricardo compared its impact on him to learning of his own death. It was not possible; it did not happen. The Mexican people had lost a friend and co-worker whom they did not fully appreciate.[11] The PLM had lost one of its most important leaders. Gutiérrez de Lara followed Guerrero into the field in Chihuahua and kept the PLM insurgency alive.[12]

While other uprisings occurred in Mexico, both by PLM followers and incipient Maderistas, the PLM wanted to open a second major front in Baja California. A remote, sparsely populated, and lightly defended state, its capture would provide an environment for creating the anarchist revolution. Chihuahua represented a means both to defeat Díaz and to rally the Mexican people to seize their liberty. Baja California represented an opportunity to show Mexicans the possibility of living as an anarchist communist.

The Baja front was to be an international venture of Mexicans and their supporters. Socialist John Kenneth Turner even smuggled arms.[13] Insurgent forces consisted of Mexicans, Canadian and Mexican Indians, IWW members (Wobblies) of many backgrounds, a Welsh soldier-of-fortune, and a deserter from the U.S. Marine Corps. A Mexican Fabian socialist and fourteen companions took Mexicali on January 28, 1911. Other victories followed: Algodones in early February and, later that month, Tecate. On May 9, the Welshman—with a force comprised mainly of Americans as well as a few Mexicans—disobeyed Ricardo's orders and captured Tijuana. Anarchism's black flag now rose, at least figuratively, over the border city, and the experiment could begin.[14]

Madero, however, had not been idle. Díaz asked American authorities to arrest Madero for violation of U.S. neutrality laws. By using the October 5 date for his Plan of San Luis Potosí, Madero claimed to have written it in Mexico and, therefore, not violated American law. This dodge got him bail, which he forfeited, and he returned to Mexico. Even though the major victories had been won by the PLM, Madero remained optimistic about his movement despite his poor beginnings.

Madero went to Guadalupe, Chihuahua, on February 14, 1911, where three days earlier PLM partisans had raised the red flag of "Land and Liberty." Madero greeted them warmly, openly embraced their leader, and later had him arrested. Gutiérrez de Lara arrived with PLM reinforcements and honored the arrest, joining Madero and abandoning Ricardo. As a socialist, Gutiérrez de Lara had no reservations about working within the system. Thus began Madero's policy of arresting those PLM adherents who would not be co-opted into recognizing him as provisional president.[15]

Madero, however, needed a victory. He boldly joined the forces attacking Casas Grandes on March 6, but they were soundly defeated at the very place Praxedis Guerrero had prevailed two months before. Madero became more cautious. Orozco, who led the largest and most successful fighting force in Chihuahua, wanted a bold assault against Juárez. Madero expressly forbade it. Orozco launched the attack anyway on May 8 and, two days later, claimed the city. Over his own objections, Madero's forces had won the most important victory of his career.

The fall of Juárez coincided with the PLM capture of Tijuana. The uprisings across Mexico represented the culmination of PLM preparations since 1906 and field action since late 1910. With the loss of the northern port, Díaz could not prevail, and so the dictator entered into negotiations with Madero's representatives. The victory at Juárez prompted independents and Floresmagonistas alike to pledge their adherence to the provisional president. In Los Angeles, an angry Ricardo railed against Madero and his phony movement that sought only to replace one Díaz with another. As Madero planned his trip to Mexico City and the assumption of political power, he knew that he would have to deal with PLM remnants. At least initially, he allowed Ricardo to rave.

Ricardo Flores Magón denounced Madero to a progressively smaller audience largely because of the confusion he had sown about PLM goals. The initial defection, seemingly minor, actually presaged substantial shifting of sides: on December 15, 1910, Alfred Sanftleben, the first editor of the English-language section of *Regeneración*, resigned, claiming that he could "not fathom the economics and the policies nor reconcile the utterances with the tactics of the Liberal party of Mexico."[16]

Alfred Sanftleben had donated his time to the newspaper even though he worked another job. He did so out of a spirit of comradeship. Earlier, in New York, he had been an associate of anarchist firebrand Johann Most, one of those who converted Emma Goldman to anarchism. Johann Most, more than any other nineteenth-century radical in the United States, symbolized the bomb and knife of violent anarchism. Sanftleben had become disillusioned with that thinking and had come to Los Angeles as a socialist.[17] He had written a book on anarchist communes and ought to have known the intricacies of radical political thought,[18] but apparently he had not seen Ricardo's anarchism. Sanftleben had helped organize a defense fund for the PLM after the 1907 arrests, and he had published stories to keep their plight before the public. He had been misled by the circular of November 1910, however, and erroneously reported in *Regeneración* on December 10, 1910, that the PLM had joined Madero.

A week later Ricardo printed a correction of the story, but he had already secured Sanftleben's resignation. On December 24, Ricardo wrote a sensitive and gently worded article about Sanftleben, praising his loyalty and selflessness, and published Sanftleben's resignation letter. Ricardo then attempted further clarification of the differences between the PLM and Maderista goals. Generously but erroneously conceding that Madero's forces had begun the revolution, he nevertheless insisted that "our own personal representatives are on the ground . . . we wish the revolution to succeed . . . but as a Liberal revolution and not as a middle-class revolution."[19] The distinction was lost to many readers. If an observer of Sanftleben's intellectual sophistication became disillusioned and confused by Ricardo's tactics, then other, less sophisticated people were likely to have similar experiences. This would be the last time in this phase of his career that Ricardo displayed generosity to those differing with him.

Ethel Duffy Turner replaced Sanftleben on January 7, 1911. To retain socialist allies, copies of her husband's book *Barbarous Mexico* were promised to every *Regeneración* subscriber. This move, designed to reinforce

American support for the PLM, had its counterpoint in Ricardo's Mexican propaganda. He stockpiled Spanish-language copies of Kropotkin's *The Conquest of Bread*, the blueprint for implementing anarchist communism, to be shipped to Mexico.[20] These political discrepancies could not be maintained indefinitely—nor could yet another socialist editing the English-language page.

The crisis precipitating the unveiling of Ricardo's anarchism in the United States began with Madero's mid-February arrest of the PLM adherents in Guadalupe, Chihuahua. In a front-page headline across seven columns, *Regeneración* proclaimed Madero "a traitor to the cause of Liberty" and included Gutiérrez de Lara in the denunciation. Ricardo explicitly denied the "presumed right of Capital to expropriate for itself a portion of what workers produce." Exchanging Madero for Díaz constituted no victory. If Madero now arrested people for not pledging fealty to him as provisional president, what would he do as "legal" president?[21]

Ricardo apparently kept the front-page article confidential until printed. The headline and story caused a sensation. The night after it appeared, Villarreal confronted Ricardo and his inner circle in the presence of Ethel Duffy Turner, and demanded an explanation. After an acrimonious exchange, Villarreal left to join Madero.[22] American authorities stopped him at El Paso. Gutiérrez de Lara joined him and together they assumed control of PLM operations there, converted them to Maderista activities, and earned further fiery blasts from Ricardo's pen.

Ricardo's denunciation of Madero on February 25 found its way into English very quickly. *The New York Call*, the largest circulating socialist newspaper in America, featured the story. Labeling the PLM inaccurately as socialist, *The Call* castigated the Los Angeles junta for disavowing Madero, asserting that the junta's action threatened to divide the anti-Díaz forces over insignificant details.[23] Ricardo was being pinched both by his long-time American supporters and by their government.

On March 6, President Taft ordered large military forces deployed along the border in Texas and California, obviously to protect American lives and property in the wake of the growing military actions in Mexico.[24] Ricardo responded with an appeal to Samuel Gompers and the American Federation of Labor to protect this thinly disguised preparation to invade Mexico by the forces of their common enemy, the "money power." To insure wider publicity against the American military maneuvers, he sent a copy of the appeal to Emma Goldman to print in her journal, *Mother Earth*.[25]

Ricardo had accused Madero of shedding a sheepskin to reveal the wolf inside when he had arrested PLM followers at Guadalupe. Now Ricardo acted in a similar manner with his "Manifesto to the Workers of the World," dated April 3, 1911. An excerpt from the Manifesto is quoted as the epigraph for this chapter. With its disavowal of government, its pledge to direct action as the means of returning land to the people, and its insistence upon worker and campesino solidarity, the Manifesto represented a clear anarchist statement of intent and plea for support. Ricardo circulated it widely.[26] Furthermore, he began to establish an important distinction between individual acts of violence, usually conspiratorial, such as propaganda by the deed, and the collective action of the people, embodied for him in direct action.

Nonetheless, Ricardo also wanted to maintain socialist support and so proved disingenuous in his letter to Debs pleading for help. Claiming that the leading newspaper had misled the American people into thinking that the struggle in Mexico was political rather than economic and social, Ricardo charged that the complex issues had been reduced to the claim that socialists support Madero and anarchists the PLM. He continued:

> Indeed, I myself was called on recently by a Socialist committee and asked to inform it whether personally I was a Socialist or Anarchist; the intimation being that if I was the latter support would be withdrawn. Could anything be more absurd or deplorable? We are not concerned with "isms." We are practical people, engaged in a most sternly practical task—the recovery of their natural inheritance by the disinherited.[27]

Still evading the issue of ideology and firmly believing in international solidarity, he asked for money and accurate coverage of PLM goals.

Defections continued. As the letter to Debs indicated, the Los Angeles Socialist Party had been deeply distressed by Ricardo's split with Madero. John Kenneth Turner, especially, showed concern. He could not fathom the reasons for it and decided "that it was time to write articles and even fiction."[28]

Many other socialists thought that the Mexican insurgents' goal had been "the overthrow of Díaz for the purpose of establishing fair elections, free speech and a free press."[29] To them, government could be reformed; hence, Ricardo, rather than Madero, seemed to be placing personal issues above labor interests. Socialist criticism of the PLM increased as Ricardo became more belligerent.

Shortly after Ricardo's initial salvo, William C. Owen entered the Socialist Party office seeking the author of *Barbarous Mexico*. The book had drawn his attention to the Mexican question. In the course of their conversation, Turner prevailed upon Owen to replace his wife on the *Regeneración* staff.[30] Turner had chosen to withdraw from Mexican politics.

Owen's arrival proved fortuitous for Ricardo. In Owen he found a like-minded colleague of serious purpose and equal mental ability. Owen became Ricardo's closest English-speaking comrade. An Englishman, Owen had been born in India of an aristocratic family in 1854, and brought back to England for school. He studied law and languages at Wellington College, but his conscience would not permit him to practice. He believed that law reinforced privilege at the expense of the poor.[31]

In 1882, Owen came to San Francisco and, while there, became influenced by the quirky radicalism of Burnette G. Haskell's International Workmen's Association (IWA). The Association succinctly described its goal as "[t]he reorganization of Society independent of Priest, King, Capitalist or Loafer."[32] Ostensibly socialist, the IWA organized along secret lines then popular among European revolutionary societies; each group consisted of nine members, each of whom in turn would form another group of nine. From the IWA, Owen learned the organizing patterns that the later PLM would pursue. During this period, Owen also participated in filing the land claims from which Haskell would create his socialist commune, the Kaweah Colony.[33]

In 1890 Owen, then in New York, helped found the Socialist League. In 1893, back in England, he met Kropotkin, who edited *Freedom*. The aristocratic Owen and the aristocratic Kropotkin, both men who had forsaken much to struggle for the poor, became mutual admirers. Owen shortly declared himself an anarchist. Nonetheless, he gently rejected Kropotkin's insistence on communism and instead opted for individualist anarchism—emphasizing personal over collective responsibility. Obviously restive, Owen returned to Los Angeles, where he had previously agitated for the eight-hour day, and found himself interested in Mexican affairs through Turner's book.

At fifty-six, then some twenty years Ricardo's senior, Owen wanted to understand the PLM position clearly if he were to be of help. As he recalled:

> Prior to my assumption of the editorship of the English section there were several interviews between the junta and myself at which we found ourselves agreed that the Mexican movement was part of the worldwide economic revolution; that, consequently, an international propaganda should be set afoot; that we should get nothing from the Socialists but words and apologies . . . [who] would side with Madero, inasmuch as politician always support[s] politician against those who stand for direct action. Furthermore, we considered that true wisdom lay in being unpolitic . . . in neither courting alliances nor being afraid of making enemies.[34]

Owen's understanding of his and the PLM role vis-à-vis Mexico provides powerful explanatory insights to the events which unfolded.

Owen was to handle English-language propaganda, and to make that section of *Regeneración* as combative as the remainder of the paper. He assumed his duties April 15, 1911, and, in "Away with Shams," proclaimed that Mexicans were struggling to abolish the wage system in a war against "the absentee landlord and the foreign money leach [sic]." He expressed confidence that Debs would answer Ricardo's request for aid favorably. Thus, in his *Regeneración* debut, Owen was clear. Abolition of the wage system was Kropotkin's idea, a central tenet of his anarchist communism, and Debs would not fail to know now that the PLM embraced anarchism.

While Owen prepared to battle PLM enemies in English, Ricardo turned to the international propaganda their cause needed. He sought to create an International Committee of the Mexican Liberal Party Junta in every major American and European city.[35] His vehicle would be his voluminous correspondence, which Owen estimated consumed eight working hours daily.[36] The remainder of the junta recruited an army for the campaign in Baja California, where Ricardo's anarchist dream could be realized.

Unfortunately for Ricardo, recruitment involved the PLM bane of yet more mixed messages. Mexicans were urged to participate voluntarily to free themselves from the wage system and to seize the land. Non-Mexicans were promised land and a cash bonus upon success. Such a practice violated Ricardo's principles and he would not have approved it. Nevertheless, the tangible incentives undoubtedly accounted for the preponderance of foreigners in the effort.[37]

When the Welshman seized Tijuana against orders, Ricardo watched his plans begin to crumble. The battle ended on May 9 in wholesale looting of Mexican shops. Rebels looted far less than did San Diego tourists, but the former charged the latter a dollar to cross the border and take what they could carry. Within a few days, more than a thousand tourists had passed through Tijuana gawking at the PLM forces and taking or buying cheap goods.[38]

Ricardo tried to calm the situation and direct events from Los Angeles. In a proclamation to "Seize the Land," he urged Mexicans to redeem their rightful inheritance and colonize in Baja. Following Kropotkin closely, he estimated that the communal effort would reduce the work day to four hours and leave time for personal cultivation. The colonists, however, would need to come armed and to remain alert lest the capitalists return to deprive them again of their land.[39] Apparently he envisioned a transition to full anarchist communism in stages,[40] but time and events did not permit it.

The rebel force flew the PLM and American flags, drilled, and loafed in public. The non-Mexican, predominantly American faction—perhaps ninety percent of the total—acted independently of the Mexican "administration" headed by Antonio de Pío Araujo, a member of Ricardo's inner circle. Pío Araujo found himself powerless to implement the program. Most Mexicans had fled the area in the wake of the looting and enticing them back failed. Those who had arms had power, and they were not Mexicans. Celebrated Wobblies such as Joe Hill visited the Tijuana encampment and extolled its virtues, but to the popular press it looked like a scruffy, motley, vagabond band.

Lack of troop discipline stemmed partly from lack of leadership. The Welshman had sent money, supply requests, and reports to Los Angeles but had received only silence in return. So, on June 1, he left. At that moment, a Hollywood actor seeking publicity entered Tijuana with a new flag, proclaimed himself head of the army, and announced an independent New Republic of Lower California dedicated to capitalism. Anarchism and socialism were abolished.[41] This preposterous shenanigan, coupled with the previous military high-jinks and indifference by the non-Mexican majority toward the Mexican "administration," combined to reduce *The Conquest of Bread* to comic opera performed in Tijuana as street theater.

By June 3, the Floresmagonista elements had "triumphed" over the Hollywood actor's counterrevolution by narrowly electing the Marine deserter to be general and head of the force. He and the junta quickly disavowed the scheme but the image of filibuster filled the local press.[42] The embarrassment proved disruptive, forcing the Los Angeles junta to respond to charges from all quarters concerning the practical joke that the actor continued to promote.[43] Meanwhile, tensions within the rebel forces at Tijuana persisted.

While the Baja program unraveled, Madero sent a peace mission to the Los Angeles junta. Thinking that the Flores Magón brothers would listen to one of their own, Madero sent Jesús to talk to them; he was accompanied by Juan Sarabia, whom Madero had released from Díaz's prison. In the tradition of Mexican politics, Madero was offering Ricardo and his intimates a deal. Ricardo railed indignantly against the offer. The PLM would not lay down arms nor cease agitation until peasants had land and workers had control over the means of production. That and nothing less would satisfy him.[44]

The day after this angry and bitter interaction, June 14, 1911, American authorities entered *Regeneración*'s offices and arrested Ricardo and Enríque Flores Magón, along with two of their associates. Ricardo became convinced that Madero had betrayed them to the police through Sarabia, and he excoriated his former friend in print calling him "Juan Sarabia, the Judas."[45] No matter that Sarabia may have wondered which of them played Judas to the other's Christ, nor that Ricardo employed a religious metaphor when he hated and renounced religion. No matter that Sarabia denied it. Neither reason nor compassion could override the venom Ricardo spewed at the man who had shared Belén with him and Enríque in their struggle against Díaz. Ricardo's rage reflected his reaction to the collapse of his plans.

Federal troops, at Madero's direction, invaded Baja California and engaged the PLM forces. By June 22, a week after the peace mission and arrest, federals had routed the last of the PLM from Tijuana. Those who fled to San Diego were arrested for violating U.S. neutrality laws. They and the junta would go to court over the attempt to implement anarchism in Mexico. Ricardo's international propaganda effort in the Baja California front had failed.

The Chihuahua front had prepared the way for the fall of Juárez and Díaz' withdrawal, but the cost had been very high. Guerrero lay dead, and the PLM forces had gone over to Madero voluntarily or by force. Moreover, in Mexico City, where preparations for national elections began, Camilo Arriaga, convener of the First Liberal Convention, whom Ricardo had shunted from the PLM in 1906, emerged as Madero's campaign manager.[46] Mexicans seemed prepared to accept reform.

Many Americans seemed captivated by Madero or, at least, disenchanted with the PLM. The American Federation of Labor reacted coolly to Ricardo's appeal to Gompers to protest troop mobilization on the border. Gompers' earlier support had been won by socialists Gutiérrez de Lara and Villarreal who had since joined Madero. Gompers wrote Ricardo asking for a clear statement of his intentions in Mexico. "If the present regime is to be supplanted by another . . . without fundamentally changing the conditions which shall make for the improvement of the workers' opportunities . . . rights and interests," he concluded haughtily, "then the American labor movement can look upon such a change with entire indifference."[47]

Ricardo replied that Gompers' statement concisely summarized the PLM attitude. "Accordingly, our party adopted at the outset 'Land and Liberty' as its motto," he wrote, "and our brief declaration of principles states that we are struggling for possession of the land, reduction of the hours of labor and increased wages." Ricardo described the system imposed by Díaz as one of "chattel and wage slavery" and "against this we are in revolt."[48]

On April 8, Gompers straightforwardly sent Ricardo's request and the attendant correspondence to the members of his executive committee for their vote. He sent no written comment, pro or con. Only one of eight voted in favor of endorsing the PLM call for protest.[49] Abolishing the wage system had made Ricardo's point absolutely clear.

Debs took longer to reply, and when he did, he used a public forum. In the July 1911 issue of the *International Socialist Review*, he assayed the Mexican situation with particular reference to the PLM. He had been reading their current literature and especially the April 3 Manifesto. "If I read aright the manifesto recently issued by the Mexican Liberal Party all political action is tabooed. 'Direct action,' so called, is relied upon for results. Reading between the lines I can see nothing but anarchism in this program, and if that is what the leaders mean they should frankly say so that there may be no misunderstanding as to their attitude and program."[50]

Debs thought that direct action would lead to "a series of Haymarket sacrifices and the useless shedding of their noblest blood." To Debs, working through the system to find a political solution to economic problems was the only correct course. Owen, however, had condemned that socialist principle as an illusion "dreamed of in the opium den of politics"—a rejection of Debs' most cherished belief.[51]

Owen had been criticizing all socialists for their coverage of the Mexican question. He categorized them as boycotters and attempted a typology. Some boycotted the PLM through silence, as did the Los Angeles-based *California Social Democrat*. Some attacked the PLM indirectly; the *Chicago Daily Socialist*, which saw Madero as "Liberator," was one of these. Still others attacked the PLM directly, as had the *Appeal to Reason* and *The New York Call*. The latter accused Ricardo of attacking tyranny only with his pen. In considering the articles as a whole, Owen thought he detected a conspiracy to distort the truth.[52] George Shoaf, a shifty, blustery reporter, wrote most of the stories on Mexico for the *Appeal to Reason;* John Kenneth Turner thought Shoaf guilty of "covering his ignorance with fake stories."[53] Some deliberate deception aside, however, the root cause of the differences between socialists and PLM anarchists was profoundly ideological.

Debs returned to this difference in an essay on "The Mexican Revolution" carried in the *Appeal to Reason*. He began with a lengthy description of the PLM plight following the Baja debacle. "Six of the party's leaders [were] in jail in Los Angeles and five in San Diego." Debs denounced their arrest because the charge was intended to silence them. "It is simply monstrous that the commission of such crimes against totally innocent men should be tolerated in the United States." Manifesting his admiration for their commitment, he wrote: "That we stand for such brutal assaults upon men who have sacrificed their all in the service of their country and to emancipate their fellow men from the torments of hell, is nothing less than a disgrace to us all."[54]

He thought them men who had "sacrificed everything they have, including their freedom and almost their lives" for their beliefs. Debs appealed for money for their defense fund, giving the contact person and the address. He concluded this segment of his essay with a moving statement of his responsibility as citizen and socialist to Ricardo Flores Magón and the PLM. "Personally I am not in agreement with all the plans and tactics of these [PLM] leaders, but I am bound to admit their honesty, their sincerity, and their unselfish devotion to their enslaved people, and I am under obligation to fight for them against these fresh outrages perpetrated upon them by the Hessian hirelings of American capitalism to the full extent of my power."

Nonetheless, when PLM leaders "denounced the advocates of working class political action as steeped in depravity, 'in the opium den of politics,' " Debs wrote, "they attacked the Socialist Party and every member of it." As long as they resisted political action, instead of making the revolution they desired, they would only waste blood and treasure. "Without right education and right economic and political organization the revolution cannot succeed. With these it cannot fail."[55]

Thus, PLM criticism of political action and insistence upon direct action caused Debs to draw the line on socialist support that summer. In these two essays, Debs wrote the PLM out of the forefront of socialist solidarity. Henceforth, Socialists would aid the PLM only in matters of free speech and then only if their own priorities permitted. Moreover, Socialists, along with the conservative AFL, were facing a major challenge in Los Angeles, not from the PLM, but from an assault on unionism linked to American-initiated propaganda by the deed.

The previous year, about 1:00 A.M., October 1, an explosion had shaken the building of the *Los Angeles Times*. A fire immediately ensued and quickly engulfed the entire structure, killing twenty-one people. Harrison G. Otis, editor and long-time union opponent, immediately blamed the explosion on union dynamiters. California Governor James Gillett issued the following statement: "Whether guilty or not, the labor unionists will have to be blamed for the crime until shown that they are not guilty. . . . " At the funeral service on October 9, the pastor of the First Methodist Church told the large crowd, "the vicious act of these murderers is the logical [con]sequence of the incendiary and treasonable tirades of loud mouthed Anarchists. . . . Our watchword must be, 'The extermination of Anarchists and Anarchy.' "[56]

Otis and the *Times*, along with his supporters, pushed the dynamite theory. Police claimed to have found crudely made bombs in the shrubbery outside the Otis home, adding further speculation to the charge. Other newspapers, however, carried an alternative story. A Western Union operator who had left the destroyed office just before the explosion, reported that "throughout the night the building was filled with the fumes of gas, escaping from an unknown leak, and that the fumes were so noxious that they caused considerable annoyance to the workers."[57] The radical papers favored this view and launched a search for the evidence to confirm it.

Shoaf managed to convince the *Appeal to Reason* that the explosion theory had been his personal discovery and got assigned to the case. Over time, he convinced Debs that Otis had known of the gas leak and had hired someone to plant the bombs to blame on organized labor. In April 1911, two brothers named McNamara, members of the International Association of Bridge and Structural Iron Workers, AFL, were arrested in Indianapolis for the crime and clandestinely returned to Los Angeles to stand trial. Both Debs and Gompers were now committed to defending these workers against Otis and the antilabor forces.[58]

Ricardo's revelation of his deeply held anarchist convictions came at an inappropriate time for the AFL and Debs, locked in combat as they were in Los Angeles over the *Times* explosion. When Ricardo was arrested, his usual attorney, Socialist party member Harriman, was committed to the McNamara case and unavailable. Money had been raised to hire Clarence Darrow as defense attorney and Harriman as his assistant. Harriman had been a former running mate of Debs, and in 1911, he was the Socialist candidate for mayor of Los Angeles. Despite the case, his chances for election looked excellent. And even if Debs had some slight doubt about the McNamaras' innocence, the manner of their extradition and the anti-union stance of Otis made this an important fight to win.[59]

Out on bail raised partly by Emma Goldman and others, including socialists, Ricardo decided to abolish any possibility of future confusion about his aims. His Manifesto of September 23, 1911, became the cornerstone of all future PLM agitation and propaganda. No really new ideas were included, but, like the shedding of a cocoon, the creature inside emerged in full and clear form.

The statement followed a logical progression beginning with the evils of private property, affirming that without it government would not exist, and arguing that expropriation of property and abolition of government constituted the only correct course. "The Mexican Liberal Party recognizes that the so-called right of individual property is an iniquitous right . . . that Authority and the Church are the supports of . . . Capital and, therefore . . . has solemnly declared war against Authority, . . . Capital, and . . . Church." Following this concise statement of aims, the document enumerated fourteen states in which expropriation had taken place and advised how goods should be distributed according to anarchist communist ideas. Both land and industry should be seized at once and their benefits shared without distinction of sex.

In unmistakable language Ricardo urged:

> Mexicans! If you wish to be free . . . struggle only for the Mexican Liberal Party. All others are offering you political liberty when they have triumphed. We Liberals invite you to take immediate possession of the land, the machinery, the means of transportation and the buildings, without expecting anyone to give them to you and without waiting for any law to decree it . . . Liberty

and well being are within our grasp. The same effort and the same sacrifices that are required to raise a governor—a tyrant—will achieve the expropriation of the fortunes that the rich keep from you. It is for you, then, to choose.[60]

Yet even this clarifying manifesto, designed to replace the 1906 document, contained contradictions, a legacy of the movement's origins. Despite its name, the PLM was neither a party nor Liberal. In anarchist fashion, the "party" was now an association of like-minded individuals without the organization and direction that the term "party" implied. From this point, Ricardo began to abandon creation of new local cells; he left the existing ones as sources of financial support, but without his previous central direction. And, of course, the ideology of the group was not Liberal but anarchist with appeals both to anarchist communism and to anarchosyndicalism. Probably only long-standing name recognition caused Ricardo to retain the newspaper's title.

Ricardo's September 23, 1911 Manifesto coincided with the astonishing resolution of the McNamara case. With Darrow for the defense, the stage had been set for a dramatic confrontation between labor and capital. The *Appeal to Reason* had invested heavily in money, energy, and news coverage of the case and, based upon Shoaf's exaggerated stories, predicted vindication of the brothers. On the eve of the mayoral election, however, the McNamaras confessed. They had set the bombs that destroyed the *Los Angeles Times* building, and they were responsible for the deaths that ensued. American unionism appeared disgraced.

Angelenos, angered and outraged by the confession, resoundingly rejected Harriman and the Socialists at the polls.[61] The AFL stood to lose much from this incident, and the McNamara case prompted Gompers to redirect the organization away from confrontation to ever more conservative cooperation with capital. Debs and the *Appeal to Reason,* however, lost most. The bitter disappointment of the McNamara case seemed to have broken the power of the *Appeal,* and it began a decline that ended its advocacy three years later.[62] In this milieu, Ricardo's problems seemed irrelevant.

Ricardo's September 23 Manifesto pertained more to Mexican politics and his international standing among anarchists than to the local labor struggle in Los Angeles. He published his appeal on the eve of the first fair Mexican presidential elections in more than thirty-five years. In a carefully prescribed elections code, presidential electors were chosen on October 1, and they in turn chose the president and vice-president on October 15. The immensely popular Madero won.[63] Ironically, the reformer Madero had made an honest man of Ricardo the anarchist. Without Madero's victory, who knows how much longer Ricardo would have continued to dodge acknowledging his ideology?

Madero made one more attempt to heal the rift with Ricardo and to bring him back to Mexico. Madero sent the remarkable Mary Harris Jones—better known to American workers as "Mother Jones"—from Mexico City to Los Angeles to reconcile the PLM junta to the new order. "Mother Jones" had toiled on behalf of the junta for years, raising money for defense funds and to sustain their activities in the United States—protecting them both against Díaz's agents and U.S. authorities. She believed that Madero represented positive change for the worker, and she came to tell the junta so. Describing her meeting with them, she wrote in a letter to Manuel Calero, "they charged everyone with being a traitor, but themselves . . . We discussed the matter pro and con for an hour, but they believed only in direct action, the taking over of the lands."

After that meeting failed, she tried another—this time with the PLM's attorney Harriman present. In the same letter, she recounted that discussion: "Neither Mr. Harriman or myself could get them to accept any proposition that was made to them." For refusing to take Madero's offer, she told the junta, "if you are again arrested, the labor movement will take no hand in your defense. It has done everything honorable for you. It has delved into its Treasury and defended you when you needed a friend." She concluded, "I consider them one and all a combination of unreasonable fanatics, with no logic in their arguments . . ."[64] Ricardo had broken with yet another important American labor supporter over his ideals.

Ricardo faced a court trial for violation of U.S. neutrality statutes in June 1912, but he also faced trial in Mexican and European papers for the Baja escapade. In reply to Ricardo's earlier denunciation of his former friends, Villarreal published an article describing Ricardo as a "blackmailer, swindler, coward and a drunken pervert and scoundrel who shared his mistresses with all men of bad taste."[65] Ricardo had referred to Villarreal in print as a "homosexual" and "assassin."[66] Ricardo's venom had lowered the argument over revolution in Mexico to an ugly series of ad hominem attacks conveying untruths.

The uninformed may have accepted many of the allegations against Ricardo, for some were repeated frequently. He had, after all, lied to his followers in the PLM about his real goals, and the Baja failure seemed monumental folly or treason. Nonetheless, Ricardo rarely drank, and he was not a sexual libertarian. Anarchists could be advocates of free love—as were Emma Goldman, her former lover and co-worker Alexander Berkman, or Owen. But other anarchists were sexually conservative, living with one partner in nearly lifelong fidelity in a common-law relationship. This way of life characterized Kropotkin, Malatesta, and Ricardo.

María Brousse de Talavera lived with Ricardo most of his life. When he was imprisoned, she visited him frequently and smuggled messages in and out. When writing to American friends on his behalf she used the name Magón.[67] Her daughter Lucile, or Lucía, Norman Guidera, Ricardo accepted as his stepdaughter,[68] and when her son attended the Walt Whitman School—a Modern School patterned after Ferrer's model—he was regarded as Ricardo's grandson.[69] Periodically Ricardo tried to establish an anarchist-communist commune,[70] but his lack of funds and his prison stays disrupted the attempts. Sexual sharing of partners was not part of his communal idea.

Another problematic issue of Ricardo's sex life involved his sterility. The fact had been published originally by a close friend, after Ricardo's death, to counter claimants pretending to be his heirs.[71] When, in assessing Ricardo's character, the reader encounters "[h]is sterility may or may not have been of psychological significance,"[72] a comment is needed.

Male sterility, a sperm count insufficient to impregnate an ovum, should not be confused with impotence, the failure to achieve and sustain an erection during sex. To many, impotence means sexual failure. Sterility does not. Impotence may be caused by psychological or physiological difficulties.[73] Suggesting sexual failure as a component of Ricardo's radicalism conjures, unfairly, a comparison with one of anarchism's major figures, Bakunin. A large and powerfully built man of action who fought on the barricades of Europe, Bakunin is said to have suffered from impotence.[74] One may choose to view Bakunin's life as a compensation for his sexual impotence;[75] however, to suggest a similar approach to Ricardo Flores Magón's life is inappropriate.

Because he did not take the field in the Baja campaign, Ricardo was hounded by the charge of cowardice. At least two reasons can be adduced for his nonmilitary activity. He saw his role in the revolution as propagandist, not by the deed, but by the pen. Moreover, the Tijuana seizure had been against his orders, and events there degenerated quickly into disaster. He did not comment on the Tijuana operation except to denounce the actor's filibustering joke.[76] His embarrassment at the farce his anarchist-communist experiment had become, drove him into public silence on the subject.

That silence and his deception, however, lent further credence to the unwarranted charge that he had planned a filibuster from the beginning. As one careful student of the episode has observed, "The transfer of territory by means of a filibuster from one national sovereignty to another was the last thing that the anarchist Flores Magón, the enemy of all states, aimed for."[77] Respect for the Mexican nation and its pride in patrimony, to which his propaganda contributed, would never have permitted it. Alta California had originally been taken from Mexico in 1846 by a successful filibuster headed by John C. Frémont. Ricardo did not want to repeat the past. He wanted to overthrow states, not augment their territories.

Ricardo and Owen defended the PLM in the international anarchist press. On March 2, *Les Temps Nouveaux,* an important Parisian anarchist newspaper, carried a story denouncing Ricardo and the PLM as bandits, reactionaries, and false anarchists. The article cited as evidence the November 1910 instructions forbidding joint action with Madero and the 1906 reform program attached to those instructions. Ricardo's deception had caught up with him again.

Ricardo's reply, typical of the period, was riddled with half-truths. He claimed, correctly, that the PLM had been evolving. His contention that the "manifesto in question was old and long since abrogated" was, however, untrue. He did not actually abrogate it until he issued the September 23, 1911, document. With a disingenuousness bordering on contempt for his anarchist audience, he wrote that "copies [of the 1906 program] found their way into circulation solely because at that particular moment we were out of funds and had no other propaganda matter."[78] Ricardo expected his anarchist colleagues to believe that he, the primary PLM propagandist, lacked the money to publish the movement's true aims on the eve of its revolution! Small wonder that other European and American anarchist newspapers remained equally unconvinced.[79]

Owen confidently wrote that Kropotkin understood the real nature of the Mexican revolution and the role of *Regeneración* and Ricardo in it.[80] While Kropotkin did defend Ricardo as a legitimate anarchist and confirmed that the insurrection in Mexico constituted a genuine agrarian struggle against exploitation,[81] he refrained from giving the endorsement that Ricardo and Owen sought. They wanted acknowledgement that Mexico's struggle was not only part of the international revolution, but also its beginning.

Such affirmation would have meant international backing for the PLM in money and active volunteer support, in addition to propaganda. Kropotkin could not do that. Insufficient news coverage and Eurocentrism militated against it. Ricardo's poster representing anarchism showed the horsewomen galloping from Europe to America. Now Ricardo wanted Kropotkin to acknowledge America as model, with the Mexican example galloping across the Atlantic to Europe—the New World rejuvenating the Old. Ricardo asked too much of his European colleagues.

Nonetheless, in the United States and in Mexico, Ricardo as anarchist found succor. Some anarchists in America had known his real mind for several years, so that his full disclosure provoked no astonishment. Moreover, among those who had not known him previously, study of his work and exposure to *Regeneración* created new allies. Unquestionably, one of the most important of these was the American Voltairine de Cleyre. Born in Michigan in 1866 and educated in a Canadian convent that she regarded as a prison, Voltairine became a free thinker shortly after her graduation. The Haymarket tragedy caused her conversion to socialism, and the executions convinced her of anarchism.

In the opinion of an important anarchist historian, Voltairine's philosophical grasp "of anarchist thought, in its tolerance, breadth of outlook, high seriousness, close reasoning, and clear definition" had no equal save for Elisée Reclus.[82] Voltairine's approach derived from her acceptance of the idea of "anarchism without adjectives," as articulated by Tarrida del Marmol. The Spanish anarchist sought to heal the divisions within anarchism—mutualist, communist, individualist, syndicalist—by minimizing economic differences and emphasizing the anarchist insistence on the right to choose any path. By 1900, Malatesa too had embraced this idea, shared by both Reclus and Voltairine.[83]

She found the same spirit in *Regeneración*. Ricardo appealed to communist and syndicalist sentiments and tolerated Owen's individualist notion in order to focus anarchism on its objective—Liberty. Although sectarian about anarchism—no other way to freedom existed—he was nonsectarian within it. He believed that it was essential for people to free themselves, and he had no need to dictate precisely what economic form their freedom should assume. Tarrida del Marmol, Malatesta, and Reclus all appeared in Ricardo's 1910 poster, and his writings in *Regeneración* demonstrated his embrace of their views.

Voltairine detected "more anarchism in *Regeneración* in a week's issue than the rest of our publications put together." Moreover, it was "fighting anarchism, that means to do and is doing something to smash this whole accursed system."[84] She recognized Ricardo's intention in Tijuana and sympathized. *Regeneración*'s emphasis upon sex equality, Modern Schools, opposition to every form of tyranny, and direct action resonated with her as nothing else she had encountered previously. She was a feminist, an advocate of sex equality and free love, a devoted teacher in Ferrer Modern Schools, an implacable opponent of authority, and a woman committed to practical action. Although periodically sick from chronic sinusitis, which caused severe earaches, she found renewed inspiration in the spring of 1911 by making the Mexican revolution her cause.

As a speaker she lacked the flamboyance and skill of Emma Goldman, although at least one observer who had heard both thought that she learned more from Voltairine.[85] In a major address in Chicago on "The Mexican Revolution," which Voltairine delivered October 29, 1911, she chided anarchists for their ignorance of the situation and their gullible acceptance of Madero's election as evidence that the revolution was over. Citing the continued insurrections against Madero and the land seizures made by the peasants, she dismissed the socialist notion, advanced by Debs, that the peasant needed more education and organization before the revolution could be made. "These unlettered but determined people must be dealt with *now;* there is no such thing as 'waiting til they are educated up to it.'" Education had been denied the poor because education could be a weapon used by the weak against the powerful. "But to conclude that people are necessarily unintelligent because they are illiterate is itself . . . unintelligent."

Anarchists had been denied the truth about Mexico, she decried, because the press, including the socialists, failed to report events accurately. Social preoccupations with sports and divorce scandals, lack of knowledge of Spanish, and a presumption "that whatever happened in Mexico was a joke"—all combined to reinforce American ignorance of the great events transpiring south of the border. She did not think that her efforts could "remove this mountain of indifference." Nonetheless, she argued, every reformer of whatever school should watch the "wakening of the land workers themselves to the recognition of what all schools of revolutionary economics admit to be the primal necessity—the social repossession of the land." Concluding with feeling, she said, "whether they are victorious or defeated, I, for one, will bow my head to those heroic strugglers, no matter how ignorant, who have raised the cry, Land and Liberty, and planted the blood-red banner on the burning soil of Mexico."[86]

She used an invitation to address the Chicago Bohemian Club on March 18, 1912, to celebrate the Paris Commune, as a vehicle for appealing to Congress and to the international anarchist community. In addition to the arguments already advanced in "The Commune is Risen," she compared Mexico to the Paris Commune and found them identical. Only foreign intervention could prevent the Mexican peasants from reclaiming their land, and against this possibility she inveighed with extraordinary intensity. "Yes, honorable Senators and Congressmen, the house next door is on fire—the house of Tyranny . . . Yes, it is on fire. And let it Burn—burn to the ground—utterly. And do not seek to quench it by pouring out the blood of the people of the United States, in a vile defense of . . . financial adventurers."

With words that equalled Ricardo's eloquence she concluded: "Let it crumble to the ground, that House of Infamy; and if the burning gleeds fly hitherward, and the rotten structure of our own life starts to blaze, welcome, thrice welcome, purifying fire, that shall set us, too, upon the earth once more—free men upon free land—no tenant dwellers on a landlord's domain.' "[87]

Voltairine did more than talk. She organized the "Chicago Mexican Liberal Defense League" in response to the junta's appeal for support. Within a year she could report impressive results. "At various picnics, private gatherings, and mass meetings we have sold copies of *Regeneración* or distributed freely the unsold copies, to the number of sixteen hundred." They distributed to the city's unions four thousand copies of Owen's *The Mexican Revolt*.

She and her group pressed their views of the PLM and Mexico upon the international community. One of their representatives traveled to Canada and England lecturing and giving interviews over an eight-month period. In February 1912, Ludovico Caminita, *Regeneración*'s Italian section editor, visited Chicago and lectured in Italian. He introduced the group to some "active and self-sacrificing Spanish-speaking comrades from whose example we almost unconsciously adopted the habit of taxing ourselves a little weekly for the support of the paper."[88] Voltairine herself raised several hundred dollars for Ricardo's work and legal defense, in addition to propagandizing for the cause.

In the midst of this intense pace, and probably because of it, the sinusitis returned severely on April 17. A doctor diagnosed an infection in her middle ear and sent Voltairine to a hospital. Physicians there determined that the infection had entered her brain, and they immediately operated. When she suffered a relapse, they performed a second operation. She lost the power of speech and movement and, after nine weeks of hideous suffering, she died on June 20.[89] American anarchism had lost one of its leading articulators, and Ricardo had lost another invaluable ally.

Not all who responded to *Regeneración*'s appeal for help could do so with the dramatic intensity of Voltairine in Chicago. Yet working readers and listeners of all kinds responded with money and signatures, hoping to secure freedom for Ricardo and the PLM leaders. The trial had been scheduled for June 1912. *Regeneración* published bilingual coupons that subscribers could clip, sign, and mail to implore President Taft's justice for these men. Returned coupons rarely contained a single signature. Those which bore an April postmark illustrate. Returns came from 246 communities in the United

States and Mexico, representing 889 individuals and two "Mexican Colonies" in America of unspecified size. A random look at the returns shows: 33 Mexicans from Pénjamo, Guanajuato; 4 Italians from Stonington, Illinois; 111 signers for the Mexican Colony of Hondo, Texas; 219 signatures from La Junta, Colorado; the Mexican Colony of Austin, Texas, without enumeration; one signature from Boston, Massachusetts; and 85 representing the Mexican Colony of Phoenix, Arizona. Later arrivals came from Puerto Rico, Cuba, Argentina, and Spain.[90]

The PLM's greatest grass-roots support, in terms of these coupons, came from Mexicans and Mexican Americans in the southwestern United States. International mail as well as the violence of civil war may have meant underrepresentation from Mexico. Yet, President Taft received thousands of expressions of support for the PLM before and after their trial. Nonetheless, popular support would have no impact on the hearing and its outcome. Other radical outbursts, particularly in San Diego, would.

Ricardo's two natural allies, the IWW and Emma Goldman, were involved in a desperate struggle over freedom of speech at the time of his trial. Goldman and the Wobblies had fought the issue for years and, after each conflict, thought the victory secure.[91] In February 1912, however, in the wake of the McNamara case, San Diego authorities passed a law prohibiting free speech in Horton Plaza—a traditional site of open talk akin to Hyde Park. Wobblies and anarchists were the law's specific targets, and citizens organized themselves into vigilante bands to "help" police enforce the law. Anarchists, socialists, reformers, and other concerned citizens protested this infringement of personal rights by holding illegal street meetings in the plaza. The jails soon filled and Wobblies appealed nationally for help.

Goldman, along with her tour manager and lover, Ben Reitman, traveled west to assist. In Los Angeles she raised money for the PLM defense fund. San Diego and free speech, however, constituted her principal objectives on this trip. A young Wobbly had been killed by the police, and, following his funeral, Goldman and Reitman arrived in San Diego on May 14. An angry mob including women greeted them at the depot, threatening to strip Emma, beat her, and "rip her guts out." Before she could speak, police whisked them away separately to the U.S. Grant Hotel across from Horton Plaza. With police and hotel connivance, however, vigilantes kidnapped Reitman. They forced him into an automobile where he was held down and urinated on by one of the men before they drove him out of town.

The vigilantes forced Reitman to strip in preparation for his "lesson." They then tarred him—using sagebrush for feathers—burned IWW into his buttocks with burning cigars, twisted his testicles, and tried to sodomize him with his cane. They poured tar on his head and forced him to run a gauntlet while being beaten by the gang. After he had sung "The Star Spangled Banner" and kissed the American flag, they threw him his underpants and fled. Despite publicity and special investigations, the vigilantes remained at large.[92]

Reitman had been profoundly shaken. He had saved his sex organs at the expense of his pride. Humiliation struck deep, and Goldman did not assuage it when she expressed disappointment at his alleged cowardice. She thought he should have refused to submit. She was prepared to make the sacrifice that only he could make. Shame drove him into a deep depression; she quickly put the incident aside.[93] This marked Reitman's turning point; he later left the movement in favor of a conventional marriage, fatherhood, and social respectability. The free speech fight in San Diego had been a costly failure for radicals and, following upon the McNamara case, had prepared the climate of hostility for the PLM trial.

The Los Angeles courtroom filled with the motley collection of people who had been in the Tijuana campaign. In an atmosphere of acrimony and bitterness, charges were presented and testimony given with witnesses frequently challenged by others in the room. Some witnesses for the prosecution blithely perjured themselves; at one point Ricardo's stepdaughter interrupted a witness, called him a traitor, and slapped his face.[94]

Ricardo's alliance with American radicals stood trial more than his deeds;[95] however, if seeking to redeem the disinherited constituted crime, he accepted guilt. After two weeks, the court found that the PLM leaders had violated U.S. neutrality laws. Three days later they stood for sentencing. In June 1912, precisely a year after Madero's forces had routed the PLM remnants from Tijuana, an American judge handed Ricardo and his colleagues the maximum penalty of twenty-three months, to be served at the dank prison on McNeil Island in Puget Sound. Ricardo's enraged stepdaughter denounced the proceedings, called the authorities cowards, and "precipitated one of the wildest riots ever witnessed in the streets of Los Angeles."[96] Police quickly sent the prisoners away.

That fall, Americans seemed to prefer reform as much as Mexicans had a year earlier and, in November, elected Woodrow Wilson president. Socialists had done well, however, with Debs earning six percent of the total presidential vote—his highest mark. Socialists also held 1,200 public offices in 340 municipalities nationwide.[97] Yet disappointment prevailed in several quarters because accomplishments had fallen short of predictions.

Socialists could look at the McNamara case and San Diego as failures that tarnished their national performance. Anarchists, on the other hand, could view the McNamara case positively. In comparison with the Haymarket tragedy, the Los Angeles experience marked an improvement. "In 1887 men were hanged who were innocent of the charges against them, and a howl of exultation went up all over the country," one writer observed. "In 1911 men [were] sentenced to imprisonment who [were], according to their own statement, guilty—and they [found] many defenders. This shows progress."[98]

The *Appeal to Reason,* the newspaper that had striven to unite the Socialist party nationally, had been battered by the McNamara case and by the presidential election. Julius Wayland, the paper's founder and the coarchitect of its national prominence, spent a quiet Sunday after the election "talkin' socialism" with friends. He went to his room to retire but instead took a loaded pistol and, using a sheet as silencer, put the barrel in his mouth, aimed for his head, and pulled the trigger. His note, on the bedside table, read: "The struggle under the competitive system is not worth the effort; let it pass."[99]

Ricardo could not "let it pass"—whether in Mexico or the United States, in prison or at large. Those who pursued radicalism in America at that time either paid a heavy price for their activism or turned away. Ricardo knew the price was higher in Mexico, so he endured what he could not change. Comrades and colleagues had fallen: Guerrero in battle and Voltairine in illness. Some found the personal sacrifice too much and, like Reitman, left. For a small group, losses like these severely crippled a movement. Perhaps those closer to the political system—those such as the Socialists, who expected more from it—were more susceptible to despair. Nonetheless, despite losing the large Mexican coalition the PLM had built through deceit; despite losing broad-based American labor support that had been won by deception; despite failing to instill anarchist communism in Tijuana; despite an increasingly hostile political climate; despite prison; despite all these reverses, Ricardo persevered in the United States with a gritty hope. Ricardo's anarchism convinced him that the disinherited would not tolerate Madero much longer and that reform could never solve Mexico's ills. Even if few listened, he would soon appear to be a prophet.

CHAPTER 3

A CONTRADICTION IN TERMS

But it is full time to give up this illusion, so often proved false and so dearly paid for, of a revolutionary government. It is time to admit, once for all, this political axion [:] that a government cannot be revolutionary.
Peter Kropotkin[1]

With Ricardo and Enríque Flores Magón serving long sentences in a federal penitentiary, as were other PLM leaders, *Regeneración* fell to the able hands of Pío Araujo. He too had been indicted for his role in Tijuana but had skipped to Canada, returning to Los Angeles after the trial.[2] He began 1913 by reprinting the poster representing anarchism,[3] and he continued the vigorous anarchist propaganda begun earlier by Ricardo and Owen. Owen kept the English section as combative as ever.

Anarchists, convinced that Madero could not endure, continued exhorting Mexicans to seize their land and factories and to reject the new government. Ricardo's doomsaying seemed prophetic, as Madero proved ill suited to politics. "Díaz the Little," as Emma Goldman dubbed him,[4] stalled on the land question, angering both campesinos who wanted land and landlords who wanted their rights reconfirmed. Madero's most serious quarrel had been with Emiliano Zapata, whose followers had repossessed lands wrongfully taken from them in Morelos.

The Zapatistas acted independently of Madero. When, during the slow demobilization following Díaz's departure, overzealous federal troops shot several of Zapata's people for not disarming quickly enough, Zapata decided to keep his weapons. At this impasse, a threatening move by the federal general Victoriano Huerta caused Zapata to rebel. He disavowed Madero and followed his own course. Insurrection in Morelos, very close to Mexico City, proved a persistent irritation. It was, at various times, a serious threat to the capital for the next eight years—bedeviling Madero and his successors.[5]

Madero surrounded himself with family members, some of whom enriched themselves from public coffers, and he appointed members of the upper class to his cabinet. Madero made a token mestizo appointment—Ricardo's older brother Jesús Flores Magón—to Minister of Government (*Gobernación*), the most powerful cabinet post. When Madero realized his mistake, he tried to transfer Jesús to Development (*Fomento*), prompting the Minister's resignation.[6]

Madero treated Orozco no better. Many Mexicans thought the muleteer had defeated Díaz, thereby giving Madero power. Orozco himself thought he deserved a position in the new government. Madero, however, retained nearly all the old federal officers, and he appointed new civilians who supposedly were better prepared than Orozco for the complexities of government. Hence, Abraham González won election as Chihuahua's governor and Venustiano Carranza joined the cabinet as Minister of War and Marine. Orozco had to settle for heading Chihuahua's *rurales,* the local police, and he became disgruntled.[7]

Orozco rebelled against Madero and issued his own political plan calling for comprehensive land reform. He joined others, already in revolt, who held Juárez; this give him a base for serious opposition. He raised an army quickly, took Ciudad Chihuahua, the capital, and became master of the state. When word reached Mexico City that Orozco led a column of eight thousand prepared to march on the national capital, panic ensued. Taking drastic action, Madero recalled to service a man he had previously dismissed for alienating Zapata, General Huerta. As a condition of acceptance, Huerta demanded no civilian interference in his military campaign.

With his disciplined, regular soldiers, Huerta slowly began to retake important towns from the Orozquista irregulars. By late summer 1912, Huerta had retaken Juárez and reduced Orozco's forces to guerrilla operations around Ojinaga.[8] Yet Huerta did not crush Orozco, or rather anti-Madero sentiment, in the north. Huerta treated Orozco as a hedge against the future, when he might need a strong man in Chihuahua.

Madero faced 1913 as a troubled man. The commander of his army, which had been Díaz's army as well, disliked him. The foreign community grew impatient with his delays, wanting assurances that the old Porfirian arrangements favoring them still held. The land question burned and campesinos rebelled. The avarice of Madero family members caused scandal. Madero's popularity had fallen so steeply that, as we shall see, the only act that could save his inept government from being discarded and forgotten would bring about his political salvation at the cost of his life. He became the revolution's martyr and Apostle—the symbol of all it embodied. And who should have been there to witness the drama but the man who had quit Mexican politics over Ricardo's break with Madero, John Kenneth Turner?

Turner had decided to revisit the country whose misery he had reported and through which he had won his fame. He stayed with old friends, Manuel Sarabia of the celebrated kidnapping and his heiress wife Elizabeth Trowbridge. On January 27, 1913, he secured an interview with Madero, who greeted him saying, "You are a very famous man." Madero credited *Barbarous Mexico* with helping him to victory "as it gave the American people the knowledge that he was fighting for liberty."[9] Although Turner had learned first about Mexican problems from Ricardo and Enríque and had traveled into Mexico with their socialist associate Gutiérrez de Lara to gather the data that became *Barbarous Mexico,* the benefit of his muckraking ironically did not accrue to the PLM.

Turner was given assurance of a safe conduct and carte blanche to visit any installation and to write whatever he chose. He embarked on a sightseeing expedition around the capital when Madero's government fell. During this time, Huerta took advantage of a ten-day battle between warring factions to seize power on February 18. He had Madero, Vice-president José Pino Suárez, and the entire cabinet arrested; and then legalized his position cynically. He forced Madero, Pino Suárez, and the remaining cabinet ministers, save one, to resign. The surviving minister then appointed Huerta to the cabinet post of succession, and then himself resigned. To reinforce his "legal" claim, Huerta had Madero and Pino Suárez subjected to the *ley fuga* on February 21; they were shot to death while attempting to escape.[10]

Huerta's coup d'état and murder of Madero stunned most of Mexico. When Huerta demanded that provincial governors adhere to his government, only one thought quickly enough to refrain. In Coahuila, Madero's natal state, Governor Venustiano Carranza first defiantly refused to recognize Huerta, yet then began to vacillate.[11] Saying no officially and perhaps privately, the governor tried to stall for time to collect his scattered military forces and to plan the future. On March 7, Carrancista forces first engaged Huerta's forces, and Carranza's opposition became clear.

Defeat in battle, however, prompted Carranza to try for victory in a different medium. On March 13, he issued his Plan of Guadalupe, a simple document that disavowed Huerta and made Carranza First Chief of the Constitutionalist military forces. Carranza announced that after taking Mexico City, he would hold elections and yield his authority to the winner. In an attempt to make the incipient movement more than Coahuila's revenge for the murder of a favorite son, representatives from Sonora and Chihuahua signed for their respective states.[12]

As originally created, the Constitutionalist Army comprised two corps and one division. Alvaro Obregón commanded the Northwest Corps, Pablo González the Northeast Corps, and Pancho Villa raised the famed Division of the North. Carranza thought that González, with his subordinate Jacinto B. Treviño, was the most loyal of these men. Militarily, Obregón proved the best, and his decision to stay with Carranza eventually contributed the talent to win. Pancho Villa, however, won the greatest popularity with his sensational and reckless attacks. Each of these forces operated independently and without unified command. Carranza deliberately eschewed military rank to emphasize the civilian nature of the movement and thereby underscore its legitimacy—although he presided over the equivalent of a military coalition.[13]

Huerta's federals, better trained, armed, and equipped, proved a formidable obstacle to the provincial irregulars who developed their military strategy in campaign. Huerta regarded Chihuahua as the most potentially dangerous state, and he took special steps to insure its loyalty. Huerta made a deal with Orozco incorporating the rebels into the federal army and even paying their debts incurred while fighting Madero.[14] Moreover, Huerta engaged in a policy of political assassination, which included Chihuahua Governor Abraham González—the man who had even more influence upon Villa than Madero.[15]

Huerta's tactics made Villa a national hero. The former bandit called men to his side in a war that country people could understand. Huerta had betrayed and murdered Madero, murdered González, and bought Orozco. Villa took these acts as personal insults, wanted revenge, and recruited forces in Orozco's territory. The struggle between these two deepened into war without quarter, neither man wanting the other's prisoners, each wanting the other dead.

Initially, Orozco took the brunt of the Constitutionalist military campaign because Villa went straight after him. Despite his disadvantages, Villa fought with an unbelievable fury. His charisma bound men to him, and his valor against overwhelming odds prompted emulation from his soldiers. Much of his celebrated and real battlefield heroics sprang from his desire for vengeance rather than political outrage. Nonetheless, his soldiers followed him with extraordinary fealty and performed with superhuman prowess.

Villa's successes obscured the slower, incremental progress of Obregón and the failures of Pablo González. Yet Carranza's military campaign was always accompanied by political propaganda that pursued a single goal: to define legitimacy so narrowly that only Carranza fulfilled its requirements. Carranza insisted that he acted not out of revenge for Madero's murder but out of outrage that Mexico's laws had been violated. As a constitutionally elected state governor, Carranza had been the first to disavow the Usurper Huerta, who had taken power illegally and maintained it through assassination. Carranza stated that he sought only a return to rule by law and restoration of order under the Constitution of 1857. In effect, he claimed Madero's mantle and proclaimed civil war to get it back.

Carranza and the Constitutionalists received help from an unexpected and, to many, an unwanted quarter—the United States. Huerta had taken power in the weeks prior to the inauguration of Woodrow Wilson as president; outgoing President Taft left to the newcomer the problem of recognizing a Mexican government. Wilson, a former professor and Princeton University president, had run on a Progressive ticket for the Democratic Party; he viewed Huerta's actions with stern disapproval.

Wilson believed that Huerta had murdered a constitutionally elected president and would not countenance diplomatic relations with such a man. Wilson viewed Madero as a reformer bent on doing good, and saw Huerta, obviously in league with foreign business interests, as an evil man seeking to undo Mexican reform. Although other international governments had recognized Huerta, Wilson would not. He refused to recognize Huerta or anyone else until the contest had been decided on the battlefield, and he announced a policy of "watchful waiting" to see how Constitutionalists or Zapatistas fared against the federal forces.[16]

Addressing Congress in December 1913, Wilson described American conditions in positive terms, but noted, "There is but one cloud upon our horizon. That has shown itself to the south of us and hangs over Mexico." He continued ominously, "There can be no certain prospects of peace in America until General Huerta has surrendered his usurped authority in Mexico."[17] Wilson raised the spector of intervention in Mexican affairs—one of Ricardo Flores Magón's greatest fears.

As Ricardo neared the end of his prison term at McNeil Island, he confronted an altered Mexican situation. He also faced an American president who knew of his political activities personally. Through the intercession of friends, including Los Angeles socialists, a California representative persuaded the new president to personally review the 1912 case and to discover for himself the travesty that had been done Ricardo and the PLM. Wilson did just that but reached a different conclusion. "After looking into the case as fully as possible," Wilson wrote, "I am convinced that it would not be wise or right to grant a pardon."[18] Wilson, the democratic reformer, understood and abominated anarchism.

In January 1914, Ricardo and the other PLM leaders left prison and began again their active propagandizing through *Regeneración*. Despite the civil war engulfing Mexico, the anarchists had some reason for optimism. Zapata had maintained a sizeable following; he appeared to be an expression of his people, not a deceiving enslaver. Zapata had popularized the PLM slogan "Land and Liberty;" he subscribed to *Regeneración*, repeated Praxedis Guerrero's "tracers," and distributed land. His political document, called the Plan of Ayala, reflected some anarchism in addition to its agrarian radicalism. The anarchism was bestowed by adviser Antonio Díaz Soto y Gama, a friend of Ricardo's from the days of the First Liberal Congress.[19] While Ricardo and the PLM always remained wary of Zapata lest he degenerate into a petty tyrant, his movement represented the persistence of the direct action that they believed all Mexicans should pursue. Zapata represented the only viable alternative to Madero's successors.

Carranza and the Constitutionalists, from the PLM perspective, represented nothing more than Maderismo seeking to reassert itself—the false idea of a revolutionary government. Whereas Taft had represented business and the money power, Wilson represented something perhaps more dangerous—an impatient moralist who wanted the civil war to end and order by law restored in Mexico. And Wilson, the author of books on America's constitution and representative government, knew precisely what the PLM wanted. *Regeneración's* injunctions against possible U.S. intervention grew more shrill as the president, employing several tactics, seemed to grow dissatisfied with events in Mexico.

Wilson began meddling in domestic Mexican politics with a variety of instruments. In addition to not recognizing Huerta's government, Wilson also played with the arms embargo voted into law by Congress in 1912. That joint resolution permitted the president to prohibit arms shipments to any country where "conditions of domestic violence exist which are promoted by the use of arms or munitions of war procured from the United States."[20] It had been only selectively enforced by Taft and, in general, helped rebels with good smuggling connections and hindered established governments without them.[21]

Wilson vacillated on the embargo, announcing shortly after he took office that he was satisfied with it. In practice, policy implementation had devolved upon the secretary of state, giving him the selective power of enforcement. Wilson, always suspicious of the State Department, reversed himself several months later and decided to practice a total embargo. Huerta, knowing the tactic was aimed at him, cynically remarked that it would not affect the Constitutionalists since their arms came mainly from smuggling.[22] Therefore, Huerta placed a large munitions order in Europe.

Wilson's dislike of the State Department prompted him frequently to bypass it by sending special emissaries to various factions for personal assessments.[23] To keep up, the State Department sent its representatives, official and unofficial, to the same leaders. Thus, Carranza had a special representative, and, when he became powerful, Villa had *two*—although he was nominally under Carranza's command and should have had none. Wilson also periodically sent representatives to Zapata.

All of Wilson's meddling signaled that the president had become impatient with his own policy of "watchful waiting." And when the German steamer *Ypiranga*, loaded with weapons for Huerta, sailed the Atlantic bound for Veracruz in April 1914, the American president decided to act. Using an alleged insult to the American flag at Tampico as pretext, Wilson ordered the navy to seize the customs houses, town, and port of Veracruz. Inexplicably, he thought there would be no bloodshed. After two days of fighting, the American flag flew over Veracruz on April 22, 1914, and U.S. troops under the unified army command of Major General Frederick Funston began an occupation of unannounced duration.[24]

When the *Ypiranga* entered the outer harbor, the ship's captain learned that the cargo of 17,899 cases could not be unloaded at Veracruz. After several weeks of delay that included a journey to Mobile, Alabama, the *Ypiranga* managed to unload the weaponry two hundred miles south of Veracruz at Puerto Mexico on May 26.[25] The materiél arrived too late to help Huerta.[26] Wilson had occupied Mexican territory, rather than let his sense of the embargo be circumvented. From an international perspective, his action was less risky than stopping vessels on the high seas, but it sent a message to Mexicans of unmistakable clarity: Wilson wanted his way in Mexico and would do whatever was needed to get it.

Opposition to the occupation annoyed him. Mexicans of all political creeds opposed it. National pride had been offended and national sovereignty violated. Huerta tried to use this sensitivity to rally Mexicans to support him for nationalist reasons; however, resentment against his ugly pacification campaigns could not be overcome by patriotic calls. Carranza demanded total and immediate evacuation by the United States, and his strongly nationalistic stance won him increased support. Villa, more conciliatory toward Americans, admitted that occupation rankled but accepted it.

For Ricardo, American occupation embodied his great fear that international capital would reimpose its authority over Mexico by armed intervention. He had feared Taft's military activities along the border in 1911; now he became absorbed, nearly obsessed, by American troops in Mexico. *Regeneración* blasted away at the occupation, exhorted Mexicans to resist.

In addition to prose, Ricardo employed poster and cartoon to convey his points. The cover of the June 13, 1914, issue featured a bare-chested man, having broken his chains, raising the black flag of anarchism above the flames consuming the Clergy, the Bourgeoisie, and the Government, while behind him the rising sun of "Land And Liberty" shows the way to freedom (see Figures 2 and 3). Inside that issue, a political cartoon depicted Carranza and Villa as monkeys, dancing to the same music wherever they went, controlled by Wilson the organ grinder. In the background Mexicans endure parasites, and in the foreground those who carry the banner "Land and Liberty" challenge this mockery—woman and man alike.[27] The message of resistance to American domination is unmistakable.

To offset American influence, Ricardo again sought international aid. He appealed to the International Anarchist Congress, scheduled to meet in late June in London, to make up its mind about the Mexican revolution. He wanted the Congress either to endorse the revolution or condemn it, but stop "sitting on two stools. We want a clear-cut declaration that the Mexican peon is right in holding that economic liberty can be won only by retaking possession of the land; that he is right in expelling the land monopolist; that you urge the disinherited of all countries to imitate him."[28] To increase pressure on the Congress, Ricardo published advance copies of the letter in both *Regeneración* and Owen's new publication, *Land and Liberty*.

By the time the International Anarchist Congress met, an even more important item presented itself for consideration. On June 28, 1914, in the town of Sarajevo, a Serbian nationalist shot to death the heir to the Austrian throne; Europe began sinking into international war. The international solidarity of the working class—in which anarchists, socialists, and communists deeply believed—was about to be tested against nationalism. In the ensuing shuffle, the Mexican revolution would be forgotten in Europe, even as it continued in Mexico.

Wilson had thought that an American presence in Veracruz would settle the civil war and bring about elections to replace Huerta. Carranza's Plan of Guadalupe, however, called for Huerta's expulsion before any elections could be held and the First Chief insisted upon that condition. He would prosecute the war to victory. The Constitutionalists seemed destined to win even before Wilson's invasion because of Villa's stunning victory over superior federal forces at Torreón in the north. Villa stood poised to move south when Carranza intervened and redirected him to routing federal remnants.

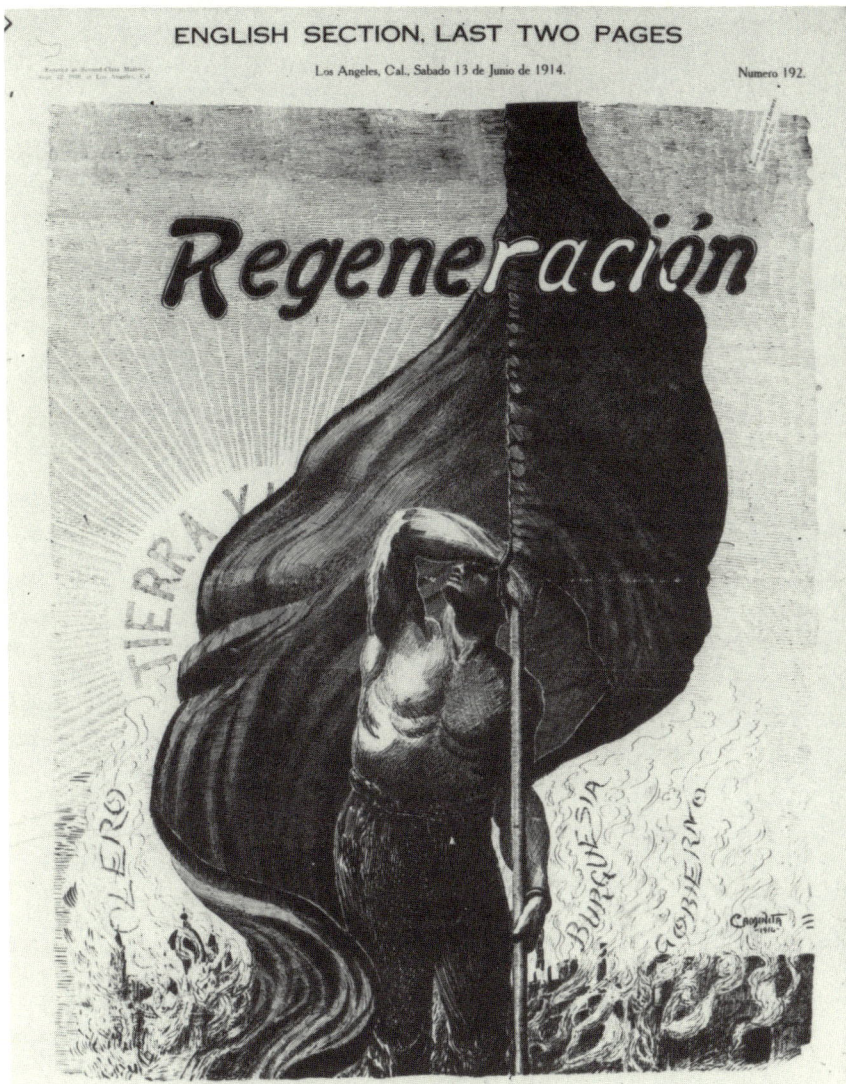

Fig. 2. Poster of Liberation (*Regeneracíon*, June 13, 1914)

Meanwhile, González continued his campaign in the northeast against Matamoros and Monterrey, while Obregón pushed down the west coast. His campaign, less impressive and costly than that of Villa or González, gave him time to learn to become a military commander and strategist.[29]

Huerta's position became untenable for several reasons. The three-

Fig. 3. Cartoon of U.S. relations with Mexican faction. Heading reads, "They send their song all over." (*Regeneracíon*, June 13, 1914)

pronged Constitutionalist military assault proved successful, in part, because of a shortage of weaponry imposed by the combined embargo and occupation of Veracruz. U.S. control of the port and the customs houses denied to Huerta the principal governmental revenue source, export duties. Huerta saw the impossibility of his position and resigned in July 1914. He immediately departed for exile on the German steamer *Dresden*.[30] Obregón continued south, accompanied by Lucio Blanco, and received the federal surrender on August 14. On August 20, Carranza entered the capital on horseback, greeted by a cheering crowd of nearly three hundred thousand.[31]

The Constitutionalists held Mexico City, and Huerta had left. According to Article VI of the Plan of Guadalupe, Carranza should have held elections and surrendered his power. Carranza, however, was not yet prepared to do that. He could find many reasons to justify his delay. Three full-fledged governments had operated the bureaucratic machinery since 1910—those of Díaz, Madero, and Huerta—besides the brief interim administrations. Rapid turnover had meant that governmental institutions did not operate smoothly or effectively. Mutual suspicion between Carranza and Villa, foreign occupation of national territory, absence of an internationally recognized regime, and the disarray of governmental structure could all be argued to prolong the First Chief's tenure.

Internal dissension among Constitutionalists, suppressed during the final days of the Huerta campaign, began to resurface. Lucio Blanco, who had won substantial victories for Carranza in the northeastern states of Tamaulipas and Nuevo León in 1913, had been ordered to merge his command with that of Carranza favorite Pablo González, the corps commander whose military failures in the northeast had forced him to withdraw to Coahuila. Blanco refused to accept a position subordinate to a man who failed to do his job. In the resulting negotiations, he won reassignment to Obregón's forces in Sonora. When Obregón negotiated the final Huertista surrender in 1914, he refused to invite González to the conferences, believing that his contribution to Huerta's downfall had been minimal. González then refused to ride in Carranza's triumphal parade into the capital.[32]

The split with Villa was even more serious. Disaffection developed almost from the beginning between the doughty, aloof governor of Coahuila and the effusive, reckless bandit from Chihuahua. Confusion of authority in Chihuahua between Villa, commander of the Division of the North, and Manuel Chao, Carranza's appointed governor, contributed further to mistrust.[33] In addition to his tendency toward independent military action, Villa was given an independent line of political action through Wilson's policy of "watchful waiting." Despite Carranza's repeated attempts to consolidate his own authority by demanding that all subordinates refer to him any foreigner with a question,[34] Villa continued to communicate with Washington via his own representatives.

Moreover, Villa's battlefield victories notwithstanding, Carranza chose Obregón, not Villa, to negotiate the federal surrender and to enter the capital first. Carranza made the arrangements through González in an agreement known as the Pact of Torreón. Assenting to the stipulations of this document, Villa agreed to recognize Carranza as First Chief and to stay out of Mexico City in return for coal, munitions, and Carranza's pledge to hold a convention of military men in the capital to decide the future of the revolution. The convention would address the issues of leadership and solutions to social and economic questions, chiefly land reform.[35]

Once in Mexico City, Carranza chose to defer elections and prolong his stewardship as First Chief, angering many of his followers. Villa, citing the Pact of Torreón, then denounced Carranza in a Manifesto to the Mexican People of September 30, 1914, and withdrew recognition from the First Chief. Carranza, in a tactic typical of him, claimed never to have ratified the pact. Public consistency was important to him, and private concessions could be publicly disavowed; he now refused to countenance any convening of military men to discuss the civilian revolution.

Despite the First Chief's objections, a convention finally assembled in Aguascalientes in mid-October 1914, representing a cross section of Constitutionalists and others who wanted immediate change in Mexico. Even the unaligned Zapata sent delegates and subscribed to the decisions of the Convention of Aguascalientes. Villa subscribed to it, as did Lucio Blanco. After much agonizing, Obregón decided to stay with Carranza, a decision the importance of which cannot be overestimated. The Convention elected a provisional president of the republic—a military man, as were most of the delegates—and pledged to hold regular elections following Carranza's defeat. Thus, in November 1914, the Constitutionalists began internecine war.[36] Ricardo had foreseen it all.

Carranza, faced with the prospect of being caught in a pincers between Villa from the north and Zapata from the south, evacuated Mexico City in November. But where could he go? At that moment, fortune provided an answer. Wilson wanted to evacuate Veracruz after Huerta's departure; however, the hoped for elections had failed to develop, and the transitory order of late summer gave way to renewed civil war.

Wilson remained uncertain to whom he should relinquish the city. He had told his secretary of state, "we are dealing with a very difficult person in Carranza,"[37] but that fall the First Chief had privately given guarantees to protect the lives and property of foreigners in his area—probably to win Wilson's support. That act, coupled with Carranza's proximity to the port, decided the president. Carranza's troops replaced the Americans at Veracruz, and General Funston left Mexico to take charge of the Southern Department in Texas.[38] By late November, Carranza held a port of entry for munitions and controlled customs houses revenues to pay for them. Together, these elements gave him a chance against his enemies.

From Veracruz, however, Carranza witnessed a specter nearly as frightening as the real armies of his opposition—the union of the poor. On December 4, Indian and peon Mexico met to join forces in the floating gardens built by the Aztecs at Xochimilco. Zapata and Villa came together and agreed to wage common war against Carranza. Zapata agreed to take Puebla and from there move up; Villa would march against the port.[39]

Zapata did take Puebla but then retreated. His intrinsic parochialism kept him from seeing that the only way to secure his gains in Morelos lay in securing them nationally. Ricardo and *Regeneración* had been unable to communicate that sufficiently to him. Villa, more aware of the national entity than Zapata, knew that power meant national control. He decided to remove any threat to his supply lines by clearing the area north and west of the capital before advancing against the coast. These decisions gave the First Chief time to regroup both militarily and politically.

The Convention of Aguascalientes, while containing a substantial number of Villistas and Zapatistas, nevertheless possessed a clear majority of Constitucionalistas disaffected with Carranza. The First Chief did not fail to read the implication—continued silence on social issues meant fewer followers. To patch his oversight or snobbery, Carranza published a series of decrees from Veracruz on January 6, 1915, by which he expanded the Plan of Guadalupe to encompass comment on social problems. In an attempt to make it appear a natural reflection of his matured opinion and not a direct response to Zapata, Villa, and his disloyal adherents, Carranza backdated the decrees to December 12, 1914.[40]

The revised Plan still maintained the old legalistic forms and theme. It identified Villa and his followers with Madero's opponents and blamed them for forcing Carranza to retain power. The land deal it offered was no more than Madero's vague promise of returning land illegally taken. Nonetheless, Carranza did go further. He promised strict applications of the Liberal Laws of Reform, bestowed upon Mexico by Juárez, and full implementation of the 1857 Constitution. A sop to the Liberals in his ranks, these decrees nevertheless proved sufficient to hold them. Carranza faced the greatest military challenge of his career in 1915, and he approached it as he had Huerta, with both a political and a military strategy. Unlike Madero, however, Carranza felt no need to try to make peace with Ricardo in America.

In Los Angeles, the close of 1914 found the PLM hard pressed in every quarter. The ever restless Owen moved from Los Angeles to Hayward, California. There he created the Bakunin Institute and published his own monthly journal, *Land and Liberty,* to propagandize for the Mexican revolution and to comment on the European war. He continued to edit the English-language section of *Regeneración,* but through the mail.[41]

Regeneración had devoted much space and money in 1914 to a defense and relief fund for PLM adherents arrested in Texas in 1913. Jesús Rangel and Charlie Cline, IWW members and PLM followers, formed a guerrilla *foco* in Texas to operate in Mexico. Rangel had previously served time in Leavenworth for his PLM activities and, upon his release, acted as emissary between Ricardo and Zapata. Rangel and Cline had organized their unit from former Orozquistas in exile. As they prepared to enter Mexico, they were confronted by U.S. cavalry and Texas authorities and, in the gunfight, lost two of their own while killing a Mexican spy. The PLM followers were tried, convicted, and given harsh terms. The court sentenced Rangel and Cline to life imprisonment.[42] Providing aid to these men proved financially costly for the impoverished PLM.

The Rangel-Cline incident underscored both continuities and significant changes affecting PLM activities. Mexican and American anarchism continued the tradition of joint action that was begun in 1910 and was most visibly demonstrated in the Tijuana seizure in 1911. The IWW-PLM connections persisted. The Mexican situation, however, had become far more complex. Gone were the days of choosing between Madero and Flores Magón. Rangel and Cline's recruitment of ex-Orozquistas in 1913 would have been dangerously foolish a year later, when Zapata and Villa made common cause against Carranza. Villa would have killed the Orozquistas and their supporters. Mexican politics by 1914 had made recruitment, for many reasons, both difficult and dangerous.

Ricardo's focus on the agrarian issues in Mexico, partly reflecting peasant discontent, had prompted some factions to confront the question more directly than Madero had. Even Huerta had created a new cabinet post for Agriculture and Colonization—supposedly to develop an appropriate agrarian policy.[43]

Constitutionalists had outstripped Carranza in dividing large estates. When in Durango, Villa had confiscated properties of the rich and parceled them out to the poor, without the First Chief's permission or approval.[44] In Matamoros, Tamaulipas, Lucio Blanco had taken the estate of Díaz's nephew and divided it among his soldiers, also without Carranza's sanction.[45] Carranza eventually called for land reform also. Even President Wilson expressed concern for the submerged Mexican peasants who had been deprived of land.[46]

Whether understood as a division of spoils or perceived from a reformist perspective, the land issue captured popular attention in both countries. Ricardo's version of it, however, did not. He wanted the disinherited to take land for themselves, not to receive it from others. He reiterated Kropotkin's sentiments exactly: "There must be EXPROPRIATION. The well-being of all—the end; expropriation—the means."[47]

Since Ricardo had identified the Mexican revolution as a primarily agrarian phenomenon, his anarchist definition of correct behavior could admit no compromise. Compromise, however, constituted Mexican reality. Hence, Ricardo's call for direct action in Mexico, like his appeals for financial aid to anarchists internationally, fell mainly upon unreceptive ears.

Response to his manifesto "To the Workers of the United States," dated November 7, 1914, illustrated his diminished position. Ricardo's desperate appeal for help underscored the severity of the PLM situation. He needed money badly and begged for financial aid to the junta. The problem, he maintained, was international.

> To deny solidarity to the Mexican workingmen who are struggling to conquer their economic freedom is to stand against the Labor cause in general, because the cause of the wage slave against his master has no frontiers; it is not a national problem but a universal conflict; it is the cause of all the disinherited of the world over, of everyone who has to work with his hands and his brains to bring his family a loaf of bread.[48]

Ricardo's call went largely unanswered, and, in December 1914, *Regeneración* suspended publication because of lack of funds.

Money, though, was a proxy for subscription, and this suspension demands consideration of the subscriber base. Subscribers, those who paid for the newspaper, must be distinguished from readership and from those influenced by a publication through hearing articles read to them. Making such distinctions is hampered by the term "circulation," which usually means total number of papers produced "exclusive of leftover, unsold, returned, file, sample, . . . and advertisers' copies."[49]

Superficially, the argument from diminished revenue seems false. Circulation figures for *Regeneración* over time seem fairly good. The year 1906 marked the high point, with circulation figures ranging between 15,000 and 20,000.[50] When Owen joined the staff he placed the figure at 12,000,[51] and from 1912 on, the editors regularly reported 10,000.[52] The transition from reformist to anarchist, then, cost *Regeneración* from one-third to one-half its following. These estimates of circulation, however, are misleading. Subscription meant payment, either in money or, if by another journal, in kind. One subscription list has survived for late 1915, and it reveals, as no other document could, *Regeneración*'s problems of viability (see Table 1).

Table 1
Regeneración Distribution by Leading Destination (Subscribers and Papers),
November 22, 1915

	Subscribers		Papers	
Total	2,619	(100%)	3,986	(100%)
Texas	1,052	(40.1%)	1,672	(41.9%)
California	451	(17.2%)	534	(13.3%)
Mexico	74	(2.8%)	500	(12.5%)
Cuba	136	(5.2%)	198	(4.9%)
Arizona	168	(6.4%)	172	(4.3%)
Subtotal	1,881	(71.7%)	3,076	(77.2%)

Compiled from "The United States vs. Enrîique and Richardo Flores Magón," 1916, Government Exhibits numbers 10, 15, 16, 17, 18, Case 1071, Record Group 21, Records of District Courts of the United States, Southern District of California, Southern Division, Federal Records Center, Laguna Niguel, California.

The list for November 22, 1915, reveals that 2,619 subscribers took 3,986 papers, the total number of that issue's circulation. In this instance, circulation was half again the number of subscribers or, phrased another way, *Regeneración* produced and distributed 1.5 papers per subscriber. Owen's circulation estimate of 12,000 in 1911 would have meant, in terms of the 1.5 ratio just deduced, 8,000 subscribers; at that point, he thought *Regeneración* made money. *Regeneración*'s claim four years later of 10,500 circulation would, in turn, have rested on a subscriber base of 7,000, a patent falsehood—nearly three times higher than the 2,619 actual figure. The four-year decline—a 67 percent subscriber loss—had been truly catastrophic. Circulation lies and desperate appeals to American workers could not cover real financial losses.

Moreover, what had begun as a newspaper aimed at influencing events in Mexico had, by 1915, assumed a substantially different character. By then, Mexico ranked third in total number of papers taken, behind Texas and California, and fifth in total number of subscribers, following Arizona and Cuba.

Regeneración had become a newspaper concerned about Mexico but read primarily in the United States within the Mexican American communities in Texas and California and by readers of other radical newspapers. Texas with 1,052 subscribers and California with 451 constituted 40.1 and 17.2 percent respectively of total subscriptions. Together, those two states accounted for 57.3 percent of all those who paid for *Regeneración*. By 1915, then, *Regeneración* had become an American anarchist newspaper.

Radical press subscriptions or exchanges with *Regeneración* reveal different ways a newspaper could exert or lose influence far beyond its circulation (see Table 2). Table 2 shows major socialist papers that subscribed to *Regeneración* in 1915, with a combined circulation of about 730,000. With the exception of the *California Social Democrat*, however, which continued to cover PLM difficulties and raised money for defense funds, *Regeneración* lost all influence with the socialist press following the conflict with Debs.

Table 2
American Socialist Press Subscribing to *Regeneracíon*, 1915, by Circulation

Name	City Published	Frequency	Circulation
Appeal to Reason	Girard, Kansas	w	500,000^e
National Rip-Saw	St. Louis, Missouri	m	150,000^e
The Rebel	Halletsville, Texas	w	26,145^e
International Socialist Review	Chicago, Illinois	m	25,424^d
New York Call	New York, New York	d	19,836^s
California Social Democrat	Los Angeles, California	w	11,000^e
		Total	732,405

Legend: Frequency: *w* is weekly, *m* is monthly, *d* is daily.
Circulation: *e* is estimated, *d* is detailed statement of publisher, *s* is statement from U.S. Post Office.
Compiled from Walter Goldwater, *Radical Periodicals in America, 1890–1950*, New Haven: Yale University Press, 1966, pp 2–3, 18, 26, 30, 34. *N. W. Ayer and Son American Newspaper Annual Directory, 1915–1916* (Philadelphia: N. W. Ayer and Son, 1915), pp. 74, 75, 87, 88, 186, 192, 208, 326. All circulation figures presented here and all *e* determinations made by Ayer.

The PLM had disavowed that 730,000 socialist circulation when Ricardo publicly unveiled his anarchism.

The anarchist press in the United States, with circulation perhaps 3 percent that of the socialists, could and did extend *Regeneración*'s influence (see Table 3). Among the most important, as shown in Table 3, were the Italian language *L'Era Nuova,* which had been edited originally by Malatesta; *Mother Earth;* Berkman's *The Blast;* and IWW publications. Emma Goldman continued to raise money for the PLM and to give the cause the benefit of her press.

But by late 1914, anarchists had become far more absorbed with the European war than with the Mexican revolution, and sharp divisions had shattered the dream of international solidarity. The gentle and retiring Kropotkin began the schism by championing the war as a means to defeat Prussian militarism.[53] Kropotkin saw Germany in France as Ricardo saw the United States in Mexico—as a powerful vehicle to crush the much needed social and economic revolution through force of arms. Kropotkin, of all people, appealed to nationalism and urged workers to join their national armies to defeat Germany.

Malatesta, among many anarchists, rejected the appeal as preposterous. That anarchists should join government violated first principles; it was a contradiction in terms. He and others broke with Kropotkin over the issue of the war.[54] By late 1914, internal dissension had figuratively taken Ricardo's poster representing anarchism and torn it to pieces—leaving individuals fragmented and adrift.

In the United States, *Regeneración* had gone down but not yet out. Texas had 40 percent of the journal's subscribers, and the state was a web of intrigue with former Mexican politicians in exile conspiring to return. Beneath the political surface, however, lay an economic and social reality which

Table 3
Select Anarchist Press in America Subscribing to *Regeneración*, 1914–1916

Name	Language	Editor	City Published	Frequency	Circulation
The Blast	English	Alexander Berkman	San Francisco, California	w	?
Chung Say Yat Po	Chinese	Ng Poon Chew	San Francisco, California	d	4,500
La Comune	Italian	?	Philadelphia, Pennsylvania	?	?
Cronaca Sovversiva	Italian	Luigi Galleani	Lynn, Massachusetts	w	?
L'Era Nuova	Italian	?	Patterson, New Jersey	?	?
Fraye Arbeter Shtime	Yiddish	Saul Yanovsky	New York, New York	w	20,000
Land and Liberty	English	William C. Owen	Hayward, California	m	3,500
Miners Magazine (IWW)	English		Denver, Colorado	m	2,750
Mother Earth	English	Emma Goldman	New York, New York	m	3,500–10,000
Revolt	Swedish	Theodor Johnson	Chicago, Illinois	m	?
Woman Rebel	English	Margaret Sanger	New York, New York	m	?

Compiled from "The United States vs. Enríque and Ricardo Glores Magón," 1916, Government Exhibits #10, 15, 16, 17, 18, Case 1071, R.G. 21, FRC Laguna, Niguel; N. W. Ayer and Son *American Newspaper Annual Directory, 1915–1916*; Weinstein, *The Decline of Socialism in America*, Table 1, pp. 94–102; Goldwater, *Radical Periodicals in America*, p. 21. Drinon, "Mother Earth Bulletin," *The American Radical Press*, Vol. 2, p. 395.

Regeneración had described with increasing cogency over the years, until, in late 1914, Ricardo's rhetoric began to bear fruit. That harvest he would attribute to the soil capitalism had prepared. Nonetheless, even he could not recognize the second coming of an anarchist-communist movement born in Mexico and seeking implementation near the border—this time in South Texas instead of Baja California.

CHAPTER 4

SOUTH TEXAS

The worker cannot arrive at anarchism in one leap. To become a convinced anarchist . . . he must begin to feel the solidarity that joins him to his comrades, and to learn to cooperate with others . . . by struggling against the bosses and against the government which supports them [and] realize that . . . the workers could manage the domestic economy by their own efforts. And when the worker has understood this, he is an anarchist even if he does not call himself such.

Errico Malatesta[1]

Cameron and Hidalgo counties in South Texas underwent profound social, economic, and demographic changes between 1900 and 1920. Those changes fractured the old social order, intensified discrimination against Mexicans to the point of violence, and permitted the anarchist Plan of San Diego, Texas, to emerge. Some background is needed to understand this transformation of South Texas. The Treaty of Guadalupe-Hidalgo, which concluded the war with Mexico, 1846–1848, made the river called the Rio Bravo by Mexicans and the Rio Grande by Americans, the international boundary. Climate, vegetation, and distance, however, combined to make the boundary and its environs a remote and isolated frontier.

The lower Rio Grande valley—in reality, not a valley—is a relatively level stretch of land that embraces the delta and its floodplains.[2] Situated a few degrees north of the tropics and characterized by a high rate of evaporation, the environment is called xeric by geographers. With no topographical changes, average annual rainfall declines from thirty inches at coastal Point Isabel to sixteen inches one hundred miles inland at Rio Grande City. Without irrigation, agriculture is impossible.[3] Generally, the soils are silty loam and become very productive when "brought under the ditch," as irrigation has been called.[4]

Soil types vary from shifting sand dunes to tight clays. The latter require tractor power to break them up, a technological improvement for effective cultivation that came only in the twentieth century, subsequent to the spread of irrigation.[5] Vegetation posed and poses serious obstacles to agriculture. The most common pattern is chaparral or thorn bush consisting of mesquite, ebony, and thorny huisache, interspersed with yucca and prickly pear cactus.

A similar complex of soils and vegetation exists on the Mexican side.[6] Growth remains dense within ten miles of the river banks, then slowly thins. Men on horses and herds of cattle can be lost to sight within several feet of the water.

Given the terrain, ranching became the most important and common pattern of land use in the nineteenth century. Warm climate and abundant grasses permitted open stock ranging without the need for shelter. In this remote area, shrewd American cattle ranchers gained economic power. The fabled King Ranch, under the stewardship of the Kleberg family, grew to nearly one million acres by 1900 and resulted in the development of a new cattle strain that was larger and more disease resistant than others.[7] Mexicans also could become wealthy and enter the upper class, but generally they served as laborers, cowboys, assistant lawmen, and occasionally as stockmen.

While relationships between white and brown could become strained, an effective social glue for the old order came from intermarriage. A corollary of intermarriage, which occurred at all levels of society, was the Roman Catholic and Hispanic convention of *compadrazgo*, the fictive kinship of godparents. These two unrelated adults renounced Satan and his works for the infant at Baptism. They pledged to treat the godchild as their own to insure its instruction in the faith and to assist it in reaching adulthood. The shared offices of *compadrazgo* created a bridge between languages and cultures. English represented the language of law, finance, and politics; Spanish represented the social language of *bailes* (dances), *fiestas* (parties), and work. The mingling of families through intermarriage and godparenthood up to 1900 produced a precarious but real social balance.[8]

After 1900, intermarriage declined and population increased, creating a social scissors that cut the old order into ribbons. Let us consider intermarriage first. As revealed in Graph 1, the mixed-blood population of Cameron County dropped from nearly 47 percent of the total in 1900 to 24 percent in 1920; Hidalgo County's decline went from 52 percent to 25 percent. These staggering proportions were unlike anything that happened in the other South Texas counties.

The proportions were intensified by the dramatic population rise the valley sustained over the same period. Population nearly doubled from 1900 to 1920, with the greatest increase coming after 1910. As Table 4 demonstrates, Hidalgo County experienced a demographic explosion of 450 percent, while the proportion of native whites of native parents rose threefold, from 12 percent in 1900 to 35 percent in 1920.

The reasons for these changes lay in the economic transformation of the valley from ranching to farming, made possible by twin developments that gained ground after 1904—the arrival of the railroad and the growth of irrigation. New settlers came to South Texas on a conveyance new to the area, the train. In July 1903, the efforts of James B. Wells, political boss of the valley, the Klebergs, and prominent citizens of lesser status such as Uriah Lott, Lon C. Hill, and others, succeeded in having rail lines laid south

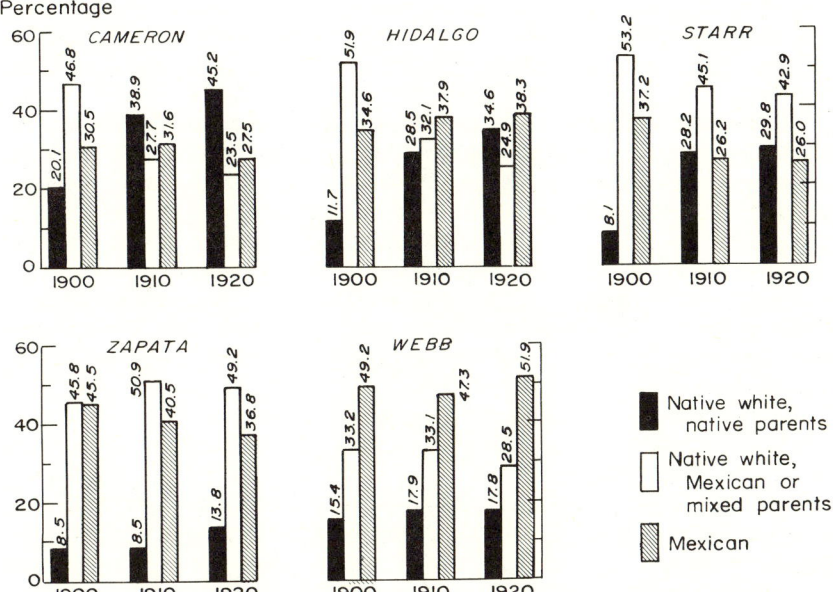

Percentage of population by origin, Lower Rio Grande Valley, 1900–1920 (From *12th, 13th, and 14th Census of the United States*)

of Corpus Christi heading toward the river. Settlements along the route generally took the names of prominent people. Norias bespoke Wells—the word being an old Spanish version of his surname. Rudolf memorialized a member of the Kleberg family who had served in the U.S. House of Representatives. The rail lines reached Brownsville on June 7, 1904—the date valley residents reckoned as marking the railroad's arrival.

From Brownsville, the line followed the river's course toward Starr County. Along the way, inhabitants of one site named their settlement Mercedes in honor of the young bride of Porfirio Díaz, explicitly invoking his protection against bandit raids. Lott designated Harlingen after his family homesite in Holland, and T. J. Hooks named Donna for his daughter, a divorcée who became the community's postmistress. McAllen, the last significant early settlement christened along the rail line, honored a Scottish pioneer whose ranch became a famous battle site ten years later.[9]

Railroad extension corresponded to irrigation growth as Maps 1 and 2 show. As settlers bought more land, developers exhausted the farm-to-market convenience of the existing lines. Sam Robertson of the San Benito Land and Irrigation Company recognized this limitation early. He overcame it by proposing and getting built a series of spur lines that expanded the amount of farmland that could be served. Simultaneously, he opened new

Table 4
Total Population and Population by County, Lower Rio Grande Valley, Texas, 1900–1920

County	1900	1910	1920
Cameron	16,095	27,158	36,662
Hidalgo	6,837	13,728	38,110
Starr	11,469	13,151	11,089
Zapata	4,760	3,809	2,929
Webb	21,851	22,503	29,152
Total	61,012	80,349	117,942

Compiled from U.S. Department of Commerce, Bureau of the Census, *Twelfth Census of the United States, 1900: Population*, 40–42, 784–789; *Thirteenth Census of the United States, 1910: Population*, 608–648, 810–850; *Fourteenth Census of the United States, 1920: Population*, 983–1028.
Note: The average annual rate of population growth from 1900–1920 was identical for both the valley and the state: 4.8%.

land for irrigation. The building of railroads in 1911–1912 was halted by the uncertainty of the Mexican revolution but resumed after 1920. The early construction, however, provided the framework for integrating regions of Cameron, Hidalgo, and Webb counties into the cash crop market.

Irrigation and the transportation revolution transformed the valley. Because the river was avulsive and the streambed meandered, early irrigation had proven risky. The first irrigation system in the valley had been built by a Frenchman from Louisiana, George Brulay, in 1876. He moved to a subtropical microclimate south of Brownsville to grow cotton and sugar. He enlarged his plant again in 1890, but his operation never attained the significance of its successors. Five years later the second man to build a system and the first to use the new stream pump, John Closner, began operating in Hidalgo County. He abandoned his plant in 1910, after it had been washed out several times by flood.[10]

Closner's pump, however, had pointed the way for the future. In those areas where the river incised below the land surface, sometimes down to thirty feet, only the steam pump and a series of lifts could draw the water up to irrigate the arid tableland. Without pumps and lifts, irrigation could never have developed as rapidly as it did, but great financial risk attended creation of a pumping station. Because the pumping station had to be built on the river, investors risked losing it in floods. After 1904, risks began to decline compared to potential returns because the railroad made irrigation profitable.

Pumps may have been expensive, costly to transport, difficult to install, and subject to loss through natural disaster, but the prospect of getting goods to an ever-expanding market overrode fears and revolutionized the basis of economic activity in less than twenty years. Table 5 depicts the increase in irrigated land in the valley in the decade 1909–1919.

When that increase in acreage is compared to the growth of the value of farmland in the lower Rio Grande valley between 1900 and 1920, as shown

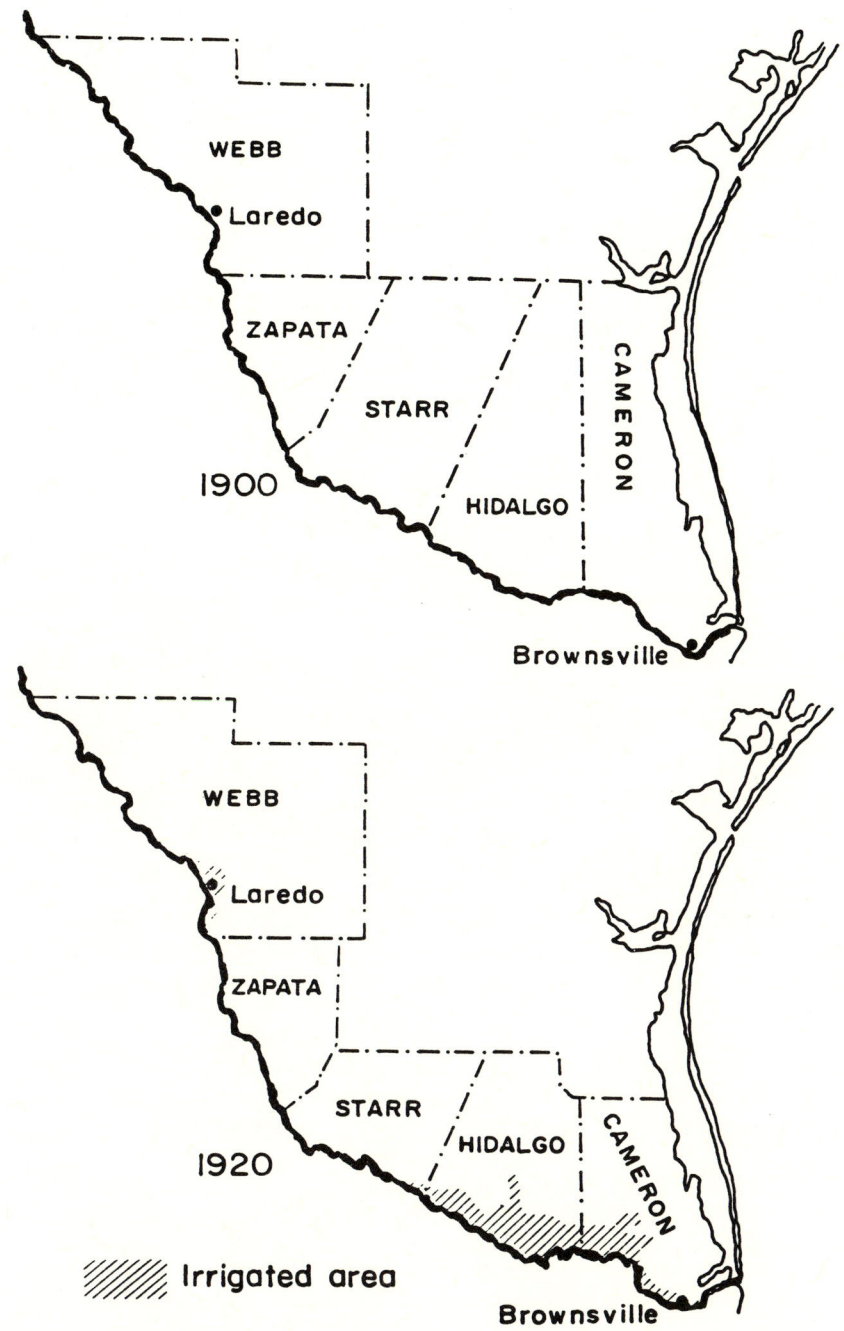

Map 1. Approximate location and extent of irrigated land, Lower Rio Grande Valley, 1900 and 1920

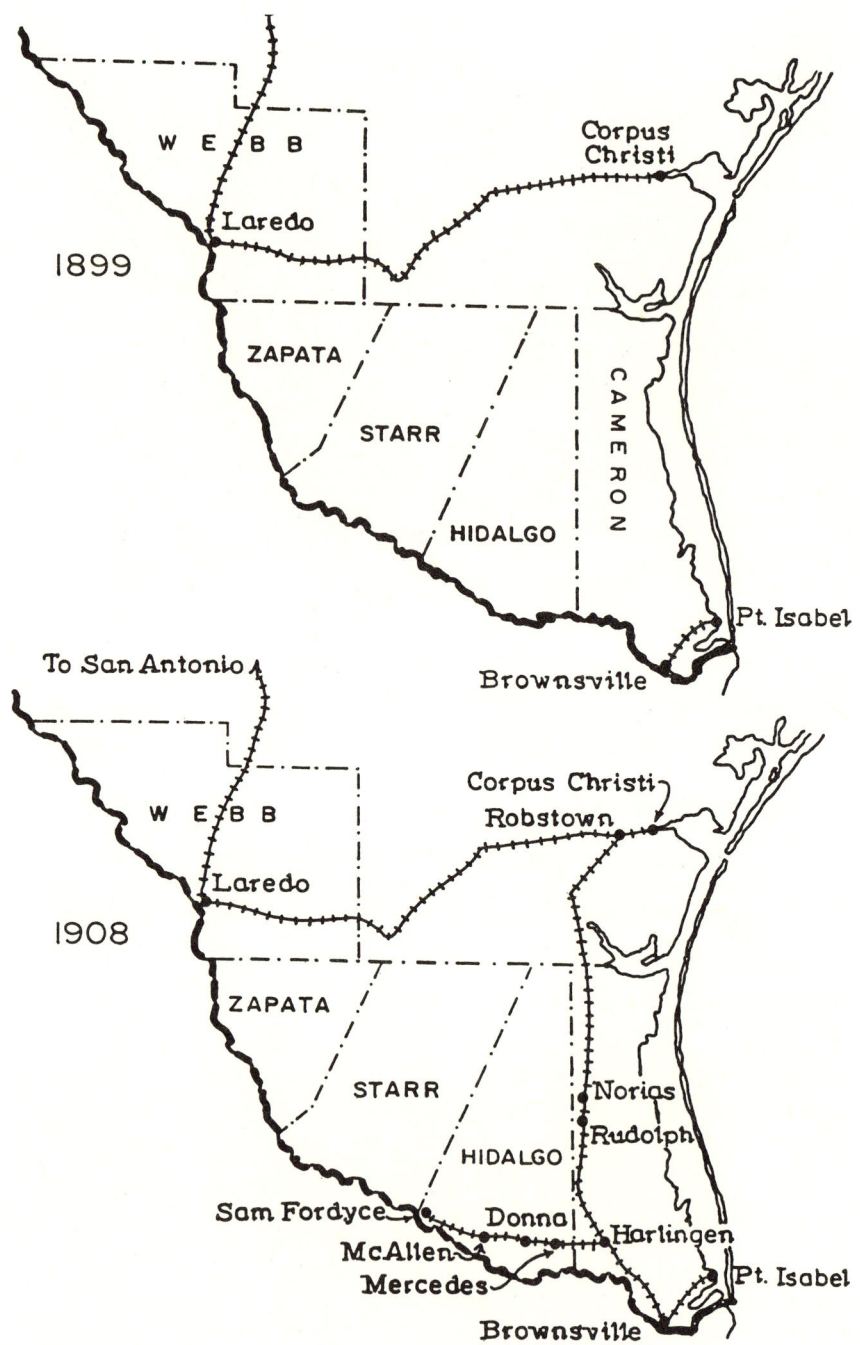

Map 2. Growth of the railroad in South Texas, 1880–1920

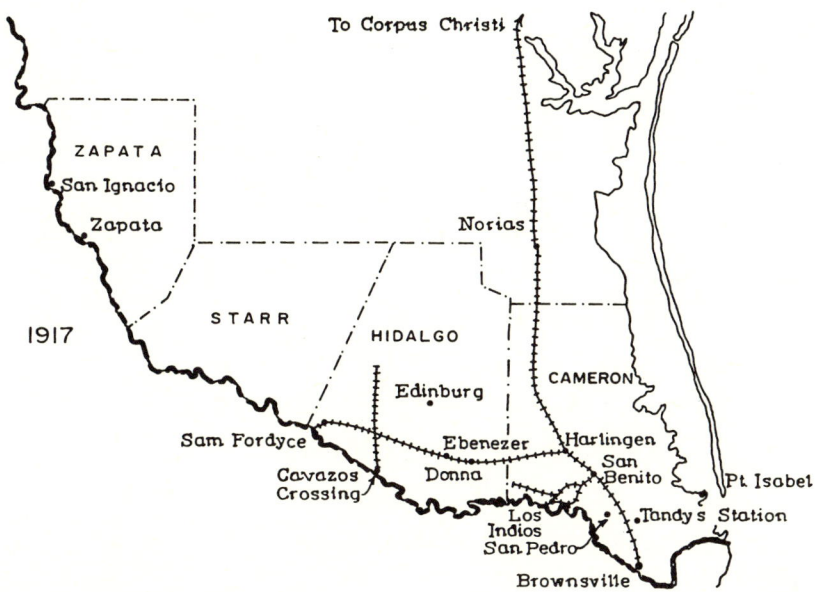

Map 2. *continued*

in Table 6, the enormous impact of irrigation on land value becomes apparent. Farmland in Hidalgo County more than tripled in value in the decade after 1910; in Cameron and Webb counties, the two other significant irrigators, value at least doubled. Farmers increased the capital they invested in irrigation in these three counties over the same decade. Table 7 shows that farm investment soared by more than 50 percent in Cameron and by more than

Table 5
Increase in Irrigated Land, Lower Rio Grande Valley and Texas, 1909–1919 [in acres]

County	1909	1919	Increase	Percent
Cameron	29,439	60,008	30,569	+ 104%
Hidalgo	21,048	160,532	139,484	+ 663%
Webb	4,186	7,480	3,294	+ 79%
Subtotal	54,673	228,020	173,347	+ 317%
All Texas	451,130	586,120	144,990	+ 32%

Compiled from U.S. Department of Commerce, Bureau of the Census, *Fourteenth Census of the United States, 1920: Agriculture: Irrigation and Drainage*, 298, 300, 302. These were the only counties in the valley which had significant acreage under the ditch to warrant report. The reconfiguration of the boundaries of Cameron and Hidalgo counties does not seem to have affected the amount of irrigated land.
Note: This was the first irrigation census made in Texas.

Table 6
Value of Farm Property, Lower Rio Grande Valley, Texas, 1900–1920
[in U.S. Dollars]

County	1900	1910	1920
Cameron	9,787,533	9,184,783	24,525,730
Hidalgo	2,740,564	10,992,746	45,049,080
Starr	2,187,879	5,468,184	2,609,182
Zapata	636,846	950,820	1,432,630
Webb	2,724,250	6,646,355	12,195,432
Total	18,077,072	33,242,888	85,812,054

Compiled from U.S. Department of Commerce, Bureau of the Census, *Fourteenth Census of the United States, 1920: Agriculture*, 6, 664–686.

300 percent in Hidalgo and Webb counties. These new farmers had land worth fighting for.

Farmers began to lobby for regulation of the river's channel by a system of flood controls which would have irrigation benefits as a by-product. The solution was seen to lie in the construction of several dams and reservoirs, similar to that at Elephant Butte, New Mexico; these would impound the floodwaters, guarantee constant streamflow, and stabilize the channel. Irrigation canals relying upon gravity instead of the expensive pump could then be used from the reservoirs and river banks to water land not immediately adjacent to the river's edge.[11] Such incentives lured new people to the river.

New farmers entered the valley in astonishing numbers after 1910, able to invest an average of $35.00 (dollars) an acre for irrigated land in Cameron County and $46.00 (dollars) an acre in Hidalgo County. Their purchases from developers meant that ranchland had been bought cheaply from Anglos, Tejanos, and Mexicans and resold dearly as farmland—all on the basis of water. The newcomers tended to stick to themselves, to regard Mexicans as menials, and to see their future in short-term agricultural prosperity.

Moreover, the Magic Valley's boom received unappreciated benefit from

Table 7
Increase in Capital Invested in Irrigation, Lower Rio Grande Valley and Texas, 1910–1920 [in U.S. Dollars]

County	1910	1920	Increase	Percent
Cameron	2,024,500	3,108,489	1,083,989	+ 54%
Hidalgo	1,961,902	8,024,550	6,062,648	+ 309%
Webb	263,312	1,098,640	835,328	+ 317%
Subtotal	4,249,714	12,231,679	7,981,965	+ 188%
All Texas	13,487,347	35,072,739	21,585,392	+ 160%

Compiled from U.S. Department of Commerce, Bureau of the Census, *Fourteenth Census of the United States, 1920: Agriculture: Irrigation and Drainage*, 298, 300, 302. These were the only counties in the valley that had significant acreage under the ditch to warrant report. The reconfiguration of the boundaries of Cameron and Hidalgo counties does not seem to have affected the amount of irrigated land.
Note: This was the first irrigation census made in Texas.

the Mexican revolution. Disturbed conditions in Mexico after Huerta's coup, the Constitutionalists' resistance, and civil war meant that some Mexicans left for the United States to avoid the fighting and to find work. South Texas provided economic opportunity close to Mexico.

In absolute numbers, the Mexican population of Hidalgo County nearly doubled between 1900 and 1910, and then nearly tripled by 1920. In the same twenty years Cameron County's Mexican population nearly doubled. Moreover, the aggregate figures do not reveal fluctuations caused by changing political fortunes or seasonal work.[12] Mexican labor, dislocated by the revolution, contributed to the South Texas farm boom.

The potential for ethnic conflict intensified as more Anglos of native parents and more Mexicans entered the valley. With no corresponding growth of the mixed population—the traditional bonding element of this historically polarized society—the cultural network could no longer function. The precarious social balance had worked as long as the mixed population was proportionately significant, for it provided evidence of and encouraged interaction between both poles. Intermarriage and *compadrazgo* had constituted a network for stability that deteriorated when new arrivals maintained exclusivity. Growing ethnic separatism came to dominate social relations after the introduction of the railroad and increased over the issue of water.

Mexico, unintentionally, contributed water for Texas irrigation. Because of mutual boundary and water problems, both countries had created the International Boundary Commission (IBC) in 1894. The IBC consisted of a commissioner, engineer, and secretary from each country and had authorization to discuss water problems as well as boundary questions.[13] To insure the presumed right of Mexico to one-half the water of the Rio Grande in that stretch of the river's course that formed the international border, active Mexican representation was necessary.

After Huerta's usurpation, however, Wilson recognized no government in Mexico and, consequently, none of its minsters. Mexico, then, had no representative on the IBC who could protect its interests at the very time that irrigation in South Texas took off. As a result, by 1920, Texans in uncoordinated and often unapproved irrigation projects took the entire dependable streamflow in the lower Rio Grande valley. Seventy percent of that water, however, had originated in Mexico.[14]

The U.S. section of the IBC tried to control the Texan diversions, but the absence of enforcement machinery and the complexities of bureaucratic responsibility thwarted its efforts. Starting with nearly equal areas of potentially irrigable land, Texans developed their side of the valley at the expense of Mexico in general and Tamaulipecos in particular. In ten years, the number of acres irrigated in South Texas jumped from 54,000 in 1909 to 228,000 in 1919 (see Table 5). In the corresponding area of Tamaulipas, little had changed. Tamaulipecos irrigated 2,000 acres in 1910 and twenty years later less than 20,000.

Crops followed water. In 1910, Texans irrigated mainly cotton. A decade later cotton remained important, but so, too, were sugarcane, broom corn for fodder, and cereal corn. The first citrus trees had been planted in Hidalgo County in 1915, and their impact—which would bring the biggest boom ever seen in the valley when it beat California to the citrus market one week early—had not yet been felt. Tamaulipeco crops, however, remained the same: beans, rice, small amounts of cotton, and sugarcane.[15]

With the revolution, Mexicans on both sides of the line and Tejanos recognized their progressive losses but were powerless to prevent them. In 1910, the commissioners of Hidalgo Drainage District Number 1 sought to build a levee along the Texas side of the river to prevent floodwaters from damaging their farms and pumping stations. The commissioners noted, "As a matter of course a large proportion of the floodwaters of the river will be deflected by this levee into Mexico."[16] The catastrophe of a flood would therefore not seriously inconvenience Americans; Mexico's only recourse lay in Texas courts, where complaints could be indefinitely delayed.

American IBC engineer W. W. Follett opposed the plan, noting that "the effects [of the levee] on lands lying on the Mexican side of the river would be disastrous."[17] The commissioners eventually altered their plan, but their original approach reflected the feelings of their water users. Even Wells, the valley's political boss, openly said that Texans had the right to all the water of the Rio Grande, basing his claim on two nonexistent Supreme Court decisions.[18]

Mexican and Tejano land owners and farmers in Texas fared little better than their counterparts across the river. For Mexicans and Tejanos in South Texas to complain, they needed English, the language of the powerful—which few commanded well enough to write. One Ramón Salinas, age sixty-eight, wrote in protest to the War Department on behalf of himself and seventy other Mexican/Tejano families living along the river in Webb County. Unable to obtain water because others diverted it first, they had sold their land cheaply to a developer—who then got water and sold the land to newcomers at a substantial profit.

Salinas, born in Brownsville and made an American citizen after the Mexican War, expressed the anger and resentment of many.

> "I have said as a Spanish adage says: that something done well is paid by something done wrong. That is what happens to me . . . I never heard of a goverment [sic] doing this before, to take something from one and give it to someone else. Money protects the ones whose [sic] got it."[19]

If Salinas had never heard of government treating the poor as he had been treated, he had not read *Regeneración*. His experiences, however, like those of his neighbors in the valley, were evidence for *Regeneración*'s argument that capital protected its interests. Others in the region had learned of Ricardo Flores Magón's thoughts and, through *Regeneración*, could express their outrage. Aniceto Pizaña had met Ricardo and Enrique Flores Magón in Laredo in 1904 and had formed a PLM *grupo* in Brownsville shortly thereafter.[20]

Pizaña maintained his loyalty to Ricardo throughout the PLM transformation from reform to anarchism; Pizaña found the more radical doctrine a better explanation of local conditions and of Mexican reality. While the PLM leadership served prison sentences for the Baja California expedition, Pizaña composed a poem demanding their release.

> Mr. Taft thought of imprisoning the Idea
> But his evil instincts were shipwrecked
> And Anarchy with Phoebean Light
> Demands from martyrs of McNeil Island, their
> Liberty.[21]

Pizaña, in 1915 a forty-five-year old stocky Tejano, about 5'9" with curly hair, worked as a stockman. In February, his thirty-one year old wife Manuela bore him a son whom they named Praxedis after the PLM warrior-poet Praxedis Guerrero. Unfortunately for the family, the infant died nine days after birth.[22] Nonetheless, two other children survived: son Guadalupe, age twelve, and six year old daughter Beatriz. The children, like the parents, were Tejanos.[23]

Pizaña had done reasonably well in the valley. He owned his own ranch along the river, Los Tulitos, and he rented a house in Brownsville for his mother Cela and his family.[24] As a Tejano stockman watching the transition from ranching to irrigated farming, however, he saw the adverse effects of change upon his segment of local society. Sensitive to issues of social and economic discrimination against Mexicans and Tejanos, he wrote a twenty-one verse poem about leaving the little valley town of San Benito after suffering anti-Mexican abuse.

> With suffering and pain that grows greater
> I say that there are Mexicans
> Who hate and despise their own race
> In order to lick the feet of the Americans[25]

For Pizaña, *Regeneración* expressed his outrage and exhorted the action he thought might correct injustice in Mexico and in South Texas. He read the newspaper aloud to illiterate friends and acquaintances at Los Tulitos on Sundays, and vigorous discussion followed the readings. Pizaña told his listeners that everything in *Regeneración* was true.[26] Reading aloud, a long-standing PLM and anarchist practice, helped to spread Ricardo's views throughout the valley.[27] Pizaña also distributed such PLM propaganda as copies of the September 23, 1911, Manifesto and buttons inscribed with the slogan "Land and Liberty."[28]

Other subscribers followed Pizaña's pattern. At Rancho del Castillo, for example, laborers Atilano Cruz and Cosmo García received *Regeneración* and shared its contents with fellow workers.[29] José Zamora, a *Regeneración* subscriber and a stockman of some accomplishment like Pizaña, owned his own ranch outside Brownsville. Born in Mexico, Zamora's parents brought him to the valley in 1871, and eventually he became a naturalized citizen. In 1910, he had been married to his second wife, a Tejana, for eight years; she had borne him three Tejano children to join the two surviving Tejano offspring from his first marriage. His workers learned of *Regeneración*'s propaganda through Sunday gatherings.

In Brownsville, Pizaña found like-minded people. Emilia Rodríguez, Mexican, had come with her husband to Texas around 1900, where she gave birth to her daughter Consuelo. In 1906 her husband died, and Emilia became a seamstress. She worked hard, and by 1910 she had purchased a house that she owned outright. As a *Regeneración* subscriber, she represented the anarchist affirmation of sexual equality, and she probably spread anarchist ideas through conversations with her customers and a women's discussion group.

Other influential subscribers within the Spanish-speaking community in Brownsville were grocer Calixto Hinojosa and barber Ismael Soza. Both were Mexican, but Hinojosa came to Brownsville in 1903, five years earlier than Soza. In 1915, Hinojosa was fifty-three and Soza, forty-three. Soza, married for nineteen years, had the larger family consisting of his wife, Manuela, and their four daughters, the youngest of whom, Concepción, had been born in Brownsville. Hinojosa, married for twenty-five years to Lucinda, had a thirteen-year-old Tejana daughter named Adela. Hinojosa through his grocery store and Soza through his barbershop came to discuss *Regeneración* with a wide range of people, both from town and the outlying countryside.

Pizaña's closest friend, Luis de la Rosa, also deeply admired Ricardo Flores Magón and *Regeneración* and had helped to establish other *grupos* in South Texas. In 1915, De la Rosa was about fifty years old, as tall as Pizaña but twenty pounds lighter, and had black hair and a mustache. His left arm, which curved in toward his body, ended in a hand missing one or two fingers—a mute testimony to injuries sustained over the years as a butcher and former Cameron County deputy sheriff. He lived about twenty-five miles north of Brownsville in the small community of Rio Hondo; Pizaña rode up there frequently to visit and discuss *Regeneración* with his Tejano friend.[30]

De la Rosa, talkative and compelling, traveled the backlands extensively, frequently in the company of Amado Garza, an active member in the Brownsville association, who established Floresmagonista *grupos* in Falfurrias and Alice. De la Rosa also fancied himself a *macho*, spending time in the bars and brothels of Brownsville's Red Light district. There he talked about both *Regeneración* and his sexual exploits—bringing anarchist thought to an area Pizaña did not frequent. Over time, however, De La Rosa became progressively more militant about the need for direct action to redress the wrongs done to Mexicans and Tejanos on both sides of the river.

Regeneración subscribers in South Texas, whether Tejano, naturalized citizen, or Mexican, represented Spanish-speaking people of some accomplishment in America. They were small entrepreneurs with investment in valley society; they were politically conscious people who abstained from valley politics because of their subordinate role to English speakers. Wells maintained his political machine by voting the Mexicans, gathering them up before an election, providing them with beer and food, and then voting them as a bloc. Most of those so voted were laborers and cowboys, people of less education and accomplishment than the *Regeneración* subscribers. Nonetheless, those subscribers served the poor as alternative examples to those Mexicans and Tejanos who secured a place in the valley by accepting its political and social life.

The Solis family typified adjustment. The family was an old and respected Mexican clan with members living both in Tamaulipas and in Texas, in the vicinity of Brownsville, since the nineteenth century. Lazaro Solis owned a large ranch near La Feria on which he ran several thousand head of sheep and goats, in addition to horses and cattle. His Tejano son Gumersindo became property manager and gradually acquired prominence as a livestock trader in Cameron and Hidalgo counties, as well as in Tamaulipas.[31] Gumersindo's aunt, Lazaro's sister, married into the French Catholic Champion family. The Champions grew to become large landholders in the Tio Cano Lake area of Cameron County.[32]

Jim Wells depended upon his *compadre*, John Closner, to deliver the vote in Hidalgo County.[33] Closner, in turn, relied upon Florencio Saenz, whose powerful family controlled much of eastern Hidalgo County's land and economy prior to the great Anglo influx. Florencio had been born in Mexico, but he resided continuously in the area of Hidalgo County after 1846. He and his kin held nearly fifty thousand acres on both sides of the line; he had inherited the Llano Grande grant in Cameron County that included the later townsites of Mercedes and Weslaco. He won election to the first Hidalgo County Board of Supervisors and won reelection continually until he resigned in 1905.

Florencio created a permanent base for his diverse operations at La Toluca Ranch in eastern Hidalgo County. There he built a house and church, both of brick, and from wood erected several dwellings for his permanent workers as well as a large mercantile store and a school. He hired a Brownsville Anglo to come and teach. His store became the major trading center for the region, enhanced during Texas elections when the corralled Mexican voters also shopped. When Florencio and his wife, Sostenes Cano, found they could not have children, they adopted one of her nieces, Manuela Champion. Manuela married Amador Fernández, who managed the store. Saenz, like Closner, grew sugar cane by irrigation, but Saenz made from it the coarser *piloncillo*, which Mexicans purchased.[34]

The Saenz-Champion-Solis interrelationships exemplified elite Mexican-Tejano-Anglo intermarriage. Such intermarriage, however, occurred at all levels. Manuela Villarreal, born in 1873 on the Nueves Ranch near what became Mission in Hidalgo County, married Abraham Dillard. He worked as a Texas Ranger and later as deputy collector of customs before accumulating enough capital to buy the Nueves Ranch. He later built a store there and a permanent house. Their bilingual son, George Dillard, served as a Hidalgo County deputy sheriff and acted as a scout for the U.S. Army during the troubles of 1915–1916. George had a small place at Ojo de Agua, near Mission, and raiders sacked it twice, the second time in retaliation for George's assistance to Anglos.[35]

The strengths and weaknesses of Anglo-Mexican interaction in the old social order are illustrated well in the case of Jim Wells. A Texan, Wells arrived in the valley in 1878, having just failed as a land speculator in Refugio County. With a law degree from the University of Virginia as his only asset, he entered into partnership in Brownsville with Judge Stephen Powers, an important figure in local Democratic party politics. One of Wells's first accomplishments involved successfully defending twenty of twenty-one contested land titles, one of which belonged to the King Ranch. When Corpus Christi friend Robert Kleberg assumed management of the King Ranch, he retained Wells as a legal adviser on land.[36]

Wells's deepening interest in the valley prompted him to learn Spanish and, after taking religious instruction, to convert to Catholicism. Wells, a man who spoke Spanish, attended Mass, and knew the American law, became much admired by people of both cultures. The key to his strength among the upper classes, both Mexican and Anglo, lay in his involvement in land. Although he personally acquired acreage, his investments never paid him their anticipated return, and he did not become wealthy. He gained power not from owning land, but from his lasting role in its turnover. He worked incessantly, validating old Spanish land grants, transferring property rights, answering boundary and water questions, and handling property transactions. His was a combination real estate and legal aid office. For the older, established families of the valley Wells was the man to consult in affairs of property.[37]

Wells became equally popular with the poor Mexican/Tejano elements in the valley. He regarded them as humble people who lacked formal knowledge of political life and who needed guidance. Acting as patriarch, he extended his care to them and asked their trust in return. He found employment for people, gave them advice, and did their legal work, usually without fee. During the drought of 1892–1893, he provided relief to the poor and homeless.[38]

Since individual poor Mexicans had tried for centuries to attach themselves to a protector to find security in an insecure world, Wells justified his continuation of such practices in South Texas on hereditary grounds. Wells thought that the Mexican "naturally inherited" dependence from the Spanish.[39] He never considered that dependence might be the involuntary result of society's economic and social structure. In his view, as long as the benefactor acted out of love and the worker behaved loyally, then both were well served.

Wells married Judge Powers's niece, acquired the Judge's political contacts, and built them into a political network embracing South Texas. Wells also insisted that his sons learn Spanish, both to assist him and to participate fully in valley life.[40] Wells, as others, used the voting of Mexicans as a means of obtaining and holding political power, but the mixed-blood population constituted a much more important segment of his political base. Wells and his associates ran South Texas from the 1880s until 1920, when the newer arrivals became the clear majority and rejected him as the last vestige of the old political order.

New arrivals coming to the valley as farmers brought different experiences and values. Beda Franksen Schultz separated from her husband in 1908 and took as settlement twenty-one acres of farmland in Hidalgo County near Sebastian. She had come from Chicago, where her marriage to Albert Schultz, a Swede, had permitted him to become a citizen. She brought her daughter Ruth with her. Beda improved the property with a five-room house, a barn, and other outbuildings and engaged in hog farming. She also acted as Sebastian's postmistress.

In five years, Beda had acquired nearly one hundred well-bred hogs, ten horses, and several head of thoroughbred Jersey cattle. She had enough to manage the farm as an absentee. She moved into Sebastian where she purchased two adjacent lots, with improvements consisting of a store building with a stock of merchandise as well as a residence. With town and country properties to manage, she no longer had time to be the postmistress. Beda found her friends among the newcomers and her interest in Mexicans/Tejanos was limited to their labor.[41]

In 1909, Alfred L. Austin bought forty acres located one and one-half miles southeast of Sebastian; there, he raised corn. He and his wife Nellie came to the valley from the Panama Canal Zone, where Austin had learned some Spanish to organize work crews and where he also developed a skeptical view of Spanish-speaking laborers. His older son Charles joined him in 1911, and they not only cultivated the rural acreage but also operated a corn sheller in Sebastian, where they could process their own and their neighbors' corn.[42]

A. L. Austin prided himself in aiding law enforcement with any "Mexican problems," and he became president of the Sebastian Law and Order League—a vigilante group credited with driving several "bad Mexicans" out of the area.[43] The hot-tempered senior Austin had a reputation for using "the toe of his boot a little too freely on those he considered laggardly in their field work."[44] Such an impatient, intolerant attitude earned him enemies among the Tejano/Mexican workers. But to most Anglo new arrivals, Mexican/Tejano discontent—like the people themselves—remained largely invisible.

In this context, *Regeneración* subscribers in the valley constituted an intellectual elite within the Mexican/Tejano community that criticized both the old social order and the new, emerging one based on change. They were able ideologically to identify exploitation readily and to rail against it. Fifty years later such anarchists would be called "weathermen." Their criticism gained an audience because of their individual accomplishments. Those who lived in Brownsville, for example, lived in wooden frame structures worth insuring, a dramatic step above the simple thatched *jacales* (huts) in which many laborers lived.[45]

During this period membership in *Floresmagonista* clubs ran to 165 in Cameron and Hidalgo counties alone[46]—a figure more than five times greater than the number of subscribers[47] and certainly far short of all those who heard *Regeneración*'s message. Given their numbers and their prominence within their communities, even as *Regeneración* suspended publication in December 1914, its partisans in South Texas were capable of mounting their own propaganda independent of its immediate voice. In those times of change in South Texas, these women and men were ready for direct action.

CHAPTER 5

THE PLAN OF SAN DIEGO

> Do you not have [race] hatred in Texas—and in other states—where a Mexican is forbidden to travel in the passenger cars of the men with white skin? Where Mexicans are not admitted to restaurants, hotels, barbershops, nor fashionable beaches. In Texas, Mexican children are excluded from the [public] schools.
>
> Ricardo Flores Magón[1]

> In Texas, [whites] have paid their workers with an unjustified race hatred that closes to the Mexican, the Negro, the Asian, the doors of the schools, the hotels, the theaters, of every public place; that segregates them on railroad cars and keeps them out of the meeting places of the "white-skinned" savages who constitute a superior caste.
>
> Preamble to the Plan of San Diego[2]

Talk of reclaiming the land Mexico lost to the United States had persisted since the mid-nineteenth century. During the Spanish-American war in 1898, a prominent Mexico City Catholic Newspaper, *El Tiempo*, called for Hispanic unity to "liberate us from the unsupportable Yankee yoke." To accomplish this aim, *El Tiempo* proposed a fifth-column operation designed to promote Indian uprisings on reservations, foment black revolts in the South, and exploit sectional divisiveness.[3] In the twentieth century, such appeals to national pride assumed greater cogency for the Mexican poor as the propaganda of the Mexican revolution spread across the countryside.

From 1910 to 1920, an estimated 230 Spanish-language newspapers, publishing from California to Texas, carried their messages to readers and listeners throughout the American Southwest. These newspapers reflected the factional divisions within Mexico and represented all persuasions of Mexican political thought. In South Texas alone, twenty-three of these journals appeared—ten percent of the total.[4]

While *Regeneración* unquestionably made itself the most radical, all the papers emphasized Mexican pride as a necessary precondition for change. Ricardo's appeal for international solidarity rested upon the fundamental call to national identity and respect for the individual Mexican. *Regeneración*'s coverage of the Rangel-Cline case, for example, focused more on ethnic discrimination against Mexicans than on ideological antipathies between labor and capital. In this milieu, anti-American talk frequently became pro-Mexican.

In late 1914, such talk could be heard across South Texas. Along the border around Laredo, a handbill circulated that was addressed to the "Sons of Cuauhtémoc, Hidalgo, and Juárez in Texas"—an open appeal to Mexico's Liberal tradition. Cuauhtémoc was the Aztec who had succeeded the woebegone Moctezuma and violently resisted the Spanish Conquest. Hidalgo, a freethinking Roman Catholic priest, had initiated the independence movement against Spain in 1810 to secure justice for Indian Mexico. Juárez, a full-blooded Indian who became the primary leader of the original Liberal movement, helped give Mexico the 1857 Constitution. He resisted the French intervention personified by Maximillian, and, after expelling the foreigners, became the first Indian president of the Restored Republic.

In the names of Cuauhtémoc, Hidalgo, and Juárez, the handbill demanded that Texas be taken by force and made an independent republic. At such time as Mexico achieved government based upon the 1857 Constitution, then a free Texas would unite. Above all, the circular stressed the need to emancipate all Mexicans living in the United States from American exploitation.[5]

At the same time, similar talk could be heard further south in the community of San Diego, Texas. There had been a PLM *grupo* there for five years.[6] San Diego's twenty-five hundred inhabitants, seventy-five percent of whom were of Mexican origin and bitterly anti-American, drew little notice from Anglos.[7] In late summer 1914, four recently arrived Mexican nationals opened a wholesale and retail beer establishment two blocks off the main plaza on Victoria Street. One of them was Basilio Ramos, Jr., a former secretary in the customs house at Nuevo Laredo who had served under Díaz, Madero, and Huerta, and who had been arrested and imprisoned by the Constitutionalists when they swept the northern border in 1914.[8]

Ramos had been accompanied by Augustin S. Garza, a 5'6" 110-lb. former school teacher who dressed well, was clean shaven, possessed a fair complexion, and had a glass eye. One observer thought that Garza "might be taken for an American Jew, although he sp[oke] very little English."[9] He had been a commission man in Monterrey and had come to San Diego, Texas, because he had a sister living there. In addition to his partnership in the beer business, Garza also bought hides for the local Finnigan.

A. A. Saenz, the only one of the four with prior beer-selling experience, had operated a saloon in Nuevo Laredo; there his best customers had been Huerta's federals when they occupied the town.[10] Saenz knew that he and his associates would need a surety bond to open and so approached the local Mexican Masonic Society for it. Claiming Masonic membership and pleading for help to get started, they succeeded in obtaining the bond. They did not design the saloon and wholesale operation only to make money, however. They wanted a forum to vent anti-American feelings and either gave the beer away as free rounds or sold it at a nominal cost. While their place was popular, it was not profitable, and, in December, they skipped town with the rent unpaid—forfeiting the bond. The Masonic Society had to honor their debts.[11]

Garza's brother-in-law, Mocario Barrera, much older than Garza's sister, typified some local attitudes. Barrera had lived in San Diego for forty years, had seen the region transformed, and had become embittered by it. If someone wanted to lead a fight against the Anglos, he would do what he could. "I am too old to fight," he told an informer, "but I can carry water for the troops."[12] Without active field leadership, though, nothing would happen.

Garza meanwhile had made a significant convert through his propaganda efforts—Luis de la Rosa. The Tejano had been predisposed to direct action for several months, but the forum at San Diego propelled him to become more militant. De la Rosa then split the Floresmagonistas into two groups, his own aggressive *sediciosos* and Pizaña's moderates.[13] With the departure of Garza and his companions, little remained but to await further developments. Although Garza and his friends made their returns to Mexico separately, each found himself rearrested as a Huertista and sent to prison in Monterrey.

On January 6, 1915, in prison in Monterrey, Garza, Ramos, Saenz, and six other low-level Huertistas signed the original document known as the Plan of San Diego, Texas. It had been written by an unidentified "friend" of the Monterrey prisoners and smuggled in by a servant with their meals. These nine Mexican nationals signed it because they agreed with its goals.[14] According to the Plan, an armed uprising against the government and country of the United States would occur on February 20, 1915.

Marching under a red banner bearing a white diagonal fringe and proclaiming "Equality and Independence," Plan supporters would reclaim for themselves the territory comprising Texas, New Mexico, Arizona, Colorado, and California. A race war was envisioned—with every North American male over the age of sixteen to be put to death. Plan membership was restricted only to "the Latin, the Negro, or the Japanese race." Once the territory had been secured and the Negroes liberated from white bondage, they would be given six additional states, bordering those already named, for their own republic. Social goals articulated in the Plan included the freedom of the Mexican and Oriental, the independence of the Negro, and a promise to the Indians that their ancestral territory would be restored to them in return for their support. Essentially, the Plan of San Diego proposed a common interracial effort against the hated Yankee.

Structurally, power was to be vested in a Supreme Revolutionary Congress, which would designate a Supreme Chief for the Armed Forces and issue commissions. The commissions could be either for military command or for organizing political juntas, or cells, to support the Plan. Membership in the Supreme Revolutionary Congress would be determined by free elections from among the representatives of the various juntas. Initially, however, actual power would be exercised by a Provisional Directorate. This group, probably the prisoners of the jail, designated Garza as commander of the military forces, which would be called the Liberating Army for Races and

Peoples. The various ranks, from subordinate to superior, would be filled and approved by the Provisional Directorate. Furthermore, the Provisional Directorate would recognize the ranks of those in other political factions who wished to join the Plan of San Diego. Field commanders would seize all necessary supplies and arms but would take no prisoners. If a city were captured, the commander would appoint a new set of municipal authorities to maintain order. When the territory had been secured and the independent republic established, that republic could, if it chose, unite with Mexico and be ruled by the same form of government then prevailing in the parent country. However, no aid, "either moral or pecuniary," would be accepted from the Mexican government, "and it need not consider itself under any obligations in this, our movement."[15]

The curious document emitted many messages. In political form, it was a Mexican Plan, part of the revolutionary Plans such as Madero's Plan of San Luis Potosí, Carranza's Plan of Guadalupe, or Zapata's Plan of Ayala. Yet it disavowed no one in Mexico. Its target was the government of the United States, and its goals were the liberation of specific minorities. Nonetheless, unlike the earlier appeals of *El Tiempo* or the circular to the "Sons of Cuauhtémoc, Hidalgo and Juárez in Texas," the Plan of San Diego was far more than irredentist in its goals. Territorial reclamation would be a means toward other ends.

Within Mexico, it appealed to all factions—to all Mexicans—to cooperate in a struggle for social justice. The Plan of San Diego would accept any Mexican—regardless of factional allegiance—who accepted the Plan. Theoretically, the bitterest of enemies could be reconciled under its banner, and transcend factionalism to pursue a higher goal. The Plan's appeals to lofty idealism distinguished it from any other Mexican Plan except the PLM reformist program of 1906 and Zapata's Plan of Ayala. Moreover, like that PLM program, the Plan of San Diego promised to restore ancestral Indian lands to specific peoples. The earlier PLM commission to engage the Yaquis to join them in fighting Díaz in return for land restoration possessed too curious an affinity with the Plan of San Diego to have been mere coincidence.[16]

The Provisional Directorate commissioned Ramos to create juntas throughout northern Mexico and the American Southwest and appointed Garza chief of military operations. Both men were released, and in mid-January, each went separately to Texas.[17] For Garza, the problem of military recruitment would have been formidable. A one-eyed man lacked depth perception, a particularly useful asset in combat, so Garza undoubtedly knew that he would have to find a replacement for field operations.

Ramos, fearing rearrest if he returned to Nuevo Laredo, went directly to Matamoros and crossed into Brownsville by the international bridge.[18] Subsequent events render it unlikely that he contacted any of the Brownsville Floresmagonistas. If he did, he would have found them in disarray over the De la Rosa–Pizaña split. Ramos continued to McAllen, where he contacted medical doctor Andres Villarreal about the Plan. Villarreal told Deodoro

Guerra, a local merchant, of Ramos' approach, disavowing any interest in it.[19]

Guerra, under investigation for receiving smuggled goods, needed no further legal problems.[20] He immediately notified Sheriff A. Y. Baker. After Ramos failed to appear at a prearranged meeting, Baker left, telling Guerra to arrest Ramos if he should appear. Deodoro and his son Modesto arrested Ramos and confiscated papers from their prisoner. The papers included his commission, letters from Garza, a copy of the Plan of San Diego, a codebook, and a safe conduct through Constitutionalist lines signed by local border commander General Emiliano P. Nafarrate.[21] When Deputy U.S. Marshal T. P. Bishop came to Guerra's store to claim him, Ramos passed into Anglo custody. From the beginning, Mexican nationals encountered difficulty in persuading their counterparts in Texas to support a movement ostensibly for their own liberation.

Basilio Ramos was in a Texas jail at 2:00 A.M., February 20, 1915—the hour and day the uprising was to begin. Nothing violent occurred, but on that date the Plan of San Diego was drastically revised without him. In a Manifesto to the Oppressed Peoples of America, the Revolutionary Congress amended the Plan of San Diego, making it more specific both tactically and ideologically. Henceforth, the struggle would center in Texas and spread from there to the other states. In unequivocal terms the document proclaimed the "SOCIAL REVOLUTION" that would emancipate all peoples and races of the United States. It decried the exploitation of land and labor by whites and denounced their racist discrimination against people of color. The revised document particularly emphasized the dignity of Mexicans; it also introduced the term "proletarian" into Plan rhetoric.

The Plan of San Diego now enumerated specific clauses describing particular objectives. Clause IV called for delivery of cultivated land to the proletarians, with preference given to tenant farmers and those fighting for the movement. Absolute communization might be proclaimed. Communal sharing and distribution of rural property, of access to communication media, and of supplies and tools—all without national distinction (VI, IX)—complemented the abolition of race hatred (II). To help build a new future, the Plan now called for creation of "Modern Schools where all children regardless of color and without class prejudice [might] prepare the future happiness of a Society whose acts would be governed by the norm of UNIVERSAL LOVE" (X).

Negro independence remained the primary objective, but the socioeconomic emancipation of the worker from Yankee capitalist exploitation became a concomitant goal. Moreover, once the Negroes had received their six states, they could organize freely—provided they chose to be communal (XXII). Simultaneously, the new Plan accepted all the provisions of the old, as well as its organizational structure, but with the stipulation that the new clauses took precedence. Nine people signed for the Revolutionary Congress: J. Z. Walcker, president; F. F. Lippi, vice-president; J. R. Becker, secretary; J. N. Nagazaqui, treasurer; P. Veeni; Jonás Bub; W. Córcega; Inctlaca Ubaqui; and León Caballo, military commander.[22]

The signers suggested the multiethnic mix of the movement. Walcker and Becker seemed German; Lippi and Veeni, Italian; and Nagazaqui (Nagasaki) and Ubaqui (Ubaki), Hispanized Japanese. This mix appeared reminiscent of PLM-IWW joint ventures at Cananea, in the Baja campaign, and in the abortive movement of Rangel and Cline. None of the signers seemed to have participated in the original Plan except for Agustín Garza who now signed as León Caballo.[23]

The February 20 revisions of the Plan of San Diego made it an anarchist document, albeit a confused one. Kropotkin's anarchist communism and Ferrer's Modern Schools, along with the term "SOCIAL REVOLUTION," bespoke classic anarchist thought. Use of the word "proletariat" in a document circulated primarily among country people suggested a larger appeal to all members of the working classes. The most obvious intellectual sources of influence on the Plan of San Diego were *Regeneración* and the PLM. Ricardo Flores Magón's emphasis on international solidarity found expression in ethnic solidarity and vindication in the struggle of exploited against exploiter. Organizationally, Plan structure closely followed the early, nonanarchist, PLM model.

Confusion lay partly in that organizational structure—a pattern difficult to reconcile with anarchist objectives except as a compromise to expediency. Land expropriation to form one or more republics also contradicted anarchist aims of decentralized, nongovernmental societies. The very nature of a Plan was antithetical to the nonpolitical galvanizing of human energy in spontaneous destruction of the existing order. Moreover, while the Plan implicitly called for concerted "direct action," it did not employ that phrase. In its appeal to all Mexican factions as well as to diverse ethnic groups, it could be seen as a flawed interpretation of the "anarchism without adjectives" principle important to Ricardo's thought. Overall, the Plan appeared to be a program composed by a diverse committee—much as the 1906 PLM program had been crafted; it lacked the coherent focus of a single mind and a single philosophy behind it.

Nonetheless, the Plan of San Diego's most remarkable affinity with the PLM lay in its different versions. People could follow it with or without knowing themselves to be furthering an anarchist cause. Just as Ricardo had issued anarchist instructions to his forces not to cooperate with the Maderistas in 1910 and then confused the issue by circulating more copies of the 1906 PLM reformist program, so too Plan of San Diego (PSD) leaders could appeal to the January 6 version for wider support if the February 20 formulation cost them followers. As an anarchist phenomenon, the PSD opposed all Mexican factions save Zapata's. Without the anarchism, it was friend to all. Its mixed messages meant that the PSD movement potentially could embrace nearly all those of Mexican ancestry along with blacks, Indians, and Japanese in both countries.

Following PSD revision, the conspirators went underground. Plan agents actively established *juntas* throughout South Texas and northern Mexico. Americans discovered a *junta* in Laredo in April but ignored it. When Anglos discussed the PSD, they generally dismissed it as preposterous. In May, when Basilio Ramos came to trial in Brownsville, the judge stated that the defendant "ought to be tried for lunacy, not conspiracy against the United States." He set a bond and released the prisoner. With his bond experience in San Diego, Texas, to guide him, Ramos skipped bail.[24]

Plan agents had a burgeoning refugee population to proselytize. Mexico's civil war forced progressively more families from their homes and fields in the interior, and by spring 1915, thousands of people had sought refuge in the northeastern frontier. Whenever rail lines could be repaired, Constitutionalists provided free passage to the border. Those who wished to emigrate and were not excluded by American law, could cross the border legally into the United States.

From the American perspective, the quality of Mexican immigrant had declined. The inspector in charge at Laredo summarized it succinctly:

> Before the revolution began and for some time after, we had each day from two to four Pullmans, most well filled; three to five first-class coaches and two to four second-class coaches. First the Pullman class disappeared, then the first-class traveler, until now we have only the second-class arrival; and even this class has deteriorated. In normal times we had many of the laboring class who were in the prime of life and fine specimens of physical manhood. This class has almost entirely disappeared, and only the ordinary laborer and a few women and children are now coming.[25]

The immigration supervising inspector for the Texas border attributed the change "to the fact that those of a higher degree of mental and physical fitness are engaged in the revolution in Mexico." He did not believe, as some had charged, that Mexican authorities engaged in "any systematic practice" of sending indigents to the border to become U.S. charges.[26]

In Brownsville, on the other hand, the inspector in charge believed that Carranza's forces did encourage "the emigration to this country of men, women and children who are unfit for service in the army or unable to work. Most of the noncombatants now in Matamoros belong to the excluded classes," he wrote, among whom were "Chinese, Japanese, Syrians, prostitutes, pimps, diseased, beggars, paupers, insane, feeble-minded, criminals, etc." He intended "to use strenuous efforts to keep these classes out of the United States." He acknowledged the role of the revolution in creating these refugees and observed, "If it were not a fact that the poorer classes of Mexicans require very little to sustain life, and can live very cheaply indeed, conditions would be far worse among them than they are.[27] . . . And if Americans were in the same plight as the peon Mexicans, the distress and starvation would be *many times* greater."[28]

People impoverished by civil strife and placed proximate to relative wealth could be tempted to raid their neighbors, especially if border crossing could be done surreptitiously and easily. The immigration service could barely cover the legal entry points in Cameron and Hidalgo counties and relied upon Mexican authorities to police their side of the line. Given the typhus quarantine then in effect, which meant that persons coming from within fifty miles of the border had to wait in Matamoros or Reynosa thirteen days before entering the United States, Mexican officials had a heavy workload without dealing with lawbreakers.[29]

In Texas, confusion over spheres of responsibility contributed to general lawlessness and eventually to the initial success of the PSD. The Southern Department, created by the army in 1913 with headquarters in San Antonio, had responsibility for guarding the boundary from the Gulf of Mexico to the California-Arizona border. In 1915, the department commander, General Frederick Funston, had fewer than twenty thousand troops to secure 1,745 miles of line. His primary duty, a legacy of earlier activities by the PLM Maderistas, and others, involved preventing violations of U.S. neutrality statutes by conspiratorial groups of Mexicans seeking to stage military operations from American soil. Preventing smuggling or banditry per se was not an army concern.

Nonetheless, Texas Governor James E. Ferguson appealed to President Wilson for help in late February, complaining of depredations from Mexico by men who were "almost daily crossing into the Texas side." Ferguson wanted $30,000 (dollars) to add thirty men to the Texas Ranger force to meet what he called "almost a reign of terror."[30] Funston regarded Ferguson's description of the situation an egregious exaggeration, and the War Department considered that Ferguson wanted federal forces to do a Texas job. Wilson made the Solomonic decision that he could provide no funds but he would change governmental policy so that after March 5, the Southern Department would view marauding bands "*as belligerents entering American territory for unlawful acts*" and deal with them accordingly. Funston was to confer with Ferguson about troop deployment in sensitive areas "so that the military can apprehend and disarm them [marauders] and turn them over to civil authority."[31]

In 1915, Governor Ferguson's Ranger force was below strength. Four years earlier, the Texas state legislature had authorized a force of eighty-five men organized into four companies of twenty, commanded by a captain and a first sergeant. One quartermaster served the entire force.[32] In June 1915, actual strength stood at thirty-four men divided into three companies.[33] As unrest increased in South Texas, the state adjutant general ordered Company "A," commanded by Captain J. J. Sanders, and Company "B," led by Captain J. M. Fox, into the valley. Later a fourth company, "D," was created under Captain R. L. Ransom.[34] By summer's end, more than seventy-five percent of the Texas Ranger force operated along the river from Brownsville to Laredo and ranged as far north as Corpus Christi.

Ranger appeal to Americans lay in their mythic reputation for frontier defense and settler protection against marauding Indians and Mexicans. Their service that summer began ominously. Ranger Winfred Bates resigned from the force, charging corruption. He accused the sergeant of Company

"B" of persistent drunkenness and claimed further that fellow Ranger E. B. Hulen, who had been killed in a skirmish with Mexican smugglers in May, had been deserted in combat by two other Rangers and left to fight alone.[35] Henry Hutchings, the state adjutant general, accepted Bates' resignation without comment and perfunctorily asked Captain Fox if there were any truth to the charges.[36]

PSD-initiated violence began on July 4, Independence Day for some, when a band of forty Mexican irregulars crossed the Rio Grande into Texas and shot to death two Anglo men on their ranch near Lyford.[37] The raiders continued to ride through the chaparral for two weeks before finally eluding their pursuers. En route they killed an eighteen year old Anglo boy near Raymondville and lost two of their own to the pursuing posse.[38] On July 25, a railroad bridge burned near Harlingen; the surrounding telegraph wires hung from their poles—cut.[39]

Reprisals quickly followed. On July 24, in separate incidents, lawmen killed two Mexicans resisting arrest.[40] In a more dramatic encounter on the evening of July 28, a group of armed, masked men stopped sheriff's officers transferring Adolfo Muñoz from jail in San Benito to the safer confines of Brownsville. Vigilantes took Muñoz and hanged him.[41] Ranger L. J. Engelking then arrested Muñoz's brother and half brother—fearing that they might attempt revenge.[42]

On August 2, twenty Mexicans crossed the river five miles above Brownsville, stole some horses, fired upon people in an automobile, and then disappeared into the brush. A posse composed of Texas Rangers, local sheriff's officers, a mounted customs inspector, a cavalry officer, and private citizens set out after them. The posse spent the night at Scrivner's Ranch. There John D. Scrivner told them to investigate Aniceto Pizaña's nearby ranch, Los Tulitos, since Scrivner thought it a nest of cattle and horse thieves. He offered to guide them, and his house guest, a furloughed U.S. Army private named McGuire, volunteered to accompany them.

At daybreak on August 3, a month after the serious trouble had begun, the posse left Scrivner's for Los Tulitos. The narrow road wound through dense vegetation; it was heavily wooded on both sides with mesquite, chaparral, and cactus. As they approached the two ranch houses, the customs inspector, Joe Taylor,— a well-known Mexican-hunter—drew his rifle from its scabbard as he prepared to dismount. Gunshots instantly rang from the buildings and killed Private McGuire. In the extended exchange of fire, three other posse members sustained wounds. Aniceto Pizaña and others escaped. The posse captured José Buenrosto and Aniceto's wife, brother, and twelve-year-old son Guadalupe, who had been wounded in the leg. Guadalupe later lost the limb, probably from delayed medical attention. Sheriff Mike Monahan recalled afterward that they had gone hunting twenty Mexicans but had found only four. With the possible exception of Buenrosto, they had found not Mexicans but Tejanos.[43]

If Scrivner's allegations about Pizaña had led the posse to suspect the people at Los Tulitos, then discoveries in the houses afterwards confirmed for authorities that Pizaña's malicious intentions far exceeded cattle rustling. Pizaña could read and write, and evidence of this linked him to Ricardo Flores Magón, the PLM, and *Regeneración*. Anglo investigators found ten years of Floresmagonista propaganda, chiefly copies of *Regeneración*; correspondence with Ricardo and other PLM leaders generally mentioning enclosure of small sums of money to sustain the newspaper; examples of Pizaña's poetry; and "an inflammatory handbill," apparently the September 23, 1911 PLM Manifesto.[44] Whether the observers were more shocked by Pizaña's literacy or by the subject matter of his literate interests, they concluded erroneously that he had been a follower of the Plan of San Diego.

Investigators had determined that Pizaña read *Regeneración* and supported the PLM; they then deduced that he had conspired to participate in the PSD—a conclusion that severely strained logic. Why would a man regarded by a long-time valley resident as "honorable, and a high-class and as straight a Mexican as there was"[45]—whose success as a stockman earned him the financial respect if not the envy of Scrivner—abandon what he had achieved if not provoked by attack? Why would a man of forty-five—married and the father of two children who were native-born Americans like their parents—conspire to overthrow the society that would be his children's future? Moreover, if he did, then why did he not remove them to safety first?

Later reports from Aniceto Pizaña and his wife Manuela claimed that the unprovoked attack at Los Tulitos drive him to join the PSD.[46] Pizaña wrote to Ricardo a few weeks after the incident and claimed that the surprise assault and his son's loss of a leg prompted him to seek revenge and to lead forces against Texas.[47] Although local authorities secured a murder conviction against Ramón Pizaña for the death of Private McGuire, Brownsville attorney José T. Canales, arguing that his client acted in self-defense, obtained a reversal of that conviction.[48] Apparently, Aniceto could have been exonerated of the charge against himself on the same ground. By the time Ramón's conviction had been overturned, however, Aniceto had made Pizaña a name of terror in the Anglo community. Moreover, he had been pushed into it by that community's lawmen.

Luis de la Rosa, on the other hand, had conspired to revolt and had removed his family to Matamoros before he began raiding. His carefully chosen targets illustrated the appeal he wanted the PSD to make. In preparation for his dramatic appearance, he, or others, ripped up rail trestles, set fire to railroad bridges, and cut telegraph lines near Sebastian the same day that the posse attacked Pizaña. PSD raiders did the same things in the area around Harlingen on August 4. General Funston responded by assigning five-man guards for trains running between Harlingen and Raymondville.[49]

Then, on August 6, De la Rosa and about fourteen other well-armed and mounted men rode into Sebastian. They robbed Thomas Alexander's small store. They also robbed Beda Schultz's store, burned some of her buildings, and stole some of her livestock. They then crossed the railroad tracks toward the Austin corn sheller. There De la Rosa seized the president of the

Sebastian Law and Order League, his son Charles, and another man. De la Rosa challenged white law and order in the valley by executing the Austins. He then released the other Anglo.[50]

Beda Schultz, a stocky woman, heard the shots, and ran through her fields in the opposite direction. She stepped in a hole which turned her foot, causing her to fall on a sharp stick that she struck forcefully with her right breast. A hernia resulted when she tried to regain her footing. She believed that the malignant breast tumor she later developed began with that incident. Certainly, her daughter Ruth developed a nervous condition from the event, and Beda shortly left the valley for Ruth's mental health.[51]

May Wagner heard the shots that killed the Austins, and she saw the blood on the ground where their bodies had fallen. The sights and sounds traumatized her into a "nervous breakdown." She lived on the farm adjacent to the Austins—whom she and her husband had known from the Panama Canal Zone. Wagner had joined her husband on the farm that January, and in June, he had returned to the zone to earn additional money as a railroad engineer. Consequently, she was alone two months later when the Austins were killed. She stayed with Beda Schultz for three weeks following the incident, then left the valley in fear. She had never suffered from nervousness before.[52]

Financially—in terms of crops, equipment, buildings, livestock, and business—the Austins, Alexander, Schultz, and the Wagners had lost everything. De la Rosa's killing of the Austins on August 6 prompted a letter signed by fifty-one valley residents to the secretary of war demanding that more troops and artillery be sent for their defense. Worried about property they valued at over $100 million (dollars), the residents lamented that it was "all easy prey for bands on [the] other side of the river aided by renegades on this side."[53] Three days later, the Brownsville Merchants Association added its request for more federal troops.[54]

Meanwhile, Texas state authorities responded. Following the Austins' murder on August 6, Adjutant General Hutchings took the train to Brownsville to investigate. He immediately joined a posse of Rangers and local officials; that evening, they skirmished with three Mexicans at a farmhouse thirty miles above Brownsville. According to an eyewitness, two Mexicans sitting on the front porch were shot by the posse upon approach, and the third was felled trying to flee. The posse left the bodies where they lay.[55] Within ten hours of their deaths, Anglos had retaliated for the attack on the Austins by killing three Mexicans.

De la Rosa had instilled terror quickly, and he was not yet finished. After leaving Sebastian, he and his force rode seventy-five miles inland to strike at one of the oldest symbols of Anglo power in South Texas, the King Ranch. On August 7, he joined a force of twenty-five Mexicans, led by a Constitutionalist major and a captain. The soldiers had crossed from Mexico—probably that day. A circular had been widely distributed throughout Matamoros that week—calling upon Mexicans to "unite with our brothers

... in Texas ... and take the same chances they are taking, for this is the solemn moment of the vindication of right and justice lost to us for so long a time."[56]

Once the two bands united, they seized Manuel Rincones, a King Ranch employee in his late seventies, to act as guide. Rincones recognized eight of the Tejanos as valley workers. Before advancing further, a uniformed officer read a declaration to the assembled group. Their purpose was to strike a blow to reclaim land taken from Mexico by the United States. This was an act of war—not brigandage—which the officer claimed had the approval of Venustiano Carranza. On August 8, the band pushed further north, taking eight horses from a wealthy Tejano's pasture before proceeding to the headquarters of the lower part of the King Ranch at Norias, the site named for James Wells (see Figure 4). There, without reconnaissance, De la Rosa and the officers ordered an attack.

In those troubled times, a substantial guard of U.S. Army troopers, Texas Rangers, deputy sheriffs, and King Ranch employees patrolled the ranch house and railroad shed at Norias. After a two-hour fight, that guard repulsed the raiders—killing five of them and losing two troopers. According to Rincones, the Mexican officers fought well, but the soldiers fled. The surviving raiders under De la Rosa reassembled in the brush on August 9; there a cowboy whom Rincones recognized joined them and led the men to water and food. On the next day, part of the band fled toward Mercedes; they skirmished with the army patrol there, killed one of the troopers, and disappeared. The remaining members of the band avoided Mercedes and

Fig. 4. Norias ranch house, 1915 (Hidalgo County Historical Museum, Edinburg, Texas)

marched to the river where they released Rincones before crossing into Mexico.[57]

Rincones had heard men talk of Aniceto Pizaña and the fight at Los Tulitos, but he did not see Pizaña at Norias. A popular Mexican folksong (*corrido*) of the time mentioned Pizaña but claimed he avoided Norias—fearing death. In a verse more descriptive of the general situation than the particular incident, the song told of Rangers surrounding and shooting down Mexicans, allowing few survivors.[58]

Following the attack at Norias, Captain J. M. Fox, from Company "B" of the state Ranger force, and two other men tied the legs of the dead raiders to their saddle pommels, dragged the bodies through the brush, and brought them into a heap. At one point, they stopped to be photographed (see Figure 5). The picture was then reduced to postcard size, and thousands of copies were sent into northern Mexico as a warning to future raiders. Instead of instilling fear, however, it provoked outrage and fueled the fire of revenge.[59]

Rangers sent out mixed messages at Norias, as they had in their general conduct. They and their apologists commented that "those horses and those ropes were nothing but the Norias hearse. No regular funeral equipment was available."[60] Nonetheless, the long-standing Ranger practice of ridding an area of Mexican "undesirables" could not be denied.[61]

As an El Paso Anglo phrased it, "Whenever they [Rangers] arrest one of the greasers, they rarely disarm him, and allow him every opportunity to

Fig. 5. Dead raiders at Norias, 1915 (U.S. War Dept. General Staff photo no. 165-CB-H-21 in the U.S. National Archives)

get away. I asked one the reason for this once and he replied, 'They might try to start something if we leave their arms on them, and a dead Mexican is always a lot less trouble than a live one. We would have to kill 'em in self-defense.' "[62]

Some Anglo farmers objected to Ranger treatment of Mexicans because it made relations with Mexico more difficult. A South Texas farmer remarked:

> A Ranger can shoot a poor peon with impunity, and he is scarcely even asked to put in the usual plea of self-defense, which is as a general rule an untrue one anyway. No race, however ignorant or downtrodden, is going to submit to this for long without feeling an overwhelming sentiment, not only against the rangers themselves, but against the race from which they come.[63]

Ranger practices told Mexicans that if they died by Ranger hands, they would be denied proper Roman Catholic burial. Their bodies would be left for the vultures or burned—not interred in consecrated ground. Thus, those who fought and simultaneously believed in at least the final sacrament of their religion had additional reason for outrage over the Norias postcard.

Moreover, bad feelings spread rapidly after the Norias fight. State Adjutant General Hutchings gave the Rangers "certain instructions" to quell the disturbances. Hereafter, they were "to shoot to disable any suspicious character on sight," a move designed to reassure the Anglo population and frighten the Mexican and Tejano raiders.[64] These orders, however, could only have encouraged the Rangers to behave as they always had toward suspected Mexican bandits. "We met two Mexicans on the road," the story of a Ranger report went, "but did not have time to bury them."[65]

In supporting traditional Ranger behavior, the *Laredo Times* editorialized, "The recent happenings in the Brownsville country indicates that there is a surplus population down there that needs eliminating."[66] In this atmosphere, valley residents coined a new verb—"rangered"—to describe summary treatment of a suspect by any law enforcement official.[67]

Criticism of "rangering" tended to be ignored. One prominent Laredo businessman wrote to a Bureau of Investigation agent, "As I view it, Americans in Mexico have more to fear from the misconduct of peace authorities in Texas, who, in the name of law and order, are running down and shooting everything they can meet in the way of Mexican suspects in the lower Rio Grande country."[68] His view, however, was not the one prevalent among Anglos.

The Norias fight, which permitted Rangers to intensify this misconduct against Mexican and Tejano suspects, also provided, indirectly, some check on their behavior. In the conflict, raiders dropped a packet of documents containing copies of the PSD. Skirmishes against army patrols at Mercedes Pump on August 9, and the next day just west of Mercedes at Palm Garden, resulted in the death of an army private and a Mexican raider. The Mexicans dropped both a banner bearing the inscription "Liberating Army of Mexico-Texas" and another copy of the PSD. Together, these materials convinced General Funston that valley troubles involved more than banditry; they also

THE PLAN OF SAN DIEGO   93

involved a conspiracy against the United States that the Constitutionalists supported.[69]

The banner was a remarkable symbol (see Figure 6). On the handmade flag, the central sign within the written border consisted of the classic symbol of national Mexico—the eagle atop a nopal with a serpent in its mouth. This symbol had been chosen by Liberals in the nineteenth century because it recalled an Aztec legend prophesying that the people would recognize their future home site when they found the eagle and serpent upon the cactus. On this banner, however, and, in contrast to the conventional display of that symbol then and now, a Liberty cap before the rays of an enlightening sun stood above the eagle. The Liberty cap came directly from the symbols of the French Revolution that began in 1789,[70] and here it appeared in the lower Rio Grande valley 126 years later. These raiders wanted to link their acts to the revolutionary struggle of the French Revolution—expressing precisely the lineage Voltairine de Cleyre had seen when she identified the PLM Baja campaign of 1911 with the French Commune. PSD followers were revolutionaries more than raiders or social bandits. These distinctions notwithstanding, Funston and the army would try in any case to stop the Mexicans and Tejanos—taking them into federal, rather than local, custody.

After the Norias raid, Constitutionalists and PSD followers began firing across the river at cavalry patrols; Mexican bandits crossed into Texas seeking booty; and Anglo civilians increased reprisals against Mexicans and

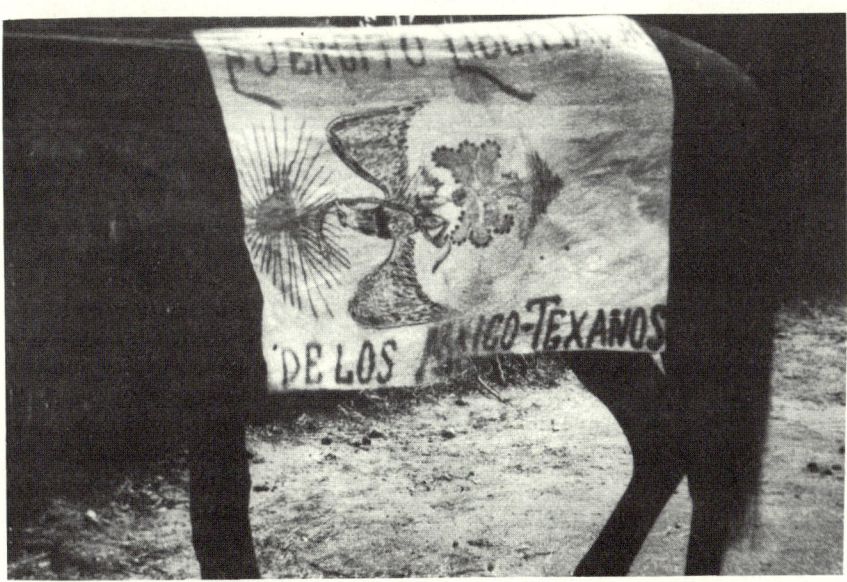

Fig. 6. Plan of San Diego banner, 1915 (Hidalgo County Historical Museum, Edinberg, Texas)

Tejanos. Violent incidents became near daily occurrences and uneasiness spread.[71] Immigrant Inspector David Warner at Brownsville, speaking primarily for the Anglo population, said, "The oldest and bravest inhabitants here are in a strain, and everyone feels he is about to face a massacre."[72] Moreover, for the week ending August 21, the military report at Brownsville recorded, for the first time, an "unusual large number of Mexicans moving with household effects from Texas to Mexico, none returning."[73]

That same week, nine Constitutionalist guards at Reynosa deserted and crossed the river into Texas. A posse of lawmen, including Rangers, pursued them immediately and engaged them in intermittent fire. After three days, four of the deserters managed to break contact and returned to their Mexican garrison. They chose certain execution rather than the risk of being "shot like coyotes" in the South Texas chaparral.[74] One contemporary report from Hidalgo, the area in which the deserters sought refuge and from which the survivors had fled, claimed "that 31 bandits had been killed in that vicinity by the rangers during the past 24 hours."[75] If some of Carranza's soldiers found death in Mexico preferable to life in South Texas, then Tejanos had little reason for hope.

As Pizaña prepared to take the field, he appealed to Tejanos and Mexicans to join him in seeking vengeance. From Mexico he issued a handbill that voiced a "true cry of indignation and anger" at the crimes and outrages "daily committed against helpless women, the aged, and children of our race, by the miserable bandits and rangers who guard the Bravo river" (See Figure 7). He sought to reach the sense of humanity and patriotism in the souls of his readers and listeners. All reasonable limits had been reached. Enough (*basta*) was enough (!*basta ya*¡).

!*Basta ya*¡ to tolerance. !*Basta ya*¡ to suffering insults and contempt from the "gringos." !*Basta ya*¡ to life as it had been. Liberating Texas and pursuing PSD aims would prove the valor and patriotism of those struggling for a better way. The handbill closed with the cry of "Long Live Independence! Land and Liberty," and described De la Rosa as first chief of military operations and Pizaña as head of the General Staff. The handbill was published in the Constitutionalist official newspaper in Monterrey on August 26;[76] Anglos quickly translated the document and circulated it throughout the valley.[77] Local federal officials sent it to their superiors in Washington, D.C.[78] Pizaña and De la Rosa had drawn national attention.

Pizaña, moreover, returned to the valley dramatically—amid a wave of PSD violence begun a month after the posse had attacked him at Los Tulitos. On September 2, raiders struck near Brownsville, Harlingen, and Ojo de Agua; they attacked soldiers and civilians—looting, burning, and killing. Around noon, a cloud of fire and smoke rose skyward from a burning storehouse at Fresnos Pump Canal, outside Harlingen (see Figure 8). By mid-morning, a group of heavily armed Mexicans and Tejanos, commanded by Pizaña, had captured S. S. Dodds and his crew who had been building the pumping station; the raiders set fire to the building and to Dodds' new Ford

A Nuestros Compatriotas
Los Mexicanos en Texas

Un grito de verdadera indignación y de ira, ha brotado de lo mas profundo de nuestras almas, al ver los crímenes y atropellos que a diario se están cometiendo en indefensas mujeres, ancianos y niños de nuestra raza, por los bandidos y miserables rangers que vigilan las riberas del Río Bravo.

Indignación justa y santa, que hace enardecer la sangre que circula por nuestras venas y que nos impulsa, nos ordena, a que castiguemos con toda la energía de que somos capaces, a esa turba de salvajes, que avergonzarían, al tigre hambriento y a la nauseabunda hiena.

¿Cómo permanecer indiferentes y tranquilos ante semejantes atentados? ¿Cómo permitir semejantes ofensas inferidas a nuestra raza? ¿Acaso ya se acabó en nosotros el sentimiento de humanidad y de patriotismo? ¡No! estará adormecido pero es fácil despertarlo.

Basta ya de tolerancia, basta ya de sufrir insultos y desprecios, somos hombres conscientes de nuestros actos, que sabemos pensar lo mismo que ellos "los gringos"; que podemos ser libres y lo seremos y que estamos suficientemente instruidos y fuertes para elegir nuestras autoridades y así lo haremos.

El momento ha llegado, es necesario que todos los buenos mexicanos, los patriotas, todos aquellos que aún les quede el resto de verguenza y de amor propio, es necesario, lo repito, acudamos a las armas, y al grito de "Viva la Independencia de los Estados de Texas, Nuevo México, California, Arizona, parte del Estado de Missisipi y Oklahoma que de hoy en adelante se llamará "República de Texas", nos unamos a nuestros compañeros de armas, que ya iniciaron el combate, dando pruebas de valor y patriotismo.

¡Viva la Independencia!
TIERRA Y LIBERTAD.

CUARTEL GRAL. EN SAN ANTONIO TEXAS.

Primer Jefe de las operaciones.   2o. Jefe de Estado Mayor.

Luis de la Rosa.   Aniceto Pizaña

Fig. 7. Plan of San Diego handbill, 1915 (U.S. National Archives)

Fig. 8. Fresnos pump station, 1915 (Hidalgo County Historical Museum, Edinburg, Texas)

Roadster (see Figure 9). and marched their prisoners toward the border—eight miles away.

During the march, Pizaña freed Dodds' Mexican employees and ordered the "gringos" taken into the brush to be shot. At that point, one of the raiders spoke up for Dodds—saying that he had worked for the Anglo and that Dodds had helped him when he had been wounded earlier as a Villista. Pizaña decided to spare Dodds. Then he asked the other two Anglos if they were German. Their negative reply, in Dodds' opinion, cost them their lives; Pizaña ordered them shot immediately. Continuing south, the band met a posse—forcing the raiders to take cover. In the ensuing exchange of gunfire, Dodds escaped.[79]

At least one of Pizaña's Mexican partisans also fled. Esmerejüldo Cruz, about twenty-four, had lived most of his life in Texas and had worked most recently for an Anglo, building irrigation canals. He joined the movement the day De la Rosa killed the Austins. He agreed with the PSD goals but did not see how they could be achieved. When he later saw Aniceto Pizaña, Cruz followed him for two reasons: he had known Pizaña for years, and "don Aniceto" gave him a rifle and ammunition—which not all followers had. In the field, Pizaña remained silent about what they were to do until it was to be done. Risk and uncertainty caused Cruz to quit within a month of joining.[80]

Pizaña's raid stirred deep fears among valley residents because he not only attacked private property that epitomized much recent change—the irrigation pumping plant and the automobile—but he raised again the prospect of German involvement. A few weeks earlier, military intelligence in Laredo reported a strange conversation. Two recent German arrivals from Mexico City had talked to a Spaniard in the Bazar Hotel in Nuevo Laredo about securing support from the local German colony for the uprising of Negroes

Fig. 9. S. S. Dodds' burned Ford Roadster, 1915 (Hidalgo County Historical Museum, Edinburg, Texas)

and Mexicans in Texas.[81] Pizaña's question during the raid at Fresno's Pump Canal raised the specter of nationality as an additional factor in the race war.

Fear, feeding upon itself, multiplied violence throughout society. To reduce untoward incidents, civilian lawmen along the border were placed under U.S. Army control on September 8, and General Funston prohibited border patrols from firing across the river, even if attacked, unless expressly ordered to do so by the local military commander.[82] Nevertheless, on September 14, a cavalry patrol found three deputy sheriffs and one Brownsville city policeman firing across the river at nothing. This being the first verifiable incident since the new arrangement, Funston wired Governor Ferguson that not only did such behavior worsen the situation, it was "impossible for the Army in its dangerous and arduous work to cooperate with peace officers who are such scoundrels."[83] Ferguson responded by demanding that Cameron County Sheriff W. T. Vann dismiss the men.[84] Because of the officers' experience and the difficult times, however, Vann felt that he needed to keep them, despite their indiscipline.[85]

Suspicion and anxiety increased in all quarters as inhabitants feared imminent invasion. Despite the posting of nearly four thousand troops in the valley by mid-September, unauthorized border crossings increased as the river rose—permitting a proliferation of illegal ferries. Immigration inspectors counted forty-nine of these sites containing sixty-three boats scattered from Sam Fordyce in Hidalgo County down to the river's mouth.[86]

Despite Funston's requests for even more troops, situational demands seemed limitless. An Anglo family near San Benito felt so fearful that all members slept in their sugar cane fields, despite their knowledge that soldiers stood guard two miles above and five miles below them. They soon fled, leaving three hundred acres to go fallow.[87] As fear spread, other Anglo families followed suit.[88] Moreover, valley Mexicans and Tejanos felt similar fear. Spokesmen for San José, an exclusively Mexican hamlet twenty-five miles upriver from Brownsville, appealed to U.S. Army Colonel Robert Bullard to guarantee their safety. They, like most Mexicans and Tejanos, saw the army as the only institution capable of treating them fairly; fewer of them died trying to escape from the army than from Anglo civilians.[89]

Nothing locals did seemed to assuage fear. The King Ranch disarmed its Mexican and Tejano employees,[90] and Anglos there slept on rooftops with their weapons—including two smooth bore canon—at the ready, in anticipation of another attack.[91] In Brownsville, seventy-five armed citizens slept in county buildings the nights of September 14 and 15, lest the celebration of Mexican Independence Day lead to attack.[92] They had as precedent the occupation led by Juan Nepomuceno Cortina fifty-six years earlier to protest Anglo discrimination.[93]

Reprisals became commonplace. Rangers composed a "blacklist" of suspected "bad Mexicans," and any important valley Anglo could add a name by denouncing someone he feared or envied.[94] Since it was rumored that Mexicans had a "blacklist" of their own hated Anglos, rumor reinforced paranoia.[95] In early September, a prominent valley newspaper observed, "The finding of dead bodies of Mexicans, suspected for various reasons of being connected with the troubles, has reached a point where it creates little or no interest. It is only when a raid is reported or an American is killed that the ire of the people is aroused."[96]

In late September, Wells and others discovered the bodies of about fifteen local Mexicans and Tejanos around the rail depot at Ebenezer. Their relatives feared to bury them lest they, too, become victims.[97] This proved the largest single group murder of the entire episode. Moreover, despite the opinion of many observers that no more than ten percent of the Mexican and Tejano population had committed a disloyal act,[98] the viciousness continued.

In September, reprisals against women suggested sexual aggression, the magnitude of which probably was concealed in silence. Cenovio Rivas, rumored but unproven abettor of both bandits and Rangers, found his fourteen year old daughter shot to death in front of their small home near Los Fresnos on September 22.[99] On the evening of September 27, a woman whose family had participated in killing a suspected "bad Mexican" walked out on her porch to see two Mexicans passing by. She drew a pistol and fired three times before they returned her fire, wounding her slightly in a forearm.[100] These incidents raised the specter of sexual violation as a form of revenge or outrage in the struggle.

Raiders took reprisals against Tejanos and Mexicans who failed to cooperate with them or who—even worse from their perspective—abetted law enforcement. On September 9, a Tejano died after being attacked by Mexican

Fig. 10. Poster of Direct Action (*Regeneracíon*, October 16, 1915)

assailants. At the same time, raiders from Mexico killed two other Tejanos near Brownsville, one positively identified and the other suspected of being pro-American.[101] And whom had Juan Nepomuceno Rodríguez—with a name reminiscent of Cortina—offended that he should have been dragged by the neck with wire wrapped to an automobile bumper before being shot dead?[102] Prominent Brownsville attorney José T. Canales, himself a descendant of Cortina, collected many notes sent to Tejanos and Mexicans by the raiders, threatening them with harm if they did not aid the movement.[103]

In Los Angeles, Ricardo Flores Magón read the Spanish-language newspaper accounts of the Plan of San Diego, along with Pizaña's letter describing the attack at Los Tulitos and his commitment to join the movement to take Texas. Ricardo, however, did not comprehend the situation. After some deliberation, he decided that there was no Plan of San Diego at all: the plan had been a bourgeois invention to conceal the realities of worker exploitation. The bourgeoisie had taken land and water away from Mexicans and Tejanos and enforced their submission through the Rangers. What occurred in South Texas, he wrote in October 1915, was nothing more than the disinherited resorting to self-defense. Rangers rather than raiders deserved to be shot.[104]

Ricardo's anarchist uprising unfolded before him without his notice. *Regeneración* had appeared only three or four times before resumption in October, and Ricardo devoted his stories to Mexican affairs and the Rangel-Cline case in Texas. The uprising in South Texas drew little attention. In irony unthinkable in fiction, the ideological father of the Plan of San Diego failed to recognize his intellectual progeny. Perhaps it was not as beautiful as expected. Perhaps Ricardo could not recognize an anarchist struggle with which he had not personally been involved. Astonishingly—for whatever reason—he practically ignored it.

Nevertheless, with the graphic symbolism that had always been *Regeneración*'s strong suit, Ricardo presented an image of "DIRECT ACTION" that October that spoke to the heart of the PSD movement (see Figure 10). Two workers jointly operated a grinding stone, labeled the September 23, 1911, PLM Manifesto, using it to crush the symbols of bourgeois dominance: cannon, drum, miter, helmet, crown, and capital. This call for direct action appeared two days before Luis de la Rosa led the most spectacular attack of the PSD assault.

CHAPTER 6

ASSIGNING BLAME

According to my belief all this trouble is caused by Mexican anarchists, Magonists, I.W.W.'s . . . and the famous Plan of San Diego.
E. P. Reynolds[1]

I think the Germans were back of the whole thing.
Marcus Hines[2]

These raids were planned by Carranza as a method of forcing recognition of himself by the United States.
U.S. Information File on Mexican History[3]

The incident that galvanized fear into terror and accelerated the flight of Anglos and Mexicans from the valley occurred the night of October 18, 1915. Valley residents told each other the story in English and Spanish, expanding and enlarging the tale with each retelling. Even stripped of exaggeration, however, the events of that night inspired horror. A train of the Saint Louis, Brownsville & Mexico line left Kingsville about 7:30 P.M., heading south to Brownsville. The engine and tender, in addition to the baggage and mail car, drew two passenger coaches: the first was divided into a first-class smoker and a second-class section for black men and the second, without divisions, was for women.

Luis de la Rosa (see Figure 11) and his followers lay in wait about eight miles above Brownsville, near Tandy's Station. They had removed the protective fish plate connecting two rails and attached wire to the rail end where it had been. They then extracted the spikes anchoring the rails in place and, with the wire wrapped around a crowbar buried in the ground as a lever, could pull the track apart. About 11:00 P.M., the engineer saw nothing in the darkness, and, when De la Rosa ordered the wire pulled, the engine derailed—killing its engineer instantly.[4]

The conductor, an Anglo, had been checking tickets in the second-class compartment when the train derailed. He and the black brakeman ran toward the front door when they heard shots from both sides of the track directed at the smoker. The first car had tilted to one side by the derailing, putting everyone in it off balance. Passengers could hear gunfire interspersed with

Fig. 11. Luis de la Rosa, 1914 (The Huntington Library, San Marino, California)

chants of ¡Viva Carranza! ¡Viva Luis De la Rosa! ¡Viva Aniceto Pizaña! and again ¡Viva Carranza! from the men outside.[5]

After the initial fusillade, two of the raiders entered the smoker. The first was a tall man wearing a red bandana over his face; he fired two shots from a Winchester into the car—severing a finger on the left hand of Henry Wallis, a former Texas Ranger. More gunshots followed, and Wallis sustained a graze. He recognized the second man and called out to De la Rosa, "Don't do this. We are friends, we have been friends." Wallis had known and liked De la Rosa from the time they had been neighbors in San Benito. De la Rosa ignored him, however, and urged the tall man to get the soldiers riding the train. The soldiers, like Wallis, were unarmed. More gunfire, more raiders entered the smoker, more violence. Wallis dropped to the floor where the tall Mexican stepped over him, continuing to shoot, and someone fired two rounds into Wallis' right leg.[6]

Down the listing aisle, District Attorney John Kleiber lay on a bench and saw Corporal Claude Brashear trying to stand; a rifle shot tore into the soldier, and blood spurted onto Kleiber—making him appear wounded. The tall man prodded Kleiber with the rifle butt, demanded money and Kleiber's watch, then demanded Kleiber's tan, military-looking shoes. Kleiber, who had been born in Matamoros, spoke to the raider in Spanish, telling him to take the shoes. The raider began untying them when De la Rosa began to curse him for his slowness and told him to move along, to get the *gringos*. Kleiber kicked his other shoe off and watched while other raiders took the corporal's shoes.[7]

Raiders took money, jewelry, and luggage from both cars but left Mexicans alone. Kleiber could hear a Mexican couple plead with the raiders not to harm them and heard the reply, "Mexicanos no, *gringos* no mas!" In the rear of the smoker, Morris Edelstein, a Brownsville merchant, fictitiously claimed to be German, and the raiders left him alone. They took the ring and money of L. I. Henninger, visiting from Council Bluffs, Iowa, and were about to kill him, when Edelstein alertly claimed that Henninger, too, was German, and they spared him.[8]

Meanwhile, Wallis had managed to crawl to the lavatory, where he found Cameron County Health Officer Dr. Eugene McCain, and a Mexican boy of about eighteen, both hiding. The three crowded in tightly, with the Mexican boy pushed to the front, facing the door. Wallis saw the tall Mexican raider force the door open enough to grab the boy and drag him out, and heard the following exchange in Spanish: "I'm a Mexican, I'm a friend of yours." "We're not bothering Mexicans, we're just after the *gringos*." "They're two behind the door."

Wallis slammed the door shut, latching it with his usable right hand. The raider tried unsuccessfully to force the door open; then he fired two rounds from his Winchester through it. One round struck Wallis in the left shoulder—rendering that arm practically useless the rest of his life. McCain must have been standing on the toilet because he took the other round in the stomach. Then, as suddenly as they had appeared, De la Rosa and his men left the train and rode into the darkness. As they escaped, they ripped up more track sections and set fire to several railroad bridges.[9]

De la Rosa had visited death and destruction upon the oppressors and left behind a bitter legacy. The derailed train (see Figure 12) symbolized the rejection of Anglo-initiated change in the valley; the engineer had been found with his arm still on the throttle.[10] Raiders had shot three soldiers, killing two; one of the dead had been shot through the head, execution style. Wallis sustained five wounds and was lucky to have survived. McCain was not so fortunate; he died the next day of the stomach wound. He left a wife, an invalid sister, and an aged mother, all of whom he had supported.[11]

Since the incident occurred close to town, Sheriff Vann and a posse arrived on the morning of October 19. The posse included Captain H. L. Ransom of Company "D," Texas Ranger force, and some of his men. Making a sweep of the general area, the posse picked up seven local Mexicans and Tejanos

Fig. 12. Train wreck, Tandy's Station, 1915 (Hidalgo County Historical Museum, Edinburg, Texas)

for interrogation. One of them, Tejano Feliciano Flores, confessed to Sheriff Vann, whom he knew. Flores admitted that he had participated in the derailment, that Pizaña had been there, and that nearly all of the sixty-man force had come from Mexico.[12] None of the men apprehended by the lawmen had been with Flores in the raid.

Nevertheless, Ransom claimed four of the men as his prisoners and invited Sheriff Vann to join him in their execution. Vann refused. He had opposed Governor Ferguson's appointment of Ransom, and he had recently been reprimanded for his subordinates' unprovoked firing across the river. Ransom, accusing Vann of lacking "guts," took the prisoners into the chaparral and shot them to death—leaving the bodies where they fell.[13] Ranger Ransom thought his act would teach the raiders a lesson; presumably, it was to be the same lesson that Ranger Fox had given more than two months earlier with the photograph of the dead raiders at Norias.

The events surrounding the train wreck underscored the worst elements in valley violence. De la Rosa and his followers were confused about the precise nature of Anglo discrimination. The preamble to the Plan of San Diego inaccurately accused the "white skinned savages" of segregating trains into sections where they sat only with one another and excluded Mexicans. Yet, in reality, whites admitted Mexicans and Tejanos to their first-class cars. By firing indiscriminately into such a car on the night of October 18, De la Rosa and his comrades could easily have struck one of their own, one of those they sought to help. Perhaps that realization prompted De la Rosa to halt the firing outside and to board the car.

Attacking U.S. soldiers proved desirable and easy for a number of reasons. First, their uniforms identified them. Moreover, army troops guarded trains, depots, irrigation pumping stations, and other targets PSD raiders wanted to strike. General Funston ordered detachments scattered along the river to dig themselves into fortified positions (see Figures 13 and 14) in attempts to thwart raiders crossing from Mexico. Thus, unlike Rangers, who were more difficult to find, soldiers made themselves available targets. But Rangers and civilians, when taking prisoners, abused Mexicans and Tejanos, whereas the army represented safe and impartial treatment for them. Of course, not all Rangers engaged in evil abuses. When De la Rosa encountered one whom he knew to be fair, as in the case of Wallis, De la Rosa could not order his execution.

When a terrified Mexican boy disclosed the hiding place of two Anglos, most white valley residents readily believed that all locals of Mexican ancestry supported the raiders. As the military commander of Brownsville observed:

> Owing to race antagonism engendered past few months in this section of the valley about fifty percent of the Mexican male population disloyal in thought and possibly ten percent of these also disloyal in action when opportunity offers.[14]

The local ranch workers murdered by Ranger Ransom seem to have been guilty of no other "crimes" than being Mexican and available. Raiders quickly provided more excuses for extremism.

Fig. 13. U.S. Army troops entrenched along the Rio Grande, 1915–1916 (Hidalgo County Historical Museum, Edinburg, Texas)

Fig. 14. U.S. Army rifle trench on the Rio Grande, 1915–1916 (Hidalgo County Historical Museum, Edinburg, Texas)

Three days after the train wreck, Pizaña and sixty men crossed the river and attacked the small army detachment at Ojo de Agua. During the protracted skirmish, Americans saw at least four Japanese in the attacking party and many raiders wearing hatbands labeled "¡Viva la Independencia de Tejas!" Pizaña and his force killed three and wounded eight of the eighteen troopers before finally being driven off. They suffered nine wounded and left five of their dead behind, along with documents, including a diary and handbills, linking them to De la Rosa and the PSD.[15] Before returning to Mexico, the band burned the home of Tejano George Dillard, as a reprisal for serving as deputy sheriff in Hidalgo County.[16]

General Funston described his guard at Ojo de Agua as "nearly annihilated"[17] and demanded both more troops and a tougher policy—one which would "make it almost certain death to engage in one of these raids."[18] The secretary of war vigorously rejected Funston's proposal, arguing that it "would result in sensational statements being made against the Army, suggesting that we were reverting to methods of barbarism."[19] The War Department had been hard on Funston earlier to insure disciplined and controlled army behavior, and it continued to exact measured performance from its troops by careful and prompt checks on local commanders.

Meanwhile, more handbills, couched in anarchist language, circulated on both sides of the river, exhorting those of Mexican ancestry to rise. One entitled "!BASTA . . .!" called for the "Redemption of the Disinherited" through "expropriation": "The moment has come to shake off the iron yoke . . . Let us destroy but at the same time build . . . War to Capital, War to the Clergy, War to the State, [to] everything that smells of oppression. War without quarter to the *gringos*. ¡*Basta Ya!*"[20]

The handbills may have been written in ungrammatical Spanish and the ideas expressed imprecisely, even confusedly, but they contained essential anarchist claims about present and future society. They showed how the inarticulate used anarchist thought to express their anger and their hope. The crudest of these expressions, entitled "¡LEVANTEMONOS!" began with an incoherent listing of abuses committed by Americans against people of color; acknowledged the Revolutionary Congress of San Diego, Texas, and the "SOCIAL WAR" in progress; and embraced the slogan "Redemption for the disinherited!" It concluded with an appeal to the memory of the Chicago Haymarket anarchists of 1886![21]

Still another poster heralding "¡A LAS ARMAS MEXICANOS!" told its audience: "Because every noble-hearted man must desire to live in a social state where one may work according to his ability and consume according to his necessities . . . it is necessary to destroy the capitalistic society . . . [and] upon its ruins to implant that [society] of the future, thus forming one . . . universal family in which peace and justice may reign."[22] These anarchist appeals testified to the enduring nature of PLM and *Regeneración* propaganda over a decade. Social conditions, not propaganda, however, made the Plan of San Diego possible and contributed to its continuation.

The severe October raids culminated 120 days of escalating violence and coincided with President Wilson's recognition of Carranza as the de facto leader of Mexico on October 19. Prominent valley men hastily called meetings to invoke federal and state protection for lives and property. Seven Cameron County officials, led by Judge Yates, telegraphed the secretary of state on October 19, demanding that valley citizens be given "at least as much consideration as the [American] oil interests [in Mexico]." The telegraph then asserted that most Mexicans believed that they had bluffed America into recognizing Carranza by terrorizing citizens in South Texas.[23]

More than two hundred people from throughout the valley assembled in a mass meeting at Brownsville the evening of October 23 to press state and national officials for greater protection. Brownsville Mayor A. A. Browne extended the invitation to people who were both pro- and anti-Wells. The group elected a representative committee from the larger townships, headed by long-time Wells antagonist D. W. Glasscock, to present its plea to Governor Ferguson in Austin. The newspapers saw the election of the committee as an act of bipartisan unity, but Wells recognized it as the first grass-roots challenge to his power. Not to be denied, Wells and others, including the aforementioned Judge Yates, went to Austin on the same mission as Glasscock.[24] Ferguson met with both groups and promised action. His solution lay in appointing more Special Rangers, those who served at no expense to the state, and pressing Washington for more troops.

Glasscock's committee carried its message beyond Austin. On October

29, all members signed a petition to President Wilson calling for help. They described the situation in Cameron and Hidalgo counties as an international problem because of the Plan of San Diego; as long as raiders found safety in Mexico, the depredations would continue. Therefore, they recommended that Carranza be pressed to police his side of the line, and, if he failed, then U.S. troops should be permitted to cross into Mexico after marauders. Glasscock's committee concluded with a plea that "Federal authorities be asked to take exclusive charge of the local situation"—a request for martial law that tacitly admitted failure. Fear had prompted desperate measures. Although Wells did not sign the petition, his old crony John Closner did, as did Caesar Kleberg of the King Ranch, the erratic Lon C. Hill, and others.[25]

Sam Robertson was among those who tried to allay local fears with different methods. Robertson, an early irrigation developer, was a leading proponent of the idea that the Mexican and Tejano population should voluntarily disarm for its own safety. He redoubled his efforts in this direction following the "rangering" done after the train wreck. He called meetings, visited *jacales* and small ranches, even drove into the chaparral to talk to any vaquero he could find—urging all to surrender their weapons in return for a receipt. When tensions subsided, arms would be returned. On at least one occasion, in early September, he met with success. At a meeting in San Benito, nearly one hundred Mexicans and Tejanos surrendered their firearms—almost half the audience.[26]

By late October, however, the attitude had changed. Mexicans and Tejanos needed their weapons; surrendering them meant dying unarmed. After a discouraging late night meeting, as Robertson and his aide, a fourteen year old Mexican goatherd, rode in his automobile through the chaparral, a group of assailants opened fire. Robertson counted five Mexicans in the attacking party, some of whom he knew. With the goatherd's help, he repulsed them.[27]

José T. Canales, a former Wells protege and descendant of Juan Nepomuceno Cortina, suspended his law practice and organized a force of thirty Mexican and Tejano scouts to patrol the river. They operated in pairs— scouting and reporting to the nearest army detachment. Canales hoped that this service would help protect all valley residents. The army appreciated the scouts' work, but some local authorities, disliking the monitoring of their behavior, did not.[28]

Some financially independent Anglos, such as Customs Inspector Frank Rabb and Lon C. Hill, secured commissions as Special Rangers.[29] Those too poor to serve at their own expense needed both an employer and a sponsor. Caesar Kleberg obtained such a commission for former Ranger Paul McAlister and sent him to operate around San Diego, where he was to chase cattle thieves and to watch the community that supposedly had spawned the PSD. Within six weeks, Kleberg received complaints about McAlister's drunkenness and excessive use of force against suspects, especially Mexicans.[30] While Kleberg defended his employee to State Adjutant General Hutchings, he admitted that McAlister was "crowding some of them just a little too close."[31] McAlister, however, backed by the King Ranch, received no reprimand.

Fearful Anglos, with or without badges, took vigorous action to repress any possible outburst from a Mexican population that outnumbered them. On October 21, the Brownsville head of the U.S. Immigration Service confiscated the entire delivery of *El Demócrata*, the Constitutionalist newspaper, because he found the articles inflammatory. The one hundred copies of the Matamoros edition indicated a large audience in Brownsville, and the chief inspector decided not to risk its potential incendiary impact.[32]

In late October, an army commander in the valley observed, "The wide use of arms by white citizens and the extreme difficulty of the civil authorities supervising their use, leading to personal aggression, revenge, and terrorism by white population upon Mexican citizens are certainly complicating the situation."[33] Near Donna, on the nights of October 28 and 31, Mexican *jacales* along the river burned; they were set afire by unknown assailants.[34]

Fear had slowly given way to terror. As early as July, Texan farmers had moved their households into nearby towns for security.[35] By August, as fear spread, families began to leave the valley. Anglos went north to Corpus Christi or returned to their original homes in the East or Midwest. Mexicans and Tejanos began to enter or reenter Mexico, preferring distressed conditions there to those in South Texas.[36] Anglo farmers experienced a labor shortage during the cotton harvest, but did nothing to allay their laborers' fears for safety.[37]

Moreover, while a Bureau of Investigation agent thought that by mid-August "conditions were in [a] very bad state, with the result that citizens, rangers and others commenced to kill all Mexicans suspected of supporting the Plan of San Diego,"[38] many long-time Anglo residents disagreed. Judge Sam Spears of San Benito wrote in September, countering criticism, "all things considered, these rangers and officers have proceeded with commendable discrimination. Much more has been said in the press and otherwise, about killing innocent Mexicans, than is justified by the facts as I have them . . . In my judgment it is better by far to have made this kind of mistake than to have had one of our own [Anglo] people killed."

Judge Spears concluded with a justification of vigilantism with which many, but not all, agreed: "Every fair-minded man, when brought face to face with a condition where the criminal element is so powerful that the laws of the land cannot be enforced through the courts, must admit that mob violence is necessary to the saving of our civilization."[39]

Ultimately, "civilization's" salvation proved temporary; mob violence exacted the cost of both a labor force and any vestiges of social cohesion. By late October 1915, General Funston estimated that more than 150 Mexicans and Tejanos had been summarily executed by local lawmen and vigilantes.[40] The *San Antonio Light* had arrived at that figure a month earlier.[41] No wonder surviving Mexicans and Tejanos, in increasing numbers, chose to flee with their lives from the terror.

When they began their exodus in August, families took into Mexico with them "their horses, mules, wagons, household furniture, farming implements, chickens, cows, and, in fact, all their effects which could be moved." Although they gave as their reasons the Constitutionalist general amnesty and promise of free land around Matamoros,[42] some Anglos disbelieved them. They had left behind whatever land and housing they owned, including crops in the field.[43]

By October, the countryside had an eerie, vacant look. George Martínez at Los Indios wrote his father, who had already left, "There are no more people on the ranch here; already all those alive have gone; the dead are gone; the mourners, the Vargas and Juárez [families are gone] for Mexico."

Agent J. B. Rogers investigated, discovered that neither the Martínez family nor anyone else mentioned in the letter had participated in the violence, and concluded, "They left because they were afraid of the Rangers. They want to come back and would do so if the Rangers were not here. They are not afraid of the soldiers. They have no work in Mexico and their families are suffering."[44]

Rogers had found Los Indios "abandoned, except by the soldiers [and] I noticed that all the houses were vacant, some of them very nice homes." At Rio Hondo, De la Rosa's home, only "nine families out of fifty or more" remained. "This is the condition as I see it all over the rural section here."[45]

As if to confirm Rogers' impressions, the *Brownsville Herald* estimated that, in September and October 1915, more than seven thousand Mexicans left Cameron and Hidalgo counties[46]—a figure representing nearly 40 percent of the Mexican population of both counties at the time.[47] This movement represented a dramatic exodus of labor and a dramatic decline in social stability.

The Wilson administration responded decisively to the crisis and, by late October, had embarked on a threefold approach to stop raiding and to restore order in South Texas. The War Department increased troop strength in the Southern Department until General Funston commanded fully half the mobile soldiers in the continental United States.[48]

The Department of Justice coordinated and pressed the investigation into the history and persistence of the disturbances, commissioning bilingual or trilingual informants where necessary, and exploring every lead developed throughout the American Southwest and northern Mexico.[49] The Department of State asked Carranza—even before he had been formally recognized—to increase his forces along the river, to restrain his local commanders from sanctioning raids, and to arrest De la Rosa and Pizaña.[50] The department did not, however, consider the problem exclusively a foreign responsibility. Secretary of State Robert Lansing sent Governor Ferguson a public letter informing him of the protestations made to Carranza and asking Ferguson's help in "allaying race prejudice and in restraining indiscreet conduct" by local lawmen.[51]

Carranza responded forcefully both to the demands of local residents—

Mexican and Anglo—and to those of the U.S. government. His ability to respond, however, was limited by the chaos of Mexico's civil strife. He could not solve his problems immediately. The Wilson administration's confidence in Carranza was riddled with suspicion, exacerbated by its recent experience with international intrigue and with the further unfolding of Mexico's civil war. The activity of former president Victoriano Huerta and his attempted return to power—also intertwined in foreign plotting—intensified this suspicion.

Huerta may have made initial preparations for his eventual return even as he departed Mexico in July 1914. After a brief stay in Cuba, he proceeded to Barcelona, Spain, where, from afar, he watched the Constitutionalists turn upon themselves. In February 1915, the former minister of foreign relations under Díaz, Enrique Creel, came to visit. Creel represented himself and his father-in-law, the wealthy Luis Terrazas, both of whom had funded the muleteer Orozco in his revolt against Madero. They, and other Mexican exiles in the United States, had recently financed the organization of a clandestine force in Texas to launch an anti-Constitutionalist invasion. Orozco would be its field commander, and the group wanted Huerta to return as its overall leader. Jointly Huerta and Orozco would pacify Mexico.[52]

Creel, apparently, also introduced Huerta to a young German captain on special assignment from the German General Staff (Abteilung IIIB).[53] Franz Rintelen von Kleist had been sent to Spain to offer Huerta a deal. Huerta could have German arms, money, and diplomatic recognition for his new government if, in return, he caused a second Mexican-American war.[54] Since the American munitions industry armed the Entente, if America became involved in a hemispheric imbroglio, then Germany would be free to deal with England and France. Huerta agreed to the proposal, or at least to the part that benefited him, and let the Germans think what they might.

In February 1915, Huerta and Creel left Barcelona for New York, where the former president took up residence to meet with other exiles, accept their adherence, and plan. Rintelen followed in April and participated in diverse plots, both to aid Huerta and to undermine American munitions production. He was aided in his espionage by the military, naval, and commercial attachés attached to the German embassy in Washington, D.C.[55]

Upon his arrival in New York, Rintelen engaged as Mexican advisors first Felix A. Sommerfeld[56] and later Federico Stallforth.[57] Both were members of the German community in Mexico and both supported Villa; Sommerfeld served as Villa's chief munitions purchaser in the United States. Stallforth, born in Mexico, operated a successful store in Parral, Chihuahua, where his brother Alberto served as German consul. Both Sommerfeld and Stallforth wanted Villa to rule Mexico.

Subsequent investigation of the Rintelen-Sommerfeld relationship by Justice Department agents revealed that from April 5 to December 1, 1915, Sommerfeld purchased over $380,000 in arms for Villa. In their opinion, Sommerfeld dispensed those funds under cover of an account of the German embassy in Washington, D.C.[58] Although Rintelen had inherited the Villista financial connection, his pursuit of further Villista support testified to profound German cultural arrogance in dealing with Mexican affairs.

Germany, in a limited way, appeared willing to support anybody in Mexico who might accomplish its desired ends. Both formal German emissaries and free lances, seeking to promote what they saw as the Fatherland's good, failed to respect the divisiveness the revolution had engendered. It was preposterous to think that Huerta and his colleague Orozco would join with Villa, or he with them, regardless of promised financial gain. At one time, Huerta had sentenced Villa to death, and only Madero family intervention had prevented it.[59] Moreover, vicious fighting between Orozquistas and Villistas had become the stuff of legends. Peace could not be made among these men and their partisans but only, possibly, among their former followers. Such basic miscalculations, rooted in contempt for those involved, plagued German policy in Mexico throughout the revolution. In addition, as Huerta and Rintelen conspired, Mexico's civil war took a turn that affected their plans dramatically.

Carranza's principal military liability, as his forces entered Mexico City in late summer 1914, lay in troop shortages. Without sufficient men in arms, his movement could be overthrown by any other faction. With Villa and Zapata opposing him, Carranza turned to the only other source of manpower, the organized workers of Mexico City who had belonged to the *Casa del Obrero Mundial*. The *Casa*, an anarcho-syndicalist organization begun in summer 1912 and dedicated to the mobilization of the Mexican working class, had been suppressed by Huerta in 1914 just before he fled.[60] Carranza, through General Obregón, offered to reopen the *Casa* and to give it a former Jesuit convent for its headquarters.

The offer tempted. *Casa* leadership had taken a position of noninvolvement with political forces, since to do otherwise would obviously be a compromise of anarchist first principles. The government support seemed more attractive than its alternatives, however, when *Casa* members viewed the provincial forces of Villa and Zapata following the Constitutionalist withdrawal. Zapata's men begged tortillas from the homes of the bourgeoisie! What kind of an anarchist-communist behaved like that? Expropriate it! And the Zapatistas wore armbands and medals with the image of the Virgin of Guadalupe. Clearly, religious "superstition" still clouded their minds. Moreover, Villa, who seemed to have Church backing, chose to meet Zapata in the National Palace. Was this not the personalism of Díaz and the promise of yet more government? Many *Casa* intellectuals came, perhaps unfairly, to identify Villa with the reaction.[61]

When Villa and Zapata left the capital to catch Carranza in a pincers, the Constitutionalists had an opportunity to press their case again with the *Casa*. This time Carranza wanted manpower in return for concessions. He would allow the *Casa* to organize Mexican labor along its anarcho-syndicalist lines, even provide resources to do it, if the *Casa* would join the army. After much deliberation, *Casa* officials signed the pact in Veracruz on February 20,

1915—ironically, the date that the Plan of San Diego was revised to reflect anarchist thought.

Casa leaders moved simultaneously to recruit men as soldiers and to create regional *Casas* across Mexico to organize the working class. By mid-March, more than seven thousand workers entrained as troopers to the Constitutionalist training facility at Orizaba, where they were organized into six Red Battalions. Their presence significantly augmented Carranza's forces.

Mexican anarchists, as some European anarchists did in supporting the war against Germany, tempered first principles for survival. Cooperation with a supportive government, they reasoned, gave them an opportunity to have a voice in the revolution that they heretofore lacked. They recognized that inevitable confrontation with Carranza must come, but they planned to be ready for it. Ricardo Flores Magón, outraged, decried the maneuvering, chastised the anarchists for their faithlessness, and exhorted the worker-turned-soldier to use the weapons against Carranza. Mexico City anarchists in turn denounced Ricardo and *Regeneración* for being out of touch and hysterical.[62]

The *Casa*-Constitutionalist alliance, as ideologically unstable as the German proposed Huerta-Orozco-Villa triad, produced anarchist rhetoric as bizarre as this anarchist behavior. *Casa* leaders began propagandizing for the Constitutionalists. Carranza was now seen as committed to the "Social Revolution," and joining the Constitutionalist army became a vehicle for "Direct Action." Such blubbering distortion of thought and language made it possible for Constitutionalists in the north to see the Plan of San Diego as compatible with their recent alliance with the *Casa*—a contradiction not otherwise explicable.

From Carranza's perspective in Veracruz, however, the *Casa* deal meant soldiers when he desperately needed them. When it became apparent that Zapata would not advance beyond Puebla, Carranza could decide how to combat his enemies. Villa, much stronger and with control of northern ports, began an advance toward Tampico. Carranza placed his politically trusted ally Pablo González in charge of that port's defense but chose the militarily superior Alvaro Obregón to take the campaign to Villa in the field. He wanted to divide Villa's forces, and the newly formed Red Battalions gave him the manpower to do so. Villa did as expected; he sent part of his force against the port—at which point, battle at El Ebano developed—and part against Obregón's column, giving battle in spectacular encounters at Celaya twice, and again at León in Guanajuato.

Tampico, port for Mexico's foreign-dominated oil industry, had as its defensive perimeter El Ebano, San Luis Potosí. Port and outpost were connected by rail line. The oil fields were held by Manuel Peláez who, with foreign money and arms, catered to oil interests operating independently of any Mexican faction. As long as no one interfered with oil production and its export, who controlled the port did not matter to Peláez. Since oil tax revenue meant hard currency in a collapsing economy, control of Tampico was vital to contending political factions. Constitutionalists held the port and first encountered Villistas around Ebano on December 21, 1914. After the skirmish, Constitutionalists began to dig trenches and erect breastworks.

Villa's forces, commanded by Generals Tomás Urbina and Manuel Chao, began a series of assaults in late March 1915, that developed into a seventy-two-day siege. The embattled Constitutionalists, led by Jacinto Treviño, a subordinate of González, managed with Red Battalion reinforcements to hold out against the repeated onslaughts. Outnumbered at times two to one, Carranza's forces withstood thirty-seven assaults before the frustrated Villistas withdrew, abandoning cannon and small arms in their departure. A counteroffensive then cleared the field. From March 21 to May 31, 1915, Treviño held at Ebano, drawing down Villista fire and giving indirect support to Obregón.[63]

Villa personally commanded the assault against Obregón. As at Ebano, he allowed himself to be drawn into attacking entrenched positions where his numerical superiority dissipated before Obregonista machine guns. On April 6–7, Villa attacked Celaya and incurred his first defeat in a year of unbroken victories. He returned again on April 13, and two days later, as he tried to withdraw, Obregón, having reserved part of the veteran Constitutionalist force for a counterattack, routed him.

Obregón then astutely offered a general amnesty, and many Villistas defected to Obregón's army. Obregón's ability to deploy his veterans at strategic points derived from having Red Battalion troops to man the trenches. Thus, Obregón's advance unit of veterans continued to maintain contact with the retreating Villistas, and a series of skirmishes between them developed into another major battle in late May and early June 1915, around León. Once again, Villa destroyed his forces with reckless charges.[64]

By mid-1915, Villa had sustained major losses. El Ebano, Celaya, and León had destroyed the myth of his invincibility. Although his power ebbed, however, Villa still remained a significant force in Mexican politics, and Carrancistas continued to fear his ability to spoil their leader's quest for control.[65] Moreover, Villa's battlefield reverses, coinciding with the German plan to restore Huerta through Orozco, also contributed to American confusion about the Plan of San Diego.

Orozco, probably through his secretary Ricardo Robelo—a former attorney in Huerta's Ministry of Justice—established contact with Huerta in exile and prepared for his return. In Washington, D.C., Orozco and Robelo tried unsuccessfully to secure an audience with a Wilson administration insider. Talking to outsiders convinced them, foolishly, that Wilson would not oppose their plans. They left for San Antonio to organize broader support.

Since Orozco contacted Huertistas in South Texas in mid-1915, and since Basilio Ramos had described himself and his cellmates as former Huertistas, American authorities—and subsequently scholars as well—erroneously concluded that the two movements were linked.[66] Ramos did not, however, contact any Huertistas when he went to South Texas, and, if the PSD were a Huerta plot, he would have. The most prominent valley Huertista, Dr.

Miguel Barragán, lived in Brownsville and his son-in-law, Juan Cross, an Afro-Mexican who owned a large lumberyard, presumably would have been interested in the Negro liberation aspect of the PSD.[67] Ramos's statement about his former affiliations distracted local officials from the larger issue of his release from a Constitutionalist prison and a safe conduct through their lines.

The Orozco-Robelo mission to San Antonio failed, however, because an ill-starred attempt to bring peace to Mexico by a coalition of disaffected followers of the various factions denied Huerta the support of his influential former followers when he needed it.[68] Rebuffed in San Antonio, the plotters turned to a city where Orozco knew he could find support, El Paso. He successfully recruited and armed a small band of men and awaited Huerta's arrival.

After two months of planning, Huerta boarded a train in New York on June 24, ostensibly headed for California. On June 27, he left the train at Newman, New Mexico, to meet Orozco. No sooner had they joined forces than a posse of agents from the Departments of Justice and Treasury, aided by army troops and local lawmen, arrested them for violation of U.S. neutrality statutes. One Bureau of Investigation agent believed that Huerta had "leaked" the news of his leaving the train precisely to precipitate the arrest. Huerta thought that if he entered Mexico unannounced, the press censorship of Villa and Carranza would make him invisible to his possible supporters and deny him their aid. Detention and temporary incarceration in the United States would mean publicity, and once the Spanish-language newspapers along the border spread the word, his followers would rally. He could then forfeit his bond and enter Mexico triumphantly.[69]

If such had been Huerta's thinking, he had miscalculated the U.S. response. Woodrow Wilson would not permit his return. Wilson, vacationing in Vermont when he learned that Huerta was headed for the West Coast, immediately wired his secretary, "It seems to me imperative Huerta should be prevented from entering Mexico and removed from border. Hope sincerely some means may be found to do this. Importance of it very great."[70] Department of Justice officials had anticipated the President's wishes and had apprehended Huerta before Wilson requested it.

U.S. authorities took Huerta and Orozco to El Paso and formally charged them with conspiracy to violate the neutrality laws. Orozco managed to escape on July 3, but Huerta remained a prisoner at Fort Bliss. Orozco's freedom proved short-lived. After two months of repeated attempts to raise a substantial force around El Paso, while continually dodging Mexican and American authorities, Orozco and four companions headed southeast. In the Big Bend region of Texas, near dusk on August 30, the five men decided to camp in an arroyo. They unsaddled their horses, unaware of the encircling movement of the posse of Texas Rangers, local constables, and army troops that had been tracking them. As the light faded, the posse, without challenge, began to shoot. By dark, Orozco and his companions lay dead. The surprise had been complete; no posse member sustained even a wound.[71] Orozco and his companions had been "rangered"—part of the wave of repression that accompanied the spread of the PSD.

In Washington, D.C., Secretary of State Lansing surveyed German support for the Huerta-Orozco-Villa alliance and wrote, "German agents have undoubtedly been at work in Mexico arousing anti-American feeling . . . the proof is not conclusive but is sufficient to compel belief." He thought Germany engaged in these activities "so that this nation will have troubles in America and be unable to take part in the European war." The foreign policy implications for relations with Mexico seemed clear to him: conditions warranted careful investigation of German plots there and in the United States, and recognition, in concert with other American nations, of the Carranza faction as government.[72]

Lansing invited representatives of seven Latin American countries to confer about recognizing a government in Mexico. Carranza's recent victories over Villa made him the likely choice. His reputation for being iron-willed, arrogant, and opinionated, however, made him unpopular with the delegates. The image of Carranza popularized by American radical journalist John Reed typified the man for many.

Reed had gone to Nogales, Sonora to interview the First Chief, and he described the encounter in his writings. Upon arrival, he was told that all questions had to be submitted first to the minister of foreign relations for approval. The allowable questions the minister would submit to Carranza. After Reed composed a list of twenty-five questions, the minister said he should strike about five that Carranza would not answer—those that dealt "rather specifically with the platform of the Constitutionalist government: such as land distribution, direct elections, and the right of suffrage among the peons." The minister promised to return with the answers in twenty-four hours. Reed would, however, be allowed to meet the First Chief but only to greet the great man and leave immediately. Reed agreed.

Reed described entering Carranza's office.

> It was so dark within that at first we could see nothing. Over the two windows blinds had been drawn . . . As our eyes became adjusted to the light, we saw the gigantic, khaki-clad figure of Don Venustiano Carranza sitting in a big chair . . . He rose to meet us, a towering figure . . . I noticed with a kind of shock that in that dark room he wore smoked glasses.

Reed broke his promise and spoke to the First Chief, which elicited the comment:

> I tell you that if the United States intervenes in Mexico . . . intervention will not accomplish what it thinks, but will provoke a war which, besides its own consequences, will deepen a profound hatred between the United States and the whole of Latin America which will endanger the entire political future of the United States.[73]

Despite the well-known warning, Lansing believed that recognition of Carranza would help thwart German trouble-making. He succinctly observed:

Germany desires to keep up the turmoil in Mexico until the United States is forced to intervene; *therefore, we must not intervene.* Germany does not wish to have any one faction dominant in Mexico; *therefore we must recognize one faction as dominant in Mexico.* When we recognize a faction as the government, Germany will undoubtedly seek to cause a quarrel between that government and ours; *therefore, we must avoid a quarrel, regardless of criticism and complaint in Congress and the press.*[74]

While Carranza waited and wondered what it would take to secure U.S. recognition, he could not know that possible American relations with Germany influenced Lansing's strategy. Word of Pizaña's and De la Rosa's treatment of suspected Germans caused observers to wonder if the PSD were also a German conspiracy. Moreover, the participation of Constitutionalist soldiers in valley raiding further qualified Wilson administration support. Recognition, however, in addition to countering German aims, would mean that Washington could hold someone in Mexico accountable for border violations.

By the time Lansing completed his arrangements, the train wreck had occurred; the formal announcement of recognition came one day after the attack. Many Americans thought that Carranza had used the raids to win recognition. The events tended to confirm existing suspicions of U.S. authorities. Wilson recognized Carranza de facto not de jure, acknowledging only the Constitutionalist military victories and placing him on probation to prove his legitimacy. Wilson simultaneously reimposed the arms embargo and, although he intended to aid Carranza, traditionally the embargo had hurt Mexican central authority and helped insurgents.[75]

Americans complained of the negative attitude shown by General Emiliano P. Nafarrate, commander of Carranza's troops across the river from Cameron and Hidalgo counties in summer and fall 1915. Nonetheless, few, if any, knew his background. Nafarrate had been one of Carranza's earliest adherents, a signer of the original Plan of Guadalupe.[76] Carranza had sent him into Tamaulipas early in the campaign, and he had remained there so long that people regarded him as a Tamaulipeco—although he was, in reality, from Sinaloa.

He defended Matamoros when Villistas lay siege in March 1915. Nafarrate skillfully lured him into a miniature Ebano and, when the exhausted Villistas began to close for a desperate attack, he knocked holes in the dikes he had built around the town—deluging the attackers with river water. Villistas, nearly chest deep in water, fled, while abandoning arms and cannon. It was said of Nafarrate's bold and brilliant defense of Matamoros that three times Carranza ordered him to evacuate the city, and, by the time the last order arrived, it was besieged.[77] Despite his refusal to follow orders, Nafarrate earned both victory and promotion; the incident underscored Carranza's difficulties in controlling distant subordinates.

Nafarrate tended toward independent action. He retained cronies and probably profited from graft and illegal financial transactions. Both Carranza's consul in Matamoros and one of Carranza's special investigators complained about the large entourage of indolent connivers with which Nafarrate had surrounded himself. Chief among these stood Francisco Barrera y Guerra, a Tejano, who got one of his Tejano sons appointed military commander (*Jefe de las Armas*) at Ciudad Mier. Francisco used his Mexican connections to export Mexican cattle to Texas—tax free.

Moreover, another of his sons, Aguirre, had made $27,000 (dollars) selling Constitutionalist ammunition.[78] Since ammunition shortages continually plagued Constitutionalist armies, such illicit sales constituted serious crime. At the time Aguirre Barrera y Guerra sold his supplies, the total reserve of 7mm cartridges available at Carranza's central munitions warehouse numbered 26,400.[79] The confidential investigator recommended to Carranza that Nafarrante and his entire "gang" (*pandilla*) be transferred to the interior where they could be more closely controlled.[80]

Frontier defense forces, however, could not be easily rearranged. General Alfredo Ricaut, Carranza's nephew, had been stationed at Matamoros, then reassigned inland to cover part of Coahuila. During the march, six hundred of his troops deserted—going over to brigade commanders offering promotion, more pay, and the opportunity to loot.[81] Although Ricaut's report did not name him, the implied reference to Nafarrate seemed clear.

Ricaut believed that prevailing practices along the northern frontier meant that he should send a commission to Mexico City to recruit new men to raise his brigade to full strength. With new men and reliable older troops, he thought he could forge a credible unit. Ricaut asked his uncle, Carranza, to support the recruiting mission and to alleviate six-month delays in shipping clothes to his soldiers.[82]

Problems of corruption, venality, and desertion plagued other northern commands. General Jacinto Treviño, hero of Ebano and commander of the line from the end of Nafarrate's district to Sonora, had similar problems. When Carranza ordered troops from Pablo González's army in Morelos to march north and join Treviño, the unit commander protested. General Francisco de P. Mariel, reflecting Ricaut's argument, informed Carranza, González, and Treviño that mixing his newly recruited men from central Mexico with those of questionable reliability in the north would produce an unstable compound that could easily dissolve under campaign stress.[83] He proved prophetic.

Given troop instability in the north, Carranza might have ignored Nafarrate's lack of discipline and his nephew's problems and focused instead on marshaling his central forces for the campaigns against Zapata, Peláez, and other serious insurgents closer to the capital. Nafarrate's relationship with the PSD, however, did not permit Carranza that luxury. Nafarrate generally disliked Americans, and he expressed a socialist radicalism close to anarchism.[84]

Although he pledged fidelity to Constitutionalism and called it "nuestra CAUSA" in his correspondence to Carranza,[85] Nafarrate encouraged the Constitutionalist newspapers in his area to criticize social discrimination in the United States. He urged them to stress that the Constitutionalist revolution sought the elevation of all Mexicans to a new "civilization" where social justice, education, and culture would prevail.[86]

In this setting, Nafarrate's use of revolutionary rhetoric was important. He attributed the raiding to "los revolucionarios en Texas,"[87] a term signifying a legitimacy that most Constitutionalists reserved exclusively to themselves. After the Convention at Aguascalientes, Villa became a "bandolero" to them and lost his status as revolutionary in their lexicon. Nafarrate's use of "revolucionarios" to describe those who fought Anglos in South Texas encouraged others to do so—especially the press. Such language had profound propaganda implications.

Carranza used the newspaper as the primary propaganda organ of his movement—as did other factions such as the PLM. In 1914, he contracted with newspaperman Rafael Martínez, better known by his pseudonym RIP-RIP, to create and subsidize a network of newspapers under the common name *El Demócrata*. They were to report Constitutionalist military victories and to represent Carranza's position on the revolution.[88] Although not the only Constitutionalist organs, they were the most important. Only semireliable in news reporting—sensational stories frequently appeared with the facts unchecked—they usually reflected official political orthodoxy.

El Demócrata, published in Mexico City, Monterrey, and Matamoros, began under Nafarrate's influence to describe the border raiders as "revolucionarios" and "rebeldes,"[89] as did *El Constitucional*,[90] official organ of the Army Corps of the Northeast. Assumed to reflect political orthodoxy, the papers thus conferred legitimacy upon the raiding. They also conferred legitimacy, perhaps inadvertently, upon the PSD. Sloppy and inaccurate reporting in Constitutionalist papers antagonized and frightened Americans.

El Demócrata, for example, reported through correspondents in El Paso and Laredo that a German national had been among the raiders killed at Norias; that the revolutionary force consisted of five thousand well-armed men who had defeated U.S. government forces several times and had even taken Brownsville; and that the rebels had seized Mercedes.[91] Americans confronting these stories had to choose; either *El Demócrata* was guilty of its customary slipshod and sensationalized reporting of events or *El Demócrata* conspired to spread disorder by propagandizing for De la Rosa, Pizaña, and the PSD. Most Americans chose the conspiracy.[92]

As criticism of Nafarrate mounted, Carranza sent General Treviño on a confidential investigation. Refusing to discuss his mission with reporters, Treviño met with the Mexican and American consuls in Brownsville and Matamoros and with several military commanders before returning to his headquarters on September 21.[93] The incident that insured Nafarrate's removal from the border occurred just two nights later.

Approximately eighty uniformed Constitutionalist soldiers crossed the river near Progreso late on the night of September 23; they then proceeded to loot the large store of Florencio Saenz at La Toluca. His store had been looted a year earlier and, despite his key role in the Wells political machine, he did not feel adequately protected by the army elements around him.

By mid-August, Saenz found country life so precarious that he moved to Brownsville, leaving his inventory at La Toluca.[94]

The Carrancistas took arms, liquor, food, and mules, and then set the stores ablaze. They tried to burn the house and chapel, but Saenz had been among the first to build with brick in eastern Hidalgo County, and so the fire failed. Their work took them through the night, and, while at their mischief about 7:00 A.M. the next morning, a U.S. army patrol happened upon them and a skirmish ensued. When the retreating Carrancistas reached the river, their compatriots on the Mexican side lay down a covering fire to protect their escape. In the course of the fighting, the Constitutionalists captured Private Richard J. Johnson, whom they took into Mexico with them. They tortured the American soldier by cutting off his ears before decapitating him, then posted his head on a spike, and paraded it along the riverbank[95]—imitating an old Spanish practice.

The State Department protested vigorously, claiming that whether Carranza's troops raided under orders or upon their own volition, the responsibility for their actions lay with Carranza. The United States demanded immediate action.[96] Unbeknownst to American officials, however, Carranza had already begun the delicate maneuver to oust Nafarrate. Because of Nafarrate's proven military abilities and his professed loyalty to Constitutionalism, Carranza wanted to retain this nominal subordinate and still defuse the situation. Carranza chose a clever strategy; he removed Nafarrate by promotion. On September 27, three days after the incident at La Toluca, Carranza promoted Nafarrate to General of Division (*Divisionario*), mandating a new command commensurate with the new rank.[97]

On October 1, Carranza privately informed the State Department that, although no direct evidence had been presented of Nafarrate's complicity in the border raids, the U.S. complaints had placed the general in a "doubtful" position, and Carranza would remove him.[98] The next day, Nafarrate announced his promotion and expected rotation but acknowledged that he did not know where he would be sent. Just before De la Rosa wrecked the train, Nafarrate and many of his troops departed for Ciudad Victoria, capital of Tamaulipas. When they arrived, Carranza announced that Nafarrate's new assignment would be Tampico.[99]

Carranza had given Nafarrate a critical post. The oil that kept the British navy afloat flowed through Tampico and the export tax revenue on the oil helped fund Constitutionalism. Nafarrate's proven military abilities could be used in the event of another attack, and, although his opportunity for graft would have been improved, he could now be more closely checked. Carranza in no way publicly rebuked Nafarrate. Both Nafarrate's removal from the tense border and his promotion wrongly convinced many Americans that Carranza had rewarded his subordinate for services rendered; that Nafarrate's support for the PSD had been on Carranza's orders.[100] That belief persisted, despite Carranza's efforts to defuse tensions.

Carranza replaced Nafarrate and his troops with another hero of the battle of Matamoros, General Eugenio López, who had led the counterattack. López assumed his post accompanied by new recruits from the interior.[101] The dire predictions of Generals Ricaut and De P. Mariel came true. New troops lacked the training and discipline to patrol effectively, and they grew bored. Some, learning of the PSD, supported it. López and his men had been on station only eight days when De la Rosa and his force crossed the river under their control and wrecked the train.

When Americans reported that De la Rosa had been seen in the streets of Reynosa two days later, they demanded his arrest. A confused López transmitted the demand to Carranza, explaining, "I have no instructions in this matter and am asking that you send me some."[102] Carranza ordered López to stop raiders from Texas who tried to enter Mexico and to arrest immediately those who might be on Mexican soil; Carranza himself would determine their fate.[103]

López, despite explicit instructions, moved slowly, hampered by his unreliable troops and his own predisposition toward the PSD. He described the raiders as "revolucionarios Texanos" in his dealing with the U.S. consul, and thought the valley situation was a Texas problem.[104] The Constitutionalist consul in Rio Grande City, who described the raiders as "bandoleros Texanos," complained to Carranza of Lopez's lackadaisical attitude. By allowing these men safe refuge in Mexico, López weakened U.S. confidence in all Constitutionalist commanders. Failure to prosecute the guilty within Mexico exacerbated the plight of Mexicans living in Texas. Moreover, although López had obtained confidential information about the location of De la Rosa's camp, the consul believed, correctly, that López would do nothing.[105]

Within a month of replacing Nafarrate, Carranza again had to change border commanders opposite Cameron and Hidalgo counties. While he considered his course, Carranza took other steps to allay U.S. fears and to bolster his sagging control over northern subordinates. On October 29, Carranza sent a public letter to Governor Ferguson stating that he had given his local commanders standing orders to arrest De la Rosa, Pizaña, and any of the other "rebeldes" who might enter Mexico[106]—a point reinforced by interactions between U.S. and Constitutionalist soldiers on the line.[107]

On November 1, Carranza's personal representative, Roberto Pesquiera, met with D. W. Glasscock, Caesar Kleberg, and the rest of the valley committee in San Antonio. Pesquiera promised that Carranza would conduct a full investigation into the disturbances and send more troops to the border.[108] Ten days later, the entire editorial staff of *El Demócrata*, Matamoros, announced its immediate resignation on orders from Mexico City. Rafael Martínez, RIP-RIP, demanded that they resign for their incendiary reporting of raiding in Texas and pledged that he would come to Matamoros to reorganize the press.[109] This act was designed to squelch the rumors of official Constitutionalist propaganda for the PSD.

On November 15, through mutual friend Carlos Bee, Carranza proposed and Governor Ferguson accepted, an invitation to meet on the line within ten days to discuss mutual problems.[110] At the time, Carranza had been traveling for nearly a month through major and minor northern cities—ostensibly to visit reclaimed territory. The State Department observer with him, however, thought the real purpose was to bring doubtful Constitutionalists back into line. With Obregón at his side, Carranza could mollify even the angriest of his followers, including Nafarrate.[111]

Carranza met Ferguson in Nuevo Laredo on November 23, in an interchange that revealed the deep misunderstanding that Americans in general and Texans in particular had of Mexicans. Initially, the English-language press reported that both men had met on the international bridge.[112] Carranza, who adamantly refused to set foot outside Mexico, received the governor in a home in Nuevo Laredo. Carranza used the occasion to announce that General Ricaut would replace General López in a new patrol area that would extend from the Gulf of Mexico to Piedras Negras, opposite Eagle Pass. Ferguson had brought Adjutant General Hutchings and, following the announcement, Hutchings and Ricaut conferred. The U.S. press account described the conference as concluding with a pledge that each nation would return outlaws to their country of origin.[113]

The pledge could not have been made, since Carranza's government would not make an agreement with an individual American state, and Wilson's government could not make an extradition treaty with a government it had not recognized de jure. The American press omitted what its Spanish-language counterpart covered: Carranza's toast. Carranza concluded the conference with a toast, not to mutual cooperation or to the border, but to the anniversary—the following day—of the U.S. evacuation of Veracruz. Carranza stated that amicable relations could be conducted only under conditions of respect for national sovereignty, and the U.S. withdrawal had permitted the Mexican-American dialogue to begin.[114] The mistake on the part of the press reflected American misjudgment of Carranza and his country.

Carranza continued to demonstrate his willingness to cooperate against raiding by traveling on to Matamoros, where he stayed from November 28 to November 30. In addition to the two thousand troops accompanying him—which helped to eliminate disturbances—Carranza brought the Governor of Tamaulipas, as well as Generals Ricaut and Nafarrate with their respective staffs, to meet the Americans. He brought the assemblage to the monument at the midpoint of the International Bridge at Brownsville, an extraordinary act of outreach (See Figure 15). The American military commander noted, "Carranza said he was doing all in his power to suppress the bandits and would continue to do so."[115]

Ricaut's appointment pleased local American officials because they thought him reliable and fair. Nonetheless, they missed the point Carranza made in having Nafarrate present. Carranza wanted publicly to impress upon Nafarrate that, even though his new command was far to the south, Carranza wanted raiding suppressed. Carranza wanted to pressure Nafarrate but not alienate him altogether. From his new base in Tampico, Nafarrate had been

Fig. 15. Mexicans and Americans on the Brownsville bridge, November 1915. Venustiano Carranza, center left, with glasses and full beard; behind his right shoulder, General Emiliano P. Nafarrate (Hidalgo County Historical Museum, Edinburg, Texas)

recruiting new men with the same tactics Ricaut had denounced in July.[116] Moreover, Nafarrate had given Constitutionalist commissions and safe refuge in Ciudad Victoria to De la Rosa, Pizaña, Basilio Ramos, and others.[117] Carranza was telling Nafarrate, albeit obliquely, to stop.

Carranza's choice of Ricaut to command the line revealed his serious commitment to resolve the border problem and secure the Wilson administration's full support. More than mere nepotism, the appointment of this reliable family member signified Carranza's attempt to control personally the frontier trouble. Ricaut assumed his post with a mix of frontier veterans and well-trained and loyal recruits from the interior. Ricaut instituted a system of regular river patrol, and untoward incidents declined. If Carranza could keep them well-supplied, perhaps the new discipline would curb the PSD leanings of some of the veterans.

Moreover, Ricaut's seriousness was reflected in the northern Carrancista press by a subtle but distinct semantic shift in reporting. Instead of "revolucionarios," De la Rosa and Pizaña became "bandoleros."[118] The attitudinal change produced results in the river patrol. By the end of December, Ricaut reported to Carranza that "complete order prevails all along the border under my command."[119] His U.S. army counterparts across the river agreed.[120] As long as Nafarrate's attitude remained doubtful, and PSD leadership remained free, however, the tranquility could only be temporary. And Americans remained ready to blame anyone but themselves for valley disturbances.

CHAPTER 7

THE PLAN OF SAN DIEGO: FOLLOWERS AND ADHERENTS

Proletarians . . . the Revolutionary Movement growing on the southern border of this country and led by the **REVOLUTIONARY CONGRESS OF SAN DIEGO, TEXAS** . . . is the **SOCIAL WAR** which, in these moments, agitates all corners of the earth. . . . Remember those martyrs who have been victims of savage beasts in this country, in the events of Chicago, in the Year 1886 . . . remember all this and let us rise with the vindicating rifle in our hands waving through towns and country fields the **RED BANNER** . . . until achieving . . . **BREAD** for all, **WELL-BEING** for all, **FREEDOM** for all.

Delegate Number 825 in Bryan, Texas[1]

De la Rosa, Pizaña, other PSD leaders, and adherents withdrew into northern Mexico following Carranza's visit to the U.S. boundary line. Their fallback and General Ricaut's commitment to patrolling the river under his command brought temporary peace. Yet despite Carranza's continued pressure to defuse the movement, PSD support lay in areas beyond his control, and powerful subalterns within his Constitutionalist army continued to give succor to the movement's leadership. Thus, PSD followers continued to prepare for further raiding and to seek new monies, as U.S. Bureau of Investigation agents soon learned. By the time PSD activity resurged in the spring of 1916, American investigators had both developed a variegated picture of the movement and pursued a two-pronged approach to quell it.

Information from which the Department of Justice composed its view of the PSD came from numerous sources, but perhaps the earliest and most conveniently offered evidence came from Carranza's agents in the United States. In the manner of Madero and Díaz before him, Carranza turned to the United States to rid him of his anarchist critics. On September 27, 1915, Consul General Teodulo R. Beltrán in a press release from San Antonio, launched a public attack on the PLM, misidentifying it as the Mexican branch of the IWW, and charging its followers with the border raids.[2] The aspiring government of Carranza thus identified a mutual threat to the social order of both countries—the PLM as tool of the IWW—and called for Wilson administration help in removing it.

That same day, Beltrán accompanied by Heriberto Barron, representing Carranza in Washington, D.C., called on the solicitor of the Post Office Department to complain. *Regeneración,* they charged, incited

> Mexicans in the United States who live near the border . . . to rise in arms against the authority of the United States . . . every issue of this publication contains matter which tends to incite arson, murder and assassination in violation of Section 211 of the Criminal Code. . . .[3]

Carranza's agents had presented the Americans with copies of the original newspapers. The Post Office Department did not have a local employee who could read Spanish and lacked funds to pay for translation. So Beltrán did the translations himself and sent them to the Americans.[4] His initial translation from *Regeneración,* later polished, became the basis for the new U.S. government case against the PLM. From the October 2, 1915, issue, Beltrán quoted Ricardo Flores Magón:

> Justice and no shots is what ought to be given to Revolutionists of Texas. And from now on all of us, we must demand that these persecutions to innocent Mexicans ought to stop and in regard to the Revolutionists we must also demand that they will not be shot. The ones who ought to be shot are THE RANGERS and the balance of fellows who are with them in their depredations.[5]

Since Ricardo's essay spoke about the Plan of San Diego and described the shoot-out at Pizaña's ranch from Pizaña's perspective, the Post Office Department and the Department of Justice believed that this proved both PLM support for the PSD and conspiracy to launch the movement. American agents recognized the ideological link between the PSD and the PLM through *Regeneración,* but could not accept that this might be the primary, perhaps only, connection. There had to be more—some clandestine plan such as had characterized the PLM armed insurrections of 1908 and 1910. Agent investigations eventually failed to produce the desired proof; the real picture was more complex than simple conspiracy.

Ironically, much U.S. misperception of PLM-PSD relations could have been clarified by reading and accepting the offending editorial in its entirety. Americans finally did secure complete translations but ignored a most important point. Ricardo wrote that the Plan of San Diego did not exist, that it was a creation of the bourgeois press. Mexicans in South Texas simply defended themselves against racist exploitation and oppression. Self-defense, he argued, not some conspiracy, prompted the uprising.[6] American authorities chose not to notice. They did not observe that Ricardo had veered away from using the PLM *focos* for action after 1908, that he had not supported the seizure of Tijuana in 1910, and that he had allowed the *focos* to function without his central direction as his commitment to anarchism, and thus to decentralization, deepened. Ricardo's absorption with the Rangel-

Cline case had blinded him to the significance of the PSD. Moreover, those PLM members and *focos* in South Texas and northern Mexico who joined the PSD did so on their own—without his order or direction. American authorities, however, pursued the fictive conspiracy.

The postal inspector sought to gather more evidence to bolster a recommendation to revoke the newspaper's use of second-class mailing privileges. Use of the mail could be restricted if the material were unmailable because obscene; obscenity was defined to include inciting others to violence and advocating the overthrow of constituted authority. The Bureau of Investigation within the Department of Justice sought to gather sufficient evidence to link the PLM in Los Angeles to the uprising in Texas and to try them together for conspiracy to overthrow the government. Should the evidence not warrant the conspiracy charge, then the indictment would be for violation of neutrality.[7]

The Post Office Department made its first intercept in November 1915, when a representative of the Revolutionary Congress of the Plan of San Diego, one L. Gante, sent a copy of the February 20th version of the PSD to comrades at the *Solidaridad Obrera* in Barcelona, Spain. Gante described the raids against Texas as part of the international "social revolution" which he saw as "the only means of redeeming the proletariat of the world." Gante told the Spanish group, "We expect your cooperation in the press, at meetings on the floor of Parliament, and by every means of propaganda." Gante concluded with the dual message that had plagued the anarchist vision of the PLM almost from its inception. "Do not wonder at a certain patriotical cant in our manifest; the ambient we are now breathing and the conditions that must be bowed to to start the struggle so demand." With characteristic PLM optimism, he concluded, "Time and the course of events will rid it of that which modern conditions must overcome."[8]

U.S. authorities tried unsuccessfully to locate Gante and to identify the *Solidaridad Obrera*.[9] Very few anarchist participants in the PSD were found in the United States; *Solidaridad Obrera,* in Spain, referred both to an anarcho-syndicalist group and to a newspaper of the same name which it published. The newspaper had been served by such important Spanish anarchists as Francisco Ferrer, who founded the Modern School movement, Anselmo Lorenzo, and José Prat.[10]

These men had all been important to Ricardo Flores Magón's thought and each appeared in the celebrated 1910 *Regeneración* anarchist poster. Ferrer was present in an aphorism, Lorenzo in a photograph, and Prat in a title in the open book.[11] Other than goodwill, however, no evidence was discovered showing that *Solidaridad Obrera* contributed to the anarchist effort in South Texas.[12]

What of this man L. Gante, whose name was a pun on *elegante?* Who was he and what did he represent? León Cárdenas Martínez used the pseudonym L. Gante in his writing. He was a PLM adherent, a *Regeneración* subscriber, the editor of *Evolución Social,* and a partisan of Praxedis Guerrero. In 1909, together with Guerrero, Gante/Cárdenas established a PLM *foco* in the West

Texas town of Toyah. There he propagandized among the Mexican railroad workers. Although the town reported only 1,052 people in the 1910 census, Toyah was the terminal point for all crews of the Texas and Pacific Railroad. In 1915, the roundhouse alone employed 110 men working in shifts around the clock. In 1915, Toyah had eight subscribers to *Regeneración*.[13]

Gante/Cárdenas was a PLM organizer and *foco* leader who propagandized for the PSD. Perhaps he was the author of the revised PSD—the writer of the February 20, 1915, anarchist-communist version. Whatever his role, Gante/Cárdenas acted on his own, as a free lance without Ricardo's direction or knowledge. Had Ricardo known more about the PSD, it seems doubtful that he would have invested his concerns about events in Texas in the Rangel-Cline case rather than in the incipient "Social Revolution," as Gante/Cárdenas had called it.

In Los Angeles, when Postal Inspector William Cookson began to investigate *Regeneración*, Ricardo countered with an old ploy. He inserted a bilingual coupon in the newspaper that could be clipped, signed, and sent to President Wilson protesting the harassment. His followers had done the same thing in 1912, when they protested to President Taft the trial of PLM leaders for the Baja expedition. *Regeneración* had not been then the unambiguously anarchist newspaper that it had become.

Although public reaction in late 1915 proved strong, it also differed from the earlier response. Now coupons came from but 16 communities rather than 246, all but one in the United States, and they carried 762 signatures as opposed to over 889. Although the responses contained the same mixture of women and non-Spanish surnamed adherents as the 1912 mailings, instead of the broad diversity of states then represented, these coupons originated overwhelmingly in California, Arizona, and Texas.[14]

Undaunted by the coupon protest, Cookson continued to gather his evidence. On November 22, 1915, he had his agents copy out *Regeneración*'s complete subscriber list.[15] Department of Justice informant Carlos Minck, professing an interest in anarchism, secured for $.75 (cents) copies of *Regeneración* dated from January 1, 1913 to October 2, 1915, from Blas Lara, a member of the editorial board.[16] The Post Office Department, with newly found funds to pay for the work, had Minck translate the newspaper,[17] while inspectors searched for inflammatory essays for potential criminal prosecution. Minck also continued the Department of Justice inquiry into anarchist life in Los Angeles.

Since late 1914, Ricardo, Enríque, their families, and those of eight other members of the PLM, had rented five acres of land in Edendale, near the Silver Lake district of northern Los Angeles.[18] They maintained peach and plum orchards and farmed communally, vainly trying to keep their living costs low enough to sustain *Regeneración*. They shared the area with a film colony that antedated the one in Hollywood. To the *Los Angeles Times,* Edendale was "a community which exists, apparently, just for the fun of making believe."[19] While some inhabitants projected other worlds on celluloid, however, the PLM leaders projected theirs in newsprint.

The Department of Justice described how to find the anarchists: "Take the 'red car' to Edendale on 6th & Main when the car is going West, get off on Fargo Street and walk left until you reach Ivanhoe Avenue and then walk three blocks until you reach the lake; in the *jacales* is the shop of *Regeneración.*"[20]

The department did not, however, comprehend what it found. The anarchists in Edendale lived in shacks and, in late September 1915, had resumed publishing *Regeneración* there. They maintained PLM headquarters, however, in a brick building near the railroad freight depot in Los Angeles at 767 San Fernando Street. The anarchists went to town in a horse-drawn cart; there they mailed letters and newspapers, sold their fruit and produce, and then returned with paper for the press and other necessities.[21]

The PLM shared its town headquarters building with several organizations and offered a reading room with current issues of many anarchist newspapers—including *Regeneración,* the IWW paper *El Rebelde,* and *Tierra y Libertad* from Barcelona—and a variety of books. A Spaniard, P. C. Paulet, acted as librarian. When Minck visited the place, he disparagingly described the dozen Mexicans in the reading room as "loafers" and thought that "this place is used at night for the homeless to sleep."[22]

Female anarchists had their own organization—"Luz y Vida" (Light and Life). On Saturday night, November 27, 1915, "Luz y Vida" held a dance to raise money for *Regeneración.* Minck attended the event at the Italian Hall on the corner of North Main and Macy Streets and considered those present "of the lower class of Mexicans." The following afternoon, Sunday, he went to the Mexican plaza on North Main Street, where he heard anarchists inveighing against the rich to the people who had gathered to listen.[23]

Minck's contemptuous reports, transmitted without comment by his superiors, conveyed the prevalent government attitude towards anarchists. While anarchists might live miserably, their dedication to their ideals—despite the lack of means to achieve them—made them potentially dangerous.

Minck's account of Los Angeles anarchist life could have applied equally to libertarian groups in Chicago, Boston, or New York.[24] He described accurately how anarchists lived and survived: by mutual aid from varied ethnic groups, communal effort, sexual equality, and frugality. They enlivened their daily struggle, however, with dances, public oratory, and other events that escaped Minck's notice, such as commemorative observances of the Paris Commune (March 18), the First of May, and the martyrdom of those accused of the Haymarket tragedy (November 11). Such events were characterized by picnics and speeches, concerts and occasional theater. In the calm of Edendale, Ricardo finished a play—a comedy entitled *Tierra y Libertad—* that Ethel Duffy Turner described as "profoundly revolutionary." It was performed in December 1915 in Los Angeles and earned money for *Regeneración.*[25]

The subscriber list that the postal inspector had compiled revealed much about those who followed *Regeneración* and Ricardo's writings, especially locally. Nonetheless, the postal authorities did practically nothing with the information. The enumeration shows local newspaper exchanges with five publications: the English-language *Daily Tribune, Pacific Press,* and *California Social Democrat,* as well as *El Rebelde* in Spanish and *La Rivolta* in Italian. The Los Angeles Public Library subscribed. Individual subscribers ran to 111, of whom 14, or 12.6 percent, were identifiable as women—9 of whom had Spanish surnames. Of the total, 39, or 35.1 percent, had non-Spanish surnames, and many of those were the Los Angeles Socialists such as attorney Job Harriman, who had represented the PLM in court, and John Murray, who had worked on *The Border* with Manuel Sarabia, Elizabeth Trowbridge, and Ethel Duffy Turner.

Many of the roster entries, with only an initial for given name, proved incomplete. With the defective ones deleted, 74 remained that potentially could be found in the individual census schedules for 1910—provided that the individuals had been living in Los Angeles that year and had been enumerated. Of the 74 names, 19, or 25.7 percent, could be identified in the census. John Murray, however, could not be found, although he lived then in the city.

The data are intriguing. Collectively, the Los Angeles *Regeneración* subscribers were a mix of women and men, native and foreign born, who contradicted popular stereotypes of anarchists as European males. Four women represented 21.1 percent of the group; the six native-born subscribers, 31.6 percent, did not have Spanish surnames. More than half reported themselves as aliens, only one had been naturalized, and two recorded no information on the subject. One alien subscriber had arrived from Cuba in 1899; the others had come from Mexico between 1898 and 1910.

Living arrangements revealed variety in income, occupation, and assets. Two of these subscribers lived alone, but the remainder lived with others in households ranging from two members to twenty-eight. Five households took boarders, and two had servants. The professionals included a physician, a journalist, an assayer, and an attorney. Workers, numbered twelve, or 63.2 percent; they painted houses and furniture, packed candy and cigars, labored on the railroad or at general tasks, and performed the tasks of power lineman, servant, or cigar maker. Three subscribers were unemployed—apparently voluntarily. Eight subscribers rented, six owned houses, and five lived with relatives. They ranged in age from 17 to 60, averaging 36.8 years; five were single and one widowed.[26]

The diversity of *Regeneración* subscribers makes it difficult to compare them with the subscribers of other left organs. The *Appeal to Reason,* one of the major socialist newspapers, had risen to prominence on the efforts of its "salesmen soldiers," whose success at selling subscriptions ("hustling subs") had brought circulation to some 750,000 by 1913. Four of the *Appeal's* top salesmen lived in Los Angeles and gave their respective occupations as railroad worker, shoemaker, carpenter, and merchant.[27] None subscribed to *Regeneración* and only the 67-year-old married carpenter could be found in the 1910 census. These Socialists, perhaps closer to the mainstream of

American socialism and agreeing with Debs's disavowal of the PLM, had nothing to do with the Mexican anarchists. The left-leaning elements among the Los Angeles socialists did continue to support Ricardo.

Curiously, both despite and because of Ricardo, Mexican anarchists in Los Angeles rallied to support Aniceto Pizaña through the pages of *Regeneración*. Carranza had been doing what he could to curb the PSD in Mexico and, in February 1916, succeeded in having Pizaña arrested in Monterrey. Los Angeles anarchists responded quickly. On March 4, 1916, *Regeneración* printed a letter to Carranza protesting Pizaña's arrest and demanding his immediate release. The letter bore 47 signatures, including that of Paulet, the librarian at the PLM reading room. Only 3 of the signers, or about 1 in 16, subscribed. Through the *City Directory*, 18 people, or 38.3 percent, could be identified. Aside from the barber and cart driver, all the others gave their occupation as laborer. When their addresses were plotted on a street map, they were found to be clustered in an area of railroad housing.

Thus, it appears that Angeleno anarchists in 1916—subscribers and sympathizers to *Regeneración* who supported Pizaña and the PSD in South Texas—were primarily railroad laborers.[28] Transportation workers in the city expressed their solidarity with campesinos in the countryside more than 1,500 miles away through *Regeneración*. A subsequently published letter from Hondo, Texas, also demanding Pizaña's release, bore 34 signatures, 11 from subscribers. One subscriber had each member of his family sign, including his four children under the age of sixteen. Those signers who could be identified worked at odd jobs, primarily in agriculture.[29] To them and to others in South Texas who demanded that Carranza set him free, Pizaña was one "of the disinherited, a hero"; his arrest made him "a martyr" for their cause.[30]

Carranza's crackdown followed significant leadership changes in the PSD. In early January 1916, Ramos, Garza, De la Rosa, Pizaña, and others met in Monterrey at the Plaza del Colegio Civil; there after much arguing, De la Rosa emerged as the new military commander of the PSD. De la Rosa's rise offended Pizaña, who had wanted the post. It also meant replacing the previous unofficial commander, Maurillio Rodríguez, a Constitutionalist lieutenant colonel highly placed in the central railroad dispatching office in Monterrey. Rodríguez provided liaison between Generals Nafarrate, then in Tampico, and González, then in Cuernavaca.[31] Because of González' closeness to Carranza, coupled with Nafarrate's actions, some have concluded erroneously that Carranza himself supported the PSD and directed its movements.[32]

Carranza, however, had informed the governor of Nuevo León that "those individuals responsible for the revolution[sic] in the State of Texas" were suspected of being in Monterrey, and he ordered them apprehended. He specifically included in his list the names of Garza, Rodríguez, Ramos, De la Rosa, and Pizaña.[33] On February 3, 1916, the governor wired Carranza that Rodríguez had been arrested and imprisoned in the state penitentiary.[34]

Simultaneously, General Ricaut apprehended Pizaña with four companions and incarcerated them at Matamoros.[35] Ricaut made the action public two weeks later.[36] American authorities had full knowledge of these arrests.[37]

Carranza knew that one of General González's associates, Major Pedro Hernández, chief of police for the headquarters of the Army Corps of the Northeast, recruited actively for the PSD in Monterrey—distributing its propaganda and broadsides, and soliciting money to fund it.[38] The Constitutionalist-anarchist-Tejano confluence in Monterrey resulted from the ebb and flow of the revolution, and Carranza moved carefully in trying to remove his subordinates from participation in a movement that ran counter to, and threatened, his political future.

Monterrey was the primary northern industrial city, and Casa del Obrera Mundial organizers quickly formed a branch there.[39] The Monterrey Casa drew adherents from among railroad and industrial workers, but also from campesinos.[40] In Monterrey, Casa organizers thought that agricultural workers needed protection, too, and so not only received the headquarters' proletarian oriented propaganda but also subscribed to *Regeneración*. Soldiers from the recently disbanded Red Battalions gathered around the regional Casa office for conversation and to seek jobs. They participated in a fluid world where the Constitutionalist army did not appear as their enemy, and where, conversely, Constitutionalist soldiers did not automatically disassociate from anarchists. Even after Carranza had the Casa closed by General Treviño in late October 1915,[41] workers and campesinos continued to gather there informally.[42]

Monterrey's proximity to the border meant people came and went frequently—their news and views of the Texas situation constantly modified by changing information. A sense of pride in being Mexican grew with the spread of revolutionary propaganda—whether anarchist or reformist. This pride in ancestry, coupled with anger at abusive treatment, fueled support for the PSD. Curbing PSD activity in Monterrey frequently meant pitting Constitutionalists against each other over issues of nationalism and politics. As we shall see, the arrest of Alfonso Domínguez Tijerina and seven companions is instructive in this regard; apprehended at the rancho "Las Espinas," outside Monterrey, on February 5, 1916, they were charged with violation of Mexican neutrality laws for participating in the PSD.

Domínguez, a twenty-one year old major in the Constitutionalist Railroad Corps, was a friend of Colonel Maurillio Rodríguez, from whom he first learned of the "revolution in Texas." Rodríguez in turn introduced Domínguez to León Caballo (Agustín Garza) in early January. Domínguez, although single and from Reynosa, Tamaulipas, had family in Hidalgo, Texas, and visited there frequently via Brownsville. From his knowledge of social conditions in South Texas, he agreed with the aims of the PSD—especially after Caballo assured him that it would help, not hurt, the Constitutionalist cause.[43]

In mid-January, Domínguez left Monterrey for the rancho, accompanied by others he had recruited. They had joined after Domínguez explained the ideals of the PSD to them and showed them the February 20th manifesto. The group included Benito González, a married twenty-seven year old smelter worker and former cavalry veteran; Julian Hernández, a single twenty-two year old day laborer (*jornalero*) introduced to Domínguez by a mutual friend; and twenty year old Nieves Riveras, broom-maker (*escobero*) friend of Hernández and also from Monterrey.

Another recruit was José Montemayor, a nineteen year old single agricultural worker, invited along by Hernández, who agreed that "North Americans have abused and exploited Mexicans living there." Montemayor was accompanied by the Villarreal brothers, Calixto and Santos; all came from Cadereyta Jiménez, Nuevo León, seventeen miles outside of Monterrey. Of the brothers, Calixto agreed with the PSD but Santos did not. They and Montemayor had been introduced to the PSD through Antonio Garza in Cadereyta Jiménez, who took ten copies of each issue of *Regeneración* and circulated PLM propaganda in the area.[44]

When Domínguez and his party reached the rancho, he became the officer in charge, and awaited the arrival of others. Only one other appeared, Juan F. Garra, a twenty-three year old businessman (*comerciante*) from Marín, Nuevo León, whom León Caballo had recruited in the plaza Hidalgo in Monterrey and sent out to join the others. Caballo had promised that when he finished recruiting, he would come to "Las Espinas" and lead them all into Texas. At the rancho, the men lived mutually, sharing their own funds, with Juan F. Garza acting as treasurer. They had to do so because the small amount of money that Caballo had contributed was quickly exhausted.

After two weeks of waiting, Domínguez began to rethink his commitment when he learned that Hilario Hinojosa, former commander of Huerta's forces in Nuevo León, had joined the PSD. Domínguez correctly reasoned that if Huertistas supported the PSD, then that movement could not help the Constitutionalists. He explained his thinking to the others; they agreed, and therefore offered no resistance when apprehended. At the time of their arrest, the eight men had eleven carbines, one thousand cartridges, and three bugles. Given the chronic arms shortages Constitutionalists faced in the north, these men may have been better armed than their captors.

At the same time as Caballo recruited in Monterrey, his agents also solicited in Tampico and in El Paso. A certain Abasta, who had served in the federal army of Díaz in Tampico and who had persevered to become a Constitutionalist lieutenant colonel, went to El Paso to elicit support from ex-federals in exile. He visited his former commander, General Ygnacio Zaragosa, and showed him the PSD, signed by Caballo and others, and various handbills. Abasta urged General Zaragosa to join. The General considered everything carefully and refused. He had persecuted the Floresmagonistas in Monterrey under Díaz, had even imprisoned Antonio Villarreal, and the PSD looked to him to be their work. Zaragosa advised Abasta to quit. Abasta did and became a stone hauler in El Paso.[45]

As Carranza cracked down on the PSD in Monterrey, so did U.S. authorities move against the PLM in Los Angeles. At about 4:00 P.M. on February 18, 1916, federal marshals, accompanied by Los Angeles policemen and detectives, entered the offices of *Regeneración* in Edendale, where Ricardo sat at his desk writing letters. They arrested him and noisily asked Enríque's whereabouts. Hearing the commotion, Enríque entered the office in shirtsleeves. As usual, the brothers were unarmed. Enríque asked to see the warrant (memory of the Sarabia kidnapping probably prompted the caution) and the arresting officer, Marshal Frank G. Thompson, grudgingly produced it. Enríque asked for his coat and hat, to which Thompson countered that he needed nothing. When one of the policemen produced the items, and Enríque reached for them, Thompson grabbed his arm and shoved him away, yelling, "Get back here, you son-of-a-bitch." Enríque criticized the vulgarity, and Thompson hit him; other policemen jumped Enríque, and, when he struggled, Thompson pistol-whipped him. The police then dragged the two prisoners away with Enríque bleeding from his head. The police had to stop at a hospital, however, where it took eight stitches to close Enríque's wounds.[46]

The Flores Magón brothers, Enríque as editor and publisher and Ricardo as author, were charged with violation of Section 211 of the U.S. Criminal Code for mailing obscene material contained in *Regeneración*. William C. Owen, in absentia, was included in the charge as editor of the English-language section. While the indictment specified three particular articles, the core of the case centered on Ricardo's essay about the PSD, which Carranza's agents had brought to the attention of American authorities. In its polished form, it began with "Justice, and not bullets is what ought to be given to the revolutionists of Texas."[47]

Ricardo's *compañera* María immediately sought help from fellow anarchists Emma Goldman and Alexander Berkman. The original bond of $3,000 (dollars) quickly raised to $7,500 (dollars), was more than the PLM could meet.[48] Berkman had left New York and *Mother Earth* to go to San Francisco where, early in 1916, he published *The Blast*. Through its pages, he called for financial aid for the Flores Magón brothers, and Goldman made the same appeal in her paper.[49]

The Los Angeles socialists organized a "Workers International Defense League" with Englishman Edgcumb Pinchon—coauthor with Gutiérrez de Lara of *The Mexican People: Their Struggle for Freedom*—as general secretary. Noting that the socialists stood opposed to the anarchists, they nevertheless pledged "to see to it that justice is secured to those who are giving their lives [the Flores Magón brothers] to emancipate the people."[50] Three other "progressive" Los Angeles socialists, who also subscribed to *Regeneración*, Dr. Percival T. Gerson, Mrs. Georgiana Kotsch, and J. D. Kaufman, joined the league. Pinchon affiliated the Los Angeles league with similar ones in San Francisco, Chicago, and New York in an umbrella group to defend freedom of speech wherever attacked.[51]

Yet, despite strong appeals, U.S. authorities frustrated solidarity efforts by suppressing other papers and arresting activists. These tactics forced radicals to fight on several fronts simultaneously. Beginning with the arrest of Margaret Sanger for "misuse of the mails" in making birth control information available through the *Woman Rebel,* federal authorities then apprehended labor organizer Elizabeth Gurley Flynn and anarchist Emma Goldman; denied mailing privileges for two issues of *The Blast;* and arrested the Flores Magón brothers. In the same ninety-day period, the U.S. government also attacked several anarchist publications—some of which they managed to suppress either completely or partially by revoking second-class mailing privileges. The papers included: *Mother Earth, The Blast, The Alarm,* and *Revolt* in English; along with the Spanish-language *Voluntad, Revindicación, Redención,* and *Regeneración.*[52] To dramatize the severity of the assault on the anarchist community in America, *Regeneración* printed a carefully drawn illustration that depicted a wild beast attacking doves flying out of a barn; the names of the victimized newspapers were inscribed on the wings (see Figure 16).[53]

Meanwhile, dissension between the PLM and IWW in Los Angeles further undermined the anarchist cause—both in the United States and in Mexico. Ricardo had to counter the influence of Juan Francisco Moncaleano, a Spanish anarchist who had come to Mexico from Cuba in June 1912, and who had been a co-founder of the Casa del Obrero Mundial in Mexico City. Moncaleano's Bakuninist anarchism favored centralized control and direction of small groups *(focos),* and he was an early admirer and defender of Ricardo. He especially applauded the September 23, 1911, PLM Manifesto. Moncaleano's activities earned him Madero's enmity, and he was expelled from Mexico in September 1912, making him the Casa's founding martyr.[54]

Moncaleano and his dynamic wife Bianca went to Los Angeles, where they continued their agitation and published their own newspaper, *Pluma Roja.* Through its pages, they vigorously denounced the Casa-Constitutionalist pact in early 1915, with the martyr accusing his former colleagues of betraying first principles in fighting for nothing more than "political and social reforms through the triumph of Constitutionalism." Moncaleano charged the Casa with supporting a faction that would become nothing less than the new state. *Pluma Roja* also denounced the PLM for failing to be more active in leading the workers to freedom, for failing to take the initiative of "propaganda by the deed."[55]

The acrimony between the Moncaleanos and the Floresmagonistas seems rooted in their differing conceptions of anarchism. As Bakuninists, the Moncaleanos favored central direction and "propaganda by the deed" to effect the social revolution. By 1915, Ricardo and the PLM leadership had discarded the old Bakuninist approach in favor of decentralization; they emphasized the collective efforts of the people in voluntary "direct action" as against the individualized and supposedly precipitous violence of "propaganda by the deed."

The Moncaleanos claimed that their differences with the PLM were those of the true believer versus the deceiver. The Moncaleanos claimed to have been sent to the Americas by anarchist comrades in Spain to ferret out the truth behind the Mexican anarchists. They charged the Flores Magón brothers with receiving and squandering over $500,000 (dollars) from various

Fig. 16. Poster of U.S. government closure of anarchist newspapers, with portraits of Ricardo and Enríque Flores Magón, 1916 (*Regeneracíon*, April 29, 1916)

anarchist groups from 1910 to 1915. The PLM anarchists were "fake" to the Moncaleanos and only participated in the movement for money. The failed Baja campaign served as sufficient proof for them that the PLM had used the IWW callously and failed to give the support needed for victory.[56] These claims, however distorted or false, nevertheless weakened the solidarity of the Spanish-speaking anarchist community in Los Angeles.

Despite Juan Francisco Moncaleano's failing health, he continued his attacks against the PLM, aided by Bianca's determination and forceful presence. They gained influence over the Spanish-language section of the local IWW and over its newspaper, *El Rebelde*. Thus, when Ricardo and Enríque were arrested, the local IWW offered them almost no support. A new coupon clipping campaign in *Regeneración* protesting the arrests garnered a poor response, 379 signatures, of which 143, or 37.7 percent, came from Los Angeles. Two-thirds of the signatures came from the PLM's women's section, "Luz y Vida" (42) and from the youth group, "El Grupo Juvenil Libertario" (50).[57]

"It is sad and disgraceful that the militant elements of Los Angeles permit Ricardo and Enríque Flores Magón to remain so long in jail, for lack of bail," wrote Berkman.[58] Labor solidarity on this issue continued to remain elusive. The PLM desperately missed the good offices of Anselmo Figueroa, who had been so important in winning early IWW support through its Spanish-speaking members. Figueroa's health had been seriously impaired during the nearly two year imprisonment he shared with the Flores Magón brothers at McNeil Island, and he died in 1915.[59]

Thus, despite an impassioned appeal in *Regeneración* to the IWW that its leadership and *El Rebelde* were mistaken about the brothers, coupled with a call for common cause against persecution by the U.S. government, the IWW remained unreconciled.[60] The Flores Magón brothers remained in jail, awaiting trial; they used the monies sent by such comrades as Emma Goldman to continue to mail *Regeneración* at the more expensive, first-class rates.[61]

In a comedy of errors, the Post Office Department thought that the Department of Justice would arrest William C. Owen[62] and Justice thought that the postal authorities would do it.[63] In the delay, Owen fled the commune in Lake Bay, Washington, where he had been living, made his way to New York, and from there returned to his native England. Owen had now quit his American adventure, and *Regeneración* had lost its most forceful English-language section editor.[64]

The Flores Magón trial began May 31, before Judge Oscar Trippet, and the issue of the defendants' anarchism arose immediately. As Enríque commanded better English, he spoke longer. "We are Indians; we are peons; . . . we are not bomb throwers . . . we became anarchists and are anarchists because we want peace on earth . . . amongst all the human race." Enríque expanded his remarks in a new direction showing his, and by extension Ricardo's, grasp of how to formulate their anarchism with reference to American symbols.

He and Ricardo left Mexico, Enríque told the court, because "there in the United States they enjoy freedom. . . . There in the United States there is a refuge for political refugees; their constitution grants freedom to all and of course, freedom of press and freedom of speech, so let us go over there. . . ." The Flores Magón brothers' experience in the United States, however, had been bitterly disappointing.

"What do you suppose," Enríque asked the judge, "[if] Tom Paine, Tom Jefferson, and Franklin had received the same treatment in France, the same treatment that we are receiving in this country[?] then [the] United States would not exist, there would not be the land of the free at all."[65]

The next day, Berkman published a photograph of the Flores Magón brothers on the cover of his newspaper, underscoring the image with excerpts from the offending articles as caption (see Figure 17).[66]

On June 6, the Flores Magón brothers were convicted on the second and third charges. On June 22, the defendants returned to the courtroom for sentencing. Judge Trippet observed:

> In the second count for which they have been convicted there is a manifest intention upon the part of the defendants to incite insurrection in the United States; . . . No one can read this article and not come to the conclusion that its every purpose was to incite, in the streets of Texas, where the paper is largely circulated, a state of insurrection against the Government, and against its people.[67]

Ricardo and Enríque had, in effect, been convicted of inciting the Plan of San Diego, Texas.

Trippet fined each man $1,000 (dollars) and sentenced Enríque to three years' imprisonment and Ricardo to a year and a day, both to be served at McNeil Island, Washington. Bail, pending appeal, stood at $5,000 (dollars) for Enríque and $3,000 (dollars) for Ricardo, which money they still did not have.

Enríque made an eloquent reply and appeal, not in the court, but in the pages of *Mother Earth*.

> The court has spoken of us as aliens to this country and its people. The court is in error. We are aliens to no country, nor are we aliens to any people on earth. The world is our country, and all men are our countrymen. It is true that, by birth, we are Mexicans, but our minds are not so narrow, our vision not so pitifully small as to regard as aliens or enemies those who have been born under other skies.[68]

Enríque continued to show just how far he and Ricardo had come as U.S. anarchists in their ability to formulate their cause in distinctly American terms:

> The lumber camps of Louisiana, the mines of Colorado and West Virginia . . . are practically the same as the hell-holes of Yucatan and the Valle Nacional. Here also you have the "commissary" which is the counterpart of our "tienda de raya," [company store]. Our massacres of Rio Blanco and Cananea have their parallel in Ludlow, Coeur D'Alene and West Virginia.

VOL. 1 SAN FRANCISCO, JUNE 1, 1916 No. 14

Ricardo and Enrique Flores Magon

JUSTICE and not bullets, is what ought to be meted out to the revolutionists of Texas; and from now on we should demand that the persecution of innocent Mexicans should cease. And as to the revolutionists, we should also demand that they be not executed.

"The ones who should be shot are the 'rangers' and the band of bandits who accompany them in their depredations.

"Enough of reforms! What we hungry people want is entire liberty based on economic independence. Down with the so-called rights of private property; and, as long as this evil 'right' continues to exist, we shall remain under arms. Enough of mockery!"

These utterances constitute the counts against the Magons. And for this they face from two to five years in the penitentiary!

Fig. 17. Ricardo and Enríque Flores Magón, with excerpts from U.S. Government's charges against them (*The Blast*, June 1, 1916)

In addition, Enríque invoked the symbols and words of Jefferson and Emerson to legitimate the work of the PLM. The Flores Magón brothers had become American anarchists.[69]

The publisher of *Mother Earth* came again to their rescue. Emma Goldman made it a point of principle that she would not return to New York from her West Coast speaking engagement until bail had been met and the brothers released. After lecturing and hectoring, she extracted that money from Angelenos, and Ricardo and Enríque returned, for the moment, to Edendale.[70]

In February 1916, the administrations of Carranza and of Wilson took decisive action against the Plan of San Diego; they apprehended leaders and followers in Monterrey and incarcerated the intellectual authors in Los Angeles. The Wilson administration had failed to make the conspiracy charge between the PLM and the PSD satisfy legal standards for prosecution. Nonetheless, an intuitive sense of conspiracy persisted among officials in the Post Office Department and in the Departments of State and Justice.

Carranza's successes proved temporary. Mexico, convulsed by civil war, could not be considered pacified despite his protests to the contrary. The men seized at "Las Espinas" and charged with violation of Mexican neutrality statutes never stood trial. Prisoners in the penitentiary in Monterrey escaped with such regularity that the guards had to be replaced frequently in hopes that men not susceptible to bribes or persuasion would keep those incarcerated in place.[71] Within that climate of disorder, American trust in Carranza would last only until the next raid; another raid would signify the further spread of anarchism.

In the predawn hours of March 9, 1916, Pancho Villa and five hundred followers crossed the border and attacked the American hamlet of Columbus, New Mexico, in an act unrelated to the PSD. The assault came at the wrong time for Carranza in his struggle for legitimacy with Wilson. Villa's raid crystalized American suspicions of foreign plots and intrigue involving Germany, Japan, Mexico, and the PSD; in the United States, it became the rallying point for those eager to strike back against America's enemies, real and imagined.

CHAPTER 8

THE PLAN OF SAN DIEGO: INTERNATIONAL CONNECTIONS AND CONFRONTATIONS

> It has become evident that the de facto government will neither use its own forces in any effectual way to protect the people of Texas, New Mexico, and Arizona nor permit us to take the steps absolutely necessary to protect them. There seems to be no alternative but to clear the northern States of Mexico, for the time being, of armed forces of every kind.
> Woodrow Wilson, To the Congress, June 1916[1]

Villa's attack upon Columbus underscored shortcomings in border security for which Americans immediately blamed Carranza. He either could not or would not keep hostile Mexicans in Mexico. Moreover, Villa's raid occurred when American officials, including the president, feared possible German intrigues to gain a naval coaling station in Mexico; they worried that German consuls in Mexico financially supported the Plan of San Diego, and they suspected German machinations behind Villa's American raid.[2] The drastic response of the United States was not to Villa per se but to the PSD and the anarchist unrest that threatened the border.

Public outrage over the murder of Americans in their own homes by Villa, building upon the previous raiding against South Texas, nudged Wilson to consider strong retaliatory action. The option of seeking Carranza's permission to send U.S. troops into Mexico in pursuit of the raiders was rejected—based upon awareness of Carranza's need to defend national honor. Wilson also mistrusted Carranza and sought an independent course. Therefore, the president tried a curious ploy. Within a day of the raid, Wilson sent a public message to the American and Mexican people that an adequate military force would be dispatched into Chihuahua after Villa with the sole object of capturing him. Nonetheless, when the president commissioned the force under General John J. Pershing, Wilson limited its objective to dispersal of Villa's forces.[3]

Wilson tied himself publicly to a policy fraught with possibilities for misunderstanding and failure. First, Villa could leave Mexico and thus leave the U.S. soldiers without a mission to fulfill or a reason to remain, unless Wilson had an ulterior motive. Second, since most of the cavalry in the continental United States had been redeployed to border duty in South Texas, Pershing's main force consisted of infantry—an ominous signal to Carranza that "capture" was occupation in disguise. Wilson's conflicting statements about the objectives of the mission could also lead to trouble. Whereas the private order for dispersal permitted the president, rather than the press, to evaluate the expedition's success, the public pledge to capture reversed this advantage and allowed the press to evaluate the outcome.[4] Moreover, maintaining the distinction between the pledge and the order depended upon a confidentiality that, if revealed, would further alienate Carranza and the Mexican people. With this inauspicious beginning, Pershing set out in pursuit five days after Villa's assault.

Despite the head start, Villa traveled slowly, suffering from a leg wound sustained at Columbus. Thus, Pershing's fast-moving advance cavalry column succeeded in surprising the retreating Villista force near Guerrero on the morning of March 29. In the five-hour engagement, the Americans killed thirty Villistas and sustained only four wounded. Carranza's troops, less organized and poorly provisioned compared to their U.S. counterparts, pursued Villa also. Carrancistas engaged Villistas at several points. Then, even as the joint pursuit continued in Chihuahua, reports from Nuevo León reached the Americans of a renewal of the Plan of San Diego.

Department of Justice agents, drawing upon their observations and conversations in Monterrey with members of the U.S. consulate, reinforced by the opinions of the Italian and Spanish consuls, concluded that the PSD would soon resurge; the PSD renewal would be funded in part by the German and Austrian consuls in Monterrey, by monies provided by the German embassy in Mexico City, and by Carranza himself.[5] Even the consul general in Monterrey, who generally ignored local rumors, was moved to write the secretary of state directly—warning of new agitation against Texas.[6]

These and numerous similar reports, including information about De la Rosa's and Pizaña's favored treatment of Germans, contributed to an American perception of a broad conspiracy against its border. The local consuls in Monterrey *were* Mexicanized Austrian and German settlers;[7] however, if they supported the PSD, they would have done so as free lances. They may even have agreed with the plan. Despite the welter of German plots in Mexico—many of them fostered by the German Minister Heinrich von Eckardt—no evidence has been uncovered of a centrally directed German conspiracy such as the Rintelen-Huerta affair. After Pershing and the Punitive Expedition invaded, however, Mexicans saw in Germans a natural ally in their shared resentment and even hatred of the Yankee.[8] Thus, Wilson administration officials viewed German activity in Mexico and Carranza with even more suspicion.

The resurgent PSD, however, contained African American and Japanese participants as the movement widened to embrace more of the ethnic elements the original ideology addressed. Jesse Mosley, an African American serving as a surgeon in the Constitutionalist army, joined the movement in Mexico City and traveled to South Texas, recruiting blacks around Austin and San Marcos. He had some limited success.[9] U.S. intelligence agents later linked his activities to support from the head of German propaganda in the United States, Heinrich Albert. Albert also spread news stories among blacks in the South of racial discrimination and lynching by whites.[10]

One Fukutaro or Fukumatsu Terasawa, representing General Pablo González, recruited among Japanese in Mexico for the Texas revolution. He promised prospective recruits between $3 and $5 (dollars) daily. In one appeal, he gathered four Japanese in Mexico City—all of whom had been working nights as guards for the Bank of London—and told them to report to the Buena Vista train station without documents and with only a single change of clothing. These men found seven or eight other Japanese—all military officers, including the son of a famous general—and fifteen Mexicans awaiting them. Terasawa, with three other Japanese, later joined them and introduced the group to its commanding officer, Lieutenant Colonel Maurillio Rodríguez—the same man who controlled the trains in Monterrey, and who provided liaison between Generals González and Nafarrate.

The group boarded a first-class coach on the Laredo train and picked up four or five more Japanese at Saltillo. After passing through Monterrey toward the border, the train stopped at a deserted station named Golondrina, where provisions had been warehoused in preparation for their arrival. Each man was issued a Winchester and one hundred cartridges. The next day, Constitutionalist soldiers brought the group horses—one for each man and extras to carry supplies. Lieutenant Colonel Rodríguez then decided to drill his assembly by staging a mock attack on the Constitutionalist forces at Lampazos. The attackers were to shout "!Viva Villa!" and the defenders were to reply "¡Viva Carranza!" while all parties fired their weapons in the air. All went as planned. Shunji Yoshida participated in the attacking party and, at Rodríguez's order, became the translator for the Japanese military men participating in this mock raid.

The group then went to the hamlet of Palofax on the river; there Yoshida saw a black guide waiting for them, sent by De la Rosa. Rodríguez readied his men to cross into Texas but sent Yoshida back to Monterrey with important messages to deliver personally. When he had completed his task, Yoshida was to return to Palofax and await Rodríguez. Yoshida watched the group cross the river at night late in January 1916, and then went about his assignment. While waiting for the group to reform at Palofax, Yoshida learned that it had crossed downriver at San Benito and that he was to rejoin it in Monterrey. In Monterrey, however, he and his companion were given tickets and pocket money, but no daily allowance, and told to go to Mexico City and hide. While in the capital, he heard that the Japanese officers in the party had gone to Veracruz en route to Cuba. Yoshida apparently did not then know about Rodríguez's arrest in Monterrey as part of Carranza's crackdown on the PSD.[11]

Although Terasawa had assured the original group that their operations against Texas had Carranza's full support, the fact that Yoshida and his companions had to hide after they got to Mexico City—beyond the effective control of the allies of González and Nafarrate—indicates the contrary. Carranza simultaneously needed to retain the loyalty of those generals and to defuse the PSD. Yet the Punitive Expedition pursuing Villa prompted González and Nafarrate to redouble their efforts in support of the PSD in Texas as a countermeasure to Pershing in Chihuahua.[12]

With the protection of Nafarrate, De la Rosa began actively recruiting around Ciudad Victoria in March and April; he was aided by Esteban Fierros, who was the superintendent of the railroad terminal at Tampico. Fierros, a Tejano, agreed with the PSD and, as an experienced staff officer, could support the movement logistically—as Rodríguez did. Moreover, with reports of renewed raids against Texas, coupled with uneasiness within the Mexican community along the border over the Punitive Expedition, general fear and suspicion increased. U.S. military authorities accused the *Brownsville Sentinel* of irresponsible journalism; and two Americans, whom the military considered reliable, said of De la Rosa's renewed activities, "he has been very ugly to Americans in [Ciudad] Victoria, even threatening their lives."[13]

Within Mexico, the tensions between the U.S. invaders and the host population degenerated into violence. While seeking supplies and forage in the town of Parral on April 12, Major Frank Tompkins and twenty men of the Thirteenth Cavalry suddenly encountered a sullen civilian crowd. At the exhortations of a woman, the crowd turned ugly, and, while the Americans tried to withdraw, gunfire rang out. Two of Tompkins's men died and six were wounded riding to safety. As a direct result of the Parral incident, President Wilson sent Army Chief of Staff General Hugh L. Scott and General Funston, commander of the Southern Department, to the border of El Paso/Juárez to confer with Carranza's representative—his new Secretary of War and Marine, General Obregón.[14]

Scott came to discuss border security and Carranza's cooperation with Pershing in Mexico; Obregón came to demand the immediate withdrawal of that expedition.[15] At one point, Scott showed Obregón the U.S. military record against Villa since Columbus. Carranza's record had been nearly as good, since, by May 3, Constitutionalists had engaged Villistas twelve times—killing 128, wounding 3, and capturing 68. Obregón, however, for unknown reasons, chose not to present the Mexican record;[16] this led Scott to regard the Constitutionalists as uncaring, incompetent, or worse. At this impasse yet another raid occurred.

A band of former Villistas, cut off from the main army and hunted in the mountains of Durango for nearly a year, broke free of their Constitutionalist pursuers and desperately rode toward the border. Their leader, Natividad Alvarez, had worked in the Big Bend region of Texas, at a place called Deemer's Store. On May 5, he divided the group of eighty men into two units and sent the larger band of sixty men to attack U.S. soldiers at Glenn Springs as a diversionary move. Meanwhile, he commanded the smaller group—which looted the store at Boquillas and kidnapped Deemer. During this action, the raiders killed two U.S. troopers, wounded three, and killed an eight year old boy.[17]

Given the raid and the impasse, Scott and Funston concluded that the conference with Obregón had been "redolent with bad faith" and urged the call-up of 150,000 U.S. militia.[18] President Wilson heeded their advice and ordered the men mobilized and sent to the border.[19] This mobilization far exceeded the 20,000 troops Taft had called up in 1911 and evoked among U.S. radicals and Mexican anarchists in the United States a fear of imminent invasion of Mexico.[20]

U.S. army troops under Major George Langhorne pursued the Glenn Springs–Boquillas raiders 168 miles into Mexico—capturing five and forcing them to release two of their kidnap victims. After ten days of pursuit, the army had scattered the survivors into two small bands. During this time, the army had not seen a single Constitutionalist, "which," the commander wrote, "goes to show the slight amount of effort that is being made in that section at least to suppress brigandage."[21] Meanwhile, the exchange of acrimonious diplomatic notes between the Wilson and Carranza governments intensified. Carranza took particular offense at the new U.S. invasion. He maintained that Langhorne's actions violated the promise made by Scott to Obregón that any future raiders would be dealt with by Constitutionalist forces.[22] As if this were not enough, PSD leaders and followers approached the border ready to fight.

For the PSD renewal, Esteban Fierros had been promoted to brevet general in the Constitutionalist army and brigadier general in the PSD. In turn, he commanded three generals: De la Rosa, the newly promoted Maurillio Rodríguez, and Gregorio Osuna. They began assembling a brigade in Monterrey in May, and then moved men and supplies into a depot at La Jarrita—nineteen miles south of Nuevo Laredo, Tamaulipas.[23]

A. Bruce Bielaski, chief of the Department of Justice's Bureau of Investigation, made an inspection of the border from May 17 to 29. Bielaski conferred with his own people and with General Funston and decided to add seven more agents to the payroll, including two in Monterrey.[24] Thus, U.S. military and civilian intelligence—augmented by information provided by Carranza's nephew, General Ricaut—tracked the PSD buildup.

In late May, one of Ricaut's subordinates arrested sixteen fully armed and mounted Constitutionalist soldiers who could produce no orders when asked. They had been discharged from Nafarrate's forces, allowed to keep their arms, ammunition, and clothing, and had been given verbal permission to approach the border. They were further instructed that they could act independently of any other command. Ricaut sent the suspicious group to Querétaro for imprisonment and further interrogation,[25] but he had already begun thwarting the PSD resurgence that all sources reported with increasing frequency.

Rumors persisted that all U.S. forces in Mexico would be attacked and that vulnerable points along the border would be assaulted—all by June 10.[26] To calm American fears and in a replay of Carranza's earlier visit, General Ricaut came to Nuevo Laredo and met at the midpoint of the International Bridge with General W. A. Mann at 8:00 A.M. on June 10. Ricaut exposed the recent buildup at La Jarrita, describing a railroad repair scheme there as a front for the formation of raiding parties by bandits. He pledged to take action against them. Although U.S. Consul Alonso Garrett believed Ricaut was operating in concert with De la Rosa, U.S. military authorities believed Ricaut was not.[27]

While Ricaut watched the activities at La Jarrita, he was also aware that De la Rosa had come to the line around June 6 with nearly three hundred men and made camp down river at Anzaldúa, across from Mission, Texas. New arrivals soon pushed the camp to over four hundred.[28] Petty bickering among the leaders at the border began to disrupt the PSD resurgence, however, even as it began. Fierros, with Rodríguez under him, commanded at La Jarrita; at Anzaldúa, Osuna began to give orders to De la Rosa that the Tejano refused. Osuna demanded command of the expedition, claiming that his rank in Carranza's army gave him authority over De la Rosa, whose commission derived from the PSD. The camp divided over the quarrel. Outraged, De la Rosa set out with a bodyguard for Monterrey, seeking vindication of his authority. And en route to Monterrey, Ricaut captured them.[29]

Nonetheless, disparate forays against Texas had already begun from La Jarrita. On June 8, a small group crossed the river and captured Simon Solis, a Laredo resident, working on a ranch outside of town. He was taken back into Mexico and impressed into service as a guide. Two nights later, the band of about thirty, commanded by Constitutionalist officers Lieutenant Colonel Villarreal, Captain Norberto Pezzatt, and two lieutenants, entered Texas.

At a point twenty miles north of Laredo, the group set about drenching with kerosene a railroad bridge near Webb, after having cut the adjacent telegraph wires. None of the men from Captain Pezzatt down learned of their mission until inside the United States. Although wearing their Constitutionalist uniforms, they carried a red flag with a white diagonal proclaiming "Equality, Independence, Liberty."

They had just begun to ignite the kerosene when a U.S. cavalry force, acting on a tip from recently hired American intelligence assets, intercepted them. In the skirmish Captain Pezzatt, Simon Solis, and one Antonio Cuevas were captured; the three other Mexican officers were killed; and the remaining force, with an undetermined number of wounded, fled. The Americans sustained no casualties.[30]

Pezzatt and Cuevas illustrated the strange composition of the renewed PSD. Pezzatt demanded to be treated as a prisoner of war and was outraged at being charged as a common criminal. He had joined Lieutenant Colonel Villarreal at the direct order of General Maurillio Rodríguez, and he had simply followed orders, as a soldier should, on the U.S. side of the border. Pezzatt even wrote a public letter to General Alvaro Obregón, Carranza's Minister of War and Marine, protesting his innocence, because he obeyed the commands of his superiors in the Constitutionalist army.

Cuevas, on the other hand, had spent time in Los Angeles where he had met the Flores Magón brothers and read *Regeneración* whenever he could; he joined the force at La Jarrita to avenge wrongs done to Mexicans and to liberate Texas. Americans, suspicious of Carranza, cited Pezzatt's protest as proof of Carranza's responsibility for border disturbances and ignored Cuevas. U.S. intelligence operatives noted that Cuevas' story confirmed their view of PLM conspiracy behind the PSD.

Five nights after the Webb raid, a group of seventy-five men under Constitutionalist Colonel Isabel de los Santos attacked a U.S. army camp at San Ignacio at 11:00 P.M. Unknown to the attackers, the detachment of Troop M of the Fourteenth Cavalry had been reinforced two hours earlier by Troop I, and the U.S. military repelled the attack despite brave leadership by Major Cruz Ruíz, who died in the fight.

De los Santos was a PSD adherent and partisan of De la Rosa who had equipped his unit well. Each man had been issued one hundred cartridges, and the Americans captured thirty-two bombs, forty-five pounds of dynamite, and five prisoners. The Mexicans, with Japanese participating, lost nine dead and four wounded; the Americans, four and fifteen respectively. The Constitutionalist commander stationed opposite San Ignacio offered to cooperate with the Americans, and he captured eighteen of the raiders, three of them severely wounded, and sent them under guard to Monterrey for trial.[31]

The San Ignacio raiders simultaneously demonstrated the breadth of PSD appeal and also its diminishing power. De los Santos had started for the border with nearly three hundred men but arrived with only sixty; desertions came upon learning the real reason they had been recruited. Those who stayed tended to be convinced of the correctness of the PSD.

José Antonio Arce, for example, sixteen or seventeen, had been a musician and orchestra member in Torreón before going to Ciudad Victoria in early June 1916. On June 5, he was sitting in the railroad depot when De la Rosa asked if he wanted work cutting wood in Matamoros. General Fierros joined them and paid Arce and others who volunteered $40 pesos in Constitutionalist money. They traveled by train to La Jarrita, where Arce was given $30 pesos more and incorporated into the command of Colonel De los Santos. He saw some men desert when they learned what they were to do, but Arce agreed with the PSD. He joined the attack at San Ignacio, but after discharging his first shot, his carbine hung fire when the spent shell would not eject. He flung the rifle aside and ran down the road, where two soldiers and two civilians later apprehended him.

Vicente Lira, seventeen, was sitting on a park bench in Ciudad Victoria when De la Rosa and Fierros came by. De la Rosa told Lira that he looked just like the kind of man he needed to go north; Lira joined. Benito Rodríguez, thirteen, came from San Luis Potosí, and, because of his youth, was left to handle horses during the attack. He became frightened after the shooting started, and, when the riders did not return immediately, he fled. The army picked him up.

Francisco de León, a twelve year old orphan, worked in the roundhouse in Monterrey when De los Santos found him and made him a house servant. At the San Ignacio raid, De los Santos and another man gave him their horses to hold. The boy held his ground until he saw two strange men running toward him; then he fled. When he got hungry, he wandered into the army camp, where soldiers collected a dollar in change for him. A native Spanish speaker with the army, possibly one of Canales's river scouts, got his story and then had him arrested.[32]

One Bureau of Investigation special agent recognized the critical role General Ricaut had played both in thwarting the PSD resurgence and in disrupting the Webb and San Ignacio raids before they could do more damage. In a report apparently not seriously considered by his superiors, the agent wrote that "Ricaut was highly instrumental in suppressing the border raids that were about to break out all along this part of the border. . . ."[33] Ricaut's absorption with the PSD activity upriver, however, left his own area unmonitored, making his territory vulnerable to disorder.

As the San Ignacio raid was beginning 180 miles away, about twenty-four Mexicans crossed the river near Brownsville. U.S. troops encountered them outside San Benito. The Americans fired into the group and later found one dead Mexican. General James Parker, in command at Fort Brown of the Brownsville District, ordered a force of fifty men, under Lieutenant A. D. Newman of the Third Cavalry, to pursue the raiders. Newman departed the fort at midnight on June 16, tracked the Mexicans to the river, and decided to cross by swimming his horses. A mile into Mexico, Newman and his troops clashed with the marauders, killing two and sustaining no casualties.

Parker had decided to reinforce Newman in Mexico. At 1:30 P.M. on June 17, he dispatched Major Edward A. Anderson with three troops of the Third Cavalry as well as a machine gun troop, accompanied by twenty infantrymen, two small boats loaded onto trucks, and a wireless transmitter. The expedition of two hundred men crossed into Mexico about 6:00 P.M. and marched toward Matamoros, making camp about seven miles west of the town. Parker, however, had exceeded his authority, and General Funston ordered the U.S. forces withdrawn next morning, June 18.[34]

Most of Major Anderson's forces, including the machine gun unit, recrossed the river without incident. With only one U.S. troop remaining, the Constitutionalist forces arrived and opened fire. Colonel Robert Bullard, the ranking officer, commanded a battalion of the Twenty-sixth Infantry regiment on the U.S. side, protecting Anderson's withdrawal. Bullard immediately ordered cover fire from the U.S. side and authorized the cavalry troop still in Mexico to return fire and give chase. The cavalry pursued the Constitutionalists, until losing them in the large dust swirl created by their horses' hooves. The Americans killed two Mexicans and suffered no casualties, adding further injury to the insult of occupation.

When Anderson's force crossed into Mexico and made camp, General Ricaut and his garrison evacuated Matamoros. Ricaut was put in a paradoxical position: to defend the national honor against foreign occupation and simultaneously to prosecute the PSD resurgence that both contributed to and was a statement against that occupation. It appeared that war was about to begin. Ricaut ordered the women and children out of the town immediately. Having presided over an orderly retreat, Ricaut ordered his men all along the line to fight the Americans if they crossed, and he so advised General Parker.[35]

Carranza's concern with the Texas border intensified after the San Ignacio raid, and in addition to his orders to Ricaut, he informed his other frontier commanders to be prepared for a conflict with the United States.[36] In Tampico, Nafarrate responded by claiming to have given orders to General Osuna both to pursue the San Ignacio raiders and to prevent Americans from crossing after them—a lying claim, since Nafarrate had endorsed Osuna's participation in the PSD resurgence. Nafarrate went further, however, offering to march to the line to battle the Americans, if Carranza would but give the order, and promising to enlist the aid of African Americans against the U.S. army if Carranza wished. The governor of Tamaulipas also offered to make armed, disaffected black Americans immediately available to fight for Mexico. Carranza refused.[37]

Carranza faced monumental problems in Mexico: a civil war that raged on several fronts, severe munitions shortages, economic collapse with attendant rising inflation, and a need for money to fund his incipient government and to buy articles of primary necessity. He faced a mighty problem on his northern border: renewed U.S. intervention. Carranza's inability to pacify the country permitted Villa to provide the pretext for the U.S. invasion; Carranza's continued inability to prevent further raiding offered renewed reasons to invade elsewhere, whether in pursuit of the Glenn Springs–Boquillas raiders or in the wake of the Webb–San Ignacio assaults.

Some of Carranza's most politically reliable subordinates, Generals González and Nafarrate, sought to tweak the Americans with the PSD; this further eroded Carranza's ability to deliver to the Americans what they demanded. Moreover, he could not appear too cooperative with the Wilson administration for fear of losing what support he had within his own faction. Carranza was truly in an untenable position. To win the domestic war, he needed foreign support in arms and money; but he could not obtain that foreign support, in part, because he had not won—he did not rule.

In coping with the frontier problem, Carranza stood firm. Publicly, Carranza insisted that Mexico's sovereignty be respected and that Pershing leave; privately, he did what he could to meet U.S. demands for action against Villa and the PSD while not alienating González, Nafarrate, and the Mexican people. Early in the pursuit of Villa, Pershing had asked for permission to resupply U.S. troops over a Mexican rail line. Carranza declined to answer publicly but privately permitted the activity as long as the consignees in Chihuahua were civilian.[38] After Parral and the failure of the Scott-Obregón conferences, however, Carranza was obliged to make more forceful demands for U.S. withdrawal, despite the border problems.

When pressed on the PSD, Carranza had Pizaña and others arrested in February. While the United States placed four requests before Carranza from May 23 to June 12 that De la Rosa be arrested for his anticipated participation in the PSD resurgence, General Ricaut succeeded in seizing him.[39]

For all his quiet cooperation, Carranza could secure no full American acknowledgment of his efforts. Americans placed in him neither confidence nor trust. Thus, he prudently prepared for hostilities between the two countries as he continued to try and survive. The clash that brought both countries to the brink of war came not along the line, however, but in Chihuahua.

The incident stemmed from the shame and resentment that many U.S. soldiers felt about Parral. In Major Tompkins' disciplined retreat, many saw a loss of "prestige" in Mexican eyes. To compensate, military patrols began to pass through towns and villages—against War Department orders to avoid all settlements. The patrols "had met with no resistance beyond remonstrance" until June 21, 1916, when Captain Charles T. Boyd and his troops tried to force their way through the town of Carrizal.

Boyd, who had joined his unit of the Tenth Cavalry in the field only a month before, deliberately disobeyed Pershing's verbal reiteration of the standing order to avoid towns. Instead, the white officer led his black troopers to Carrizal and told the Constitutionalist commander, General Félix U. Gómez, that he had been ordered to travel through the town. Gómez firmly but politely objected. Frustrated by the negotiations, Boyd turned to his interpreter and said, "Tell the son-of-a-bitch that I'm going through." The Mexicans resisted. In the battle, Boyd and six other Americans died while twenty-four fell prisoner.[40]

Since Carranza's military commander in Chihuahua had told Pershing on June 14 that the Americans could travel in only one direction—north, and since Pershing had given Boyd verbal instructions to avoid settlements, Pershing and the War Department initially presumed that the Mexicans had acted treacherously and were at fault.[41] The implications were grave. The day before the fight, Wilson had sent Carranza a long, strongly worded note in which he accused the First Chief of abetting and possibly supporting the various raiders who attacked the United States. It would be unreasonable, the note concluded, to expect U.S. forces to withdraw or not to reenter when their presence constituted "the only check upon further bandit outrages and the only way of protecting American lives and homes."[42]

When, on June 24, Carranza portrayed the Carrizal battle as the inevitable result of the failure of Wilson to withdraw U.S. troops,[43] Wilson countered with a demand for the immediate release of the prisoners and an early declaration of Carranza's intentions toward the United States.[44] Wilson followed the ultimatum with war preparations. He approved military contingency plans for an invasion and began drafting a declaration of war.[45]

Wilson's draft reveals his overarching concern for national security and the central issues as he saw them:

> If the lives of our people . . . are to be adequately defended, the daily peaceful course of their industry protected from intolerable interruption, and fear [i]s intolerable, it is necessary that the Mexican authorities be as active as we in such times as the present assuring their safety. But they are not; and they have not been. . . . Carranza opposed arguments of pride to arguments of necessity, points of form to points of fact, and offered promises in the stead of effective action.[46]

The president concluded his draft, composed and typed on his own machine, with a call for congressional authorization to use military and naval forces to protect the border and, if necessary, to enter the adjacent Mexican states and neutralize all military factions.

Wilson submitted his draft for comment to his secretary of war, Newton D. Baker, who had joined the cabinet the day of Villa's raid, and then brought it to Secretary of State Robert Lansing on the evening of June 28.[47] The president showed his message to select cabinet members, even though word had reached him by June 27 that Captain Boyd had been at fault at Carrizal.[48]

Wilson claimed that no genuine government had existed in Mexico since Madero's assassination. He saw the military action he now proposed as an assault against Carranza's pseudogovernment and other military factions, not as war against the Mexican people. In justifying the nobility of his proposal, the president wrote: "It does not lie with the American people to dictate to another people what their government shall be . . . , what laws or rulers they shall have or what persons they shall encourage and favor."

Lansing carefully wrote in the margin opposite this construction, "Haiti, S. Domingo, Nicaragua, Panama," preceded by a question mark. Before Lansing could confer with Wilson, however, the first news reached Washington that the prisoners had been released.[49] Carranza, not Wilson, had made the overture for peace.

Carranza's statesmanship in the war crisis stemmed from his appreciation of the international situation he confronted, combined with his recognition of the opportunity it presented to bolster his domestic popularity at a critical time. Had he been less politically ambitious and obstinate, he would have failed. The man who wore smoke-colored glasses in a darkened room, however, could see the glimmer of patriotism in the shadows of his faction. He had begun to accelerate his appeals to nationalism following Pershing's invasion. The real key to thwarting the PSD and his opposition, internal and external, lay in his success in appealing to national pride. If he could establish an exclusive claim as defender of national honor, then he could mobilize people to transcend their individual differences to support him.

Carranza had worked carefully since opposing Huerta to create his nationalist image. Carranza opposed the U.S. occupation of Veracruz and catered to antiforeign resentment when it helped him, as against the Spanish; he sought rapprochement where he thought it might be to his advantage, as with Japan and Germany.[50] The American pursuit of Villa gave Carranza an unparalleled opportunity to rally public support and he took it. He began to publish in Mexico, through his newspapers and official state bulletins, only those portions of his diplomatic exchanges with Washington that demonstrated his defense of the nation.[51]

Carranza's bid for renewed support within his faction bore fruit. Not only did his field commanders profess their fealty anew, but common people began to come together in the north to fight the Americans. In Tamaulipas, one thousand men volunteered to fight.[52] In Monterrey, Nuevo León, people organized a group called "Defenders of the Nation" (Defensores de la Patria),[53] and in Coahuila, a Constitutionalist officer reported that he could easily arm two hundred men if the Americans invaded.[54] In Chihuahua, where Pershing's column operated, creation of defense groups and anti-American demonstrations began in earnest after the Glenn Springs–Boquillas raids.[55]

Pershing's invasion strengthened Carranza's position within Mexico, but Carranza prudently did not aggravate the United States. As early as June 24, Carranza's foremost representative in Washington, D.C., Eliseo Arredondo, had urged the release of the American prisoners as the only way to avert war. And he continued so urging.[56] With Constitutionalist military commanders pledging loyalty,[57] but with scant food and little more to wage war than the cartridges soldiers had in the field,[58] Carranza decided to release the U.S. prisoners. He directed General Treviño to take the captives from Ciudad Chihuahua to Ciudad Juárez, where they arrived on the afternoon of June 29. Dirty and bedraggled, they crossed the international bridge into El Paso. Carranza's military commander at Juárez returned all captured equipment, including 3,236 8mm cartridges, too large to serve in the Constitutionalist rifles.[59]

Wilson found the act sufficient. The president, in an impromptu appearance before the New York Press Club on June 30, set aside the possibility of war with Mexico. Referring to a host of telegrams and advice from the American people urging that war with Mexico be avoided, Wilson remarked, "I am for the time being the spokesman for such people."[60]

Though the crisis had passed, the underlying issues had not been resolved. To Wilson, border security had to be actively maintained by Mexico; and to Carranza, the Americans had to withdraw. On June 30 and July 1, an unknown person contacted Victor Rendón, an unofficial Carranza representative in Washington, proposing that if Carranza were to appoint a commission to discuss the Mexican situation with Americans face to face, then "a result highly satisfactory to both parties can be obtained."[61] This unknown person, possibly even one of Carranza's own undercover agents operating in the United States,[62] asked that if Rendón favored the idea then Rendón should bring all his influence to bear to get Carranza formally to propose a commission to Washington. This person further suggested that Rendón approach Lansing indirectly, through a newsman called Cal O'Laughlin.[63]

As soon as he had been contacted, Lansing raised the idea with Wilson.[64] On July 8, Rendón told O'Laughlin that he had wired Carranza and others about the proposal and, although the reply had been ambiguous, Rendón thought that the commission would be appointed. He concluded, "now please get to work to get men appointed in the U.S. who are sympathetic to my country and will not put many obstacles in our way."[65] Lansing wanted to encourage the commission, and on July 9, General Treviño wired Carranza that foodstuffs could again be imported. The American secretary of state had relaxed the embargo.[66]

On July 12, Carranza proposed formation of a joint Mexican-American commission of three men from each country. The commission would be empowered to discuss U.S. troop withdrawal, negotiation of a reciprocal crossing agreement, and determination of responsibility for previous border raids. Wilson accepted, and then tried to expand the discussions to include "such other pending questions, the settlement of which would tend to improve the relations of the two countries."[67] After much pressure and intimidation, Arredondo said he thought that the commissioners would be able to discuss other subjects once Carranza's initial points had been resolved.[68] With that assurance, Wilson proceeded in his search for commissioners—a search that took nearly two months.

By the summer of 1916, anarchism in the PSD seriously threatened both the U.S. border and Carranza's leadership in Mexico. Crushing that anarchism would solve problems for both Wilson and Carranza; crushing that anarchism was what both men wanted. Yet, neither wanted to cooperate with the other to do it. Manipulation or intimidation—yes; cooperation—no. Hence, the delay to prepare for negotiations—the value of which neither leader could have been optimistic about—gave Carranza needed breathing room. The delay gave Carranza the opportunity to counter his most urgent domestic crisis—the threat of anarchism among urban labor organized under the banner of the Casa del Obrero Mundial.

CHAPTER 9

REPRESSING DISSENT AND

THE PLAN OF SAN DIEGO

As soon as Carranza felt himself the master of the situation, he kicked overboard his old friends the working men.
                                                                Enríque Flores Magón[1]

We believe that many Mexicans in this state [Texas], who have been killed without a trial lately, have been guilty of no other crime than being Mexicans.
                                     Rev. Fenón Moraida to Woodrow Wilson[2]

One of the ideas in making the further investigation was to ascertain . . . whether evidence can be produced connecting the [Flores] Magóns of California with these raids.
                                         John E. Green to U.S. Attorney General[3]

At present the Plan [of San Diego] is utterly dead and nobody is interested.
                      Marginal comment, author unknown, on report of U.S. agent Frank Fukuda[4]

Carranza's ultimate actions against the PSD went beyond the arrest of its leaders and adherents. Carranza moved against organized urban labor—his potentially most powerful factional opponent and one that contributed PSD members—by eventually denying the right to strike. Carranza claimed that strikes threatened Mexico's national security. He maintained his image in the eyes of U.S. progressives by posing as a labor reformer with a national mission to which labor must submit. Carranza also dismantled the administrative basis of PSD support within the Constitutionalist army and redeployed troops to the northern frontier to counter both the PSD and Villa. In short, Carranza's response to Wilson's demands for border security involved a comprehensive series of moves that helped Carranza eliminate the PSD and consolidate his faction. Meanwhile, repression of dissent in the United States, both against Mexicans and Tejanos in South Texas and against radicals in California and the nation, complemented Carranza's struggle in Mexico.

The search for members to fill the joint commission during the summer of 1916 gave Carranza the respite necessary to deal with organized labor in Mexico City. If he could succeed in taming the Casa del Obrero Mundial there, its branches would be silenced rather easily. His original rapprochement with the Casa had been through Obregón, the general in his faction seen as the most progressive on the labor question. Once the Red Battalions had been mobilized and the siege at Ebano won, however, Carranza moved to have them demobilized quickly. An armed labor force organized and imbued with a predominantly anarchist ideology could only become an internal threat that might defeat him. Although demobilized, however, the veterans continued to participate in their unions and to demand better wages and job security. Carranza claimed this was impossible as inflation spiraled and the civil war continued.

Casa leaders nevertheless organized demonstrations, usually in front of their headquarters at the House of Tiles, which generally ended in marches to governmental offices; frequently veterans demanded pay for having served in the Constitutionalist army. On February 1, 1916, to counter the growing unrest, Carranza had General González, an opponent of Obregón, close the House of Tiles and arrest anyone found there; Carranza had his regional commanders do the same at other Casa sites.[5]

Undaunted, Casa organizers intensified their labor-building efforts by pressing for their first national meeting in Veracruz, and convened it on the eve of Villa's assault upon Columbus. The attempt at forging a national association faltered, however, over the issue of anarchosyndicalism.[6]

Grievances persisted nonetheless, as real wages declined in the face of inflation and Carranza offered scrip instead of specie. Carranza forced private employers to do the same. The Mexico City Casa responded with the first general strike on May 22, which closed public utilities and public services for most of the day. Carranza mollified the Casa with a new meeting place and a pledge to pay workers in Constitutionalist paper money instead of scrip.[7] When June brought risk of war with the United States, Carranza needed to eliminate dissent within his faction if he were to survive.

Carranza unified his forces with an appeal to national honor and need. Even within the Casa, there had always been a strong sense of patriotism over internationalism. An erratic and sometime radical Mexican, Arnoldo Krumm-Heller, who served on one of the early directorial boards of the Casa, complained that when the workers assembled, they chose to open their meetings with the nationalist *Himno Nacional* rather than with the internationalist Song, *La Marseillaise.*[8]

The issue of Mexican national pride, which grew with the unfolding of the Revolution, had proven troublesome to internationalists such as Ricardo Flores Magón and the more radical members of the Casa; worker identification with a brotherhood beyond national borders generally required worker national identification as a first step. To recognize one's brothers, one first had to recognize oneself.

Antiforeign sentiment frequently constituted the basis of Mexican self-perception. Under Díaz, foreigners gained important economic and social advantages that ordinary Mexicans could not hope to achieve. Through actions that challenged economic discrimination against Mexican labor employed at foreign operations—which reached an explosion point at Cananea as early as 1906—Mexican workers could be organized. In the process of Mexican self-definition, to which *Regeneración* contributed and which the PSD simultaneously fed and reflected, antiforeign attitudes became more salient among disaffected Mexicans than feelings of international solidarity.

One privileged foreign group received special attention—the Americans. By 1910, Americans owned some twenty-two percent of Mexico's land surface; the Mexican Revolution can be seen as a struggle by the ordinary Mexican, rural and urban, to regain the national patrimony.[9] Carranza's appeals to national pride, in the face of a second American occupation in 1916, resonated with a broad range of Mexicans—from those who fought for the PSD or belonged to the Casa, to those who were disaffected or unaffiliated. The willingness and enthusiasm of people to form their own national defense units in the north testified to that growing sentiment, a sentiment with which Carranza sought to connect.

Within the Casa, some leaders such as Gerardo Murillo, better known by his pseudonym Dr. Atl, and Luis Morones began to see the interests of labor better served by affiliation with Carranza than by following an independent course. In effect, they accepted the need for a state, but one sympathetic to labor, in place of economic and political chaos. They cooperated with Carranza and responded to overtures from Samuel Gompers of the AFL for a meeting of labor representatives from both countries to pursue issues of mutual importance.

Gompers's interest seemed to be in creating a Pan American Federation of Labor (PAFL), whereas the Mexicans wanted aid in preventing further U.S. intervention in Mexico.[10] The conference coincided with the war crisis, and Gompers, fearing his plans would fail, sent a plea to Carranza for the release of the American prisoners. When Carranza released them for his own reasons, Gompers misinterpreted the act as a sign of his influence on Carranza.

The most important aspect of the interaction for the First Chief of the Constitutionalists, however, lay in the fact that Gompers chose to deal with Morones and Dr. Atl as the bona fide representatives of Mexican labor as opposed to the more radical members of the Casa.[11] Since Gompers represented the most conservative element in American labor, the leader most acceptable to Wilson, Gompers's acceptance of Carranza, while not in itself decisive, contributed to Wilson's acceptance of Carranza as legitimate.

By 1916, the Mexican economy had bottomed out, and the economic ravages intensified by summer.[12] Carranza strove to conserve the financial order by curbing inflation at the expense of urban workers. He again reduced real wages, and workers began to protest. When the Casa decided to call another general strike from July 31 to August 2, Carranza responded with action that unmistakably showed his determination to control organized labor.

Carranza had the Casa closed, arrested the members of the various strike committees, and issued a decree on August 1 outlawing labor organizing and cancelling the right to strike; henceforth, violators would be subject to the death penalty. Although only one Casa leader was sentenced to death—a prescription later commuted and reduced—the victory had been won by Carranza. He justified his act in the name of national interest—for the good of Mexico. Obregón had not interfered; Carranza now had claim to rule.[13]

Denying the working class the right to organize or strike should have been an important issue to U.S. labor; however, U.S. labor and some radicals accepted Carranza's act with little remonstrance. Gompers, whose AFL embraced nearly two million workers, had been preoccupied with his international conference and his attempt to get a labor man appointed to the Mexican-American Joint Commission.[14]

President Wilson chose not to respond to Gompers' lobbying and instead appointed Franklin K. Lane, his secretary of the interior; John Mott of the YMCA; and Judge George Gray. Carranza had appointed his representatives earlier. They were Luis Cabrera—his former confidential agent in Washington, D.C. and an attorney and writer—and two engineers, Ygnacio Bonillas, who had studied in the United States, and Alberto Pani, who had worked previously with Cabrera there.[15] Because of Wilson's delay in appointing commissioners, the first meeting of the joint commission took place on September 4, more than a month after Carranza's labor decree.

Gompers went to Atlantic City to meet with Cabrera and to get an accounting of Carranza's no-strike law. Cabrera assured Gompers that the issue was not one of labor—Carranza was still on the side of the workers—but rather one of national stability. The workers' demand to be paid in specie was a ruse; what they really wanted was the overthrow of the government. Gompers, after some wrangling, accepted the explanation, as did other Americans who could see no real alternative to Carranza.[16]

John Murray, one of the Los Angeles Socialists who had assisted Ethel Duffy Turner and Elizabeth Trowbridge on *The Border* in 1908–1909, had continued to sympathize with Mexican labor over the years but had come to support Gompers' idea of a PAFL. Murray had been in Mexico as an observer from late 1914 to early 1915 and been appointed to the Comité Revolucionario of the Casa. He had watched stonemasons being sworn into the Constitutionalist Army and shipped north for duty at Ebano. He had been at the joint conference in the United States in July 1916. While he approved of Gompers's visit to Cabrera to protest Carranza's no-strike edict, Murray's attitude toward Carranza still was to "wait and see."[17]

There was no other position, really, for U.S. labor to take. Eugene V. Debs, the leading socialist, had written off Ricardo Flores Magón, the PLM, and the anarchist approach five years earlier; Gompers had dropped them then, too. Carranza had made the pact with the Casa against Villa and Zapata, and that fact persuaded most of those in the American labor movement that Carranza should win U.S. support.

When Gompers presented the AFL's demand to President Wilson to extend diplomatic recognition to Carranza in late September 1915, nearly all major socialist newspapers reported the action favorably; some even endorsed it.[18] Carranza was the only faction leader who seemed to have a favorable position on organized labor, and it was this latter group, rather than the campesino, with whom American labor, for the most part, seemed able to identify.

Even former Los Angeles Socialist John Kenneth Turner, whose muckraking exposé of Yaqui Indian exploitation in the Yucatan had been made possible by his contact with Ricardo Flores Magón, came to endorse Carranza and the Constitutionalists.[19]

Thus, the border raids against Texas appeared to U.S. radicals to be a conspiracy by plutocrats to dupe the American people into supporting armed intervention in Mexico, an intervention disguised as national security but really aimed at protecting U.S. financial interests. Prominent radical writer and political cartoonist Robert Minor drew an image published in the *New York Call,* the socialist newspaper with the largest daily circulation, that depicted a fat American capitalist offering money to an armed Mexican and pleading, "For the Love of Mike, Raid Us!" (see Figure 18).

That American radicals failed to recognize in the PSD a movement by the

Fig. 18. Cartoon, "For the Love of Mike, Raid Us!" (*New York Call*, August 16, 1915)

disinherited to retake their land may have been due to a lack of familiarity with the Spanish language and the relative absence of socialists in South Texas.[20] U.S. radicals were not alone, however, in their lack of appreciation of the movement's significance. Even Ricardo Flores Magón, whose writings were as important to the articulation of the PSD in its formative stages as some of Carranza's subordinates were to maintaining it later, failed to understand its intent and misread it as self-defense.

If for American radicals the raids against Texas were instigated by American big business to produce intervention, then Villa's attack upon Columbus, which actually brought U.S. troops into Mexico after him, epitomized Wall Street conniving. An essay from *The National Rip-Saw* characterized the thinking of many:

> President Wilson well knows that the raids on the border are plotted by American conspirators to force intervention for the conquest of Mexico. He has himself issued warning against the false reports circulated by the newspapers controlled by these looting interests and calculated to inflame the American people against the Mexicans. Harrison Gray Otis and William Randolf Hearst are among these arch-conspirators who have secured fat concessions from the Mexican rulers to lend their support in suppressing the revolt of the Mexican people. . . . Otis and Hearst and their gang of American buccaneers are the conspirators and criminals responsible for Columbus and the border warfare.[21]

Continuing U.S. radical support for Carranza, despite his antilabor actions of early August, became necessary to counteract the schemes of American capital to exploit Mexico further. Lincoln Steffens had been a Carranza enthusiast for over a year and apparently persuaded Max Eastman, editor of *The Masses,* to publish a piece in the September issue praising Carranza's labor policy. It was written by a Constitutionalist propagandist.

The essay did not mention the August 1 decrees and falsely gushed, "under Carranza the workers are not only encouraged to organize, but their organization is part of his plan for the new State which he is trying to create."[22] Thus, misrepresentation of Carranza's attitude toward labor, coupled with the need for American radicals to resist further capitalist designs on Mexico by supporting a government there, combined to reinforce their support for the Constitutionalists.

Anarchists in the United States were not deceived, but they had a limited circulation to inform. Alexander Berkman saw through the article in *The Masses* and, in *The Blast,* printed as a rebuttal Carranza's decrees against labor organizing and the right to strike. Enríque Flores Magón, unable to print and ship *Regeneración* for lack of money, railed against Carranza's labor laws in the pages of *Mother Earth.*[23]

These organs, however, did not reach anywhere near as many people as the socialist papers. The anarchists, clinging to first principles, offered Americans no other party or leader whom they could support. In effect, anarchists told Americans to choose between correct behavior or Venustiano Carranza, between ideology or a person. It was not an American choice.

Just as radicals in Mexico had to confront the realities of growing nationalism, radicals in the United States in 1916 faced rising patriotism agitated by the Great War. International labor solidarity in Europe, sundered by national patriotism, failed to prevent or to stop that war.

In the United States, Preparedness parades were held in cities across the country to demonstrate readiness to participate in Europe's madness. At the time, Emma Goldman was making her annual summer lecture tour to California. In addition to her usual talks on birth control and women's rights and her impromptu pleas for funds for the Flores Magón brothers' bail and trial expenses, she had prepared a lecture on Preparedness from the anarchist perspective.

Goldman went to San Francisco, where she was scheduled to deliver her speech on July 22, but she deferred to others in that city who had planned a counterdemonstration to a large Preparedness parade. During the cavalcade down Market Street, a bomb exploded, killing ten and injuring forty more. The incident conjured the Haymarket specter of thirty years earlier. "I hope we anarchists will not again be held responsible," she exclaimed, but her hope was futile.[24] If she had given her speech on the subject, she might have been arrested for the bombing.

The police at first did try to blame her friend Berkman, since he was an anarchist, an ex-convict who had tried to assassinate a prominent businessman, an opponent of Preparedness, and publisher of a newspaper with an ominous name. Unsuccessful in bringing charges against Berkman, they trumped up a case against two men, Tom Mooney and Warren Billings, who were trade unionists but not anarchists. Berkman gallantly rallied to their defense and made theirs a national and international cause.

Overshadowed by the campaign to defend Mooney and Billings, the Flores Magón case receded into the background of anarchist and radical concerns. This was reminiscent of events five years earlier, when the trial of the McNamara brothers for the bombing of the *Los Angeles Times* building had diverted energies and monies from the Flores Magón and PLM trial for the Baja campaign. Government suspension of second-class mailing privileges meant that *Regeneración,* if it could be produced, would have to be shipped by an express company rather than by the postal service. In the wake of the Mooney case, lack of money prevented both, as the newspaper appeared only a few times in 1916 after the July 8 issue.

While national governmental repression of *Regeneración* and shifting anarchist priorities caused the PLM remnants and its newspaper to languish in obscurity, vicious local repression of Mexicans and Tejanos in South Texas became a scandal that drew Wilson administration censure. The Texas Ranger force operated in the lower Rio Grande with impunity, "rangering" suspects as individuals and company commanders saw fit.

In April and May of 1916, Department of Justice agents in San Antonio learned of another plot against Texas—this one to be led by former Constitutionalist and later Villista General José Morin. He had been recruited by a cousin of De la Rosa and had agreed to organize a band to cut rail and telegraph connections around San Antonio and then attack and burn the city. Morin pledged to do the same to other valley towns including Brownsville, Mission, and Kingsville.

When Morin decided to make Victoriano Poncé his chief operative in Kingsville, Poncé informed on him. Poncé, a former soldier turned baker, wanted no part of the conspiracy to promote an uprising among Mexicans and Tejanos living in South Texas. When Morin boarded a train in early May bound for Kingsville, Agent Howard P. Wright followed him, and arrested him when he tried to leave the train.

Wright took Morin to Kingsville and turned him over to local authorities. Wright also requested that Poncé be placed in protective custody. On the night of May 23, however, the sheriff of Willacy County took both prisoners from the Kingsville jail. Morin was charged with murder and Poncé with train wrecking. Outside of town, the sheriff turned them over to Texas Rangers from Captain J. J. Sanders' Company "A," and they were not heard from again. They were presumed dead.[25]

When a Laredo Spanish-language newspaper reported the "rangering" on its front page,[26] Mexicans and Tejanos in the valley found themselves desperate enough to protest. In Kingsville, a reverend Fenón Moraida brought a petition from his congregation protesting the incident to Circuit Judge T. Wesley Hook and asked that he write to the president of the United States.

Hook agreed with their complaint, signed it, translated it into English, and sent it to Woodrow Wilson. Describing the treatment of Morin and Poncé as typical, the petitioners claimed that many men being killed without trial were guilty only of being Mexican. The appeal concluded by "asking for the protection to which [we] are entitled under the laws of this country."[27]

Wilson, having been fully informed the previous fall about abuse of Mexicans in South Texas by lawmen, called for a full investigation of the incident by the Department of Justice. After receiving the department's report, he instructed Attorney General Gregory to confer with Texas authorities to find a way "in which we might effectively avoid any repetition of these distressing performances."[28] Wilson so advised Judge Hook and told him to thank local Mexicans for their law-abiding behavior.[29] Privately, the president instructed the War and Justice Departments not to surrender any further prisoners to Texas authorities.[30]

Unfortunately for Mexicans and Tejanos in South Texas, this incident was not yet closed. Captain J. J. Sanders, whose men had been responsible for Morin and Poncé, became enraged when he learned that Judge Hook had complained to the president. After several months of brooding—and following a morning of drinking alone in his hotel room—Sanders accosted the judge in his chambers in the courthouse at Falfurrias. Sanders demanded to know if Hook were the "son-of-a-bitch" who had written the president about the Mexicans. Hook acknowledged writing, whereupon Sanders drew his pistol and began striking the judge with it. Hook believed that if he had been armed, Sanders would have killed him. Upon discovering that Hook was unarmed, Sanders muttered an apology for drawing on a man without a gun and lumbered off.[31] He suffered no repercussions for assaulting the judge.

If a senior Ranger captain could pistol whip an Anglo circuit court judge in chambers with impunity, in the isolation of the chaparral he could do as he pleased with any Mexican. Ranger behavior scarcely improved. A Long Island chaplain, assigned to border duty in South Texas as part of Wilson's mobilization of the National Guard, reported a grim tale to the Department of Justice. Three rangers in an automobile visited a suspected raider in McAllen. "[T]hey invited the man to get into the car with them and without saying a further word to him, drove out into the country and shot him dead." When the chaplain protested to the Rangers that they should have gone through the courts, he received a preposterous response. "[T]hey said they could not do that because he would have been tried before a jury of Mexicans who would have acquitted him without regard to the evidence."[32]

Widespread fear among the Anglo population sanctioned such drastic Ranger acts. For local protection in the valley, General Parker encouraged the formation of "Civilian Home Guards" that summer. In Hidalgo, the immigration inspector reported, "The Americans sleep in the court-house, which is well guarded by U.S. soldiers and a machine gun."[33]

A real estate agent in San Diego wrote to the Department of Justice asking that a local newspaper, *La Gaceta,* be suppressed because of its inflammatory tone. It had "published an article branding the State Rangers as murders [sic] and called them assins [sic] too. This was on account of the good work they have done in this part of the country."[34]

As the repression of radicals, Mexicans, and Tejanos continued in California and Texas, the dialogue between Mexico and the United States, through the Mexican-American Joint Commission, grew uglier. The joint commission lasted only four months and adjourned sine die on January 15, 1917, without issuing a formal statement. Because of its failure to resolve the questions of border security and troop withdrawal, its import in other respects has been overlooked.[35]

The significance of the joint commission lay both in the intelligence provided to the American commissioners and in the pressure Wilson exerted through them upon the Mexican government. During the course of deliberations, reports from the Departments of War and State as well as Bureau of Investigation material were made available. Some of the U.S. suspicions were communicated to the Mexican commissioners. Thus, both sides learned of the actual orders that had been given to Pershing to disperse rather than capture Villa; both were shown evidence of complicity by some Constitutionalists in the border raiding and in the Plan of San Diego; both were told that Carranza had manipulated the PSD to gain diplomatic recognition; and both were shown damaging interpretive reports written by Agent J. B. Rogers. All of this information and conjecture reinforced the Americans' perceived need for border security.[36]

At the same time, Wilson tried to expand the joint commission's agenda to include a discussion of internal Mexican matters such as religious freedom and protection of foreigners' property rights. As could have been expected, the Mexican commissioners could discuss nothing until the U.S. troops were out of Mexico.

Nevertheless, the deliberations of the joint commission bought time for Americans to test Carranza's commitment to border security and for Carranza to consolidate his power. Carranza's first overt test came from Villa. Following the clash at Carrizal, Pershing pulled back and established a permanent base camp at Colonia Dublán, essentially allowing Villa free reign in the state of Chihuahua. With smuggled arms, Villa now slowly began mounting military actions against Carranza favorite General Treviño to discredit the hero of Ebano.

Treviño's military reputation actually rested on a slender base: he had survived a protracted siege in an entrenched position. Attacking was rather a novel experience to him. He was as militarily incompetent and venal as Pablo González. Villa clashed with Treviño's forces at Satevo on September 1, inflicted more than two hundred casualties, and routed the Constitutionalists north to the safety of the capital.

On the evening of September 15, while the joint commission met in Atlantic City, Villa struck Treviño at his headquarters in Ciudad Chihuahua. Treviño's personal bodyguard defected to Villa and Treviño fled. Upon retiring from the city, Villa took with him sixteen automobile loads of Constitutionalist weapons and ammunition. Treviño falsified the battle report on Satevo to read as a Constitutionalist victory and minimized the attack upon the state capital.[37]

Villa persisted in striking Constitutionalists both in garrison and in the open. He attacked quickly, showed his strength, and withdrew, probably because he lacked sufficient strength for occupation. In late October, he dealt Treviño's troops crushing blows at Cusihuiriachic and Santa Isabel. Treviño's ineptitude could no longer be tolerated, especially with the pressure on the Mexican commissioners to allow Pershing to move anew against Villa. Minister of War Obregón dispatched General Francisco Murguía north to take the campaign to Villa in the field.[38]

Murguía had a reputation for boldness and military perspicacity. He recognized that Villa repeated against Treviño the campaign he had waged successfully against Huerta in 1913. Villa had begun by isolating Ciudad Chihuahua, cutting its rail line as far south as Torreón, feinting against Torreón, and taking it if possible—only to fall back on the real goal, the unprotected and now unreinforceable Ciudad Chihuahua. Once ensconced there, Villa could take the state. Therefore, Murguía began by clearing Torreón, and then moved north against Villa, who was marching back against Ciudad Chihuahua. Villa bested a Treviño subordinate in a fierce contact and began to assault the city on November 23. After four days, Treviño evacuated Ciudad Chihuahua, abandoning cannon and supply trains to the enemy without a fight.[39]

Murguía had intended to catch Villa in a pincers between his forces and Treviño's, but the latter's retreat frustrated the plan. Although low on ammunition, Murguía boldly, perhaps desperately, pressed the attack. He engaged Villa's forces at Horcasitas on December 1 and, after bloody fighting, sent Villa reeling. Murguía, with his ammunition virtually exhausted, then entered Ciudad Chihuahua on December 2. Although Murguía vigorously denounced Carranza favorite Treviño to Carranza for cowardice and corruption,[40] Carranza nevertheless continued to resupply Murguía, provided him with scarce ammunition, and gave him a free hand in pacifying Chihuahua. With new supplies, Murguía returned to the fight, retaking Torreón, and giving Villa a pitched battle on January 3, 1917, that resulted in a decisive defeat for the Centaur of the North.

Carranza continued to fulfill his commitment to pacify the border by endorsing Murguía's campaign in Chihuahua; the campaign provided a second anchor to General Ricaut's stabilizing force in Tamaulipas. While the weak spot remained in Monterrey, Nuevo León, Carranza nevertheless found success there. In January 1917, Luis de la Rosa, along with others disaffected by the demise of Constitutionalist support for the PSD, conspired to seize the state government and to disavow Carranza and the Constitutionalists. Carranza's agents succeeded in infiltrating the movement, however, and arrested the conspirators before the plot could be implemented.[41]

The inherent incompatibility between the anarchist PSD and the Constitutionalist faction had been fully revealed. A dispirited Augustín Garza, speaking to a Japanese American who he did not know was working for U.S. intelligence, denounced De la Rosa's conspiracy, saying, "he is a fool and a drunkard. I did so much for him until now." Garza felt betrayed but was powerless to resuscitate the PSD.[42]

By supporting Ricaut and Murguía, Carranza had proven that he could protect the border and cope with domestic violence in Mexico. By mid-January 1917, all U.S. intelligence sources agreed that the border had experienced more than six months without a raid from Mexico, more than six months of relative peace. The reasons for improved conditions were more vigilant Mexican and U.S. military patrols and the effective elimination of the PSD.[43]

While Carranza pursued his enemies militarily, he also pushed toward the political victory of his faction. Beginning in mid-1916, as he moved to control organized labor, he simultaneously launched a propaganda campaign to declare the revolution over and himself the victor. He announced that to return to "legal order" municipal elections would be held in August in the territory under Constitutionalist control. Despite the narrowness of the franchise and local difficulties, Carranza went ahead with the charade.[44] The next step, according to his own Plan of Guadalupe, would have been the election of a national congress to whom the First Chief of the Constitutionalists would give an account of his service and surrender his power.

Instead, Carranza decided to convoke a constituent assembly to forge a new constitution. The Constitutionalists, like the original Liberals before them, had begun with the idea of restoring the Constitution of 1857. Whereas Ricardo Flores Magón and the anarchist splinter of the PLM had then gone on to reject all constitutions, Carranza now called for a new one to reflect the altered realities of Mexican life. The formation of a national congress would be determined later by the procedures set forth in the new law.

By a decree on September 14, Carranza scheduled the election of the constituent assembly for October 22, with the body to meet for two months in Querétaro beginning December 1. As with the municipal elections, Carranza restricted eligibility for office to those loyal to him. He declared ineligible anyone who had held military or political office in an opposing faction, or who had lived under enemy rule subsequent to Huerta's coup d'etat on February 22, 1913.[45]

Carranza's electoral moves, despite the flim-flam, played well in the White House. During the Carrizal crisis, Wilson remarked, "we do not know whether it [the de facto Government] represents the people of Mexico or not. We shall not know until it has been judged at the polls."[46] Carranza's actions helped build the basis for U.S. acceptance of the legitimacy of his regime. Moreover, through radical elements in the newly formed Constituent Assembly, Carranza secured the intersection of his traditionalism with militant nationalism in one of the most powerful political symbols created in the Revolution: Article 27.

Article 27 of the new constitution pledged to return the subsoil rights to the nation. This act promised to elevate the power of the Mexican state before the community of nations that had previously enriched itself at Mexico's expense. Article 27 simultaneously stimulated national pride and solidified the growing bond between the Mexican people and Carranza's Constitutionalists. In addition to Article 27, the draft constitution also promised a very liberal policy toward organized workers, helping to mollify the disaffected segments of labor. Carranza publicly appeared to resist the more liberal proposals winning the day at Querétaro but privately encouraged their articulation.[47]

This was a cunning strategy, because the constitution, whether in draft or after it was promulgated, would need enabling legislation to implement its articulated goals. A president would have to call upon a congress for the legislation to make the constitutional vision a reality. By itself the constitution changed nothing but promised a great deal. Carranza's faction appealed to much popular sentiment with the new document, but the redemption of the promises depended upon future political acts. While the draft constitution won friends for the Constitutionalists in Mexico, it earned enemies in the United States who feared loss of foreign assets to a "Bolshevick" Carranza.

The theory behind Article 27 owed nothing to Bolshevism, however, and everything to ancient Hispanic practice by which the king owned the nation's subsoil and conceded use only of the surface. Díaz had repudiated that concept in 1884 when he opened Mexico to foreign investment; Carranza now wanted the right restored but did not want to appear responsible. The convention at Querétaro also extended the process of return to "legal order" that Carranza had announced both to Mexico and to Wilson. Thus, the convention seemed like an act of national unity and healing.

By mid-January 1917, despite the failure of the joint commission to solve mutual problems, Wilson had reason to be satisfied with Carranza's recent performance. Carranza had at last dealt effectively with Villa and with the PSD, proving his willingness to secure the border, and he was returning Mexico to rule by law. Given the American president's concern with the European war and with German submarine warfare, Mexico's problems were of secondary importance as long as the boundary was not violated. Wilson decided to withdraw Pershing and, by February 5, the last U.S. troops departed Mexico—the very day that the new Mexican Constitution of 1917 was promulgated. Nevertheless, if tensions in the American-Mexican dialogue had seemingly relaxed, mutual suspicion soon resurfaced with the disclosure of a strange German offer to Mexico.

Germany had decided to resume unrestricted submarine warfare and to announce that strategy on February 1. Among the German leadership were some who feared that the announcement would make Wilson finally decide to enter the war on the side of the Allies. To thwart that effort, and in light of Pershing's inability to capture Villa, German Secretary of State Arthur Zimmermann sent a secret telegram to Carranza. Zimmermann proposed that in the event of a German-American war, Mexico should join the conflict as an ally of Germany "on the following basis: joint pursuit of the war, joint conclusion of peace. Substantial financial support and an agreement on our part for Mexico to reconquer its former territories in Texas, New Mexico, and Arizona." Mexico was to invite Japan to join this alliance.[48]

The British intercepted the telegram in mid-January 1917, decoded it, and gave it to U.S. Ambassador Walter Hines Page in London in mid-February. The British hoped that it would bring the United States into the war but feared a compromise of their intelligence collection sources and their cryptographic capabilities in releasing it. Nevertheless, a highly indignant Wilson chose to release it to the U.S. press on February 28, and the ensuing outcry against Germany overcame previous pro-German or anti-interventionist feelings.

The Zimmermann Telegram, with its curious affinity to aspects of the PSD, revived the question of German ancestry posed by Pizaña to Dodds' companions and by De la Rosa's accomplices aboard the derailed train. The proposed inclusion of Japan invoked the issue of Japanese participation in PSD raiding. The telegram confirmed the worst U.S. fears of foreign conspiracy against property and order and appealed to the deep hopes of some Mexicans that a powerful ally against the *gringo* could be found to redress their grievances.

Carranza claimed not to have received the Zimmermann Telegram and so refused American pressure to disavow publicly that which he said he did not have. Privately, he admitted that he feared that the risk of war with the United States was very high.[49] Carranza continued with his version of the electoral process, running unopposed for president and winning the election on March 11; it was the first presidential election in Mexico since Madero's. He took office formally on May 1, and, there being no one in Mexico legally above him, he administered the oath to himself.[50]

Carranza, despite some pressure from Wilson through his new ambassador Henry P. Fletcher, had won the U.S. president's sufferance. The Zimmermann Telegram brought the United States into the Great War, and Wilson left Mexico to Carranza, but with reservations. The arms embargo remained, causing Carranza much difficulty in providing his forces with the arms and ammunition needed for victory. Moreover, the PSD and Villa's resurgence had forced Carranza to rearrange his battlefield priorities—to put the campaigns against Zapata and a host of other insurgents on hold—while he dealt with the security concerns of the United States.[51]

Across the border, as the United States mobilized for war abroad, the Wilson administration sought to minimize dissent at home. Radicals, foreign-born or native, would have to be limited in their political expression. The administration had already established a link between the PLM and the PSD that it could not, however, prove in court. Thus, a war footing entailing suspension of conventional guarantees was required to make accusations toward the Flores Magón brothers and *Regeneración* tenable.

Proving a conspiracy became easier after the passage of the Espionage and Trading with the Enemy laws in 1917. The powers of each of these acts were extended by the Sedition Act of 1918. Mere discussion of radicalism sufficed to send speakers to jail and to suppress newspapers and magazines. Moreover, radicals in the United States, as elsewhere, responded with great enthusiasm in the spring of 1917 to the revolution erupting in Russia that eventually removed that country from the war. The United States, engulfed in a "Red Scare," vigorously denied freedom of speech to radicals and dissenters—and deported aliens among these groups en masse.

Attorney General Gregory and Postmaster Burleson worked quickly against domestic critics, having acquired their skills through the PSD and PLM investigation and trial in 1916. A weakened PLM, which could publish *Regeneración* only fitfully, however, was not their central concern. Their chief initial target was long-time PLM ally, the IWW. Burleson secretly created an index of "any anticapitalist remarks" it had published that could make IWW material unmailable.[52] This standard applied equally to the PLM and eventually was used against it.

On March 16, 1918, *Regeneración* carried a Manifesto addressed to the PLM Organizing Junta, anarchists of the world, and all workers. It announced, in part, that the days of capitalism were coming to an end, and that the revolution in Russia would affect the world. The Manifesto was signed by Ricardo and by Librado Rivera. Although by PLM standards the message was fairly mild, the new laws enabled the U.S. government to make this the last issue ever of *Regeneración*.

On July 19, 1918, Ricardo was sentenced to twenty years in jail for his conviction on charges that included conspiracy; publishing false statements tending to interfere with the success of U.S. military and naval forces and to incite mutiny among the same; mailing indecent materials and using the mails to transmit unmailable materials; and printing in a foreign language matters dealing with politics without filing a translation with the Post Master!⁵³ The sentence was to be added to the one Ricardo was waiting to serve for his 1916 trial; the verdict represented the real judgment that the government had wanted against *Regeneración*'s publishers then but could not secure.

Ricardo's trip to prison must have been filled with even greater bitterness as the revolution in Mexico continued to go Carranza's way. Through General González, who used a subordinate, Carranza was able to secure Zapata's assassination from ambush. Carranza eliminated a charismatic rival and left Mexican agrarian anarchists in disarray.⁵⁴ From Leavenworth Penitentiary, however, Ricardo also watched Carranza fall. In 1920, the Mexican president could not fully relinquish his power as the Maderista "no reelection" slogan had commanded. Carranza tried to impose upon the country one of his own men, Ygnacio Bonillas, formerly of the 1916 Mexican-American Joint Commission.

Obregón thought that the presidency should belong to him, and he declared against Carranza—initiating the possibility of renewed civil war. It is difficult to tell precisely at what point Carranza's fierce determination and persistence—traits that had enabled him to weather the extraordinary crises within his own faction and with the United States from 1915 to 1917—had become megalomania.

With his attempt to impose Bonillas, Carranza even alienated González. Most of the army rallied to Obregón, and González joined his former enemy in rising against Carranza. The former First Chief tried to repeat his earlier successes by fleeing to Veracruz by train with a small military group commanded by the valiant General Murguía. Forced from the train by Obregonista soldiers, Carranza sought refuge in the mountains. But his ersatz savior, one Rodolfo Herrero, murdered him in the night.⁵⁵

Obregón's political instincts had been to heal, to extend pardons, and to make deals to assure peace. Mexico had seen too much struggle, too much devastation, and too much bitterness. Obregón even offered Carranza a pardon, one that would have saved Carranza's life, but the old man was too stubborn to take it.⁵⁶

Through an interim government, Obregón made peace with most of his old enemies, including Villa. The Centaur of the North received a pension and a ranch in the state of Durango, outside of Chihuahua and its politics. Obregón wanted to reconcile dissidents to consolidate his rule, and he encouraged a rapprochement with Ricardo through Antonio Díaz Soto y Gama, former advisor to Zapata.

Díaz Soto y Gama had been an admirer of Ricardo's from the days of the First Liberal Congress in 1900, and, although he professed anarchist communism, he was malleable enough to run for office and to win election to the Chamber of Deputies. He was not rigid in his radicalism.⁵⁷ Thus, he secured from the congress approval to award a pension for Ricardo Flores Magón and Librado Rivera in 1920, following the Obregonista peace.

Ricardo could not accept it, of course, but he answered Díaz Soto y Gama in a way that was gentle but clear. He described a view that differed from his own without the sarcasm and disdain that had been the hallmark of his earlier writings.

> They [the Chamber of Deputies] are right because they believe in the State, and consider it honest to impose taxes on the people in order to sustain the State; but my point of view is different. I do not believe in the State; I support the abolition of international boundaries; I fight for the universal brotherhood of man; I consider the State as an institution created by capitalism to guarantee the exploitation and subjugation of the masses. Consequently, all money obtained by the State represents the sweat, anguish, and sacrifice of the workers. If the money would come directly from the workers, I would accept it with pleasure, even pride, because they are my brothers. But coming through intervention of the State, after having been demanded—according to my conviction—from the people, it is money that would burn my hands and fill my heart with remorse. My appreciations to Antonio Díaz Soto y Gama in particular, and to the generous deputies in general. They can be sure that with all my heart I appreciate their good wishes; but I cannot accept the money.[58]

Ricardo remained true to the first principles of his anarchism without denouncing the offer as an example of moral turpitude. He seemed to have modified his traditional penchant for bile.

His prison letters reveal both a growing facility with English and a tendency to poetic expression in the language. At the same time that he declined Díaz Soto y Gama's offer, he wrote to an American anarchist:

> How far we are from the cave man and yet how near, too. We can sail the air; we are able to talk [to] each other through space; we know how to wind up the lightning round a spool, and compel it to work for us; we have even chased the gods away from the heavens and have suspended from the stars the silvery hammock of our dreams to voluptuously rock in the blue. . . . Yet, our jurisprudence does not differ in essence to that founded on the night of time by a thief at the shout: "This is mine!"[59]

Ricardo also, however, remained proud and stubborn. Friends tried to secure a pardon for him after the war but were thwarted in their efforts—in part, because he refused to ask for one. He would ask the State's pardon for nothing![60] Moreover, he commanded the respect of a wide spectrum of political prisoners at Leavenworth, ranging from Mexicans and Mexican Americans to IWW poet and writer Ralph Chaplin. The "Kropotkin of Mexico," as Ricardo came to be known, was admired for his devotion to his ideals.[61]

His health, however, which had been severely tested during his early prison days in Mexico, deteriorated further in American cells. Both he and U.S. government officials knew that the 1918 conviction carried a sentence that would last long enough for death to take him before he saw freedom. He apparently had diabetes and received only desultory care for it. His eyesight faded because of cataracts, and in mid-1922, he began coughing up blood. In the early morning hours of November 21, a prison aid found him suffering from convulsions in his cell. Before a doctor could arrive, Ricardo died, apparently of a heart attack. He was forty-nine or fifty.[62] Despite charges by Rivera, and later Enríque, that Ricardo had been murdered in his cell by prison guards, there is no evidence to sustain their accusations, other than their wish to view Ricardo as a martyr.[63]

News of Ricardo's death stirred strong reaction in Mexico. Obregón wanted to bring him back for burial, but María Magón would not allow it until the Railway Workers offered to bring his body back at their expense. In January 1923, Ricardo returned to the country he had fled nineteen years earlier. Everywhere the train traveled, crowds assembled to pay their respects. In death, he became vastly more popular than in life.

In the Chamber of Deputies, Díaz Soto y Gama eulogized his friend in words that have persisted ever since. "Ricardo Flores Magón . . . is the precursor of the revolution, the true author of it, the intellectual author of the Mexican Revolution. . . ."[64] The warmly motivated and generous encomium for a friend—and a man whom Díaz Soto y Gama deeply admired—ultimately, however, eroded that friend's legacy. It was the word "precursor" that created the damage. Ricardo could have been a "precursor" only to Madero, and in the Mexico of Obregón, nothing could have been better. The label became a subtle but progressively more pronounced semantic swindle.

The term "precursor" is an example of the historical fallacy of "presentism"—of mistaking how things turned out for how they were supposed to turn out. Madero won the initial stages of the Mexican Revolution for many reasons—not the least of which was the Bakuninist, conspiratorial Ricardo was turning to Kropotkin and adopting a more open approach to anarchism and its realization. Ricardo did not precede Madero the way John the Baptist preceded Jesus of Nazareth. Ricardo competed with Madero and represented an alternative to him, but an alternative that failed. PLM-initiated violence began the overthrow of Díaz and antedated the movement that Madero eventually claimed.

By making Ricardo a "precursor," Díaz Soto y Gama softened Ricardo's differences with Madero and underscored his reformist stance. In short, the "precursor" label made it possible for Ricardo's enemies, who wanted to consolidate the power of the State, and his well-intended, but tender-minded, friends to agree.

This image of "precursor" aptly suited the need of Obregón and his successors, who had won the Revolution, to consolidate power by minimizing the factional differences of the past. As years passed, Zapata became the symbol of the agrarian revolution, and his rejection of Madero and Carranza overlooked, so that his opposition to Díaz could be stressed. In the retelling, Villa, the symbol of vaquero Mexico, who also died from ambush in 1923, became the arch opponent of Díaz, devoted follower of Madero, and implacable hater of Huerta. Villa's defection from the Constitutionalists and his battles with Obregón and Carranza were downplayed. From Obregón on, the official governmental view of the revolution has slowly homogenized into an alliance of high-minded men who made common cause against the two certifiable villains of the story, Díaz and Huerta. This is a memory useful to the State.

Since the victors needed peace to rule, an orderly change of government became imperative to preserve the State. Following Obregón's assassination, his successor and collaborator Plutarco Calles created the National Revolutionary Party (PNR) in 1929 as a single umbrella organization embracing, supposedly, the entire political spectrum. In 1938, the charismatic leftist President Lázaro Cárdenas, who implemented Article 27 of the Constitution of 1917 and expropriated foreign oil holdings, changed the structure and name of the organization to the Party of the Mexican Revolution (PRM). To carry the "precursor" definition to its logical extension, Ricardo had to become in death what he had never been in life—a supporter of the State.

Thus, Ricardo's remains were reburied on May Day of 1945, in the Rotunda of Illustrious Men in Dolores Cemetery in Mexico City.[65] Ricardo—the reformer—was now a national hero. Seven months later, the one-party system was renamed the Institutionalized Revolutionary Party (PRI), completing the pacification with a deception that Kropotkin had warned revolutionaries against so many years before—a contradiction in terms.

CHAPTER 10

CONCLUSION

> Who is he who does not bear in his soul an overcrowded graveyard of withered hopes and dead dreams?
> Ricardo Flores Magón[1]

The Plan of San Diego did not die a natural death; it was strangled by the military and political authorities of the U.S. and Mexican governments. The two governments, however, did not work together as had those of Taft and Díaz. Although Wilson and Carranza sought similar ends, they worked in an atmosphere charged with mutual distrust. It is an atmosphere that has never fully cleared, a climate that has permeated U.S. relations with Mexico for more than seventy years. Despite banishing the PSD and the anarchism that informed it from the national consciousness of both countries, the residual consequences of the movement have lingered.

Ricardo Flores Magón and his followers could never have foreseen this alienation between governments dedicated to the same end: capitalism. To Ricardo, capitalism meant an international conspiracy characterized by coherent recognition of self-interest and logical pursuit of its ends. For Wilson and Carranza to mistrust one another and for Wilson to fail to aid Carranza consistently in pacifying Mexico to restore order for business, seemed beyond belief from an anarchist perspective. Perhaps it is because so many aspects of the history of the PSD go against expectations and challenge stereotypes that assessing the movement and its impact has been particularly difficult.[2]

The central conundrum is that the Plan of San Diego was simultaneously a particularly Mexican and a singularly American expression. Yet, it has been denied a place of recognition among the great political Plans of the Mexican Revolution, and it has earned no place in the history of U.S. working-class radicalism. The PSD has been orphaned, abandoned by the practice of writing national histories that stop at national boundaries. Nonetheless, the PSD constitutes an unknown but significant chapter in the history of international anarchism. It is only by viewing the PSD and frontier anarchism in the larger context of Borderlands history, a perspective that permits a binational, bicultural focus, that the full complexity of the phenomena emerge.

The significance of the PSD for Mexican history lies primarily in its impact upon the events now called the Mexican Revolution. To quell the PSD, a goal insisted upon by the United States under the threat and eventual act of invasion, Carranza had to invest his efforts against border raiding rather than against domestic factional rivals. At the insistence of the U.S. government, Carranza had to make his first priority the stopping of a movement that was allegedly acting on his behalf.

Given his limited resources, Carranza could only comply by restricting campaigns against his sworn enemies. Thus, coping with the PSD from 1915 to 1917 prolonged the civil war by at least two years. Wilson's lack of confidence in Carranza further extended the duration of the war; the American president withheld aid and full support, thus delaying even more Carranza's pacification of Mexico. The PSD, through its influence on U.S. diplomacy toward Mexico, helped to shape Carranza's ultimate victory. Wilson, however, saw that victory as tainted, because he suspected that Carranza himself, as well as Germany and Japan, had manipulated the PSD.

For the United States, the PSD was a nightmare of Mexican national and international intrigue. The revelations of the Zimmermann Telegram simply confirmed Wilson in the course he was already pursuing in Europe. The telegram, however, seemed also to confirm earlier suspicions of a different nature. Japanese involvement in Mexico, including relations with the PSD, played a part in the Lansing-Ishii negotiations of 1917.

On the surface, the agreements reached in those talks ostensibly recognized Japanese interests in China. Yet the discussions also encompassed U.S. interests in Latin America, particularly Mexico. Lansing explained the Wilson administration position to the Chinese minister: "It was manifestly an axiom that geographical propinquity necessarily gave nations special interests in their neighbors . . . the axiom held good the world over, [and] . . . we . . . recognized it in our relations on this continent."[3]

Thus, the Lansing-Ishii accords acknowledged the United States' "special interest" in Mexico as much as Japan's "special interest" in China and signaled the Japanese to back away from military activity in Mexico. Great power rivalry in the Borderlands characterized the era of the Mexican Revolution as much as it did the Spanish Empire.[4]

Anarchism had unrecognized success in the United States–Mexico borderlands. Despite the repression by Díaz-Taft and Carranza-Wilson, Mexicans and Americans attempted to implement anarchism twice between 1910 and 1917. The PLM-IWW Baja California campaign that ended in the seizure of Tijuana was the forerunner of the PSD movement in South Texas. The PSD represented a second chance, an opportunity to correct what had gone wrong in Tijuana.

The second chance, however, came in different circumstances and was directed at different conditions. While, from an anarchist perspective, both actions attacked capitalism, the PSD aimed specifically to smash an American form of exploitation. The PSD represented an American anarchist response—South Texas anarchist style—to a specifically American condition.

Pizaña and De la Rosa were Tejanos who led other Tejanos and Mexicans[5] in a cry of "¡Basta Ya!" against the encroaching forces of white economic and social discrimination. Collectively these women and men shouted "¡Basta Ya!/No Further!" against the taking of their land and water; against the decline in intermarriage and the accompanying intensification of subordination and exclusion; against the advance of the railroad and steam pump; and against the erosion of the positions they had won in this American frontier society.

Their cry of outrage and defiance came both from the American tradition of protest against injustice and from the Mexican sense of *justicia,* combined with emerging national pride. *Regeneración* and the PLM helped these Tejanos and Mexicans articulate their complaint and direct their anger.

By 1915, *Regeneración,* with its circulation overwhelmingly in the United States, had become an American newspaper. *Regeneración* had increased its attention to American ethnic and economic discrimination against Mexicans and Mexican Americans and propagandized against those injustices. By 1915, the propaganda of *Regeneración* had helped to mobilize marginalized Americans and Mexicans for political action against the governments of the United States and Mexico.

By the time of their 1916 trial, the Flores Magón brothers demonstrated that they had become American anarchists; they made their propaganda by invoking American as well as Mexican symbols. Their appeals were genuinely binational and bicultural. The Flores Magón brothers had indeed become dangerous men.

Moreover, they were recognized and treated as dangerous by Carranza and Wilson alike. Carranza used U.S. neutrality statutes to rid himself of the PLM and sent his own representatives to finger the Flores Magón brothers for U.S. authorities. The Americans saw the link between the PLM and the PSD, which Ricardo did not, and eventually put Ricardo away permanently for it.

While Ricardo and Enríque were not bomb-throwing anarchists, they were serious about overthrowing the state; they succeeded in influencing people to rise violently against capitalism in South Texas. The Flores Magón brothers succeeded in getting Tejanos and Mexicans, African Americans and Japanese, to protest with armed force against American economic exploitation and social discrimination.

The Americanization of *Regeneración* and the Flores Magón brothers raises important questions for those who study the formation of the community of Mexican ancestry in the United States. What happened to the anarchist elements in those individual communities? Were they swept away in the repression accompanying the PSD?[6] Did they change their minds, becoming more conservative over time? Did they, alternatively, go underground, preserving their ideals privately within their families, thereby giving the

Chicano community a later militancy? Seeking answers to these questions suggests a new direction in Chicano scholarship.[7]

The Plan of San Diego was a potentially international revolution, led and made by people who were Americans by birth, and informed by Mexican anarchists who, through their life experiences in the United States and their command of English, had become American anarchists. The PSD was not an external conspiracy directed by enemies of the United States, but a domestic response to exploitation. PSD repression required the cooperation of the armed forces of both Mexico and the United States, just as the repression of Ricardo and Enríque Flores Magón and the PLM required the legal apparatus of both countries.

For Borderlands history, the PLM anarchist Manifesto of September 23, 1911, is a document Mexicans as well as Americans need to confront; so also is the February 20, 1915, version of the Plan of San Diego. Americans need to recognize their role in the shaping of the Mexican Revolution and in closing off dissent against it. Perhaps the topic of anarchism and the Plan of San Diego offers an appropriate starting point from which Americans and Mexicans might discuss, and embrace, our shared past; an appropriate starting point for considering what happened to frontier anarchism.

Repressing anarchism in Mexico and the United States from 1900 to 1922 did not destroy the ideas or the ideals of anarchism. In his pathbreaking study *The Anarchists,* James Joll devotes a chapter to discussing leading nineteenth-century libertarian thinkers as "secular saints." He argues that, in their personal lives, Kropotkin, Malatesta, and others embodied nearly aesthetic devotion to their ideals.[8] By Joll's standard, the Flores Magón brothers would have qualified as well.

In the twentieth century, however, the legacy of libertarian thinkers has taken an ironic turn. Anarchism failed in the Russian Revolution and in the Spanish Civil War, not to mention in Mexico and the United States. Whereas secular political victory has eluded the anarchist movement, the libertarian emphasis on the dignity of the individual and on personal liberation has found expression in the late twentieth century in religious thought. To invert Joll's observation, libertarian thought has helped to produce contemporary Christian saints; they can be found among the practitioners of Liberation Theology.

Liberation Theology, with its emphasis on personal dignity, equality of the sexes, and freedom from economic exploitation, shares many objectives of libertarian thought. The "preferential option for the poor" of Liberation Theology differs little from anarchist concern for the "disinherited of the earth." Developing awareness among the oppressed is similar in both approaches. As one of the major works on Liberation Theology describes the process:

> The poor can break out of their situation of oppression only by working out a strategy better able to change social conditions: the strategy of liberation. In liberation the oppressed come together, come to understand their situation through the process of conscientization,[9] discover the causes of their oppression, organize themselves into movements, and act in a coordinated fashion.[10]

Liberation Theology's focus on empowering the poor is frequently explicitly Marxist in its analysis, and anticapitalist in its criticism of existing economic conditions. Liberation Theology is also implicitly antistatist in its condemnation of government that perpetuates the status quo and does not alleviate poverty and suffering.

None of this is to say that Liberation Theology is simply anarchism. Anarchist communism, however, is very close to the concept of Christian Base Communities, the building blocks for putting Liberation Theology into practice. This religious movement, developing strongly in Latin American countries, has been influenced significantly by anarchist history.[11] The more militant exponents of Liberation Theology call for use of force against oppression—for revolution—a call that is virtually identical with Ricardo Flores Magón's sense of "direct action"; some militants even claim to have found religious justification for communism in the Bible.[12]

The emergence of Liberation Theology in Mexico and elsewhere in the mid-1960s can be understood, in part, as a consequence of the repression of anarchist ideas and movements in the opening decades of the twentieth century. People have feared their loss of personal freedom as the power of the state has grown. As the French philosopher Jacques Ellul noted, every successful revolution since the celebrated French eruption of 1789 has resulted in increased power for the state and diminished freedom for the individual.[13] Anarchism and libertarian thought rail against that trend; such railing protest has been the source of anarchism's enduring power.

Dismissing anarchism as impractical because it has never succeeded is a bit like dismissing Christianity because the teachings of the Sermon on the Mount have not been realized. The normative power of each philosophy endures despite the seemingly endless struggle towards fulfillment. Repressing anarchism succeeded for a time as long as anarchism was misperceived as unruly violence. The power of anarchism resurges at the close of the twentieth century but this time reinforced by a new, unexpected authority: religion.

As a philosophy, anarchism's claim to truth lay in its analysis of economic and social exploitation coupled with a sweet-spirited belief that raising consciousness would bring the downtrodden to seize their liberty. This belief depended upon unlimited confidence in the perfectibility of human nature. As long as anarchism was a philosophy, its first principles rested upon a system of thought; in the form of Liberation Theology, first principles rest upon a system of individual conscience motivated by commitment to protect the sacred.

While practitioners of Liberation Theology are every bit as convinced of the righteousness of their cause as any anarchist, they differ from anarchists in a fundamental way: the source of their belief. Liberation Theology is rooted in faith in the Christian God, which God, along with all others, anarchists denounce. Yet that God and Christianity not only justify but compel the behavior of those practicing Liberation Theology. Since their individual behavior, their personal sincerity, is an outward sign of their internal commitment to God, no personal sacrifice is too great. The potential body of believers in Liberation Theology is far greater than the potential body of believers in anarchism, because Liberation Theology identifies with the Christian tradition—that tradition anarchists condemn.

Repressing Liberation Theology, then, will be even harder than repressing anarchism; success can only be temporary. Thus, an accurate assessment of anarchism in the past, of the success and failure of the PLM and of the PSD in the U.S.–Mexico Borderlands, is essential to inform our thinking about anarchism, in its varied forms, in the future.

NOTES

A NOTE ON TERMINOLOGY

1. Waldseemüller, *Cosmographaie Introductio*, passim. The Italian navigator was Amerigo Vespucci.
2. Carl Degler in his presidential address to the American Historical Association in December 1986 indicated that "No one, so far as I know, has suggested an alternative term, such as 'United Statesian'—a literal translation of *estadounidense*. See his "In Pursuit of an American History," p. 1, n. 1.

INTRODUCTION

1. I use his first name many times in the text to differentiate him from his brother Enríque and to alleviate the cumbersome requirement to use his full name, Flores Magón. In Spanish, Ricardo's father's name is Flores and his mother's maiden name is Magón; his full last name is a combination of the two and an abbreviated version would be Flores. In the United States, Americans generally and mistakenly called him Magón, taking the second name, his mother's, to be his father's. To call him Magón would perpetuate a mistake, and to refer to him repeatedly by his full name is awkward. My compromise is based upon the Brazilian practice of refering to politicians by their first name to imply familiarity, not the American practice which might seem patronizing.
2. Sandos, "The Plan of San Diego: War and Diplomacy on the Texas Border, 1915–1916," p. 8.
3. The Bureau of Investigation preceded the Federal Bureau of Investigation in the Department of Justice. R. L. Barnes, agent in charge of investigating the Plan of San Diego, described his thinking in a "hasty outline of the department's view of the Plan of San Diego" in his letter to John Green, U.S. Attorney, Houston, November 28, 1916, Mexican Claims, #139, RG 76, WNRC.
4. Barnes called it "the official organ of the movement." Ibid.
5. Salvatore, *Eugene V. Debs*; Weinstein, *The Decline of American Socialism*; Cantor, *The Divided Left*; Kraditor, *The Radical Persuasion*; Goodwyn, *Democratic Promise*.
6. For example, see Avrich, *The Modern School Movement; An American Anarchist; The Haymarket Tragedy;* and *Anarchist Portraits*.

CHAPTER 1

1. Guerrero, *Artículos literarios y de combate*, p. 104.
2. Among the large body of literature on Ricardo Flores Magón, see Amezcúa, *¿Quien es Flores Magón?* p. 15; Abad de Santillán, *Ricardo Flores Magón*, pp. 1–4; and Langham, *Border Trials*, p. 7.
3. Avrich, *The Haymarket Tragedy*, pp. 204–205. This is the finest account of the incident and its aftermath.

NOTES TO PAGES 4–14

4. Avrich, *The Haymarket Tragedy*, pp. 270–272, 415–427.
5. *Mother Earth*, November 1916, pp. 674–675.
6. Langham, *Border Trials*, p. 7.
7. On the Liberal–Conservative background see Hale, *Liberalism in the Age of Mora*; on Díaz' popularity see Ruíz, *The Great Rebellion*.
8. Bartra, *Regeneración, 1900–1918*, p. 55. The title means regeneration in English.
9. Amezcúa, *¿Quien es Flores Magón?* p. 20. Langham, *Border Trials*, p. 7 follows him.
10. Cockcroft, *Intellectual Precursors of the Mexican Revolution*, pp. 92–116.
11. Poole, *Land and Liberty*, p. 126.
12. Hart, *Anarchism and the Mexican Working Class, 1860–1931*, pp. 60–87. This is the best study of the subject in any language.
13. Cockcroft, *Intellectual Precursors of the Mexican Revolution*, pp. 65–95.
14. Cockcroft, *Intellectual Precursors*, pp. 96–97.
15. For sound general and specific discussions of anarchism and its relationship to other political thought on the left, see Woodcock, *Anarchism*, and Joll, *The Anarchists*.
16. Poole, *Land and Liberty*, p. 126. Belén de los Mochas, a former nunnery, had been appropriated by the Liberals in 1862 and made into a prison. See *Diccionario Porrúa*, primera ed., p. 180. Some writers have mistakenly labeled it Belem.
17. Cockcroft, *Intellectual Precursors*, pp. 251–252.
18. *The New Republic*, July 5, 1922, p. 162, an excerpt from one of Ricardo's letters.
19. Larralde, *Mexican American: Movements and Leaders*, pp. 114–115.
20. Cockcroft, *Intellectual Precursors*, pp. 77–80.
21. Cockcroft, *Intellectual Precursors*, pp. 118–119.
22. Raat, *Revoltosos*, pp. 17–19.
23. Woodcock, *Anarchism*, pp. 154–155.
24. Joll, *The Anarchists*, pp. 76–79; Avrich, *Anarchist Portraits*, pp. 32–52.
25. Cockcroft, *Intellectual Precursors*, pp. 119–120.
26. Raat, *Revoltosos*, p. 190, n. 38 corrects Cockcroft who claimed that Díaz used Pinkerton detectives.
27. Raat, *Revoltosos*, p. 27.
28. Gómez-Quiñones, *Sembradores*, p. 50.
29. A convenient English-language translation can be found in Cockcroft, *Intellectual Precursors*, pp. 239–245.
30. Cockcroft, *Intellectual Precursors*, pp. 123–124.
31. Cited in Raat, *Revoltosos*, p. 27.
32. Raat, *Revoltosos*, pp. 65–91 is the best available treatment of the incident.
33. Raat, *Revoltosos*, p. 81.
34. Raat, *Revoltosos*, pp. 121–122.
35. In June the PLM issued a circular, "General Instructions to the Revolutionaries" which called for an armed uprising if and when a strike occurred at Cananea or any other PLM active site. Similarly, armed insurrection should follow any arrest of a junta member. Raat, *Revoltosos*, p. 93. Instructions exceeded capabilities.
36. Gutiérrez de Lara and Pinchon, *The Mexican People*, p. 329.
37. Cockcroft, *Intellectual Precursors*, p. 147.
38. Raat, *Revoltosos*, pp. 142–145.
39. Ferrua, *Gli Anarchici nella Rivoluzione Messicana*, is the best analysis of his life. See also *Diccionario Porrúa*, primera ed. p. 659.
40. Guerrero, *Artículos literarios*, p. 107.
41. Guerrero, *Artículos literarios*, pp. 103, 101, in order of presentation. The Zapata shrine in Chapultepec Park, Mexico City so mistakenly attributes it.
42. Guerrero, *Artículos literarios*, pp. 106, 97, 100, in order of presentation.
43. Gómez-Quiñones, *Sembradores*, pp. 33, 79 n. 91. He places the total number of *grupos* between forty and sixty-four, with thirty armed *focos*.
44. Ricardo Flores Magón to Enríque Flores Magón and Praxedis Guerrero, June 13, 1908, cited in Cockcroft, *Intellectual Precursors*, pp. 162–163. Albro, "Ricardo Flores Magón and the

Liberal Party," pp. 122–123, identifies the offending Sarabia as Tomás, Manuel's brother. Many conspiratorial letters were written in this period and later revealed. See Abad de Santillan, *Ricardo Flores Magón*, pp. 44–45.

45. Cockcroft, *Intellectual Precursors*, pp. 152–153. Hart, *Anarchism and the Mexican Working Class, 1860–1931*, pp. 100–101.

46. Albro, in "Ricardo Flores Magón and the Liberal Party," p. 174 and n. 27, says that he heard Guerrero's version separately from Ethel Duffy Turner and Nicolás T. Bernal in Mexico in 1965. Ferrua, in *Gli Anarchici nella Rivoluzione Messicana*, p. 108, discusses the incident and concludes that the episode remains "somewhat enigmatic" and is marginal to his study of Guerrero. Nevertheless, the issue seems critical to understanding future relations among the brothers and Guerrero. Had Guerrero expressed his view of Enríque's cowardice to Ricardo then, Ricardo, despite his extraordinary admiration and love for Guerrero, would undoubtedly have unleashed the full fervor of his venom against Guerrero. It is also quite possible that Guerrero had contradictory thoughts on the matter. Malingering is hard to prove. Enríque's inexperience and anxiety could have led to an accident. Even experienced gunmen such as the Texas Rangers inadvertently inflicted wounds upon themselves during the course of the uprising in South Texas. See Capt. H. L. Ransom, Texas Ranger force, to Adjutant General Henry Hutchings, November 27, 1915, reporting a private accidentally shooting himself in the fleshy part of the thigh while putting his rifle in its scabbard. See also Hutchings' reply November 29, 1915, Adjutant General's Records, General Correspondence, TSA, stating that a similar incident had recently occurred in another Ranger company. It seems that once Guerrero decided that Enríque had malingered, Guerrero held his suspicions to himself for the most part but allowed the incident to distance himself gradually from Ricardo.

47. Albro, "Ricardo Flores Magón and the Liberal Party," p. 137 and n. 27. Many of these same Spanish speakers joined the IWW and through Figueroa supported the PLM.

48. Turner, *Barbarous Mexico*, p. 5.

49. Turner, *Barbarous Mexico*, p. 6.

50. *Diccionario Porrúa* (primera ed.), p. 666. Pinchon, *Viva Villa*, second page of [an unpaginated] Forward.

51. Sinclair Snow, Introduction, to Turner, *Barbarous Mexico*, pp. xv–xvii. Hart, in *Revolutionary Mexico*, p. 308 and in his Introduction to MacLachlan, *Anarchism and the Mexican Revolution*, p. v, makes the point that Murray was a spy who informed to American authorities on anarchosyndicalist and radical labor organizations in the United States and Mexico during the first two decades of this century. Murray's case was a bit more ambiguous than the term "spy" suggests. He was a Los Angeles socialist who gradually came to adopt the more conservative labor views of Samuel Gompers and the American Federation of Labor (AFL). While he did, in time, inform on the activities of radical organizations, it does not appear that he did so clandestinely, as did the spy for the Furlong Detective Agency who had infiltrated the PLM print shop in St. Louis. Murray's involvement with radicals was not an automatic case of betrayal to governmental authorities.

52. Snow, Introduction, to Turner, *Barbarous Mexico*, pp. xv–xvii. Langston, *Border Trials*, p. 25.

53. Eugene V. Debs to Fred Warren, March 7, 1910, Debs Papers, M 565, r 1.

54. Snow, Introduction, to Turner, *Barbarous Mexico*, pp. i, xix–xxv.

55. Gompers, *Seventy Years of Life and Labor*, vol. 2, pp. 307–309.

56. Raat, *Revoltosos*, p. 51.

57. Eugene V. Debs to Fred Warren, February 1, 1910; in the same vein see also the correspondence of February 5 and 8, which indicates that Warren agreed, Debs Papers, M 565, r 1.

58. Eugene V. Debs to Fred Warren, July 8, 1910, Debs Papers, M 565, r 1. Underlining in the original.

59. Dubofsky, *We Shall Be All*, p. 81.

60. Salvatore, *Eugene V. Debs*, pp. 207–209.

61. Ruth Teiser interview with Ethel Duffy Turner, BL.

62. Raat, *Revoltosos*, p. 116. Cockcroft, *Intellectual Precursors*, p. 161.

63. *Regeneración*, September 3, 1910.

NOTES TO PAGES 20-29

64. Here I follow some of the semiotic ideas articulated in Nadin, ed., "The Semiotics of the Visual: On Defining the Field," pp. 174–177, 187–211, 215–225.
65. Joll, *The Anarchists*, p. 142.
66. Woodcock, *Anarchism*, pp. 338–339.
67. *Via Libre* (1905), *El Proletariado Militante* (1901), and *El Pueblo* (1909). Tarrida del Marmol does not appear to be represented.
68. Woodcock, *Anarchism*, pp. 187–188.
69. Another of his titles, *Mis exploraciones en América* (1909), is visible in the book in the top border.
70. My thinking has been provoked by Hobsbawm, "Man and Woman: Images on the Left," especially pp. 84–87, 96–98.
71. Well-discussed in Avrich, *The Modern School Movement*, pp. 3–50.
72. The original title could have been written by any one of a number of anarchosyndicalists in French, Spanish, or Italian. See also Joll, *The Anarchists*, pp. 180–182.
73. Mexican Liberal Party, *Land and Liberty: Mexico's Battle for Economic Freedom and Its Relation to Labor's World-Wide Struggle*, frontispiece.
74. Anselmo Figueroa, Librado Rivera, and Antonio de Pío Araujo were the others represented with the Flores Magón brothers. For more on them see Cockcroft, *Intellectual Precursors*, pp. 71, 79–80, 146, 162.
75. Joll, *The Anarchists*, p. 143.
76. Kropotkin, "Revolutionary Government," in Baldwin, ed., *Kropotkin's Revolutionary Pamphlets*, p. 247. Emphasis added.

CHAPTER 2

1. Manifesto to the Workers of the World, April 3, 1911, by the Organizing Junta of the Mexican Liberal Party, reprinted in *Solidarity*, April 22, 1911, official organ of the IWW.
2. Cumberland, *Mexican Revolution: Genesis under Madero*, pp. 46–54. Womack, *Zapata and the Mexican Revolution*, pp. 10–14.
3. Anderson, "Mexican Workers and the Politics of Revolution, 1906–1911," pp. 94–113.
4. Cumberland, *Mexican Revolution: Genesis under Madero*, pp. 114–115.
5. Cumberland, *Mexican Revolution: Genesis under Madero*, pp. 116–118.
6. Cumberland, *Mexican Revolution: Genesis under Madero*, pp. 121–123.
7. Reprinted in Abad de Santillán, *Ricardo Flores Magón*, pp. 65–66. Among those joining the Flores Magón brothers in signing the document were Antonio Villarreal and Praxedis Guerrero.
8. Cumberland, *Mexican Revolution: Genesis under Madero*, pp. 125–126.
9. See Chapter 1, n. 46. Guerrero told two people of his suspicion about Enríque and it seems significant that one of them was both a *gringa* and a socialist. Thus, Guerrero communicated his concerns *outside* the junta, signifying his unhappiness with that group's actions. In addtion, he could not have been happy with the mixed messages conveyed in the September 10, 1910 issue of *Regeneración*.
10. Cockcroft, *Intellectual Precursors*, pp. 178–179.
11. Ferrua, *Gli Anarchici nella Rivoluzione Messicana*, reprints Ricardo's articles from *Regeneración*, pp. 127–133, and gives his own assessment, pp. 121–124.
12. Raat, *Revoltosos*, pp. 58–59.
13. Ruth Teiser interview with Ethel Duffy Turner, BL.
14. Raat, *Revoltosos*, p. 57.
15. Cockcroft, *Intellectual Precursors*, pp. 179–183.
16. *Regeneración*, December 24, 1910.
17. Abad de Santillán, *Ricardo Flores Magón*, p. 59.
18. Sanftleben, *Utopie und Experiment* (1897).
19. *Regeneración*, December 24, 1910.
20. *Freedom*, December 1922, p. 81.
21. *Regeneración*, February 25, 1911.
22. Turner, *Ricardo Flores Magón y el Partido Liberal Mexicano*, p. 239.

23. *The New York Call*, February 27, 1911.
24. Cumberland, *Mexican Revolution: Genesis under Madero*, pp. 132–133.
25. Reprinted in *Mother Earth*, April 1911, pp. 47–49.
26. *Regeneración*, April 8, 1911. See also note 1 above.
27. Ricardo Flores Magón to Eugene Debs, April 6, 1911, in *Regeneración*, April 15, 1911.
28. Ruth Teiser interview with Ethel Duffy Turner, BL.
29. *The New York Call*, April 12, 1911.
30. *Regeneración*, September 30, 1911.
31. Good descriptions of Owen are found in Reichert, *Partisans of Freedom*, pp. 512–519, and the two obituaries in *Freedom Bulletin*, September 1929, pp. 4–6.
32. The IWA, its structure and methods are discussed by Cross, *History of the Labor Movement in California*, pp. 158–165.
33. Hine, "A California Utopia: 1885–1890," pp. 391–392 and n. 11.
34. *Regeneración*, October 7, 1911.
35. Debs, "The Crisis in Mexico," *Writings and Speeches*.
36. *Freedom*, December 1922, p. 8.
37. The best study of the Baja campaign and its consequences remains Blaisdell, *The Desert Revolution*. On recruitment, see pp. 44–45.
38. Blaisdell, *The Desert Revolution*, pp. 120–121. Griswold del Castillo, "The Discredited Revolution: The Magonista Capture of Tijuana in 1911," pp. 265–266.
39. *Regeneración*, May 20, 27, 1911.
40. Blaisdell, *The Desert Revolution*, p. 125.
41. Griswold del Castillo, "The Discredited Revolution," p. 269.
42. Griswold del Castillo, "The Discredited Revolution," p. 269. Blaisdell, "Was It Revolution or Filibustering? The Mystery of the Flores Magón Revolt in Baja California," pp. 147–164.
43. Blaisdell, *The Desert Revolution*, pp. 152–162.
44. Cockcroft, *Intellectual Precursors*, pp. 192–194.
45. *Regeneración*, July 2, 1911.
46. Cockcroft, *Intellectual Precursors*, p. 201.
47. Samuel Gompers to Ricardo Flores Magón, March 18, 1911, AFL Papers.
48. Ricardo Flores Magón to Samuel Gompers, [undated], AFL Papers.
49. Samuel Gompers to the Executive Council, April 8, 1911 and undated tally sheet of names and remarks, AFL Papers.
50. Debs, "The Crisis in Mexico," *Writings and Speeches*.
51. Debs, "The Crisis in Mexico," *Writings and Speeches*.
52. *Regeneración*, October 7, 1911.
53. Shore, "Talkin' Socialism," p. 178.
54. *Appeal to Reason*, August 19, 1911.
55. *Appeal to Reason*, August 19, 1911.
56. Owen, "The Los Angeles Times Explosion," pp. 310–314. Shapiro, "The McNamara Case: A Window on Class Antagonism in the Progressive Era," pp. 69–95.
57. Owen, "The Los Angeles Times Explosion," pp. 310–314.
58. Blaisdell, *The Desert Revolution*, pp. 27–28. Shore, "Talkin' Socialism," pp. 203–204, 208–211. Another man, Ortie McManigal of the same union, was also arrested, but the McNamaras were the principal defendants. Shapiro, "The McNamara Case: A Window on Class Antagonism in the Progressive Era," pp. 69–95.
59. Shore, "Talkin' Socialism," pp. 203–204, 208–211.
60. Reprinted in *Regeneración*, January 20, 1912. A convenient English-language translation is in *Mother Earth*, March 1912, pp. 15–23.
61. Kraft, "The Fall of Job Harriman's Socialist Party: Violence, Gender and Politics in Los Angeles, 1911," pp. 43–68, argues that the newly enfranchised female voters were not favorably disposed towards socialists and their votes decided the election.
62. Shore, "Talkin' Socialism," pp. 208–232.
63. Cumberland, *Mexican Revolution: Genesis under Madero*, pp. 168–170.

64. Mother Jones to Manuel Calero, October 25, 1911, in Steel, ed., *The Correspondence of Mother Jones*, pp. 97–100.
65. *Diario del Hogar*, September 27, 1911, cited in Poole, *Land and Liberty*, p. 137.
66. Blaisdell, *The Desert Revolution*, p. 193.
67. Raat, *Revoltosos*, p. 32. Ruth Teiser interview with Ethel Duffy Turner, BL. *Mother Earth*, July 1916, p. 558.
68. Blaisdell, *The Desert Revolution*, p. 191. Langham, *Border Trials*, p. 23.
69. Avrich, *The Modern School Movement*, p. 252.
70. Langham, *Border Trials*, p. 6–7.
71. Amezcúa, *¿Quién es Flores Magón?* pp. 31–32.
72. Blaisdell, *The Desert Revolution*, p. 10.
73. *The Modern Medical Encyclopedia*, vol. 6, p. 736.
74. Joll, *The Anarchists*, pp. 67–68, 71–72. Woodcock, *Anarchism*, p. 134. Bakunin's impotence is disputed by Marshall Shatz in "Bakunin and His Biographers."
75. Carr, *Michael Bakunin*, p. 24.
76. Blaisdell, *The Desert Revolution*, pp. 192–194.
77. Blaisdell, *The Desert Revolution*, p. 192.
78. *Regeneración*, April 6, 1912.
79. *Regeneración*, April 27, 1912. Among the newspapers were: *Cronaca Sovversiva* in Lynn, Massachusetts; *The California Social Democrat* in Los Angeles; *Wohlstand fur Alle* in Austria; and *Vorwaerts* in Berlin.
80. *Regeneración*, May 25, 1912.
81. Poole, *Land and Liberty*, p. 138.
82. Max Nettlau cited in Avrich, *An American Anarchist*, p. 157.
83. Avrich, *An American Anarchist*, pp. 149–150.
84. Voltairine de Cleyre to Joseph Cohen, cited in Avrich, *An American Anarchist*, p. 227.
85. Avrich, *An American Anarchist*, p. 221.
86. *Mother Earth*, December 1911, pp. 301–306; January 1912, pp. 335–341; February 1912, pp. 374–380. Emphasis hers.
87. *Mother Earth*, March 1912, pp. 10–15.
88. *Mother Earth*, April 1912, pp. 60–62.
89. Avrich, *An American Anarchist*, pp. 235–236.
90. Department of Justice, SNF #90755, RG 60, USNA.
91. Dubofsky, *We Shall Be All*, pp. 179–197.
92. Goldman, *Living My Life*, vol. 1, pp. 499–501. Foner, *History of the Labor Movement in the United States*, vol. 4, p. 202.
93. Wexler, *Emma Goldman*, pp. 179–181.
94. Blaisdell, *The Desert Revolution*, p. 191.
95. Raat, *Revoltosos*, pp. 242–243.
96. Blaisdell, *The Desert Revolution*, p. 191.
97. Weinstein, *The Decline of Socialism in America, 1912–1925*, pp. 93, 103.
98. *Mother Earth*, January 1912, p. 334.
99. Shore, "Talkin' Socialism," pp. 220.

CHAPTER 3

1. "Revolutionary Government," in Baldwin, ed., *Kropotkin's Revolutionary Pamphlets*, p. 249.
2. Poole, *Land and Liberty*, p. 138. Raat, *Revoltosos*, p. 58.
3. *Regeneración*, January 1, 1913.
4. *Mother Earth*, February 1912, p. 358.
5. Cumberland, *Mexican Revolution: Genesis under Madero*, pp. 180–181. Womack, *Zapata and the Mexican Revolution*, passim.
6. Cumberland, *Mexican Revolution: Genesis under Madero*, p. 217.
7. Meyer, *Mexican Rebel*, pp. 41–50.

8. Meyer, *Mexican Rebel*, pp. 81–88.

9. John Kenneth Turner to Ethel Duffy Turner, January 28, 1913, cited in Snow, Introduction, to Turner, *Barbarous Mexico*, p. xxvi.

10. Cumberland, *Mexican Revolution: Genesis under Madero*, pp. 234–241. Meyer, *Huerta*, pp. 70–82, argues unconvincingly that the absence of direct evidence of Huerta's order implies that the murders occurred without his approval.

11. Carranza's decree of February 19, 1913, in González Ramírez, *Planes políticos*, p. 134.

12. Text and signers in González Ramírez, *Planes políticos*, pp. 138–147.

13. Lozoya, *El ejército mexicano (1911–1965)*, pp. 37–38.

14. Meyer, *Mexican Rebel*, pp. 97–98.

15. Meyer, *Huerta*, p. 135.

16. Link, *Woodrow Wilson*, vol. 3, pp. 232–266, 456–494. Cumberland, *Mexican Revolution: The Constitutionalist Years*, pp. 85–89.

17. "An Annual Message to Congress," December 2, 1913, Link, ed., *The Papers of Woodrow Wilson*, vol. 29, p. 4.

18. Woodrow Wilson to John P. Nolan, July 22, 1913, cited in Blaisdell, *The Desert Revolution*, p. 192.

19. Cockcroft, *Intellectual Precursors*, pp. 71–77.

20. Holcombe, "United States Arms Control and the Mexican Revolution, 1910–1924," p. 30.

21. Holcombe, "United States Arms Control and the Mexican Revolution, 1910–1924," pp. 31–33.

22. Holcombe, "United States Arms Control and the Mexican Revolution, 1910–1924," pp. 64–73.

23. Hill, *Emissaries to a Revolution*, passim.

24. Quirk, *An Affair of Honor*, pp. 25–105.

25. Meyer, "The Arms of the *Ypiranga*," pp. 543–555.

26. Cumberland, *Mexican Revolution: The Constitutionalist Years*, pp. 124–125, n. 34.

27. *Regeneración*, June 13, 1914.

28. *Regeneración*, June 13, 1914.

29. Cumberland, *Mexican Revolution: The Constitutionalist Years*, pp. 111–127.

30. Report of Agent L. S. Perkins, July 9, 1919, enclosing translation of a deciphered German dispatch of December 9, 1914, MID, File #9343-251, RG 165, USNA.

31. Cumberland, *Mexican Revolution: The Constitutionalist Years*, pp. 149, n. 121; 150.

32. Cumberland, *Mexican Revolution: The Constitutionalist Years*, pp. 46–47, 146–150.

33. Cumberland, *Mexican Revolution: The Constitutionalist Years*, pp. 129–131.

34. See various circulars, letters, and telegrams to this effect in AREM, L-E-1441R, and AVC.

35. Quirk, *The Mexican Revolution, 1914–1915*, pp. 33–43.

36. Quirk, *The Mexican Revolution, 1914–1915*, pp. 87–105. Womack, *Zapata and the Mexican Revolution*, pp. 213–217. Cumberland, *Mexican Revolution: The Constitutionalist Years*, pp. 161–162.

37. Woodrow Wilson to William Jennings Bryan, August 25, 1914, cited in Baker, *Woodrow Wilson*, vol. 6, p. 57.

38. Quirk, *The Mexican Revolution, 1914–1915*, pp. 129–131. Carranza failed to keep his promise not to punish those Mexicans who had cooperated with the Americans during the occupation. See Quirk, *An Affair of Honor*, pp. 167–170.

39. Womack, *Zapata and the Mexican Revolution*, pp. 219–223.

40. Richmond, *Venustiano Carranza's Nationalist Struggle, 1893–1920*, pp. 67–71 sees Carranza's reforms as sincere and initiated by the First Chief himself.

41. *Land and Liberty*, May, December, 1914. Owen cofounded the Bakunin Institute with the Indian revolutionary Har Dayal. Avrich, *Anarchist Portraits*, p. 30.

42. Raat, *Revoltosos*, pp. 259–260. Rangel had worked with Praxedis Guerrero in Chihuahua, and the *foco* probably was established with Guerrero's aid.

43. Cumberland, *Mexican Revolution: The Constitutionalist Years*, pp. 141–142.

44. Katz, *The Secret War in Mexico*, pp. 139–145.

NOTES TO PAGES 58–72

45. Richmond, *Venustiano Carranza's Nationalist Struggle, 1893–1920*, pp. 49–50.
46. Woodrow Wilson, "The Meaning of the Declaration of Independence," July 4, 1914, in Gauss, ed., *Democracy Today*, pp. 63–74.
47. Kropotkin, *The Conquest of Bread*, p. 16.
48. *Mother Earth*, April 1915, pp. 85–88.
49. *N.W. Ayer & Son's, American Newspaper Annual and Directory 1915*, p. 6. I have excluded exchange from this definition because that is a form of payment, a type of subscription.
50. Raat, *Revoltosos*, p. 27.
51. *Mother Earth*, April 1911, p. 45. In his obituary of Ricardo Flores Magón, written eleven years later, Owen recalled the figure at 17,000, *Freedom*, December 1922, p. 81. Abad de Santillán, *Ricardo Flores Magón*, p. 75, transposed the figure as 27,000. It is the latter number Blaisdell, *The Desert Revolution*, p. 45, repeated and interpreted as subscriptions.
52. *N. W. Ayer & Son's, American Newspaper Annual and Directory, 1915*, p. 75.
53. Paul Avrich, Editor's Introduction, to Kropotkin, *The Conquest of Bread*, p. 13.
54. See, for example, his essay "Pro-Government Anarchists," reprinted in *The Blast*, May 15, 1916.

CHAPTER 4

1. *L'Agitatzione*, June 18, 1897, cited in Richards, ed. and comp., *Errico Malatesta*, pp. 89–90.
2. Physiographically, it is a synclinal embayment. Foscue, "The National Vegetation of the Lower Rio Grande Valley of Texas," pp. 25–30.
3. Foscue, "The Climate of the Lower Rio Grande Valley of Texas," pp. 207–214, and "Historical Geography of the Lower Rio Grande River Valley of Texas," pp. 1–15.
4. Foscue, "Land Utilization in the Lower Rio Grande Valley of Texas," pp. 1–11; "Physiography of the Lower Rio Grande Valley," pp. 263–267; "Irrigation in the Lower Rio Grande Valley of Texas," pp. 457–463,
5. Schoffelmayer, "The Magic Valley—Its Marvelous Future," pp. 16–31.
6. Spaight, *The Resources, Soil, and Climate of Texas*, pp. 49–51, 146–187, 289–291, 252–253. Smith, "The Lower Rio Grande Region in Tamaulipas, Mexico," pp. 210–219, 243–247.
7. Schreiner, III, "Background and Development of Brahman Cattle in Texas," pp. 427–443.
8. Sandos, "The Mexican Revolution and the United States, 1915–1917," pp. 45–122. In addition to my discussion, cited here, of the nineteenth-century background to the land struggles in South Texas, see Montejano, *Anglos and Mexicans in the Making of Texas, 1836–1986*, pp. 13–100.
9. Foscue, "The Distribution of Population in the Lower Rio Grande Valley of Texas," pp. 40–42. Stambaugh and Stambaugh, *The Lower Rio Grande Valley of Texas*, pp. 163–181.
10. Follett, "Report on the Use of Water for Irrigation on the Rio Grande below the El Paso Valley," p. 27, TSA. Stambaugh and Stambaugh, *The Lower Rio Grande Valley of Texas*, pp. 182–183.
11. Sandos, "International Water Control in the Lower Rio Grande Basin, 1900–1920," p. 493.
12. Sandos, "The Mexican Revolution and the United States, 1915–1917," p. 137.
13. Day, *Managing the Lower Rio Grande*, p. 5.
14. Elwood Mead, Chairman, International Water Commission (IWC), to Secretary of State, December 1, 1929, M 314, r 23, 711.1216 A/283 1/2, RG 59, USNA. The IWC succeeded the IBC.
15. Sandos, "International Water Control in the Lower Rio Grande Basin, 1900–1920," pp. 498–501.
16. J. C. Scott to Secretary of State, November 1, 1910, M 314, r 21, 711.1216 A/57, RG 59, USNA.
17. Secretary of State to J. C. Scott, enclosing Follett's observations, January 24, 1911, Ibid.
18. J. R. Monroe to John W. Gaines, U. S. Commissioner to the IBC, May 15, 1915; John W. Gaines to J. R. Monroe, May 20, 1915, IBC, RG 76, USNA.

19. Ramón Salinas to War and Navy Department [sic], June 23, 1915, Office of the Chief of Engineers, #98156, RG 77, USNA.
20. Raat, *Revoltosos*, p. 264.
21. Aniceto Pizaña, "Protest," Los Tulitos Ranch, Texas, May 2, 1913, Bureau of Investigation, #232-84, RG 65, USNA.
22. Ricardo Flores Magón to Aniceto Pizaña, February 11, 1915, translated and enclosed with Report of Agent R. L. Barnes, December 6, 1915, Ibid.
23. "Thirteenth Census of the United States," T 624, r 1536, NARS.
24. *The Brownsville, Texas City Directory, 1913–1914*, p. 193.
25. Attachment to the Report of Agent R. L. Barnes, November 25, 1915, Mexican Claims, #139, RG 76, WNRC.
26. Informant Amaro Rodríguez, included in Report of Agent J. P. S. Mennet, January 17, 1917, Bureau of Investigation, # 232-84, RG 65, USNA.
27. Turner, *Revolution in Baja California*, p. 3; Hart, *Anarchism and the Mexican Working Class, 1860–1931*, pp. vi–viii.
28. Report of Agent J. B. Rogers, September 29, 1915, Bureau of Investigation, #232-84, RG 65, USNA.
29. Report of Agent J. B. Rogers, November 9, 1915, Ibid., contains the list of Brownsville subscribers derived from the Post Office investigation. I have used that list supplemented, where possible, by the 1910 individual census returns and the city directory (cited in notes 23 and 24 above) to develop the information presented in the text.
30. Testimony of Agent R. L. Barnes, *Investigation of Mexican Affairs*, SD 285, 66th Cong., 2nd Sess., vol. 1, p. 1233; Link, ed., *The Papers of Woodrow Wilson*, vol. 37, p. 255, n. 6; Report of Agent R. L. Barnes, November 5, 1915, Mexican Claims, #125, Ag #5383, Doc #1313, RG 76, WNRC; Report of Agents J. B. Rogers, September 23, 1915 and J. P. S. Mennet, January 17, 1917, Bureau of Investigation, #232-84, RG 65, USNA. All references to De La Rosa and Pizaña's backgrounds and activities, unless already cited, are from these sources.
31. Deposition of Gumersindo Solis, July 24, 1925, Mexican Claims, #125, Ag #6222, Doc #1322, RG 76, WNRC.
32. Depositions of J. A. and George Champion, April 9, 1927, Ibid.
33. The term literally means godfather but here they used it in their correspondence to mean friend and protector. See the Closner-Wells correspondence in The Wells Papers, UTA. Hildebrand, "The History of Cameron County," p. 67.
34. Depositions of Florencio Saenz, August 20, 1925 and E. R. Jefferds, August 24, 1925, Mexican Claims, #125, Ag #2393, Doc #1113, RG 76, WNRC.
35. Deposition of Manuela Villarreal Dillard, February 15, 1929, Mexican Claims, #125, Ag #5496, Doc #2073, RG 76, WNRC.
36. Davenport, "Life of James B. Wells," Davenport Papers, UTA. See also Anders, *Boss Rule in South Texas*, passim.
37. Sandos, "The Mexican Revolution and the United States, 1915–1917," pp. 64–67.
38. Davenport, "Life of James B. Wells," Davenport Papers, UTA.
39. Testimony of James B. Wells, *Glasscock versus Parr*, p. 161.
40. See the report cards of Joseph and Robert Wells from St. Joseph's Academy for boys, Wells Papers, UTA. On the school, see Hildebrand, "The History of Cameron County," p. 95.
41. Deposition of Ruth Schultz Himes, October 6, 1928, Mexican Claims, #125, Ag #2393, Doc #1113; Deposition of W. H. Mead, December 3, 1927, Mexican Claims, #125, Ag #2393, Doc #1942, both in RG 76, WNRC.
42. Affidavit of Lewis D. Austin, August 29, 1925, Mexican Claims, #125, Ag #5004, Doc #1942, RG 76, WNRC.
43. Report of Agent J. B. Rogers, November 15, 1915, Bureau of Investigation, #232-84, RG 65, USNA.
44. Rocha, "The Influence of the Mexican Revolution on the Mexico-Texas Border, 1910–1916," p. 266 and n. 9.
45. *Sanborn Fire Insurance Maps*, Texas, #8445, Cameron County, July 1885–May 1919.

See also Sandos, "On Grassroots Hispanic Society: *Regeneración* Adherents in Los Angeles and Brownsville, 1910–1916," p. 9.

46. Deathbed confession of Jesús Garcia, brother-in-law of Aniceto Pizaña, reported by Sam Robertson, included in Report of Agent R. L. Barnes, November 3, 1915, Mexican Claims, #139, RG 76, WNRC.

47. From the source cited in note 29 above, I have derived twenty subscribers in Cameron and Hidalgo counties in late November 1915.

CHAPTER 5

1. Ricardo Flores Magón, "El miedo de la burguesía es la causa de la intervención," speech given July 4, 1914, Santa Paula, California, printed in *Regeneración*, cited in Bartra, *Regeneración, 1900–1918*, p. 346.

2. MANIFESTO: ¡A los Pueblos Oprimidos de América! from the Congreso Revolucionario de San Diego, Texas, February 20, 1915, Concluidos 1916, caja 1, AGNL.

3. Sandels, "Silvestre Terrazas, The Press and the Origins of the Mexican Revolution in Chihuahua," pp. 71–72.

4. Ross, *Fuentes de la historia contemporánea de México*, vol. 1, pp. xxxiv–1.

5. A Los Hijos de Cuauhtémoc, Hidalgo y Juárez en Texas, November [1914], included in Leonor Villegas de Magnón, Laredo, Texas to Venustiano Carranza, May 12, 1915, AVC, carpeta 59, doc 4263.

6. Department of Justice, SNF #90755, RG 60, USNA.

7. Report of Agent M. Sorola, August 7, 1916, Bureau of Investigation, #232-84, RG 65, USNA.

8. Interrogation of Basilio Ramos, Jr. by E. P. Reynolds, Inspector in Charge, Immigration Service, Brownsville, Texas, January 28, 1915, Adjutant General's Records, General Correspondence, TSA. Hereafter, Interrogation of Basilio Ramos, January 28, 1915, TSA.

9. Report of Agent R. L. Barnes, December 2, 1915, Mexican Claims, #139, RG 76, WNRC.

10. Interrogation of Basilio Ramos, January 28, 1915, TSA.

11. Report of Agent C. S. Weakley, June 14, 1916, Office of the Counselor, Box 221, RG 59, USNA.

12. Report of Agent M. Sorola, August 25, 1916, Ibid.

13. Larralde, *Mexican-American: Movements and Leaders*, pp. 114–115, 122–131. Report of Agent F. Fukuda, January 27, 1917, Bureau of Investigation, #232-84, RG 65, USNA.

14. Interrogation of Basilio Ramos, January 28, 1915, TSA. The Monterrey prisoners and signers were A. S. Garza; A. L. Ferrigno, President; and A. G. Almaraz. The other six, Ramos, Saenz, A. González, Manuel Flores, E. Cisneros, and Porfirio Santos, all came from Nuevo Laredo.

15. The full text of this version of the Plan of San Diego is in *Investigation of Mexican Affairs*, SD 285, 66th Cong., 2nd Sess., vol. 1, pp. 1205–1207. Gómez Quiñones, "Plan de San Diego Reviewed," pp. 124–130.

16. Commission of the Organizing Junta of the Mexican Liberal Party to Javier Guitemea, August 31, 1906, signed by Ricardo Flores Magón and Antonio Villarreal, Exhibit #10, Department of Justice, SNF #90755, RG 60, USNA.

17. Interrogation of Basilio Ramos, January 28, 1915, TSA. I could not locate Ramos' arrest record in the Monterrey archives, but he claimed to have been incarcerated only about five days. Short-term detention may have meant that he and the other conspirators were held in the municipal jail, rather than at the prison, and the records of the former institution have not survived. Since he responded candidly to all questions posed by his American interrogators, there is no reason to doubt his story of arrest and confinement.

18. Interrogation of Basilio Ramos, Jr. by E. P. Reynolds, Inspector in Charge, Immigration Service, Brownsville, Texas, March 20, 1915, Fall Collection, HL. After spending one night at the San Carlos Hotel, Ramos took a room for two days with a "Mrs. Rodríguez, on Adams Street." *The Brownsville, Texas City Directory, 1913–1914*, p. 203, shows a Mrs. Pilar Rodri-

guez [sic] with a residence at the rear of 205 Adams. Mrs. Emilia Rodríguez, seamstress and *Regeneración* subscriber, received her newspaper through Manuel Cueto, a grocer who maintained a home at his store located at 523 Adams. *Ibid.*, pp. 129, 202.

19. Deposition of Deodoro Guerra, February 4, 1915, and other documents in *The U.S. vs. Basilio Ramos, Jr., et al*, Criminal #2152, Southern District of Texas, RG 21, FWFRC.

20. Judge's Bench Docket, Criminal #2151, Ibid., reveals that Guerra and two others were charged with smuggling and receiving smuggled goods. After a year of continuances, charges were dropped for want of testimony. Guerra may have traded his freedom for that of Ramos.

21. On the documents, see Sandos, "The Plan of San Diego: War and Diplomacy on the Texas Border, 1915–1916," p. 9, n. 7. See also Plan of San Diego, Office of the Counselor, Box 208, RG 59, USNA.

22. Manifesto: ¡A Los Pueblos Oprimidos de América! Another copy can be found in the Archivo de Samuel Espinosa de los Monteros, INAH. An English translation is in Mexican Claims, #142, RG 76, WNRC, and another included in "The Annual Report of the Southern Department, 1916," RAGO, RG 94, USNA.

23. J. W. Shaw, Postmaster, San Diego, Texas to R. L. Barnes, March 2, 1916, in Report of Agent R. L. Barnes, March 6, 1916, Bureau of Investigation, #232-84, RG 65, USNA.

24. Sandos, "The Plan of San Diego: War and Diplomacy on the Texas Border, 1915–1916," pp. 10–11.

25. Inspector in Charge, Laredo, to Supervising Inspector, Immigration Service, El Paso, March 23, 1916, INS, File #53108/71-N, RG 85, USNA.

26. Supervising Inspector, El Paso, to Commissioner General of Immigration, March 30, 1915, Ibid.

27. Inspector in Charge, Brownsville, to Supervising Inspector, Immigration Service, El Paso, March 25, 1915, Ibid.

28. Inspector in Charge, Brownsville, to Supervising Inspector, Immigration Service, El Paso, June 18, 1915, Ibid. Underlining his.

29. Immigrant Inspector, Hidalgo, to Inspector in Charge, Brownsville, June 17, 1915, Ibid.

30. James E. Ferguson to Woodrow Wilson, February 25, 1915, Wilson Papers, r 216, series 4, case #95T.

31. Memorandum for the Chief of Staff, June 19, 1915, Wilson Papers, r 335, series 4, case #2446. Underlining in original.

32. General Order #5, October 2, 1911, Adjutant General's Records, General Correspondence, TSA.

33. State Adjutant General to Hugh Miller, June 7, 1915, Ibid.

34. State Adjutant General to Capt. J. J. Sanders, July 26, 1915, Ibid.

35. Winfred Bates to James E. Ferguson, June 9, 1915, Ibid.

36. Capt. J. M. Fox to State Adjutant General, June 14, 1915, and response, June 17, 1915, Ibid.

37. *Corpus Christi Caller*, July 6, 1915. PSD violence can be distinguished from general banditry by its targets. PSD followers attacked Anglos; attacked symbols of change in the valley such as equipment associated with the railroad, telegraph, automobile, and irrigation; and visited reprisals on Mexicans and Tejanos who helped Americans. Since the Plan required followers to live off the land, some theft and robbery also occurred, but they were incidental to the main target.

38. *Brownsville Herald*, July 6, 8, 19, 1915, called it the biggest raid in the valley in twenty years but carried no account of the killings near Lyford.

39. Weekly Report on Border Conditions #124, RAGO, RG 94, USNA.

40. *Brownsville Herald*, July 24, 1915.

41. *San Antonio Light*, July 30, 1915; *Corpus Christi Caller*, July 30, 1915; *Brownsville Herald*, July 29, 1915.

42. Report of Agent R. L. Barnes, November 15, 1915, Mexican Claims, #142, RG 76, WNRC.

43. Sources for account of events surrounding Los Tulitos are: Testimony of Joe Taylor, Mounted Inspector of Customs and 2nd Lt. Harold Lutz, 12th Cavalry, stationed at San Benito, in Complete Statement of Facts in Case #3613, *ex parte* Ramón Pizaña, District Court of

Cameron County, Texas, December 1, 1915, Mexican Claims, #125, Ag #5004, Doc #1942 (misfiled with Ag #2393, Doc #1113), RG 76, WNRC; Weekly Report on Border Conditions, #124-125, RAGO, RG 94, USNA (#125 giving Lutz's description of Scrivner's attitude); Sam Spears to Thomas W. Gregory, September 2, 1915, Burleson Papers, Cont 15, LC; *Brownsville Herald*, August 2, 3, 1915; Testimony of Mike Monahan, *Investigation of Mexican Affairs*, SD 285, 66th Cong., 2nd Sess., vol. 1 pp. 1265-1270. Citizenship data on Aniceto Pizaña, his wife Manuela, his son Guadalupe, and brother Ramón are derived from the individual census schedules, "The Thirteenth Census of the United States," T624, r 1536, NARS.

44. Reports of Agent R. L. Barnes, November 15, 25, 1915, Mexican Claims, #139, RG 76, WNRC.

45. Testimony of Lon C. Hill, *Investigation of Mexican Affairs*, SD 285, 66th Cong., 2nd Sess., vol. 1, p. 1263. Hill also described Pizaña financially as "unusually well-fixed."

46. Two claims of interviews with the Pizañas have been reported. Larralde, *Mexican American: Movements and Leaders*, pp. v, 114-145, reports having had conversations with Aniceto in Matamoros, Mexico on March 12, May 10, June 12, August 13, 1954 and January 1, 1955. The account Larralde presents in his text is rambling and, at points, incoherent. At the time of the conversations, Pizaña would have been eighty-five and possibly senile. Materials from these reminiscences must be used carefully and obvious absurdities dismissed (e.g., Pizaña's claim to have molded Ricardo Flores Magón's thinking! p. 126). Rocha, "The Influence of the Mexican Revolution on the Mexico-Texas Border," pp. 264-265, n. 7, reports having interviewed a Mrs. Aniceto Pizaña in Matamoros on June 14, 1980. In the 1910 census enumeration cited in note 43 above, the given name of the then Mrs. Pizaña was Manuela and her age recorded as twenty-six. In 1980, were she still alive, Manuela Pizaña would have been ninety-six.

47. Bartra, *Regeneración 1900-1918*, pp. 436-439.

48. Testimony of José T. Canales, *Proceedings of the Joint Committee of the Senate and the House in the Investigation of the State Ranger Force*, vol. 1, pp. 856-870, TSA. Hereafter, *Investigation of the State Ranger Force*.

49. Weekly Report on Border Conditions, #124, RAGO, RG 94, USNA.

50. Affidavits of Thomas J. Alexander, September 11, 1925 and Roscoe Lee Smith, September 2, 1925, Mexican Claims, #125, Ag #5004, Doc #1942, RG 76, WNRC.

51. Deposition of Ruth Schultz Hines, October 6, 1928 and Affidavit of Thomas J. Alexander, December 2, 1927, Mexican Claims, #125, Ag #2393, Doc #1113, RG 76, WNRC.

52. Deposition of May Wagner, December 3, 1927, Mexican Claims, #125, Ag #5004, Doc #1942, RG 76, WNRC.

53. Citizens of Lower Rio Grande Valley, Brownsville, to Secretary of War, August 7, 1915, RAGO, File #212358, RG 94, USNA.

54. S. A. Wayne and the Brownsville Merchants Association, Brownsville, to Secretary of War, August 10, 1915, Ibid.

55. *Brownsville Herald*, August 6, 7, 1915. Sheriff W. T. Vann was the eyewitness who gave details to the press.

56. Translation of circular enclosed in Inspector in Charge, Brownsville, to Supervising Inspector, El Paso, August 10, 1915, INS, File #53108/71-N, RG 85, USNA.

57. Testimony of Caesar Kleberg, which included a Deposition of Manuel Rincones, August 12, 1915, in *Investigation of Mexican Affairs*, SD 285, 66th Cong., 2nd Sess., vol. 1, pp. 1282-1286; Weekly Report on Border Conditions, #126, RAGO, RG 94, USNA; Claim of Natalia Martin, widow of Frank, who was wounded by raiders at Norias, Mexican Claims, #125, Ag #5892, Doc #2745, RG 76, WNRC.

58. McNeil, "Corridos of the Mexican Border," pp. 27-29. Aniceto Pizaña was mistakenly transcribed as Aneste Pasano.

59. James B. Rogers to Albert Burleson, August 30, 1915, Burleson Papers, Cont 15, LC. Rogers also served as an agent for the Bureau of Investigation and kept President Wilson's Texas cabinet members, Postmaster General Burleson and Attorney General T. W. Gregory, informed of developments in the valley.

60. Lon C. Hill, quoted in Sterling, *Trails and Trials of a Texas Ranger*, p. 35.

61. Sterling, *Trails and Trials of a Texas Ranger*, p. 30.

62. Lewis, *Along the Rio Grande*, p. 177.
63. Lewis, *Along the Rio Grande*, p. 178.
64. *Brownsville Herald*, August 9, 1915.
65. Lewis, *Along the Rio Grande*, p. 176.
66. Reprinted in the *San Antonio Express*, August 12, 1915. In this era complete runs of English-language valley newspapers are nearly as scarce as their Spanish-language counterparts.
67. *San Antonio Light*, September 10, 1915.
68. T. H. Austin, Laredo to J. B. Rogers, August 26, 1915 attached to James B. Rogers to Albert Burleson, August 30, 1915, Burleson Papers, Cont 15, LC.
69. "The Annual Report of the Southern Department, 1916," RAGO, RG 94, USNA. Frederick Funston to War Department, August 11, 1915, Ibid. Cumberland, "Border Raids in the Lower Rio Grande Valley," pp. 285–311.
70. Hunt, *Politics, Culture, and Class in the French Revolution*, pp. 59–119, sensitively discusses popular symbols including the Liberty cap. The cap in the Mexican/Tejano banner is Scythian, as is the one Hunt depicts on p. 61 atop Liberty's lance. The evolved form of the cap is Phrygian, however, as Hunt depicts it atop Liberty's head on p. 118.
71. Weekly Report of Border Conditions, #125-128, RAGO, RG 94, USNA; Pierce, *A Brief History of the Lower Rio Grande Valley*, pp. 90–93.
72. Sandos, "The Plan of San Diego: War and Diplomacy on the Texas Border, 1915–1916," p. 16.
73. Weekly Report on Border Conditions, #127, RAGO, RG 94, USNA.
74. *Brownsville Herald*, August 21, 25, 1915.
75. Inspector in Charge, Brownsville, to Supervising Inspector, El Paso, August 12, 1915, INS, File #53108/71-N, RG 85, USNA.
76. Monterrey, *El Demócrata*, August 26, 1915. A brief run, from July 12 to December 2, 1915, can be found in the Hemeroteca Alfonso Reyes in Monterrey.
77. *Brownsville Herald*, August 28, 1915; *Corpus Christi Caller*, August 28, 1915.
78. U. S. Consul, Nuevo Laredo, temporarily in Laredo, to·Secretary of State, August 26, 1915, Department of Justice, SNF #90755, RG 60, USNA. "The Annual Report of the Southern Department, 1916," RAGO, RG 94, Ibid., inaccurately called the newspaper *El Democratica*, but cited and translated the editions from Monterrey and Matamoros of August 26 and 27 respectively.
79. Affidavit of S. S. Dodds, undated, Mexican Claims, #125, Ag #5383, Doc #1313, RG 76, WNRC; Testimony of S. S. Dodds, *Investigation of Mexican Affairs*, SD 285, 66th Cong., 2nd Sess., vol. 1, pp. 1250–1252.
80. Interrogation of Esmerejüldo Cruz, included in Report of Agent J. B. Rogers, November 10, 1915, Mexican Claims, #125, Ag #5383, Doc #1313, RG 76, WNRC.
81. Weekly Report on Border Conditions, #127, RAGO, RG 94, USNA.
82. *Brownsville Herald*, September 8, 1915; *San Antonio Light*, September 9, 1915.
83. Frederick Funston, San Antonio, to Adjutant General, September 16, 1915, transmitting Funston to Ferguson, same date, RAGO, RG 94, USNA.
84. James E. Ferguson, Austin, to Frederick Funston, September 20, 1915, transmitting Ferguson to Vann, same date, and Ferguson to Vann, October 1, 1915, Ferguson Papers, TSA.
85. *Brownsville Herald*, September 16, 1915, carried Vann's remarks in which he apologized for his men's behavior—blaming it on nothing more than carelessness and thoughtlessness.
86. Inspector in Charge, Brownsville, to Supervising Inspector, El Paso, September 10, 1915, INS, File #53108/71-N, RG 85, USNA.
87. Interview with Mr. Fearnow and Mr. I. H. Seyler, seven- and three-year valley residents respectively, included in Report of Agent J. B. Rogers, September 29, 1915, Bureau of Investigation, #232-84, RG 65, USNA.
88. Sterling, *Trails and Trials of a Texas Ranger*, pp. 36, 44.
89. *Brownsville Herald*, September 17, 1915.
90. Statement of Ygnacio Rodríguez included in Report Agent of H. P. Wright, May 11, 1916, Bureau of Investigation, #232-342[?], RG 65, USNA.
91. *Brownsville Herald*, August 20, 1915.

NOTES TO PAGES 98–104

92. *Corpus Christi Caller*, September 15, 1915. *San Antonio Light*, September 16, 1915, reported a similar armed precaution in San Benito.
93. I have summarized Cortina's protest against racism in Sandos, "The Mexican Revolution and the United States, 1915–1917," pp. 33–35, 42–43, n. 57–64.
94. Testimony of R. B. Creager, *Investigation of the State Ranger Force*, vol. 1, p. 355.
95. *San Antonio Light*, September 22, 1915.
96. *San Antonio Express*, September 11, 1915, cited in Cumberland, "Border Raids in the Lower Rio Grande Valley," p. 300.
97. Testimony of James B. Wells, *Investigation of the State Ranger Force*, vol. 2, pp. 672–678, 690.
98. Testimony of R. B. Creager, *Investigation of the State Ranger Force*, vol. 1, p. 355.
99. [Frank C. Pierce], "Partial List of Mexicans Killed in Valley since July 1, 1915," undated, Foreign Service Post Records, Matamoros, 1915, RG 84, USNA. Hereafter "Partial List of Mexicans Killed in Valley." Pierce, a Brownsville attorney and local historian, prepared this document at the request of U. S. Consul Jesse Johnson, but the chronicle only runs through early October 1915. In sending the list to Washington on February 9, 1916, Johnson apologized for its incompleteness saying, "It was the only data available." The copy cited here contains numerous penciled corrections and additions not found in the version in M 274, r 51, 812.00/17186, RG 59, USNA, or in Pierce's *A Brief History of the Lower Rio Grande Valley*.
100. *Brownsville Herald*, September 28, 1915.
101. Weekly Report on Border Conditions, #130, RAGO, RG 94, USNA.
102. "Partial List of Mexicans Killed in Valley."
103. Testimony of José T. Canales, *Investigation of the State Ranger Force*," vol. 2, pp. 856–870.
104. *Regeneración*, October 16, 1915.

CHAPTER 6

1. Inspector in Charge, Brownsville, to Supervising Inspector, Immigration Service, El Paso, August 12, 1915, INS, File #53108/71-N, RG 85, USNA.
2. Testimony of Mounted Inspector of Customs, *Investigation of Mexican Affairs*, SD 285, 66th Cong., 2nd Sess., vol. 1, p. 1311.
3. Records of Research and Information Section, Mexican Claims, #145, RG 76, WNRC.
4. Deposition of Cora Kendall, wife of train engineer Henry Kendall, May 1, 1919 and Deposition of P. A. Horan, train conductor, March 20, 1919, Mexican Claims, #125, Ag #1386, Doc #604, RG 76, WNRC.
5. Testimony of John Kleiber, *Investigation of Mexican Affairs*, SD 285, 66th Cong., 2nd Sess., vol. 1, pp. 1270–1271.
6. Deposition of Henry Wallis, February, 13, 1926, Mexican Claims, #125, Ag #1386, Doc #604, and Testimony of Henry Wallis, *The State of Texas vs. Rogerio Cavallero*, #3655, District Court of Cameron County, Texas, March Term, 1916, Mexican Claims, #125, Ag #94, Doc #115, both in RG 76, WNRC.
7. Testimony of John Kleiber, *Investigation of Mexican Affairs*, SD 285, 66th Cong., 2nd Sess., vol. 1, pp. 1272–1274.
8. *Brownsville Herald*, October 19, 1915.
9. Testimony of Henry Wallis, *Investigation of Mexican Affairs*, SD 285, 66th Cong., 2nd Sess., vol. 1, pp. 1342–1344. This amplifies the Wallis materials cited in note 6 above.
10. Pierce, *A Brief History of the Lower Rio Grande Valley*, p. 97.
11. Affidavit of Allie Heard McCain, undated, Mexican Claims, #125, Ag #94, Doc #115, RG 76, WNRC.
12. Testimony of W. T. Vann, *Investigation of Mexican Affairs*, SD 285, 66th Cong., 2nd Sess., vol. 1, pp. 1297–1298. Affidavit of "Chano" [diminutive of Feliciano] Flores, September 21, 1925, Mexican Claims, #125, Ag #5004, Doc #1942, RG 76, WNRC.
13. Testimony of W. T. Vann, *Investigation of the State Ranger Force*, vol. 1, pp. 573–574. In his memoir, *Trails and Trials of a Texas Ranger*, p. 43, William Warren Sterling claimed that Ranger Ransom had physical evidence connecting these four men with the wreck, thereby

justifying their summary execution. No such claim was made on Ransom's behalf during the investigation of the Texas Ranger force in which Vann testified.

14. Weekly Report on Border Conditions, #136, RAGO, RG 94, USNA.

15. Frederick Funston, San Antonio, to Adjutant General, October 21, 1915, 1:20 P.M.; October 22, 1915, 2:40 P.M.; Weekly Report on Border Conditions, #135, Ibid.

16. Deposition of Manuela Villarreal Dillard, February 15, 1929, Mexican Claims, #125, Ag #5496, Doc #2073, RG 76, WNRC.

17. Frederick Funston, San Antonio to Adjutant General, October 22, 1915, 2:00 P.M., RAGO, RG 94, USNA.

18. Frederick Funston, San Antonio to Hugh L. Scott, October 22, 1915, 6:45 P.M., Ibid.

19. Lindley Garrison to Frederick Funston, October 23, 1915, Ibid.

20. "¡BASTA!," Concluidos 1916, caja 1, AGNL.

21. "Let Us Rise In Revolt," The Revolutionary Congress, October 1915, translation only, no original, attached to War Department to A. Bruce Bielaski, July 25, 1916, Bureau of Investigation, #232-84, RG 65, USNA. I found a faded copy of the original in Concluidos 1916, caja 1, AGNL, and corrected the translation with the assistance of María Onestini.

22. "¡A LAS ARMAS MEXICANOS!" Rebel Group in Arms in Texas, October 1915, original (almost too faint to read) and translation, attached to Report of Agent C. G. Beckham, October 13, 1915, Bureau of Investigation, #232-84, RG 65, USNA.

23. H. L. Yates, et al., Brownsville to Secretary of State, October 19, 1915, M 274, r 49, 812.00/16573, RG 59, USNA.

24. *Brownsville Herald*, October 24, 25, 1915; *San Antonio Light*, October 24, 27, 1915.

25. D.W. Glasscock, et al., Brownsville, to Woodrow Wilson, October 29, 1915, M 274, r 49, 812.00/16654, RG 59 USNA.

26. *Brownsville Herald*, September 8, 1915.

27. *Brownsville Herald*, October 26, 1915.

28. Testimony of José T. Canales, *Investigation of the State Ranger Force*, vol. 2, pp. 856-870. Weekly Report on Border Conditions, #137, RAGO, RG 94, USNA. For criticism of the system, see "What Caused the Trouble along the Lower Border in 1915 and 1916," undated, Adjutant General's Records, Detached Records, Camp Mabry, TSA.

29. *Investigation of the State Ranger Force*, vol. 3, p. 1464.

30. Charles Hoffmann, President, San Diego State Bank, to Caesar Kleberg, November 29, 1915, and John Ball to Caesar Kleberg, November 27, 1915, Adjutant General's Records, General Correspondence, TSA.

31. Caesar Kleberg to State Adjutant General, November 30, 1915, Ibid.

32. *Brownsville Herald*, October 21, 1915.

33. Weekly Report on Border Conditions, #137, RAGO, RG 94, USNA.

34. Weekly Report on Border Conditions, #138, Ibid.

35. Captain J. J. Sanders, Co. "A," Texas Ranger Force to Henry Hutchings, July 22, 1915, Adjutant General's Records, General Correspondence, TSA.

36. Weekly Report on Border Conditions, #127, RAGO, RG 94, USNA.

37. Inspector in Charge, Brownsville, to Supervising Inspector, Immigration Service, El Paso, August 12, 1915, INS, File #53108/71-N, RG 85, USNA.

38. R. L. Barnes to John E. Green, November 28, 1916, Mexican Claims, #139, RG 76, WRNC.

39. Sam Spears to J. B. Rogers, September 25, 1915, attached to Report of Agent J. B. Rogers, October 1, 1915, Bureau of Investigation, #232-84, RG 65, USNA.

40. Frederick Funston, San Antonio, to Hugh Scott, October 22, 1915, 6:45 P.M., RAGO, RG 94, USNA.

41. *San Antonio Light*, September 22, 1915.

42. Inspector in Charge, Brownsville, to Supervising Inspector, Immigration Services, El Paso, September 14, 1915, INS, File #53108/71-N, RG 85, USNA.

43. Attorney General to Secretary of War, September 20, 1915, Department of Justice, SNF #90755, RG 60, USNA.

44. Report of Agent J. B. Rogers, November 9, 1915, including a translation of George Martínez to Jesús Martínez, October 8, 1915, Bureau of Investigation, #232-84, RG 65, USNA.

45. Report of Agent J. B. Rogers, October 1, 1915, Ibid.
46. *Brownsville Herald*, November 3, 1915, using Immigration Service estimates for Brownsville and Hidalgo official crossings—obviously not the only places where people could pass.
47. Sandos, "The Mexican Revolution and the United States, 1915–1917," pp. 274, 296–298, nn. 54 and 55.
48. Adjutant General to Chief Clerk, War Department, November 4, 1915, RAGO, RG 94, USNA.
49. Bureau of Investigation, #232-84, RG 65, USNA was the main file on the Plan of San Diego but the reader will notice that many of these agent reports were scattered to other departments during the 1920s and not returned to the central file. Many are in the Mexican Claims material.
50. Robert Lansing to John R. Silliman, August 28, 1915, 1:00 P.M. M 274, r 48, 812.00/15956; John R. Silliman to Robert Lansing, September 1, 1915, 5:00 P.M. Ibid., r 48, 812.00/16000; Robert Lansing to John R. Belt, October 23, 1915, Ibid., r 49, 812.00/16545, all in RG 59, USNA. Silliman and his assistant, Belt, were State Department representatives assigned to Carranza.
51. *Brownsville Herald*, November 1, 1915; *San Antonio Express*, November 1, 1915.
52. Meyer, *Huerta: A Political Portrait*, pp. 213–214.
53. Creel had been pro-German since at least 1900. While serving as governor, he encouraged German investment in the state of Chihuahua and got the German minister to Mexico to invest in the Compañía Humboldt there. Schiff, "German Interests in Mexico in the Period of Porfirio Díaz," p. 134.
54. Rintelen, *The Dark Invader*, pp. 7–25, 84, 91–92, 175–183.
55. These subjects are well covered in many sources such as Tuchman, *The Zimmermann Telegram*, passim, and Meyer, "The Mexican German Conspiracy of 1915," pp. 76–89.
56. Special Assistant to Attorney General, July 5, 1918, and Report of Lt. John R. Winterbottom, June 27, 1918, MID, File #9140-1754, RG 165, USNA.
57. Statement of Federico Stallforth, April 22, 1917, and "Memorandum: Stallforth and Company," undated, MID, File #9140-878, RG 165, USNA.
58. Sandos, "German Involvement in Northern Mexico, 1915–1916: A New Look at the Columbus Raid," p. 84.
59. Clendenen, *The United States and Pancho Villa*, pp. 23–24.
60. Meyer, *Huerta: A Political Portrait*, pp. 174–175.
61. See the excellent discussion in Hart, *Anarchism and The Mexican Working Class, 1860–1931*, pp. 128–135.
62. Hart, *Anarchism and The Mexican Working Class, 1860–1931*, pp. 128–135.
63. Much of the information on Ébano comes from field reports in AVC, Telegramas: Tamaulipas 1915. See also Treviño, *Memorias*, pp. 85–96. Richmond, *Venustiano Carranza's Nationalist Struggle, 1893–1920*, pp. 71–75.
64. Alvaro Obregón, Celaya, to Venustiano Carranza, April 18, 1915, partial report, Operaciones Militares, Ramo de Revolución, AGN. Obregón, *Ocho mil kilómetros en campaña*, pp. 454–566.
65. Conventional wisdom, based on the fallacy of "presentism," holds that these defeats removed Villa from Mexican political life. This argument ignores the powerful impact of the American Punitive Expedition, to be discussed in the next chapters, and discounts the abundant archival evidence in Mexico of Carranza's continued monitoring of Villa's activities.
66. Report of Agent E. B. Stone, July 9, 1915, Bureau of Investigation, #232-162, RG 65, USNA. I am among the guilty. See my "The Plan of San Diego: War and Diplomacy on the Texas Border, 1915–1916," p. 10, n. 9.
67. Ygnacio Bonillas to Robert Lansing, July 23, 1918, Department of Justice, SNF #90755, RG 60, USNA.
68. See the discussion of the Asamblea Pacificadora Mexicana in Sax, *Los mexicanos en el destierro*, pp. 17–20.
69. Report of Agent E. B. Stone, July 8, 1915, Bureau of Investigation, #232-162, RG 65, USNA.

70. Woodrow Wilson to Joseph Tumulty, July 6, 1915, Department of Justice, SNF #90755, RG 60, USNA.

71. Meyer, *Mexican Rebel*, pp. 126 ff.

72. "Consideration and Outline of Policy," July 11, 1915, Lansing Papers, Private Memoranda, r 1, LC.

73. "Carranza—An Impression," in Reed, *Insurgent Mexico*, pp. 241–253.

74. "The Conference in Regard to Mexico," October 10, 1915, Lansing Papers, Private Memoranda, r 1, LC. Underlining Lansing's.

75. Holcombe, "United States Arms Control and the Mexican Revolution, 1910–1924," pp. 112–116.

76. He signed five days after its promulgation, on March 30, 1913, at Tlanepantla, México. See González Ramírez, *Planes políticos*, pp. 140–141.

77. Ignacio Muñoz, Villista who participated in the siege, "Nuestra guerra civil: El sitio de Matamoros, México," *Todo*, February 9, 1937. See also AMG, carpeta 20, doc 2804.

78. Mario Uribe to Venustiano Carranza, June 8, 1915, AVC, carpeta 41, doc 4506.

79. Major Jerónimo Hinojosa, Chief of the Arms and Munitions Warehouse, to Venustiano Carranza, July 6, 1915, AVC, carpeta 44, doc 4819.

80. Mario Uribe to Venustiano Carranza, June 8, 1915, AVC, carpeta 41, doc 4506.

81. General Alfredo Ricaut to Venustiano Carranza, July 8, 1915, AVC, carpeta 44, doc 4848.

82. Ricaut to Carranza, Ibid.

83. General Francisco de P. Mariel to Venustiano Carranza, October 5, 1915, AVC, carpeta 54, doc 5991.

84. Inspector in Charge, Brownsville, to Supervising Inspector, Immigration Service, El Paso, November 4, 1915, INS, File #53108/71-O, RG 85, USNA.

85. General Emiliano P. Nafarrate to Venustiano Carranza, August 8, 1915, AVC, carpeta 47, doc 5249.

86. *El Demócrata*, Monterrey, July 12, 22, 25, August 15, 1915.

87. General Emiliano P. Nafarrate to U. S. Consul Jesse Johnson, September 13, 1915, Foreign Service Post Records, Matamoros, 1915, RG 84, USNA.

88. "Memorándum," Rafael Martínez, August 21, 1914, Colección Jorge DeNegre, r 2, INAH.

89. For example, *El Demócrata*, México, D.F., September 8, 9, 1915; Monterrey, August, 18, 26, 27, 1915.

90. Luis F. Bustamante, "Carranza invadio E. E. U. U.," México, D.F., *Todo*, October 27, 1936. As Chief of Information for that corps, Bustamante claimed never to have been ordered to report favorably on the raiding but he personally agreed with PSD objectives.

91. *El Demócrata*, Monterrey, August 18, 27, 29, 1915; México, D.F., September 9, 1915.

92. Consul Alonzo Garrett, Nuevo Laredo, to Secretary of State, undated, received August 28, 1915, 6:15 P.M., M 274, r 48, 812.00/15946, RG 59. "The Annual Report of the Southern Department, 1916," RAGO, RG 94, USNA.

93. *Brownsville Herald*, September 21, 1915. *El Demócrata*, Monterrey, September 22, 1915.

94. Deposition of Florencio Saenz, August 20, 1925, Mexican Claims, #125, Ag #4812, Doc #850, RG 76, WNRC.

95. "Report on Affair Near Progreso," Capt. A. V. P. Anderson, C. O., Troop "B", Twelfth Cavalry, September 24, 1915, RAGO, RG 94, USNA. Pierce, *A Brief History of the Lower Rio Grande Valley*, pp. 95–96.

96. Frank L. Polk to John R. Belt, October 1, 1915, 7:00 P.M. M 274, r 49, 812.00/16329, RG59, USNA.

97. *Brownsville Herald*, September 27, 1915,

98. David Lawrence, Carranza confidential agent in Washington, D. C., to Secretary of State, October 1, 1915, M 274, r 49, 812.00/16348-1/2, RG 59, USNA.

99. *Brownsville Herald*, October 2, 20, 1915; Weekly Report on Border Conditions, #135, RAGO, RG 94, USNA.

100. Testimony of Major R. L. Barnes and Caesar Kleberg, *Investigation of Mexican Affairs*, SD 285, 66th Cong., 2nd Sess., vol. 1, pp. 1233, 1282–1286.
101. *San Antonio Light*, October 5, 1915.
102. General Eugenio López to Venustiano Carranza, URGENT, October 21, 1915, AVC, Telegramas: Tamaulipas 1915.
103. Venustiano Carranza to General Eugenio López, October 24, 1915, Ibid.
104. General Eugenio López to Consul Jesse Johnson, November 12, 1915, Foreign Service Post Records, Matamoros, 1915, RG 84, USNA.
105. Leonicio Reveles to General Eugenio López, and, separately, to Venustiano Carranza, November 1, 1915, AVC, carpeta 58, doc 6528.
106. *Brownsville Herald*, October 29, 1915.
107. Weekly Report on Border Conditions, #139, RAGO, RG 94, USNA.
108. *Brownsville Herald*, November 1, 1915.
109. *El Demócrata*, Monterrey, November 11, 1915; *Brownsville Herald*, November 11, 1915.
110. James Ferguson to Carlos Bee, November 15, 1915, AVC, carpeta 59, doc 6688.
111. John R. Belt, accompanying Carranza, to Robert Lansing, October 22, 1915, M 274, r 49, 812.00/16568, RG 59, USNA.
112. *San Antonio Express*, November 24, 1915, first edition.
113. *San Antonio Express*, November 24, 1915, final edition.
114. *La Prensa*, San Antonio, November 24, 25, 1915.
115. Weekly Report on Border Conditions, #142, RAGO, RG 94, USNA.
116. Inspector in Charge, Brownsville, to Supervising Inspector, Immigration Service, El Paso, November 4, 1915, with attached translations of Constitutionalist newspaper articles, INS, File #53108/71-0, RG 85, USNA.
117. Weekly Report on Border Conditions, #140, RAGO, RG 94, USNA.
118. For example, *El Regiomontano*, Monterrey, December 21, 1915.
119. General Alfredo Ricaut to Venustiano Carranza, December 29, 1915, AVC, carpeta 64, doc 7092.
120. Weekly Report on Border Conditions, #142-146, RAGO, RG 94, USNA.

CHAPTER 7

1. ¡LEVANTEMONOS! undated [October, 1915], Concluidos 1916, caja 1, AGNL.
2. *New York Times*, September 28, 1915.
3. Solicitor to Chief Inspector, Post Office Department, September 27, 1915, Post Office Department, CF #44548, RG 28, USNA. They also charged two San Antonio newspapers, *La Prensa* and *El Presente*, with writing inflammatory material against Carranza.
4. Teodulo R. Beltrán to Solicitor, Post Office Department, October 23, 1915, Post Office Department, CF #44548, RG 28, USNA.
5. William M. Cookson, Inspector, Los Angeles, to Inspector in Charge, San Francisco, December 4, 1915, Ibid. The Department of Justice Found that the article in question had been intended for the September 25, 1915 issue, but only about one thousand copies of that issue were mailed. Hence, the article was reprinted in the October 2, 1915 mailing. See Albert Schoonover, U. S. Attorney, Southern District of California, Los Angeles, to Attorney General, November 22, December 7, 1915; and Postmaster General Albert S. Burleson to Attorney General Thomas W. Gregory, January 3, 1916; both in Department of Justice, SNF #90755, RG 60, USNA.
6. *Regeneración*, October 2, 1915. For the translation of the entire essay see *U.S. versus Ricardo and Enríque Flores Magón*, Case #1071, 1916, RG 21, LNFRC.
7. Agent R. L. Barnes to John E. Green, U. S. Attorney, Houston, November 28, 1916, Mexican Claims, #139, RG 76, WNRC. Report of Agent J. B. Rogers, December 12, 1915, Bureau of Investigation, #232-84, RG 65, USNA.
8. L. Gante to *Solidaridad Obrera*, November, 1915, translation, no original, Mexican Claims, #142, RG 76, WNRC.

9. "The Annual Report of the Southern Department, 1916," RAGO, RG 94, USNA.

10. Kern, *Red Years/Black Years*, pp. 22–25.

11. See discussion in Chapter 1, and Figure 1. Prat's book is *La burguesia y el proletariado* (1909) visible on the right page, second line from the bottom.

12. The Post Office had no record of intercepted mail entering the United States, so it is possible that Europeans or Mexicans mailed money to the movement.

13. Ferrua, *Gli Anarchici nella Rivoluzione Messicana*, pp. 83, 87, 149, n. 70–71; Toyah is incorrectly given as Tohay. The Toyah Historical and Centennial Committee, *Toyah Taproots*, pp. 2, 6, 9, gives the population in 1910 as 771. For the governmental figures see Thirteenth Census of the United States, 1910, under Reeves County, Texas. Toyah *Regeneración* subscribers have been taken from *U. S. versus Enríque and Ricardo Flores Magón*, Case #1071, 1916, RG 21, LNFRC. Hereafter cited as *Regeneración* subscriber list, November 22, 1915.

14. The coupons, dated between November 20, 1915 to January 10, 1916, are scattered throughout Post Office Department, CF #44548, RG 28, USNA.

15. William M. Cookson, Inspector, Los Angeles, to Inspector in Charge, San Francisco, February 21, 1916, Ibid.

16. Report of Agent E. M. Blanford, December 18, 1915, Bureau of Investigation, #232-84, RG 65, USNA.

17. Albert Schoonover, U. S. Attorney, Los Angeles, to Attorney General, February 16, 1916, Department of Justice, SNF #90755, RG 60, USNA.

18. Report of Agent E. M. Blanford, December 7, 1915, Bureau of Investigation, #232-84, RG 65, USNA. Langham, *Border Trials*, pp. 54–55.

19. *Los Angeles Times*, January 14, 1912. Weaver, *Los Angeles*, pp. 72, 78–79.

20. Report of Agent R. L. Barnes, November 9, 1915, Bureau of Investigation, #232-84, RG 65, USNA.

21. Turner, *Ricardo Flores Magón y El Partido Liberal Mexicano*, p. 297.

22. Report of Agent E. M. Blanford, November 19, 1915, Bureau of Investigation, #232-84, RG 65, USNA.

23. Report of Agent E. M. Blanford, November 29, 1915, Ibid.

24. See, for example, Avrich, *Anarchist Portraits*, pp. 164–199.

25. Turner, *Ricardo Flores Magón y El Partido Liberal Mexicano*, p. 298.

26. The Los Angeles subscribers have been taken from *Regeneración* subscriber list, November 22, 1915. Personal details are from the individual census schedules of the Thirteenth Census of the United States, T 624, rs 79–87.

27. *Who's Who in Socialist America* identified John Clifford, W. W. Cummings, E. L. Osgood, and Louis A. Spengler as the Angelenos of note, but only Osgood could be located.

28. *Regeneración*, March 4, 1916. *The Los Angeles, California City Directory, 1915–1916*. Los Angeles Investment Company, *MAP* [Los Angeles], 1913, by Felix Viole. Five of the signers could be located in the 1910 Census; four of those worked for the railroad and the fifth farmed.

29. *Regeneración*, April 8, 1916. Hondo was then too small to warrant a *City Directory*. Three of the signers could be identified in the 1910 Census, one of whom, Sebastian Rico, subscribed.

30. Marcos Mendoza, Geronimo, Guadalupe County, Texas, to Venustiano Carranza, March 4, 1916, AVC, carpeta 69, doc 7559. Mendoza did not appear on the November 22, 1915 subscriber list for *Regeneración*.

31. Juan Garcia (Agent Juan Cisneros) to F. Ligardi (Agent R. L. Barnes), January 25, 1916; Report of Informant A. Oosterveen, Jr., January 25, 1916; R. L. Barnes to A. Bruce Bielaski, February 26, 1916; all in Office of the Counselor, box 221, RG 59, USNA. Rodríguez had replaced Garza sometime in 1915.

32. Harris and Sadler, "The Plan of San Diego and the Mexican–United States War Crisis of 1916: A Reexamination," have presented the most detailed reconstruction of the intrigues yet published. They have found no direct link with Carranza.

33. Venustiano Carranza to General Pablo A. de la Garza, undated. Written on the letter is the notation that on February 1, 1916, the governor ordered all military commanders to apprehend them if they appeared in Nuevo León, Concluidos 1916, caja 1, AGNL.

NOTES TO PAGES 131–37

34. General Pablo A. de la Garza to Venustiano Carranza, February 3, 1916, Ibid. This action belies the allegation that Rodríguez was Carranza's nephew. See Testimony of Captain W. M. Hanson, *Investigation of Mexican Affairs*, SD 285, 66th Cong., 2nd Sess., vol. 1, p. 1227.

35. General Alfredo Ricaut to Venustiano Carranza, February 1, 1916, AREM, Topográfico 16-17-8.

36. Monterrey, *El Regiomontano*, February 14, 1916.

37. John R. Silliman to Secretary of State, February 12, 1916, 5:00 P.M., M 274, r 51, 812.00/17262, RG 59, USNA; the same at 6:00 P.M. adjacent Report of Agent E. M. Blanford, March 4, 1916, Bureau of Investigation, #232-84, RG 65, USNA. In the 5:00 P.M. telegram, Silliman said that Carranza's private secretary informed him personally and noted "all these arrests follow [State] Department's instructions of a few weeks ago."

38. Lt. Colonel Ramón Gómez, on the train accompanying the First Chief, to General Pablo A. de la Garza, February 5, 1916, Concluidos 1916, caja 1, AGNL. Adjacent to this letter are copies of various handbills, previously cited, and a voucher signed by Hernández and dated October 23, 1915, to reimburse expenses incurred for the PSD.

39. Salazar and Escobedo, *Las pugnas de la Gleba 1917–1922*, Part 1, pp. 116–118.

40. De la Cerda Silva, *El movimiento obrero en México*, p. 116.

41. Salazar and Escobedo, *Las pugnas de la Gleba 1917–1922*, Part 1, pp. 134, 148.

42. *Regeneración* subscriber list, November 22, 1915 shows the *Casa del Obrero Mundial* in Monterrey taking ten papers, a month after Treviño had formally closed it.

43. The description of Domínguez and, subsequently, of his associates, is drawn inter alia from Police Reports, February 8, 14, 17, 1916, Concluidos 1916, caja 1, AGNL.

44. *Regeneración* subscriber list, November 22, 1915.

45. Report of Agent Stone, July 13, 1916, Bureau of Investigation, #232-84, RG 65, USNA.

46. Testimony of Enríque Flores Magón, in *U. S. versus Ricardo and Enrique Flores Magón*, Case # 1071, 1916, RG 21, LNFRC.

47. The first count involved an article accusing Carranza of conniving with Wilson to deliver the Mexican people over to exploitation by U.S. plutocrats, and the third count contained an article urging Mexicans to take up arms against Carranza. *U.S. versus Ricardo and Enrique Flores Magón*, Ibid.

48. María Magón to Alexander Berkman, printed in *The Blast*, February 26, 1916.

49. *The Blast*, February 26, 1916; *Mother Earth*, March 1916.

50. *California Social Democrat*, March 25, 1916. Gutiérrez de Lara had accompanied John Kenneth Turner to Mexico in 1908 and showed him conditions in the Yucatan.

51. *Mother Earth*, April 1916.

52. *Mother Earth*, April 1916; *The Blast*, April 15, 1916; *California Social Democrat*, May 6, 1916.

53. *Regeneración*, April 29, 1916.

54. See Huitrón, *Orígenes e Historia del Movimiento Obrero en México*, pp. 198–206, which includes a reprint of Moncaleano's defense of Ricardo published in ¡LUZ! August 5, 1912. Huitrón mistakenly described Moncaleano as a Colombian because he had been a university professor there before going to Cuba en route to Mexico. See also Hart, *Anarchism and The Mexican Working Class, 1860–1931*, pp. 111–114.

55. Salazar and Escobedo, *Las Pugnas de la Gleba 1917–1922*, Part 1, p. 120.

56. Deathbed interview of Juan Francisco Moncaleano, assisted by Bianca de Moncaleano, with Carlos Minck, transmitted in Report of Agent E. M. Blanford, December 13, 1915, Bureau of Investigation, #232-84, RG 65, USNA. Moncaleano died from complications following surgery for stomach ulcers. The anti-PLM sentiment in southern California to which they appealed had its roots in the Baja campaign controversy. See Langham, *Border Trials*, pp. 34–35.

57. The coupons, dated from March 27 to April 30, 1916, are scattered in Post Office Department, CF #44548, RG 28, USNA.

58. *The Blast*, April 15, 1916.

59. Raat, *Revoltosos*, pp. 242–243.

60. *Regeneración*, May 14, 1916. The appeal was printed in both Spanish and English.

61. *Mother Earth*, July 1916.

62. William M. Cookson, Inspector, Los Angeles, to Inspector in Charge, San Francisco, February 21, 1916, Post Office Department, CF #44548, RG 28, USNA.
63. Report of Agent E. M. Blanford, March 14, 1916, Bureau of Investigation, #232-84, RG 65, USNA.
64. *Mother Earth*, April 1916; *Freedom Bulletin*, September 1929.
65. Testimony of Enríque Flores Magón, in *U. S. versus Ricardo and Enríque Flores Magón*, Case #1071, 1916, RG 21, LNFRC.
66. *The Blast*, June 1, 1916.
67. "Remarks of Court Prior to Pronouncing Sentence," June 22, 1916, in *U. S. versus Ricardo and Enríque Flores Magón*, Case # 1071, 1916, RG 21, LNFRC.
68. *Mother Earth*, August 1916. Goldman or one of her assistants undoubtedly helped correct the English grammar in Enrique's essay.
69. *Mother Earth*, August 1916. MacLachlan, *Anarchism and the Mexican Revolution: The Political Trials of Ricardo Flores Magón in the United States*, Chapter 4.
70. *Mother Earth*, August 1916; *The Blast*, July 15, 1916.
71. Jailer José Moncayo Ybarra to Director of the State Penitentiary of Nuevo León, June 10, August 4, 1916, Penitenciaría del Estado 1916, AGNL.

CHAPTER 8

1. Wilson Papers, series 7B, r 479.
2. Sandos, "German Involvement in Northern Mexico, 1915-1916: A New Look at the Columbus Raid;" Sandos, "The Plan of San Diego: War and Diplomacy on the Texas Border, 1915-1916." Villa's motives are still debated. See Katz, "Pancho Villa and the Attack on Columbus, New Mexico," and my comment coupled with his reply in the *American Historical Review*, vol. 84, February 1979, pp. 304-307.
3. Sandos, "Pancho Villa and American Security: Woodrow Wilson's Mexican Diplomacy Reconsidered," pp. 293-295.
4. Sandos, "Pancho Villa and American Security: Woodrow Wilson's Mexican Diplomacy Reconsidered," pp. 293-295.
5. Agent R. L. Barnes to A. Bruce Bielaski, January 22, 1916, and Agent J. B. Rogers to A. Bruce Bielaski, April 2, 1916, both in M 274, r 52, 812.00/17212, 17734, RG59, USNA. Report of Agent J. B. Rogers, February 5, 1916, Gray-Lane Files, #319, RG 43, USNA. All of these originally would have been in the Bureau of Investigation file #232-84.
6. Consul General Phillip Hana to Robert Lansing, February 3, 1916, M 274, r 51, 812.00/17260, RG59, USNA.
7. Consules Extranjeros en México, Concluidos 1916, caja 1, AGNL.
8. Friedrich Katz is the primary authority in this matter; his original 1964 study *Deutschland, Díaz und die Mexikanische Revolution*, and the substantially new 1981 book in English based upon it, *The Secret War in Mexico*, pp. 340 ff, contain no argument for nor evidence of a centrally directed German conspiracy in this affair. Katz's findings have been reinforced by another German scholar working on the same topic, Reinhard Doerries. See Doerries, *Imperial Challenge*, pp. 165-190.
9. R. L. Barnes to John E. Green, November 28, 1916, Mexican Claims, #139, RG 76, WNRC.
10. Testimony of Captain George Lester, Military Intelligence, *Hearings on Brewing and Liquor Interests and German and Bolshevik Propaganda*, SD 62, 66th Cong., 1st Sess., vol. 3, pp. 1784-1785. An army patrol found Mosley's body south of Laredo in July 1916. See Frederick Funston, San Antonio, to Adjutant General, October 11, 1916, AGO, #2377632, RG 94, USNA.
11. Yoshida, "Tekisasu-shū Dokuritsu undō ni Sanka Shita Nihonjin" ("Japanese Who Attended the Movement of Independence in the State of Texas"), pp. 121-123. Yoshida gives the date of Rodríguez' return to Mexico as "around February 6 [1916]" but by then, as presented in the previous chapter, he had been arrested by Carranza's governor in Nuevo León. Kunimoto, "Japan and Mexico, 1888-1917," pp. 202-206, has a slightly different translation of the title of Yoshida's memoir and gives the name Fukutaro Terasawa; whereas my translator, Satomi Kurosu, gave it as Fukumatsu Terasawa. Katz, *The Secret War in Mexico*, pp. 345-346, also

uses Fukutaro. Senator Albert Bacon Fall claimed that the Japanese who had accompanied Rodríguez into Texas returned to Mexico upon the orders of the Japanese minister in Mexico, who did not want them involved with the PSD. See Statement of Senator Fall, *Investigation of Mexican Affairs*, SD 285, 66th Cong., 2nd sess., vol. 1, p. 1228.

12. Harris and Sadler, "The Plan of San Diego and the Mexican–United States War Crisis of 1916: A Reexamination," pp. 392 ff., view the resurgence of the PSD as undertaken at Carranza's direction.

13. Weekly Report on Border Conditions, #157–160, quoted at #160, RAGO, RG 94, USNA. Harris and Sadler, "The Plan of San Diego and the Mexican–United States War Crisis of 1916: A Reexamination," pp. 395–396.

14. Sandos, "Pancho Villa and American Security: Woodrow Wilson's Mexican Diplomacy Reconsidered," pp. 303–304.

15. Sandos, "The Mexican Revolution and the United States, 1915–1917," pp. 351–354.

16. "Encuentros de las tropas constitucionales con fuerzas villistas en la época de la 'expedición punitiva,'" in Alvaro Obregón to Venustiano Carranza, May 4, 1916, cited in Salinas Carranza, *La expedición punitiva*, pp. 421–423.

17. "The Annual Report of the Southern Department, 1916," RAGO, RG 94, USNA; Constitutionalist confidential agent report, Del Rio, Texas, May 13, 1916, AREM, L-E-801 R, leg 7; C. Flores Tijerina to Venustiano Carranza, May 10, 1916, AVC, carpeta 77, doc 8458.

18. Hugh Scott and Frederick Funston to Secretary of War, May 8, 1916, M 274, r 53, 812.00/18125, RG 59, USNA.

19. *New York Times*, May 10, 1916.

20. For example, *The New York Call*, May 13, 15, 1916; *The Appeal to Reason*, April 29, May 13, 14, 1916; *Regeneración*, May 13, 1916.

21. Frederick Funston to Adjutant General, May 22, 1916, 9:42 P.M., AGO, #2377632, RG 94, USNA. See also Teodulo Beltrán to Francisco Pérez Abreu, May 19, 1916, AREM, L-E-801R, leg 15.

22. Link, *Wilson: Confusion and Crises*, pp. 283–299. On Carranza's pique see two separate telegrams, both with the same date and time from James Rodgers, Mexico City, to Secretary of State, May 23, 1916, 5:00 P.M., AGO, #2377632, RG 94, USNA.

23. Harris and Sadler, "The Plan of San Diego and the Mexican–United States War Crisis of 1916: A Reexamination," pp. 396–398.

24. Charles Warren, Assistant Attorney General to Secretary of State, June 7, 1916, Personal and Confidential, Office of the Counselor, box 241, RG 59, USNA. The Department of State, not Justice, was to pay for these temporary agents.

25. Weekly Report on Border Conditions, #168, RAGO, RG 94, USNA.

26. For example, Agent R. L. Barnes to A. Bruce Bielaski, June 8, 1916, Mexican Claims, #139, RG 76, WNRC; Agent R. L. Barnes to A. Bruce Bielaski, June 9, 1916; and Consul Alonso Garrett to Secretary of State, June 1, 1916, 10:00 P.M. and June 8, 1916, 4:00 P.M., AGO, #2377632, RG 94, USNA.

27. Weekly Report on Border Conditions, #169, RAGO, RG 94, USNA.

28. Ibid.

29. Report of Agent A. Oosterveen, Jr., June 18, 1916, Mexican Claims, #139, RG 76, WNRC.

30. Discussion of the Webb raid and of the involvement of Captain Pezzatt and Antonio Cuevas is based on the following sources: Weekly Report on Border Conditions, #170, RAGO, RG 94, USNA; Reports of Agents C. N. Idar, June 14, 1916, and T. Ross, July 8, 1916, Mexican Claims, #139, RG 76, WNRC; R. L. Barnes to A. Bruce Bielaski, June 12, 1916, Office of the Counselor, box 221, RG 59, USNA, for the tip.

31. Weekly Report on Border Conditions, #170, 171, RAGO, RG 94, USNA. John L. Rowe to Luis Cabrera, October 4, 1916, AREM, L-E-729, leg 1.

32. Reports of Agents C. N. Idar, June 19, 20, 1916, and T. Ross, July 7, 1916, Mexican Claims, #139, RG 76, WNRC.

33. Ibid. The report was undated, unsigned, and followed Ross's of July 8, 1916.

34. Special Reports, Brownsville District, June 17–23, 1916; Frederick Funston to Adjutant General, June 18, 1916, 2:20 and 5:51 P.M., RAGO, RG 94, USNA. Unless otherwise cited,

my discussion of this segment of the border disturbances around Brownsville comes from these reports. For a convenient summary, but which praises Parker, see Pierce, *A Brief History of the Lower Rio Grande Valley*, pp. 100–102. For Parker's view see his *The Old Army*, pp. 424–425.

35. Reynaldo Garza, Chief of Arms, Nuevo Laredo to Venustiano Carranza, June 19, 1916, 2:49 P.M.; Emiliano Nafarrate, Tampico to Venustiano Carranza, June 16, 1916, AREM, L-E-1443R, leg 1.

36. For example, Venustiano Carranza to General Jacinto Treviño at Juárez, June 19, 1916, Ibid. Carranza also instructed that in the event of hostilities the railroad be destroyed.

37. Emiliano Nafarrate to Venustiano Carranza, June 16, 18, 1916; Luis Caballero, governor and military commander of Tamaulipas, to Venustiano Carranza, June 17, 1916; Venustiano Carranza to Emiliano Nafarrate, June 28, 1916, Ibid.

38. Records of the Ferrocarril Nor-Oeste de México (Mexico Northwestern Railway Company) cited in Sandos, "Pancho Villa and American Security: Woodrow Wilson's Mexican Diplomacy Reconsidered," pp. 300 n. 36, 303, n. 49.

39. James L. Rodgers to Cándido Aguilar, May 23, 25, and June 6, 12, 1916, AREM, Topográfico 16-19-155.

40. "Action Between Troops C and K, 10th Cavalry, and Troops of the De Facto Government of Mexico, June 21, 1916," AGO, #2377632, RG 94, USNA. Recollection of interpreter Lemuel Spillsbury cited in Wharfield, *10th Cavalry and Border Fights*, p. 35. For most of the Mexican documents see *DHRM*, 12, pp. 9–116.

41. John Pershing to Frederick Funston, June 22, 1916, Southern Department Telegrams, RG 120, USNA; Memorandum for the Chief of Staff, June 22, 1916, Wilson Papers, series 2, r 80.

42. Robert Lansing to Eliseo Arredondo, June 20, 1916, *Foreign Relations 1916*, pp. 580–592. Wilson read and approved the note before it was sent, Desk Diary, June 18, 1916, Lansing Papers.

43. Eliseo Arredondo to Robert Lansing, June 24, 1916, *Foreign Relations 1916*, p. 595.

44. Robert Lansing to James Rodgers, June 25, 1916, *Foreign Relations* 1916, p. 595.

45. Link, *Wilson: Confusions and Crises*, pp. 307–311.

46. To the Congress, June [27], 1916, Wilson Papers, series 7B, r 479.

47. Desk Diary, June 28, 1916, Lansing Papers.

48. Frederick Funston to Adjutant General, June 27, 1916, Wilson Papers, series 2, r 80.

49. James Rodgers to Secretary of State, June 28, 1916, *Foreign Relations 1916*, p. 597.

50. Richmond, "Confrontation and Reconciliation: Mexicans and Spaniards During the Mexican Revolution, 1910–1920," pp. 215–228; Katz, *The Secret War in Mexico*, pp. 344–350.

51. For examples, see the Mexico City and Monterrey editions of *El Demócrata*, March–June, 1916; Nuevo León, *Periódico Oficial*, March–June 1916.

52. Alfredo Ricaut to Venustiano Carranza, July 8, 1916, AREM, L-E-1443R, leg 1.

53. José Saldana to Governor Pablo A. de la Garza, June 26, July 17, 1916, Concluidos 1916, caja 1, AGNL.

54. Lt. Col. M. Carranza to Venustiano Carranza, June 10, 1916, AREM, L-E-1443R, leg 1.

55. In Camargo, fifty-six people formed "Defensa Nacional" after the Glenn Springs raid, according to its president, Gregorio Solis to Venustiano Carranza, [May or June, 1916], AVC, carpeta 78, doc 8668. In Jímenez in mid-June, people gathered in a three-hour demonstration to protest the U.S. presence, Emiliano Triana to Venustiano Carranza, June 14, 1916, AVC, Telegramas: Chihuahua 1916.

56. Eliseo Arredondo to Venustiano Carranza, June 24, 26, 28, 1916, AREM, L-E-1443R, leg 1.

57. All of carpetas 85 and most of 86 in the AVC contain responses of support to Carranza endorsing his circular warning of June 19 to prepare to resist an invasion and his statement about Carrizal.

58. The report of Luis Frias, Storekeeper, General Artillery Storehouse, June 30, 1916, AVC, carpeta 84, doc 9693, indicated that his empty warehouse had that date received 150,000

NOTES TO PAGES 152–57

7mm cartridges, total June production from the severely damaged National Munitions Factory. Domestically produced cartridges were considered inferior to those of American manufacture.
  59. *LIRC*, p. 270.
  60. Speech to New York Press Club, June 30, 1916, Wilson Papers, series 7, subseries A, r 477.
  61. "S" to Victor Rendón, June 30, 1916, O'Laughlin Papers.
  62. For example, Edmundo F. Cota Osuna, Expediente Personal, AREM, 27-7-13, an undercover agent working from Los Angeles to San Diego spreading Constitutionalist propaganda and involved with fomenting the Moncaleano-Flores Magón feud discussed in the previous chapter.
  63. "S" to Victor Rendón, July 1, 1916, O'Laughlin Papers.
  64. Desk Diary, July 3, 1916, Lansing Papers.
  65. Victor Rendón to John C. O'Laughlin, July 8, 1916, O'Laughlin Papers.
  66. Jacinto Treviño to Venustiano Carranza, July 9, 10, 1916, AVC, Telegramas: Chihuahua 1916. Despite the relaxation, Treviño's forces remained "profoundly short" of food, and the arms embargo continued in effect. Holcombe, "U.S. Arms Control and the Mexican Revolution," p. 132.
  67. Eliseo Arredondo to Robert Lansing, July 12, 1916 and Frank L. Polk to James Rodgers, July 20, 1916, *Foreign Relations* 1916, pp. 601, 603–604.
  68. Polk Diary, July 10–August 9, 1916, Polk Papers.

CHAPTER 9

  1. *Mother Earth*, September 1916.
  2. Judge T. Wesley Hook to Woodrow Wilson, June 4, 1916, transmitting a petition he translated from Spanish from Rev. Fenón Moraida to the president and bearing thirty-six signatures protesting Texas Ranger treatment of Mexicans in the lower Rio Grande valley, Department of Justice, SNF #90755, RG 60, USNA. A copy is in the Wilson Papers, series 4, case 95z, r 216.
  3. U. S. Attorney, Houston, to Attorney General, December 21, 1916, Department of Justice, SNF #90755, RG 60, USNA.
  4. Report of Agent F. Fukuda, December 22, 1916, Office of the Counselor, box 221, RG 59, USNA.
  5. See the discussion in Chapter 7 involving the closing of the Monterrey Casa in late October 1915. Hart, *Anarchism and The Mexican Working Class, 1860–1931*, pp. 132–133.
  6. Hart, *Anarchism and The Mexican Working Class, 1860–1931*, pp. 140–141.
  7. Hart, *Anarchism and The Mexican Working Class, 1860–1931*, pp. 140–141.
  8. Ejoff [signature, probably of a spy], Alto Reportazgo, undated [late 1914], AREM, L-E-794, leg 19. Americans mistakenly thought Krumm-Heller a German propagandist for Carranza and a recruiter for the PSD. See Randolf Robertson to Robert Lansing, August 12, 1915; May 19, 1916, M 274, r 47 and 53, 812.00/15622, 18257, RG 59, USNA. For an accurate view of Krumm-Heller see Katz, *The Secret War in Mexico*, pp. 348–349, 428–429.
  9. Hart, *Revolutionary Mexico: The Coming and Process of the Mexican Revolution*, p. x and passim.
  10. Levenstein, *Labor Organizations in the United States and Mexico*, pp. 30–62.
  11. Levenstein, *Labor Organizations in the United States and Mexico*, pp. 30–62.
  12. Womack, "The Mexican Economy During the Revolution," pp. 80–123.
  13. Hart, *Anarchism and The Mexican Working Class, 1860–1931*, pp. 151–155; Salazar and Escobedo, *Las pugnas de la Gleba, 1917–1922*, Part 1, pp. 181–184; Ankerson, *Agrarian Warlord: Saturnino Cedillo and the Mexican Revolution in San Luis Potosí*, pp. 86–87; Hall, *Alvaro Obregón: Power and Revolution in Mexico, 1911–1920*, pp.110–117, 161–162.
  14. Levenstein, *Labor Organizations in the United States and Mexico*, pp. 46–49.
  15. For the appointments, see Woodrow Wilson to Franklin K. Lane, Gregory Gray, and John Mott, August 31, 1916; and Eliseo Arredondo to Robert Lansing, August 4, 1916, *Foreign Relations*, 1916, pp. 606–608.

16. Levenstein, *Labor Organizations in the United States and Mexico*, pp. 53–54, says Gompers was not persuaded by the argument. Yet he continued to support Carranza.

17. Murray, "Behind the Drums of Revolution: The Labor Movement in Mexico as Seen by an American Trade Unionist," pp. 37, 237–244. By this time, Murray had become a labor spy for the AFL and U.S. governmental authorities. See Hart, *Revolutionary Mexico*, pp. 308, 335, and Chapter 1, above.

18. *New York Call*, September 22, 1915; *Appeal to Reason*, October 16, 1915; *The National Rip-Saw*, October, 1915; *The Rebel*, November 20, 1915; *California Social Democrat*, September 25, 1915.

19. *Appeal to Reason*, January 22, 1916.

20. Green, *Grass-Roots Socialism: Radical Movements in the Southwest, 1895–1943*, does not discuss the PSD. While there were literate Spanish-speaking socialists in the Southwest, none seems to have discovered the PSD during its existence. *Who's Who in Socialist America* listed twenty-six Texans, or 5.2 percent of the 498 enumerated—none of whom lived in the area of South Texas where the raiding occurred. *The Rebel*, the major Texas socialist newspaper, which had a reciprocal subscription with *Regeneración*, made no mention of the PSD or its leaders.

21. *The National Rip-Saw*, July 1916. In the same vein, see *Appeal to Reason*, May 13, July 1, 1916; *California Social Democrat*, April 1, 8, 15, 1916; *The Rebel*, March 8 [misprint], 1916.

22. Edmundo Martínez, "The Mexican Labor Movement," *The Masses*, September 1916. Martínez had been ingratiating himself with Gompers on Carranza's behalf and monitoring Mexican radical labor attempts to woo AFL support. See Levenstein, *Labor Organizations in the United States and Mexico*, pp. 25–26, 33–34, 51–52.

23. *The Blast*, September 1, 1916; *Mother Earth*, September 1916.

24. Frost, *The Mooney Case*, is the best study of the incident and its consequences.

25. Charles Warren to L. S. Rowe, August 29, 1916, Gray-Lane Files, Doc #56, RG 43, USNA.

26. *El Demócrata Fronterizo*, May 27, 1916.

27. See above, note 2.

28. Woodrow Wilson to T. W. Gregory, June 21, 1916 and Gregory to Wilson, June 16, 1916, Wilson Papers, series 4, case 95z, r 216. Gregory guaranteed fairness in federal cases but could only use moral suasion upon the Texans.

29. Woodrow Wilson to T. W. Hook, July 8, 1916, Wilson Papers, series 3, r 146.

30. Secretary of War to Attorney General, July 17, 19, 1916, AGO, #2377632, RG 94, USNA. After June 19, 1916, all federal prisoners were surrendered to the U.S. Army.

31. Testimony of Captain J. J. Sanders, *Investigation of the State Ranger Force*, vol. 3, pp. 1396–1398; Testimony of T. W. Hook, Ibid., vol. 1, pp. 242–246.

32. William E. McCord to Department of Justice, December 9, 1916, Department of Justice, SNF #90755, RG 60, USNA.

33. Inspector in Charge, Brownsville, to Supervising Inspector, Immigration Service, El Paso, June 17, 1916, INS, File #54159/79-A, RG 85, USNA.

34. Philip T. Wright to Department of Justice, June 9, 1916, Department of Justice, SNF #90755, RG 60, USNA.

35. Sandos, "Pancho Villa and American Security: Woodrow Wilson's Mexican Diplomacy Reconsidered," pp. 308–309.

36. Gray-Lane Files, numbered docs 2, 11, 16, 17, 19 and lettered docs F, H, J, RG 43, USNA. See also the Franklin K. Lane file, consisting of two boxes, Fall Collection. These two sources reveal the real work of the American commissioners not contained in the published *Foreign Relations*, 1917, pp. 916–938.

37. See inter alia Cumberland, *Mexican Revolution: Constitutionalist Years*, p. 324; Clendenen, *The U. S. and Pancho Villa*, pp. 288–289; various reports, AREM, L-E-722R, leg 1.

38. Cumberland, *Mexican Revolution: Constitutionalist Years*, pp. 324–325. On the proposal to have Pershing attempt capturing Villa in September 1916, see Tasker Bliss to Adjutant General, September 21, 1916 and Robert Lansing to Franklin K. Lane, September 25, 1916, 8:27 P.M., Fall Collection. Bliss was military advisor to the U. S. commissioners, and the commission was then meeting in New London, Connecticut.

39. For the campaign, see Juan Barragán, "La brillante campaña del General Murguía en Chihuahua," *El Universal*, November 10, 16, 24, 1955; Delgado Ortíz, "Breve narración sobre acontecimientos de la Revolución," *El Legionario*, November 15, 1957.

40. Francisco Murguía to Venustiano Carranza, December 13, 1916, cited in Cumberland, *Mexican Revolution: Constitutionalist Years*, p. 325, n. 15. Murguía acused Treviño of crimes ranging from cowardice to padding his enlistment roster with the names of the dead in order to collect their pay. See his letter to Treviño, May 9, 1917, cited in Antero de Mendoza, "Treviño juzgado por Murguía," *Nosotros*, October 6, 1956.

41. Report of Agent M. Sorola, January 22, 1917, and Report of Agent R. L. Barnes, January 30, 1917, Mexican Claims, #139, RG 76, WNRC.

42. Reports of Agent F. Fukuda, January 26, 27, 1917, Bureau of Investigation, #232-84, RG 65, USNA.

43. Sandos, "Pancho Villa and American Security: Woodrow Wilson's Mexican Diplomacy Reconsidered," p. 309. See above, note 4.

44. Cumberland, *Mexican Revolution: Constitutionalist Years*, pp. 325–330.

45. The decree is reprinted in González Ramírez, *Planes políticos*, pp. 197–202.

46. Baker, *Woodrow Wilson*, vol. 6, p. 77.

47. Meyer, *México y los Estados Unidos en el conflicto petrolero (1917–1942)*, pp. 107–114; Niemeyer, *Revolution at Querétaro*, passim.

48. By far the best account of the celebrated Zimmermann Telegram, with all of its complexities, is by Katz, *The Secret War in Mexico*, pp. 348–367, and the notes on pp. 612–615, especially n. 115. I have quoted his translation of the text as given in that work on p. 354.

49. Katz, *The Secret War in Mexico*, pp. 348–367.

50. Cumberland, *Mexican Revolution: The Constitutionalist Years*, pp. 362–364.

51. Sandos, "The Mexican Revolution and the United States, 1915–1917," pp. 442, 449.

52. Preston, *Aliens and Dissenters*, pp. 144–146.

53. Judgment, *United States versus Ricardo Flores Magón and Librado Rivera*, Case #1421, 1918, LNFRC. Librado was sentenced to fifteen years. For a good discussion of this case see MacLachlan, *Anarchism and the Mexican Revolution*, Chapter 5.

54. Womack, *Zapata and the Mexican Revolution*, pp. 323–329.

55. Richmond, *Venustiano Carranza's Nationalist Struggle, 1893–1920*, pp. 228–235.

56. Richmond, *Venustiano Carranza's Nationalist Struggle, 1893–1920*, p. 234.

57. Cockcroft, *Intellectual Precursors*, pp. 86–87, 95, 230–232.

58. Ricardo Flores Magón to Nicolás T. Bernal, December 20, 1920, cited in Albro, "Ricardo Flores Magón and the Liberal Party," p. 237.

59. Ricardo Flores Magón to Lilly Sarnoff, December 28, 1920, in Avrich, "Prison Letters of Ricardo Flores Magón to Lilly Sarnoff," p. 392.

60. Albro, "Ricardo Flores Magón and the Liberal Party," pp. 237–238.

61. Albro, "Ricardo Flores Magón and the Liberal Party," pp. 237–238. Raat, *Revoltosos*, pp. 277–286.

62. Langham, *Border Trials*, p. 59. MacLachlan, *Anarchism and the Mexican Revolution*, Chapter 7, discusses the contributing role diabetes would have played in the heart attack. Raat, *Revoltosos*, pp. 286–287 and n. 31, disagrees with the diabetes diagnosis. The real point is that Ricardo died of a myocardial infarction.

63. Raat, *Revoltosos*, pp. 287–289.

64. Cited in Albro, "Ricardo Flores Magón and the Liberal Party," p. 240, and in MacLachlan, *Anarchism and the Mexican Revolution*, Chapter 7.

65. Avrich, *Anarchist Portraits*, p. 213.

CHAPTER 10

1. Ricardo Flores Magón to Lilly Sarnoff, March 14, 1922, in Avrich, "Prison Letters of Ricardo Flores Magón to Lilly Sarnoff," p. 419.

2. See the discussion in the "Essay on Sources."

3. Memorandum by the secretary of state of an interview with the Chinese minister, November 12, 1917, in *The Lansing Papers*, vol. 2, pp. 451–453. See also *Foreign Relations*,

1917, pp. 258–274. De Conde, *A History of American Foreign Policy*, 2nd ed., pp. 417–418. For the background of Japanese activity with Mexico, see Sandos, "The Mexican Revolution and the United States, 1915–1917," pp. 404–412.

4. For further discussion see Katz, *The Secret War In Mexico*.

5. They also led African Americans and Japanese.

6. This point is suggested by Romo, *East Los Angeles: History of A Barrio*, chapter 5, in which he argues that in Los Angeles, a "Brown Scare" repressing Mexican and Mexican American radicals, preceded and paralleled the "Red Scare."

7. A similar set of questions could be posed about African American participation in the PSD and the consequences for the black community.

8. Joll, *The Anarchists*, 2nd ed., chapters 1 and 6, restate points made in the 1st edition.

9. This term, coined by Paulo Freire in Portuguese as *conscientização* and discussed extensively in his *Pedagogy of the Oppressed*, refers to the twin processes by which a person becomes conscious of economic and social exploitation *and* has his conscience aroused to the point of action to abolish that exploitation.

10. Boff and Boff, *Introducing Liberation Theology*, p. 5. This is the best general survey in English.

11. Boff and Boff, *Introducing Liberation Theology*, chapters 3 and 4. See also Berryman, *Liberation Theology*.

12. Berryman, *The Religious Roots of Rebellion*, especially chapters 7 and 9. Miranda's *Communism in the Bible* is, as the author describes it, a manifesto.

13. Ellul, *Autopsy of Revolution*, pp. 160–163. For an interesting comment on this passage see Johnson, *Autopsy on People's War*, p. 105.

ESSAY ON SOURCES

> Memory is actually a very important factor in struggle. . . . If one controls people's memory, one controls their dynamism. . . . It is vital to have possession of this memory, to control it, administer it, tell it what it must contain.
>
> Michel Foucault[1]

Perhaps the most disturbing aspect of this story of anarchism in the U.S. frontier and in the Mexican Revolution is the fact that most of the information presented here, and some of the interpretations as well, seem new, even to specialists. What is excluded from national memory is easily as important as what is included. To understand how the Plan of San Diego became lost and Ricardo Flores Magón misunderstood in the national consciousness of two cultures requires an inquiry into the process by which information is retained in scholarly dialogue. Since, in this instance, the problem is intertwined in the history of two countries, we must consider each in turn.

The entrance of the United States into the Great War permitted the Wilson administration to silence radical domestic critics with the weapon it had lacked against the PLM and the PSD: the charge of treason. Threats to U.S. national security raised by PSD raiding and galvanized by Villa's attack upon Columbus made it possible to take the Zimmermann Telegram seriously. With the declaration of war against Germany and the Entente, the U.S. government could attack its critics successfully for speaking against it.

Ricardo as "precursor" served a useful purpose in anticipating the Mexican Constitution of 1917. Howard F. Cline, in *Mexico: Revolution to Evolution,* discerned fifty-two specific points in the PLM 1906 platform that "nearly all eventually worked their way into the Constitution of 1917."[2] A later refinement by James Cockcroft reduced the number adopted in the Constitution to twenty-three and identified twenty-five more that exceeded the document's wording.[3] Yet these valuable studies, and others, tacitly accept the importance of Ricardo's political life in terms of his contribution to the Constitutionalist victory. Even that view of his importance, however, came late among Americans.

Shortly after the Revolution, U.S. observers in Mexico scarcely thought of Ricardo at all. In the Mexico of Obregón and Calles, they did not notice the PLM. In 1923, the first American observations appeared: Carleton Beals wrote *Mexico: An Interpretation* and Howard Alsworth Ross issued *The Social Revolution,* which, despite its title, was nonideological. The "Red Scare" had made Mexico an appealing and intriguing place for progressives to visit: while Beals was sympathetic and Ross not, both men reckoned the revolution as having begun with Madero. Beals and Ross differed little from previous radicals who had come to accept Madero and Carranza, and who ignored Ricardo, rejecting his criticisms as mere personalism.

Herbert I. Priestley, in the first scholarly history to include the Revolution, reduced the Flores Magón brothers to an afterthought in a description of those who prepared the way.

> *Socialist agitators, the brothers Ricardo and Enríque Flores Magón, and the brothers Vásquez Gómez, with their anti-Porfirism, also contributed to the preparation of the minds of the people for the wave of remonstrance against the atrophied government [of Díaz] which began to sweep over the land during the year of the Centennial [of Independence from Spain in 1810].*[4]

Priestley's misidentification of Floresmagonista ideology testified to the eclipse of the brothers and the PLM in American consciousness.

Further contributing to the eclipse in the United States of the Flores Magón brothers and their thought was the celebrated case of anarchists Nicola Sacco and Bartolomeo Vanzetti. These Italian anarchists were convicted in 1921 for the robbery and murder of a paymaster and his guard in South Braintree, Massachusetts, a year earlier. The Sacco-Vanzetti case became an international *cause célèbre,* as their partisans decried the conviction as a miscarriage of U.S. justice, and their antagonists upheld it as just and necessary.

Ricardo and his inner circle had never been tried for a capital offense in the United States and their cause, no matter how desperate it may have seemed to them, was obscured by the cases of the McNamara brothers, Mooney, and Sacco and Vanzetti. Ironically, Sacco and Vanzetti fled to Mexico in 1917, after the United States entered the war, to try and find passage through that neutral country to Italy; they expected revolution to break out there at any moment. Sacco and Vanzetti eventually gave up and returned to the United States. Their trip to Monterrey had been made with the aid of Mexican anarchist comrades, undoubtedly some of Ricardo's PLM followers—perhaps even former PSD adherents. One of the inner circle of their defense committee on propaganda was Frank López, a Spanish anarchist who had been a subscriber to *Regeneración.*[5] With Ricardo's death, there was no other cause more important to the American left than Sacco and Vanzetti, and their execution in 1927 effectively silenced discussion of anarchism for years.

Ignoring Ricardo and his work in Mexico and the United States, probably because the "return to normalcy" meant that discussion of such topics was inappropriate, became the norm in writing of the late 1920s and early 1930s. J. Fred Rippy in a work published in 1926, *The United States and Mexico,* made no mention of the PLM or Ricardo. Neither did Ernest Gruening in 1928 in *Mexico and Its Heritage.* Frank Tannenbaum wrote *The Mexican Agrarian Revolution* in 1929 without referring to Ricardo and the PLM; Tannenbaum began his account of the upheaval with Madero. Even Wilfrid Hardy Callcott, who wrote a lengthy monograph entitled *Liberalism in Mexico: 1857 to 1929*—which ought to have included some mention of Ricardo and the PLM—failed to remark upon them at all. American leftist writers and scholars embraced the agrarian aspect of the Mexican Revolution,[6] but accepted the Constitutionalist version of what had happened.

Memory of the Plan of San Diego suffered an analogous fate in the two countries. It was first noted in the Mexican press in 1940, but the information about the Plan was, as may be expected, fragmented. The author thought it essentially an affair of *pochos,* the derogatory Mexican term for those of Mexican ancestry who live in the northern frontier.[7] Manuel González Ramírez compiled the various political pronouncements and plans issued by the multiple factions that participated in the Revolution and published them in 1954 as *Planes políticos y otros documentos*. Included were Madero's Plan of San Luis Potosí, Zapata's Plan of Ayala, and Carranza's Plan of Guadalupe, among many others. The Plan of San Diego, however, was omitted, even though copies existed in Mexico of the revised document—clearly anarchist-communist in ideology—of February 20, 1915.[8] The PSD was not seen by Mexicans as part of their Revolution.

In the United States, information about the PSD became scattered in many different locations. In South Texas, the Tejano and Mexican populations dispersed in the wave of violence and repression. The population of Mexican ancestry turned over in the last half of 1915 and again in 1916–1917 as the untoward incidents continued unabated. This violence and the diaspora, in the view of folkloricist José Limón, undoubtedly accounts for the virtual absence of *corridos*—popular ballads of the border area—about the PSD and its leaders.[9]

Texas Ranger outrages continued as members of the force harassed suspected war dissenters, radicals, German plotters, and draft dodgers in 1917–1918. In January 1919, José T. Canales, representative from Brownsville, requested an investigation into alleged Ranger wrongdoings that unleashed a torrent of resentment. A joint committee of the Texas state legislature convened on January 31 to hear testimony. The committee found uncontradicted evidence that Ranger captains of Companies "A," "B," and "D" had committed criminal acts. Sanders of "A" had pistol-whipped a judge; Fox of "B" had desecrated Mexican corpses by dragging them through the brush and making a postcard of the act; Ransom of "D" had murdered four Mexican and Tejano suspects after the train derailment of October 18, 1915. The committee concluded that "the Rangers have become guilty of, and are responsible for, the gross violation of both civil and criminal laws of this State, and deserve the condemnation of all law-abiding citizens for so doing."[10] The committee then recommended that the Ranger force, its size reduced, be placed under a separate authority responsible to both the state adjutant general and the governor. The committee ordered its own three volumes of testimony sealed,[11] but a copy was sent to Washington later for use by the Mexican Claims Commission.

Local historians, generally Anglo, lumped the PSD together with general brigandage from Mexico, and the era from 1910–1916 became known as that of the "Bandit Wars" or border raids.[12] When some Texas Rangers wrote their memoirs, they justified their behavior in terms of the threat to local safety that the "bad Mexicans" posed.[13] Scholars too echoed the border raid theme, with little discussion of the PSD.

Scholarship was limited for many years because of various governmental restrictions on access to information collected by its agencies, and by the dispersal of materials from central files in those agencies to other organizations. The first instance of this latter activity occurred when the Mexican-American Joint Commission of 1916 met. Materials from the Department of State and the Adjutant General's Office were made available to the U.S. commissioners, and some of it was relayed to their Mexican counterparts. Since J. B. Rogers worked as a special agent for the Department of State, in addition to the Bureau of Investigation, some of the reports he sent to State, especially negative interpretive ones, were shown to the commissioners.

Rogers's more accurate descriptive reports went to the Bureau of Investigation within the Department of Justice, and that agency sent many of them, along with reports from other agents, to the Mexican Claims Commission. Under a special convention of September 10, 1923, the Mexican Claims Commission was created to settle U.S. claims for damages arising from the violence of the Mexican Revolution. Many of those Texans aggrieved during the violence of the PSD sought financial redress through that agency; Bureau of Investigation reports, along with those from the Adjutant General's Office and the Department of State, were submitted as evidence of the alleged Carranza conspiracy to secure diplomatic recognition by fostering the PSD and border unrest.[14]

Together, the 1916 Mexican-American Joint Commission and the 1923 Mexican Claims Commission clearly communicated the suspicion with which the Wilson administration viewed Carranza, and both deliberative bodies continued to perpetuate ill will toward Mexico. The records of these commissions, however, were not made available to scholars until the 1940s. A decade later the general Department of State records were also opened. The more restricted files, especially those of the Office of the Counselor, were opened only in the early 1970s. In 1977, the Federal Bureau of Investigation (FBI) provided access to the Bureau of Investigation files relating to WWI, which the FBI had microfilmed during the 1950s. Some of those records cannot be read in that file due to poor filming; copies must be sought in Mexican Claims or in the Department of Justice Straight Numerical File. Thus, at any given point in the search into the history of Ricardo and the PLM in America, or of the PSD, scholars have had fairly limited access to all the relevant information. As a result, historical memory among scholars in the United States on these subjects has been restricted.

For many years scholars had only the public document created by Senator Albert Bacon Fall, a noted interventionist, to guide them. Fall convened a special Investigation of Mexican Affairs in 1920 and published its two volumes of testimony under that title. He called a wide range of witnesses, including former agents of the Bureau of Investigation and the Military Intelligence Division of the War Department, in addition to private citizens and local lawmen. Fall's informants detailed aspects of the U.S. government's conspiracy theory alleging Carranza's manipulation of the PSD and the Floresmagonista connections. Fall even reproduced a translation of the January 6, 1915, version of the PSD, a document that contains some anarchist references but that interested Americans primarily for its race war and irredentist elements. The PSD material, however, was wedged in among a far greater range of information and misinformation designed to support the case for U.S. intervention in Mexico. Early scholarly writing was based upon either Fall's report or a combination of it and some archival material from the Departments of State and War.[15]

I contributed to the confusion about the PSD when I published an article based upon my reading of the Gray-Lane files from the records of the 1916 joint commission, Fall's report, and Department of State and War documents. I accepted the conspiracy theory and extended discussion of the PSD to 1916.[16] I had not then read material in the Mexican archives. When I did read the materials in Carranza's archive, the Mexican Foreign Relations Archive, and several others, I revised my view of Carranza. I wrote my revision in 1978, the same year that Charles Harris and Louis Sadler advanced the Carranza conspiracy argument another notch.[17]

Chicano scholars were interested in the PSD, and Juan Gómez-Quiñones, one of the founders of the journal *Aztlán*, published the Fall report's version of the PSD, along with his analysis, in 1970. He argued that it seemed unlikely that Carranza would have used the PSD to gain recognition from Wilson when a more probable consequence of such manipulation would have been intervention.[18]

Subsequent Chicano scholarship on the PSD went in many directions. Douglas Richmond, in 1980, pressed the Carranza conspiracy argument, whereas a year later, Rodolfo Rocha, following the lead of Eric Hobsbawm, argued that Pizaña and De la Rosa were "social bandits" who acted alone and used Mexico only as a refuge.[19] David Montejano, in his arresting 1987 book, viewed the PSD as part of labor resistance to capitalist coercion, the repression of which was necessary to insure a docile work force.[20]

ESSAY ON SOURCES

Treatment of Ricardo Flores Magón and the PLM in the United States tended to concentrate on the Baja incident and on the varied PLM encounters with U.S. law. Lowell Blaisdell, in *The Desert Revolution: Baja California, 1911,* issued in 1962, used some trial records to inform his work. In 1981, Thomas Langham pursued this tack further in *Border Trials: Ricardo Flores Magón and the Mexican Liberals;* by then more of the judicial records were available. Colin MacLachlan, in *Anarchism and the Mexican Revolution: The Political Trials of Ricardo Flores Magón in the United States* (1991), has made the most far-ranging use of the court records. He has drawn upon all the cases to demonstrate Ricardo's development as a perceived political threat to the U.S. government.

In his 1973 monograph, *Sembradores, Ricardo Flores Magón y el Partido Liberal Mexicano: A Eulogy and Critique,* Gómez-Quiñones sought to assess Ricardo's influence upon the community of Mexican ancestry in the United States. The fragmentation of information into so many scattered sources, however, frustrated attempts at completeness. Even Dirk Raat's richly informed and specialized work, *Revoltosos: Mexico's Rebels in the United States, 1903–1923,* devoted but two pages to the PSD— described as "one of the most bizarre of rebel events"—and did not pursue its relationship to Ricardo and the PLM.[21]

The failure of historical memory in America to recall accurately Ricardo and the PSD has analogs in the study of the Mexican Revolution. Two studies that won the Bolton Prize in the 1980s illustrate the point. Friedrich Katz in 1981 published *The Secret War in Mexico: Europe, the United States, and the Mexican Revolution,* in which he argued that Mexico was the site of the first international struggle by the great powers in the third world in the twentieth century. He accepted the Carranza conspiracy theory of the PSD and gave the movement scant attention. Four years later, Alan Knight's two volume *The Mexican Revolution* appeared; Knight argued that the Revolution had been a domestic affair with all important decisions affecting it made in Mexico. Both books won the same prize, both are richly informed and clearly written, and they view the Revolution in profoundly different ways. Knight did not mention the PSD.

Even John Hart, who earlier had written an important study of Mexican anarchism,[22] did not then consider the PSD. In his 1987 study, *Revolutionary Mexico: The Coming and Process of the Mexican Revolution,* Hart argued that the Mexican Revolution was the first of the twentieth century's "wars of national liberation," a struggle to reclaim the national patrimony from foreign exploitation. Nonetheless, Hart made no mention of the PSD.

This essay and the sources that follow are designed to facilitate further research. Perhaps, when more is known of the movement and its impact, revisionist histories of both the United States and Mexico will include discussion of the Plan of San Diego, Texas.

NOTES

1. Cited in Baker, "Memory and Practice: Politics and the Representation of the Past in Eighteenth-Century France," p. 134.
2. Cited in Albro, "Ricardo Flores Magón and the Liberal Party," p. 65.
3. Cockcroft, *Intellectual Precursors,* pp. 239–245.
4. Priestley, *The Mexican Nation: A History,* p. 395.
5. Russell, *Sacco and Vanzetti: The Case Resolved,* p. 91; *Regeneración* subscriber list, November 22, 1915. Russell claims, based on the rembrances of the son of Giovanni Gambera

of the defense committee, that Sacco was guilty and Vanzetti innocent. See Avrich, *Anarchist Portraits,* pp. 162–175, and his *Sacco and Vanzetti,* for the Italian anarchist background.

6. Britton, *Carleton Beals,* pp. 30–50.

7. Luis F. Bustamante, "El Plan San Diego y la Revolución pocha," *Jueves de Excélsior,* January 18, 1940.

8. Manifesto: A Los Pueblos Oprimidos de América!, February 20, 1915, San Diego, Texas, El Congreso Revolucionario, in Archivo de Samuel Espinosa de los Monteros, Tomo II, following p. 60, INAH, México, D.F.; Concluidos 1916, caja 1, AGNL.

9. Conversation with José Limón, University of Redlands, March 7, 1988.

10. Texas State Legislature, House, *Journal,* 36th Leg., Reg. sess., p. 537.

11. Webb, *The Texas Rangers,* had seen the *Investigation of the State Ranger Force,* but I was told in Austin in 1975 that I was the first other than he to see the report. I knew of its existence because I had found two of the three volumes in the Mexican Claims files.

12. For example, Robertson, *Wild Horse Desert,* pp. 239–50; Anders, *Boss Rule in South Texas,* pp. 215–239.

13. Peavey, *Echoes from the Rio Grande,* pp. 93–129; Sterling, *Trails and Trials of a Texas Ranger,* pp. 21–52.

14. In addition to all the citations previously given, please note especially the third epigraph in Chapter 6, Records of Research and Information Section, Mexican Claims, #145, RG 76, WNRC.

15. For example, Cumberland, "Border Raids in the Lower Rio Grande Valley, 1915;" Hager, "The Plan of San Diego: Unrest on the Texas Frontier, 1915;" Gerlach, "Conditions along the Border, 1915: The Plan de San Diego."

16. Sandos, "The Plan of San Diego: War and Diplomacy on the Texas Border, 1915–1916."

17. I filed my dissertation, "The Mexican Revolution and the United States, 1915–1917: The Impact of Conflict in the Texas–Tamaulipas Frontier upon the Emergence of Revolutionary Government in Mexico," on March 31. Harris and Sadler's "The Plan of San Diego and the Mexican War Crisis of 1916" appeared in August.

18. Gómez-Quiñones, "The Plan of San Diego Reviewed," pp. 124–130.

19. Richmond, "La Guerra de Texas se renova: Mexican Insurrection and Carrancista Ambitions, 1910–1920;" and Rocha, "The Influence of the Mexican Revolution on the Mexico-Texas Border, 1910–1916," pp. 264–265, 344–345.

20. Montejano, *Anglos and Mexicans in the Making of Texas,* pp. 117–128.

21. Raat, *Revoltosos,* pp. 262–263.

22. Hart, *Anarchism and the Mexican Working Class, 1860–1930.*

BIBLIOGRAPHY

UNPUBLISHED SOURCES

ARCHIVES: MEXICO

Archivo General del Estado de Nuevo León (AGNL)

Sección Histórica
   Concluidos 1916.
   Correspondencia con el Estado de Tamaulipas, 1910–1918.
   Inspección General de Policía, 1914–1917.
   Minutas, 1917.
   Penitenciaría del Estado, 1916.
   Periódico Oficial, 1916–1917.
   Ramo Militar, 1914–1917.

Archivo General de la Nación (AGN), México, D.F.

Ramo de Gobernación.
Ramo de la Revolución.

Colegio de México (CDM), México, D.F.

Relaciones Diplomaticas Hispano-Mexicanas 1826–1917 (RDHM).

Centro de Estudios de Historia de México, Departamento Cultural de Condumex, S.A. (Condumex), México, D.F.

Archivo de Venustiano Carranza (AVC).
Archivo de Manuel W. González (AMG).

Instituto Nacional de Antropología e Historia (INAH), México, D.F.

Biblioteca
   Colección Jorge DeNegre.
   Serie Miscelánea.
Departamento de Investigaciones Históricas (DIH).
   Archivo de Samuel Espinosa de los Monteros (AEM)

Secretaría de Relaciones Exteriores de México (AREM), México, D.F.

Revolución Mexicana, L-E-721-851.
Varios Expedientes, labeled "Personal" and "Tópico" selected by unrestricted access to the central catalog of the archive.

Secretaría de Recursos Hidráulicos de México (ASRHM), México, D.F.

Archivo de Aprovechamiento

ARCHIVES: UNITED STATES

Bancroft Library (BL), University of California, Berkeley.

German Diplomatic Service, Mexico, 1822–1941.
Sylvestre Terrazas Collection (STC).
Samuel G. Vásquez Papers.

Barker Texas History Center, University of Texas, Austin.

Harbert Davenport Papers.
Leonidas C. Hill Papers.
Morris L. Sheppard Papers.
Texas Rangers Papers.
James B. Wells Papers.

Huntington Library (HL), San Marino, California.

Albert Bacon Fall Collection.

Library of Congress (LC), Washington, D.C.

Chandler P. Anderson Papers.
Newton D. Baker Papers.
Albert S. Burleson Papers.
Henry P. Fletcher Papers.
James R. Garfield Papers.
Thomas W. Gregory Papers.
Robert Lansing Papers.
William P. McAdoo Papers.
John C. O'Laughlin Papers.
Charles Warren Papers.
Woodrow Wilson Papers.

George Meany Memorial Archives, American Federation of Labor and Congress of Industrial Organizations, Washington, D.C.

American Federation of Labor Papers.

William Russell Pullen Library, Georgia State University, Atlanta.

Papers of Eugene V. Debs, Microcopy 565, Reel 1,
Fred Warren Papers.

Sterling Memorial Library, Yale University, New Haven.

Edward M. House Papers.
Frank L. Polk Papers.

Texas State Archives (TSA), Austin.

Adjutant General's Records (AGR).
   General Correspondence (GC).
     Mexican Border Trouble, 1915–1917, detached records, Camp Mabry.
     Rangers, 1901–1935.
James E. Ferguson Papers.

William D. Hornaday Collection.

Records of the State Legislature.
Proceedings of the Joint Committee of the Senate and the House in the Investigation of the State Ranger Force, January 31, 1919. 3 vols.

United States National Archives (USNA), Washington, D.C.

RG (Record Group) 28. Records of the Post Office Department.

RG 43. Records of International Conferences, Commissions, and Expositions. Records of the United States Commissioners of the American and Mexican Joint Commission, 1916. (Gray-Lane Files).

RG 45. Naval Records Collection of the Office of Naval Records and Library.

RG 56. General Records of the Department of the Treasury.

RG 59. General Records of the Department of State.
  Microfilm series: M 274, M 314, M 336

RG 60. General Records of the Department of Justice.

RG 65. Records of the Federal Bureau of Investigation.

RG 76. Records of Boundary, Commissions, and Arbitrations.
  Records of the International Boundary Commission (IBC).

RG 84. Records of the Foreign Service Posts of the Department of State.

RG 85. Records of the Immigration and Naturalization Service.

RG 94. Records of the Adjutant General's Office, 1780s–1917 (AGO).

RG 120. Records of the American Expeditionary Forces (World War I), 1917–1923.

RG 165. Records of the War Department General and Special Staffs.

National Archives and Records Service (NARS).

T 624. Thirteenth Census of the United States.

USNA, Fort Worth Federal Records Center (FWFRC).

RG 21. Records of District Courts of the United States. Southern District of Texas, Brownsville, Texas.

USNA, Laguna Niguel Federal Records Center (LNFRC).

RG 21. Records of District Courts of the United States. Southern District of California, Southern Division, Los Angeles, California.

USNA, Washington National Records Center (WNRC).

RG 76. Records of the Special Claims Commission, United States and Mexico, Created under the Claims Convention of September 10, 1923 (Mexican Claims).

University of California, Los Angeles, Theater Arts Library

Twentieth Century Fox Film Corporation Archives

University of Texas, Austin, Latin American Collection (UTLA).

Pablo González Archive.
Miscellaneous manuscripts.

Unpublished Theses and Dissertations

Albro, Ward S., III. "Ricardo Flores Magón and the Liberal Party: An Inquiry into the Origins of the Mexican Revolution of 1910." Ph.D. diss., University of Arizona, 1967.

Baulch, Joe R. "James B. Wells: South Texas Economic and Political Leader." Ph.D. diss., Texas Tech University, 1974.
Da Camara, Kathleen. "The History of the City of Laredo." Master's thesis, Texas College of Arts and Industries, 1944.
Gilderhus, Mark T. "The United States and the Mexican Revolution, 1915–1920: A Study of Policy and Interest," Ph.D. diss., University of Nebraska, 1968.
González, Jovita. "Social Life in Cameron, Starr, and Zapata Counties." Master's thesis, University of Texas, 1930.
Hildebrand, Walter W. "The History of Cameron County, Texas." Masters thesis, North Texas State College, 1950.
Holcomb, Gertrude B. "Early Transportation in the Brownsville, Texas Area, with Historical Background." Master's thesis, Texas College of Arts and Industries, 1948.
Holcombe, Harold E. "United States Arms Control and the Mexican Revolution, 1910–1924." Ph.D. diss., University of Alabama, 1968.
Johnson, Robert B. "The Punitive Expedition: A Military, Diplomatic and Political History of Pershing's Chase After Pancho Villa, 1916–1917." Ph.D. diss., University of Southern California, 1964.
Kunimoto, Iyo I. "Japan and Mexico, 1888–1917." Ph.D. diss., University of Texas, 1975.
Maddox, Winnie. "History of the Donna Community." Master's thesis, Texas College of Arts and Industries, 1955.
Paredes, Raymund A. "The Image of the Mexican in American Literature." Ph.D. diss., University of Texas, 1973.
Rocha, Rodolfo. "The Influence of the Mexican Revolution On the Mexico-Texas Border, 1910–1916." Ph.D. diss., Texas Tech University, 1981.
Sandels, Robert L. "Silvestre Terrazas, the Press and the Origins of the Mexican Revolution in Chihuahua." Ph.D. diss., University of Oregon, 1967.
Sandos, James A. "The Mexican Revolution and the United States, 1915–1917: The Impact of Conflict in the Texas-Tamaulipas Frontier upon the Emergence of Revolutionary Government in Mexico." Ph.D. diss., University of California, 1978.
Schiff, Warren. "German Interests in Mexico in the Period of Porfirio Díaz." Ph.D. diss., University of California, 1957.
Shore, Elliot. "Talkin' Socialism: Julius A. Wayland, Fred D. Warren and Radical Publishing, 1890–1914." Ph.D. diss., Bryn Mawr College, 1984.
Smith, Margaret H. "The Lower Rio Grande Region in Tamaulipas, Mexico." Ph.D. diss., University of Texas, 1961.

PUBLISHED SOURCES

GOVERNMENT PUBLICATIONS AND DOCUMENTS: MEXICO

Fabela, Isidro, ed. *Documentos historicos de la revolución mexicana* (DHRM). Tomos XII and XIII, *La expedición punitiva*. Josefina E. de Fabela, ed. México, D. F.: Editorial Jus, 1967–1968.
González Ramírez, Manuel, ed. *Fuentes para la historia de la revolución mexicana.* Tomo 1, *Planes políticos y otros documentos.* México, D.F.: Fondo de Cultura Economica, 1954.
Salinas Carranza, Alberto. *La expedición punitiva.* Seg. ed. México, D.F.: Ediciones Botas, 1937.
Secretaría de Relaciones Exteriores. *Labor internacional de la revolución constitucionalista* (LIRC). México, D.F.: Secretaría de Gobernación, n.d. [1918].

GOVERNMENT PUBLICATIONS AND DOCUMENTS: UNITED STATES

Texas Legislature. House. *Journal.* 36th Leg., Reg. sess., 1919.
———. Senate. *D. W. Glasscock vs. A. Parr.* 36th Leg., Reg. sess., 1919. *Supplement to the Senate Journal.*
U.S. Congress. House. *Congressional Record.* 67th Cong., 4th sess., 11 and 19 December 1922, 298–300, 684–697.
U.S. Congress. Senate. Committee on Foreign Relations. *Investigation of Mexican Affairs.* 66th Cong., 2nd sess., 1920. S. Doc. 285. 2 vols.
———. Judiciary Committee. *Hearings on Brewing and Liquor Interests and German and Bolshevick Propaganda.* 66th Cong., 1st sess., 1919. S. Doc. 62. 3 vols.
U.S. Department of Commerce and Labor. Commission on Industrial Relations. *Final Report and Testimony.* 1916. Vol. 9.
U.S. Department of State. *Papers Relating to the Foreign Relations of the United States, 1915, 1916, 1917.* Washington, D.C.: Government Printing Office, 1924–1928. (*Foreign Relations* followed by the year)
———. *The Lansing Papers, 1914–1920.* 2 vols. Washington, D.C.: GPO, 1940.

MEMOIRS AND CONTEMPORARY ACCOUNTS

Baker, Ray Stannard. *Woodrow Wilson: Life and Letters.* 8 vols. Garden City: Doubleday, Page and Co., 1927–1968.
Baldwin, Roger N., ed. *Kropotkin's Revolutionary Pamphlets.* 1922. Reprint. New York: Dover Publications, 1970.
Bartra, Armando, ed. and comp. *Regeneración, 1900–1918: La corriente más radical de la revolución mexicana de 1910 a través de su periódico de combate.* México, D.F.: Ediciones Era, 1977.
Debs, Eugene V. *Writings and Speeches of Eugene V. Debs.* Introduction by Arthur Schlesinger, Jr. New York: Hermitage Press, 1948.
Gauss, Christian F., ed. *Democracy Today: An American Interpretation.* Chicago: Scott, Foresman and Company, 1917.
Goldman, Emma. *Living My Life.* 2 vols. New York: Alfred A. Knopf, 1931; Dover, 1970.
Gompers, Samuel. *Seventy Years of Life and Labor: An Autobiography.* 2 vols. New York: E. P. Dutton, 1925.
González, Pablo, Ing. *El centinela fiel del constitucionalismo.* Saltillo, Coahuila: Textos de Cultura Historiográfica, 1971.
Guerra y García, José. *Apuntes históricos de la revolución constitucionalista en Tamaulipas.* Tampico, Tamaulipas: n.p., 1918.
Guerrero, Praxedis. *Artículos literarios y de combate: pensamientos; crónicas revolucionarias, etc.* México, D.F.: Edición del Grupo Cultural "Ricardo F. Magón," Centro de Estudios Históricos del Movimiento Obrero Mexicano, 1977.
Gutiérrez de Lara, Lázaro, and Edgcumb Pinchon. *The Mexican People: Their Struggle for Freedom.* Garden City: Doubleday, Page and Co., 1914.
Hendrick, Burton. *The Life and Letters of Walter Hines Page.* 3 vols. New York: Doubleday, Page and Co., 1922–1925.
Huitrón, Jacinto. *Orígenes e historia del movimiento obrero en México.* México, D.F.: Editores Mexicanos Unidos, 1974.
Kropotkin, Peter. *The Conquest of Bread.* Edited by Paul Avrich. New York: New York University Press, 1972.
Lewis, Tracy Hammond. *Along the Rio Grande.* New York: Lewis Publishing Co., 1916.

Link, Arthur S., ed. *The Papers of Woodrow Wilson.* 64 vols. Princeton: Princeton University Press, 1966–1991.
Malatesta, Errico. *A Talk Between Two Workers.* Translated by Aurora Aleva. N.p., 1933.
Mexican Liberal Party. *Land and Liberty: Mexico's Battle for Economic Freedom and Its Relation to Labor's World-Wide Struggle. Selected from the Writings of Ricardo Flores Magon, A. de P. Araujo, and Wm. C. Owen.* Los Angeles: Mexican Liberal Party, n.d.
Murray, John. "Behind the Drums of Revolution: The Labor Movement in Mexico as Seen by an American Trade Unionist," *Survey* 37 (December 1916): 237–244.
N. W. Ayer and Son's American Newspaper Annual and Directory. Philadelphia: N. W. Ayer and Son, 1915.
Obregón, Alvaro. *Ocho mil kilómetros en campaña.* Paris and México: Libreria de la Vda de Ch. Bouret, 1917.
Owen, William C. "The Los Angeles Times Explosion." *Mother Earth,* December 1910, 310–314.
Parker, James. *The Old Army: Memories, 1872–1918.* Philadelphia: Dorrance and Co., 1929.
Peavey, John R. *Echoes from the Rio Grande.* Brownsville, Texas: Springman-King, 1963.
Pierce, Frank C. *A Brief History of the Lower Rio Grande Valley.* Menasha, Wisc.: George Banta Publishing Co., 1917.
Poole, David, ed. and comp. *Land and Liberty: Anarchist Influences in the Mexican Revolution—Ricardo Flores Magón.* Orkney, U. K.: Cienfuegos Press, 1977.
Prat, José. *La burguesía y el proletariado: apuntes sobre la lucha sindical.* Valencia: F. Sempere y Compañía, n.d. [1909].
Rand School of Social Science. The Department of Labor Research. *The American Labor Year Book 1916.* New York: The Rand School of Social Science, 1916.
Reed, John. *Insurgent Mexico.* New York: International Publishers, 1969.
Richards, Vernon., ed. and comp. *Errico Malatesta, His Life and Ideas.* London: Freedom Press, 1965.
Rintelen von Kleist, Franz. *The Dark Invader.* New York: MacMillan Co., 1933.
Salazar, Rosendo, and José G. Escobedo. *Las púgnas de la Gleba 1917–1922.* 2 vols. México, D. F.: Editorial Avante, 1923.
Sax, Antimaco. *Los mexicanos en el destierro.* San Antonio: n.p., 1916.
Scott, Hugh L. *Some Memories of a Soldier.* New York: The Century Co., 1928.
Steel, Edward M., ed. *The Correspondence of Mother Jones.* Pittsburgh: University of Pittsburgh Press, 1985.
Sterling, William W. *Trails and Trials of a Texas Ranger.* Norman: University of Oklahoma Press, 1968.
Tompkins, Frank. *Chasing Villa.* Harrisburg, Penna.: The Military Service Publishing Co., 1934.
Treviño, Jacinto B. *Memorias.* 2nd ed. México, D.F.: Editorial Orion, 1961.
Turner, Ethel Duffy. "Writers and Revolutionists." An interview with Ruth Teiser. University of California, Bancroft Library, Regional Oral History Office, 1967.
Turner, John Kenneth. *Barbarous Mexico.* Introduction by Sinclair Snow. Austin: University of Texas Press, 1968.
Who's Who in Socialist America. Girard, Kansas: *Appeal to Reason* Press, 1914.
Wilson, Woodrow. *Congressional Government.* 15th Printing, 1900. New York: Meridian Books, 1956.

BIBLIOGRAPHY

———. *Constitutional Government in the United States.* New York: Columbia University Press, 1908.

Yoshida, Shunji. "Tekisasu-shū Dokuritsu undō ni Sanka Shita Nihonjin (Japanese Who Attended the Movement of Independence in the State of Texas)." *Nihonjin Mekishiko Ijū-shi* (History of Japanese Immigration to Mexico). Tokio: Nihonjin Mekishiko Ijū-shi Hensan Iinkai (Editorial Committee of Japanese Immigrants in Mexico). 1971.

ARTICLES

Anderson, Rodney D. "Mexican Workers and the Politics of Revolution, 1906–1911." *Hispanic American Historical Review* 14 (February 1974): 94–113.

Avrich, Paul, ed. "Prison Letters of Ricardo Flores Magón to Lilly Sarnoff." *International Review of Social History* 22 (1977): 379–422.

Baker, Keith Michael. "Memory and Practice: Politics and the Representation of the Past in Eighteenth-Century France." *Representations* 11 (Summer 1985): 134–164.

Blaisdell, Lowell L. "Was It Revolution Or Filibustering? The Mystery of the Flores Magón Revolt in Baja. California." *Pacific Historical Review* 23 (May 1954): 147–164.

Cumberland, Charles C. "Border Raids in the Lower Rio Grande Valley, 1915." *Southwestern Historical Quarterly* 57 (January 1954): 285–311.

Deeds, Susan M. "New Spain's Far North: A Changing Historiographical Frontier?" *Latin American Research Review* 25 (1990): 226–335.

Degler, Carl N. "In Pursuit of an American History." *American Historical Review* 92 (February 1987): 1–12.

Foscue, Edwin J. "The Climate of the Lower Rio Grande Valley of Texas." *Monthly Weather Review* 60 (November 1932): 207–214.

———. "The Distribution of Population in the Lower Rio Grande Valley of Texas." *Field and Laboratory* 2 (April 1934): 40–42.

———. "Historical Geography of the Lower Rio Grande Valley of Texas." *Texas Geographic Magazine* 3 (Spring 1939): 1–15.

———. "Irrigation in the Lower Rio Grande Valley of Texas." *Geographical Review* 23 (July 1933): 457–463.

———. "Land Utilization in the Lower Rio Grande Valley of Texas." *Economic Geography* 8 (January 1932): 1–11.

———. "The Natural Vegetation of the Lower Rio Grande Valley of Texas." *Field and Laboratory* 2 (April 1934): 40–42.

———. "Physiography of the Lower Rio Grande Valley." *Pan American Geologist* 58 (May 1932): 263–267.

Gardner, Lloyd C. "Woodrow Wilson and the Mexican Revolution." In *Woodrow Wilson and a Revolutionary World, 1913–1921*, edited by Arthur S. Link. Chapel Hill: University of North Carolina Press, 1982.

Gerlach, Alan. "Conditions Along the Border, 1915: The Plan de San Diego." *New Mexico Historical Review* 43 (July 1968): 195–212.

Gómez-Quiñones, Juan. "Plan de San Diego Reviewed." *Aztlán* 1 (Spring 1970): 124–130.

Griswold del Castillo, Richard. "The Discredited Revolution: The Magonista Capture of Tijuana in 1911." *Journal of San Diego History* (Fall 1980): 256–273.

———. "The Mexican Revolution and the Spanish-Language Press in the Borderlands." *Journalism History* 4 (Summer 1977): 42–47.

Hager, William A. "The Plan of San Diego: Unrest on the Texas Frontier in 1915." *Arizona and the West* 5 (Winter 1963): 327–336.

Harris, Charles, III, and Louis Sadler. "The Plan of San Diego and the Mexican War Crisis of 1916; A Re-Examination." *Hispanic American Historical Review* 57 (August 1978): 381–408.

Hine, Robert V. "A California Utopia: 1885–1890." *Huntington Library Quarterly* 11 (August 1948): 387–405.

Hobsbawm, Eric. "Men and Women On the Left." In *Workers: Worlds of Labor*, edited by Eric Hobsbawm, 83–102. New York: Pantheon Books, 1984.

Katz, Friedrich. "Labor Conditions on Haciendas in Porfirian Mexico: Some Trends and Tendencies." *Hispanic American Historical Review*, 54 (February 1974): 1–47.

Kraft, James P. "The Fall of Job Harriman's Socialist Party: Violence, Gender and Politics in Los Angeles in 1911." *Southern California Quarterly* 70 (Spring 1988): 43–68.

Limón, José. "La Llorona, the Third Legend of Greater Mexico: Cultural Symbols, Women, and the Political Unconscious." *Renato Rosaldo Lecture Series Monograph* 2 (Spring 1986): 59–93.

Link, Arthur S. "The Wilson Movement in Texas." *Southwestern Historical Quarterly*, 48 (October 1944): 169–185.

McKinley, Blaine. " 'The Quagmires of Necessity': American Anarchists and Dilemmas of Vocation." *American Quarterly* 24 (Winter 1982): 503–523.

McNeil, Brownie. "Corridos of the Mexican Border." In *Mexican Border Ballads*, edited by Mody C. Boatwright, 1–34. Dallas: Southern Methodist University Press, 1967. Facsimile ed.

Meyer, Michael C. "The Arms of the *Ypiranga*." *Hispanic American Historical Review* 50 (August 1970): 543–556.

———. "The Mexican-German Conspiracy of 1915." *The Americas* 23 (July 1966): 76–89.

Richmond, Douglas W. "Confrontation and Reconciliation: Mexicans and Spaniards During the Mexican Revolution, 1910–1920." *The Americas* 41 (October 1984): 215–228.

———. "La guerra de Texas se renova: Mexican Insurrection and Carrancista Ambitions, 1900–1920." *Azlán* 11 (Spring 1980): 1–32.

Sandos, James A. "German Involvement in Northern Mexico, 1915–1916: A New Look at the Columbus Raid." *Hispanic American Historical Review* 50 (February 1970): 70–88.

———. "International Water Control in the Lower Rio Grande Basin, 1900–1920." *Agricultural History* 54 (October 1980): 490–501.

———. "Northern Separatism During the Mexican Revolution: An Inquiry into the Role of Drug Trafficking, 1910–1920." *The Americas* 41 (October 1984): 191–214.

———. "Pancho Villa and American Security: Woodrow Wilson's Mexican Diplomacy Reconsidered." *Journal of Latin American Studies* 13 (November 1981): 293–311.

———. "The Plan of San Diego: War and Diplomacy on the Texas Border, 1915–1916." *Arizona and the West* 14 (Spring 1972): 5–24.

———. "Prostitution and Drugs: The United States Army on the Mexican-American Border, 1916–1917." *Pacific Historical Review* 49 (November 1980): 621–645.

Schoffelmayer, Victor H. "The Magic Valley—Its Marvelous Future." *Texas Geographic Magazine* 3 (Spring 1939): 16–31.

Schreiner, Charles, III. "Background and Development of Brahman Cattle in Texas." *Southwestern Historical Quarterly* 52 (April 1949): 427–443.

Shapiro, Herbert. "The McNamara Case: A Window On Class Antagonism in the Progressive Era." *Southern California Quarterly* 70 (Spring 1988): 69–95.
Shatz, Marshall S. "Michael Bakunin and His Biographers: The Question of Bakunin's Sexual Impotence." In *Imperial Russia 1700–1917: State, Society, Opposition*, edited by Ezra Mendelsohn and Marshall S. Shatz, 219–240. De Kalb: Northern Illinois University Press, 1988.
Vanderwood, Paul J. "An American Cold Warrior: *Viva Zapata!* (1952)." In *American History/American Film: Interpreting the Hollywood Image*, edited by John E. O'Connor and Martin A. Jackson. New York: Frederick Ungar Co., 1979.
Womack, John, Jr. "The Mexican Economy During the Revolution, 1910–1920: Historiography and Analysis." *Marxist Perspectives* 4 (Winter 1978): 80–123.
———. "The Mexican Revolution, 1910–1920." In *The Cambridge History of Latin America*. Vol. 5, *1870–1930*, edited by Leslie Bethell, 79–154. Cambridge: Cambridge University Press, 1986.

BOOKS AND MONOGRAPHS

Abad de Santillán, Diego. *Ricardo Flores Magón, El ápostol de la revolución social mexicana*. México, D.F.: Grupo Cultural "Ricardo Flores Magón," 1925.
Amezcúa, Jenaro, *¿Ouien es Flores Magón y cuál su obra?* México, D.F.: Editorial Avance, 1943.
Anders, Evan. *Boss Rule in South Texas: The Progressive Era*. Austin: University of Texas Press, 1982.
Ankerson, Dudley. *Agrarian Warlord: Saturnino Cedillo and the Mexican Revolution in San Luis Potosi*. De Kalb: Northern Illinois University Press, 1984.
Avrich, Paul. *An American Anarchist: The Life of Voltairine de Cleyre*. Princeton: Princeton University Press, 1978.
———. *Anarchist Portraits*. Princeton: Princeton University Press, 1988.
———. *The Haymarket Tragedy*. Princeton: Princeton University Press, 1984.
———. *The Modern School Movement*. Princeton: Princeton University Press, 1980.
———. *Sacco and Vanzetti: The Anarchist Background*. Princeton: Princeton University Press, 1991.
Barrera Fuentes, Florencio. *Historia de la revolución mexicana: la etapa precursora*. México, D.F.: Editorial Bib, 1955.
Beals, Carleton. *Mexico: An Interpretation*. New York: B. W. Huebsch, 1923.
Berryman, Phillip. *Liberation Theology*. New York: Pantheon, 1987.
———. *The Religious Roots of Rebellion*. New York: Orbis Books, 1984.
Blaisdell, Lowell L. *The Desert Revolution: Baja California, 1911*. Madison: University of Wisconsin Press, 1962.
Boff, Leonardo, and Clodovis Boff. *Introducing Liberation Theology*. Translated by Paul Burns. New York: Orbis Books, 1987.
Braddy, Haldeen. *Pershing's Mission in Mexico*. El Paso: Texas Western Press, 1966.
Britton, John A. *Carleton Beals: A Radical Journalist in Latin America*. Albuquerque: University of New Mexico Press, 1987.
Callcott, Wilfrid Hardy. *Liberalism in Mexico, 1857–1929*. Stanford: Stanford University Press, 1931.
Cantor, Milton. *The Divided Left: American Radicalism, 1900–1975*. New York: Hill and Wang, 1978.
Carr, Edward H. *Michael Bakunin*. New York: Octagon Books, 1975.

Cerda Silva, Roberto de la. *El movimiento obrero en México*. México, D.F.: Instituto de Investigaciones Sociales U.N.A.M., 1961.
Clendenen, Clarence C. *The United States and Pancho Villa: A Study in Unconventional Diplomacy*. Ithaca: Cornell University Press, 1961.
Cockcroft, James D. *Intellectual Precursors of the Mexican Revolution, 1900–1913*. Austin: University of Texas Press, 1968.
Coerver, Don M., and Linda B. Hall. *Texas and the Mexican Revolution: A Study in State and National Border Policy, 1910–1920*. San Antonio: Trinity University Press, 1984.
Conlin, Joseph R., ed. *The American Radical Press, 1880–1960*. 2 vols. Westport, Conn.: Greenwood Press, 1974.
Cross, Harry E., and James A. Sandos. *Across the Border: Rural Development in Mexico and Recent Migration to the United States*. Berkeley: Institute of Governmental Studies of the University of California at Berkeley, 1981.
Cross, Ira B. *A History of the Labor Movement in California*. Berkeley: University of California Press, 1935.
Cumberland, Charles C. *Mexican Revolution: Genesis under Madero*. Austin: University of Texas Press, 1952.
———. *Mexican Revolution: The Constitutionalist Years*. Austin: University of Texas Press, 1972.
Day, John C. *Managing the Lower Rio Grande: An Experience In International River Development*. Chicago: University of Chicago, Department of Geography, Research Paper no. 125, 1970.
Doerries, Reinhard R. *Imperial Challenge: Ambassador Count Bernstorff and German-American Relations, 1908–1917*. Translated by Christa D. Shannon. Chapel Hill: University of North Carolina Press, 1989.
Dubofsky, Melvyn. *We Shall Be All: A History of the Industrial Workers of the World*. Chicago: Quadrangle Books, 1969.
Ellul, Jacques. *Autopsy of Revolution*. Translated by Patricia Woolf. New York: Alfred A. Knopf, 1971.
Ferrua, Piero, *Gli Anarchici nella Rivoluzione Messicana: Praxedis G. Guerrero*. Ragusa: Edizioni La Fiaccola, 1976.
Foner, Philip S. *History of the Labor Movement in the United States*. 4 vols. New York: International Publishers, 1947–1965.
Freire, Paulo. *Pedagogy of the Oppressed*. Translated by Myra Bergman Ramos. New York: Continuum Publishing Corp., 1981.
Frost, Richard H. *The Mooney Case*. Stanford: Stanford University Press, 1968.
Goldwater, Walter. *Radical Periodicals in America, 1890–1950*. New Haven: Yale University Press, 1966.
Gómez-Quiñones, Juan. *Sembradores, Ricardo Flores Magón y el Partido Liberal Mexicano: A Eulogy and Critique*. Los Angeles: Aztlán Publications, Monograph Number 5, University of California at Los Angeles, 1973.
González Ramírez, Manuel. *La revolución social de México*. Vol. 1, *Las ideas: la violencia*. México, D.F.: Fondo de Cultura Económica, 1960.
Goodwyn, Lawrence. *Democratic Promise: The Populist Movement in America*. New York: Oxford University Press, 1976.
Green, James R. *Grass-Roots Socialism: Radical Movements in the Southwest, 1895–1943*. Baton Rouge: Louisiana State University Press, 1978.
Gruening, Ernest H. *Mexico and Its Heritage*. New York: D. Appleton Century Co., 1928.

Hale, Charles A. *Mexican Liberalism in the Age of Mora, 1821–1853*. New Haven: Yale University Press, 1968.
Hall, Linda B. *Alvaro Obregón: Power and Revolution in Mexico, 1911–1920*. College Station: Texas A&M University Press, 1981.
Hart, John M. *Anarchism and the Mexican Working Class, 1860–1931*. Austin: University of Texas Press, 1978.
———. *Revolutionary Mexico: The Coming and Process of the Mexican Revolution*. Berkeley: University of California Press, 1987.
Henderson, Peter V. N. *Félix Díaz, The Porfirians, and the Mexican Revolution*. Lincoln: University of Nebraska Press, 1981.
———. *Mexican Exiles in the Borderlands, 1910–1913*. Southwestern Studies, Monograph Number 58, 1979.
Hernández Padilla, Salvador. *El Magonismo: historia de una pasión libertaria 1900–1922*. México, D.F.: Ediciones Era, 1984.
Hill, Larry. *Emissaries to a Revolution: Woodrow Wilson's Executive Agents in Mexico*. Baton Rouge: Louisiana State University Press, 1974.
Hine, Robert V. *California's Utopian Colonies*. San Marino: The Huntington Library, 1953.
Hinkle, Stacy C. *Wings and Saddles: The Air and Cavalry Punitive Expedition of 1919*. Southwestern Studies, Monograph Number 19, 1967.
Hunt, Lynn. *Politics, Culture, and Class in the French Revolution*. Berkeley: University of California Press, 1984.
Johnson, Chalmers. *Autopsy on People's War*. Berkeley: University of California Press, 1973.
Joll, James. *The Anarchists*. 2d ed. Cambridge, Mass.: Harvard University Press, 1980.
Katz, Friedrich. *The Secret War in Mexico: Europe, the United States, and the Mexican Revolution*. Chicago: University of Chicago Press, 1981.
Kern, Robert W. *Red Years/Black Years: A Political History of Spanish Anarchism, 1911–1937*. Philadelphia: Institute of the Study of Human Issues, 1978.
Knight, Alan. *The Mexican Revolution*. 2 vols. Cambridge: Cambridge University Press, 1986.
Kraditor, Aileen S. *The Radical Persuasion 1890–1917: Aspects of the Intellectual History and the Historiography of Three American Radical Organizations*. Baton Rouge: Louisiana State University Press, 1981.
Langham, Thomas C. *Border Trials: Ricardo Flores Magón and the Mexican Liberals*. Southwestern Studies, Monograph Number 65, 1982.
Larralde, Carlos. *Mexican American: Movements and Leaders*. Los Alamitos, Calif.: Hwong Publishing Co., 1976.
Levenstein, Harvey A. *Labor Organizations in the United States and Mexico: A History of Their Relations*. Westport, Connecticut: Greenwood Press, 1971.
Link, Arthur S. *Woodrow Wilson*. 5 vols. Princeton: Princeton University Press, 1947–1965.
Lozoya, Jorge Alberto. *El ejército mexicano (1911–1965)*. México, D.F.: El Colegio de México, 1970.
MacLachlan, Colin. *Anarchism and the Mexican Revolution: The Political Trials of Ricardo Flores Magón in the United States*. Berkeley: University of California Press, 1991.
Mandel, Bernard. *Samuel Gompers: A Biography*. Yellow Springs, Ohio: The Antioch Press, 1963.

Marsh, Margaret S. *Anarchist Women, 1870–1920.* Philadelphia: Temple University Press, 1981.
Meyer, Lorenzo. *México y los Estados Unidos en el conflicto petrolero, 1917–1942.* Seg. ed. México, D.F.: El Colegio de México, 1972.
Meyer, Michael C. *Huerta: A Political Portrait.* Lincoln: University of Nebraska Press, 1972.
———. *Mexican Rebel: Pascual Orozco and the Mexican Revolution, 1910–1915.* Lincoln: University of Nebraska Press, 1967.
Miranda, José. *Communism in the Bible.* Translated by Robert R. Barr. New York: Orbis Books, 1982.
Montejano, David. *Anglos and Mexicans in the Making of Texas, 1836–1986.* Austin: University of Texas Press, 1987.
Nadin, Mihai, Guest ed. "The Semiotics of the Visual: On Defining the Field." *Semiotica* 52 (1984).
Niemeyer E. Victor. *Revolution at Querétaro: The Mexican Constitutional Convention of 1916–1917.* Austin: University of Texas Press, 1974.
Pinchon, Edgcumb. *Viva Villa!: A Recovery of the Real Pancho Villa, Peon, Bandit, Soldier, Patriot.* New York: Harcourt, Brace and Co., 1933.
———. *Zapata the Unconquerable.* New York: Doubleday, Doran and Co., 1941.
Preston, William, Jr., *Aliens and Dissenters: Federal Suppression of Radicals, 1903–1933.* New York: Harper and Row, 1966.
Priestley, Herbert I. *The Mexican Nation: A History.* New York: Macmillan, 1923.
Quirk, Robert E. *An Affair of Honor: Woodrow Wilson and the Occupation of Veracruz.* Lexington: University of Kentucky Press, 1961.
———. *The Mexican Revolution, 1914–1915: The Convention of Aguascalientes.* Bloomington: Indiana University Press, 1960.
Raat, W. Dirk. *Revoltosos: Mexico's Rebels in the United States, 1903–1934.* College Station: Texas A&M University Press, 1981.
Reichert, William O. *Partisans of Freedom: A Study in American Anarchism.* Bowling Green, Ky.: Bowling Green University Press, 1976.
Richmond, Douglas W. *Venustiano Carranza's Nationalist Struggle, 1893–1920.* Lincoln: University of Nebraska Press, 1983.
Robertson, Brian. *Rio Grande Heritage: A Pictorial History.* Norfolk: The Donning Co., 1985.
———. *Wild Horse Desert: The Heritage of South Texas.* Edinburg, Tex.: New Santander Press, 1985.
Romo, Ricardo. *East Los Angeles: History of a Barrio.* Austin: University of Texas Press, 1983.
Ross, Edward Alsworth. *The Social Revolution in Mexico.* New York: The Century Co., 1923.
Ross, Stanley R. *Fuentes de la historia contemporánea de México: Periódicos y revistas.* 2 vols. México, D.F.: Colegio de México, 1965–1967.
Ruiz, Ramón. *The Great Rebellion: Mexico, 1905–1924.* New York: W. W. Norton & Co., 1980.
Russell, Francis. *Sacco and Vanzetti: The Case Resolved.* New York: Harper and Row, 1986.
Salvatore, Nick. *Eugene V. Debs: Citizen and Socialist.* Urbana: University of Illinois Press, 1982.
Smith, Robert F. *The United States and Revolutionary Nationalism in Mexico, 1916–1932.* Chicago: University of Chicago Press, 1972.

Spaight, Arthur W. *The Resources, Soil, and Climate of Texas.* Galveston: A. H. Belo and Co., 1882.
Stambaugh, J. Lee, and Lilian Stambaugh. *The Lower Rio Grande Valley of Texas.* Austin: The Naylor Co., 1954.
Stimson, Grace H. *Rise of the Labor Movement in Los Angeles.* Berkeley: University of California Press, 1955.
Toyah Historical and Centennial Committee. *Toyah Taproots: A Memory Book of Those Who Put Down Their Roots in Toyah.* Austin: Nortex Press, 1984.
Tuchman, Barbara. *The Zimmermann Telegram.* New York: Dell Publishing Company, 1965.
Turner, Ethel Duffy. *Ricardo Flores Magón y el Partido Liberal Mexicano.* Translated by Eduardo Limón G. Morelia, México: Editorial "Erandi," 1960.
Waldseemüler, Martin. *Cosmographiae Introductio.* Facsimile. Edited by Charles Herbermann. New York: The United States Catholic Historical Society, 1907. Originally published with two world maps, St. Die, Lorraine, 1507.
Weaver, John D. *Los Angeles: The Enormous Village, 1781-1981.* Santa Barbara: Capra Press, 1980.
Weber, David J. *Myth and the History of the Hispanic Southwest.* Albuquerque: University of New Mexico Press, 1988.
Webb, Walter P. *The Texas Rangers: A Century of Frontier Defense.* Boston: Houghton Mifflin, 1935.
Weinstein, James. *The Decline of Socialism in America, 1912-1925.* New York: Monthly Review Press, 1967.
Wexler, Alice. *Emma Goldman: An Intimate Life.* New York: Pantheon Books, 1984.
Wharfield, H. B. *10th Cavalry and Border Fights.* El Cajon, Calif.: Privately printed, 1965.
Wilkie, James W. *The Mexican Revolution: Federal Expenditure and Social Change since 1910.* 2d rev. ed. Berkeley: University of California Press, 1970.
Womack, John, Jr. *Zapata and the Mexican Revolution.* New York: Alfred A. Knopf, 1969.
Woodcock, George. *Anarchism: A History of Libertarian Ideas and Movements.* Cleveland: The World Publishing Co. Meridian Books, 1962.

NEWSPAPERS

England

[London] Freedom
[London] Freedom Bulletin
[London] Liberty

Mexico

[México, D.F.] El Demócrata
[México, D.F.] El Legionario
[México, D.F.] El Universal
[México, D.F.] Excélsior
[México, D.F.] Impacto
[México, D.F.] Novedades
[México, D.F.] Todo
[Monterrey] El Demócrata

[Monterrey] El Porvenir
[Monterrey] El Regiomontano

United States

[Brownsville, Texas] Herald
[Chicago] International Socialist Review
[Chicago] Revolt
[Cleveland] Solidarity
[Corpus Christi] Caller
[Denver] The Miner's Magazine
[Girard, Kansas] Appeal to Reason
[Hallettsville, Texas] The Rebel
[Hayward, California] Land and Liberty
[Laredo] El Demócrata Fronterizo
[Los Angeles] California Social Democrat
[Los Angeles] Hollywood Citizen News
[Los Angeles] Regeneración
[McAllen, Texas] Monitor
[New York] Mother Earth
New York Call
New York Times
[New York] The Woman Rebel
[New York] World
[Saint Louis] The National Rip-Saw
[San Antonio] Express
[San Antonio] La Prensa
[San Antonio] Light
[San Francisco] Chung Sai Yat Po (China West Daily News)
[San Francisco] The Blast
[Zapata, Texas] El Demócrata

INDEX

In subentries, Casa del Obrero Mundial is abbreviated as Casa; Plan of San Diego, as PSD; and Ricardo Flores Magón, as R.F.M.

Abad de Santillan, Diego, 185n.51
Abasta (Constitutionalist officer), 133
AFL (American Federation of Labor), 29, 180n.51; anti-union pressures on, 35; and *L.A. Times* disaster, 35, 36; and Mexican refugees, 16; and PLM, 33. *See also* Gompers, Samuel; International Association of Bridge and Structural Iron Workers; PAFL (Pan American Federation of Labor)
Aguascalientes, Convention of, 55–56, 119
Alarm, The, 135
Albert, Heinrich, 143
Albro, Ward S., III, 180n.46
Alexander, Thomas, 88, 89
Algodones, Mex., 27
Alice, Tex., 74
Aliens, deportation of U.S., 167
Almaraz, A. G., 187n.14
Alta California, 39
Altgeld, John P., 4
Alvarez, Natividad, 145
American Federation of Labor. *See* AFL
American Magazine, 16
Amnesty, Constitutionalist, 110
Anarchism: Bakuninist, 135; brands of, 40; Debs disdain for, 34, 157; enduring power of, 176; individualist, 31; Liberation Theology and, 175–77; Mexican interest in, 5, 175; nature of, 6–7; PSD espousal of, 106–107; *Regeneración* poster personifying, 18–23, 40, 46, 60, 127; U.S. fear of, 3–4, 7; victories of U.S., 173–74; and World War I, 113. *See also* Anarchosyndicalism; Communism, anarchist
Anarchists: female, 129; French, 21; Italian, 14, 21; life-style of U.S., 129; of Los Angeles, 129, 131, 196n.28 (*see also* Flores Magón, Enríque; Flores Magón, Ricardo; PLM [Mexican Liberal Party]); Spanish, 14, 21, 127. *See also* Anarchism; Bakunin, Michael; Berkman, Alexander; Cleyre, Voltairine de; Czolgosz, Leon; Flores Magón, Enríque; Flores Magón, Ricardo; Goldman, Emma; Haymarket; Kropotkin, Peter; Malatesta, Enrico; Owen, William C.; Proudhon, Pierre-Joseph; Reclus, Elisée
Anarchists, The (Joll), 175
Anarchosyndicalism, 37; as Casa stumbling block, 155; origin of, 22. *See also* Casa del Obrero Mundial
Anderson, Edward A., 148, 149
Antireelectionist Party, 25, 26
Anzaldúa, Mex., 146
Appeal to Reason, 44; decline of, 37; and *L.A. Times* disaster, 36, 37; and PLM, 17, 34; success of, 130; Turner exposés in, 16
Arango, Doroteo. *See* Villa, Pancho
Arbeiter Zeitung, 3
Arce, José Antonio, 147
Arizona, state of: Mexicans discriminated against in, 18; Mexican radicals' designs on, 81; *Regeneración* strength in, 60, 128
Arredondo, Eliseo, 152, 153
Arriaga, Camilo, 5, 6; Madero and, 24, 33; R.F.M. conflict with, 8, 10; in U.S., 8, 9
Atheism, Guerrero championing of, 13
Atl, Dr. *See* Murillo, Gerardo
Atrocities. *See* Ebenezer, Tex.; Johnson, Richard J.; Lynching; Reitman, Ben; Rodríguez, Juan Nepomuceno; Tandy's Station (Tex.), De la Rosa attack on; Texas Rangers, brutality of; Vigilantes; Yaqui Indians
Atson, retributive, 109
Austin, Alfred L., 77; murder of, 89, 96
Austin, Charles, 77; murder of, 89, 96
Austin, Nellie, 77
Austin, Tex., 107
Avrich, Paul, 178n.3
Aztecs, 56, 93
Aztlán, 208

Baja California, state of: PLM activity in, 27, 30–33, 34, 84, 93, 173, 197n.56, 209. *See also* Alta California; Tijuana, Mex.
Baker, A. Y., 83
Baker, Newton, D., 151
Bakunin, Michael, 9, 20, 21; impotence of, 39, 183n.74
Bakunin Institute, 57, 184n.41
Bakuninism. *See* Anarchism, Bakuninist
Banditry: in Diaz Mexico, 26; PSD violence differs from, 188n.37; along U.S.–Mexican border, 86, 93–94. *See also* Villa, Pancho
Banner, PSD, 92–93
Baptism, 64
Barbarous Mexico (Turner), 16, 28; Madero debt to, 47–48
Barragán, Miguel, 114–15
Barrera, Mocario, 81
Barrera y Guerra, Aguirre, 118
Barrera y Guerra, Francisco, 118
Barron, Heriberto, 126
Bates, Winfred, 86–87
Beals, Carleton, 205
Beans, of Tamaulipas, 72
Becker, J. R., 83, 84
Bee, Carlos, 121
Belem. *See* Belén de los Mochas
Belén de los Mochas, Mex., 7, 8, 179n.16
Belt, John R., 193n.50
Beltrán, Teodulo R., 125, 126
Berkman, Alexander, 7, 60, 134, 138, 159; as Flores Magón supporter, 137; and free love, 38; and Preparedness bombing, 160
Bernal, Nicolás T., 180n.46
Bielaski, A. Bruce, 145
Billings, Warren, 160
Birth control, Goldman on, 160. *See also* Sanger, Margaret
Bisbee, Ariz., 11
Bishop, T. P., 83
Blacklist, Texas Ranger, 98
Blacks: German propaganda focused on U.S., 143; Nafarrate commitment of U.S., 149; of PSD, 143, 204n.5; PSD and U.S., 81, 83, 96–97; as U.S. cavalrymen, 150
Blaisdell, Lowell, 185n.51, 209
Blanco, Lucio, 54, 55; land reforms of, 57–58
Blast, The, 60, 134; U.S. government vs., 135
Bliss, Tasker, 202n.38
Bolton Prize, 209
Bonfield, John, 3
Bonillas, Ygnacio, 157, 168
Boquillas, Tex., 145, 149, 152
Border, The, 15, 157
Boyd, Charles T., 150, 151
Brashear, Claude, 103

Brousse de Talavera, María, 17, 38, 134, 170
Browne, A. A., 107
Brownsville, Tex., 82; Carranza on bridge at, 122; counter-PSD precautions in, 98; mass meeting at, 107; Mexican emigrants through, 193n.46; Mexicans of, 72–75, 77; Mexican vs. Mexican at, 100; Morin plot against, 161; PLM *grupo* in, 72; press censorship in, 109; PSD activity near, 87, 94, 148, 200n.34; PSD "seizure" of, 119; railroad to, 65; Red Light district of, 74; Treviño in, 119. *See also* Canales, José T.; Wells, James B.
Brownsville Sentinel, 144
Brulay, George, 66
Bub, Jonás, 84
Buenrosto, José, 87
Bullard, Robert, 98, 148
Burguesia y el proletariado, La (Prat), 196n.11
Burleson, Albert, 167, 189n.59
Bustamante, Luis F., 194n.90

Caballo, León. *See* Garza, Agustín S.
Cabrera, Luis, 157
Calero, Manuel, 38
California, state of: Constitutionalist agents in, 201n.62; Mexican radicals' designs on, 81; *Regeneración* circulation in, 60, 128. *See also* Edendale; Los Angeles; San Diego
California Social Democrat, 34, 60, 130, 183n.79
Callcott, Wilfrid Hardy, 206
Calles, Plutarco, 171, 205
Camargo, Mex., 200n.55
Cameron County, Tex.: changes in, 63–78, 108; intermarriage in, 64; Mexican evacuation of, 109–10; Mexicans of, 71. *See also* Brownsville; Harlingen; San Benito; Vann, W. T.
Caminita, Ludovico, 42
Canales, José T., 88, 100, 108, 148, 207
Cananea (Mex.), labor unrest in, 10–12, 13, 15, 17, 84, 138, 156, 179n.35
Cananea Consolidated Copper Company, 10
Cano Saenz, Sostenes, 75
Capitalism: Liberation Theology vs., 176; to R.F.M., 172
Cárdenas, Lázaro, 171
Cárdenas Martínez, León, 127–28
Carranza, Venustiano, 47, 173, 206; ascendant, 54–57; and border crisis, 108, 110–11, 164 (*see also* Carranza, Venustiano—and U.S. war threat); dilemma of, 149; election of, 166; and Ferguson, 122; and Gompers, 202nn.16,22; and González, 131; vs. Huerta, 48–50, 52–54, 57, 151; and land re-

INDEX 227

form, 58; murder of, 168; and Nafarrate, 120; new constitution advocated by, 164–65; persona of, 116; press manipulated by, 119, 194n.90; and PSD, 90, 120–25, 131–33, 140, 144, 145, 149, 151, 154, 162, 166, 173, 196nn.32,33, 197n.37, 208; and R.F.M., 47, 52, 57, 197n.47; and Rodríguez, 197n.34; U.S. and, 51, 110 (*see also* Carranza, Venustiano—and Wilson); and U.S. collaborationists, 184n.38; vs. U.S. occupation, 52; U.S. radicals and, 158–59; U.S. recognition of, 107, 117; and U.S. war threat, 149, 150, 151–53, 155, 156, 166, 200nn.36,57 (*see also* Carranza, Venustiano—and border crisis); and Villa, 54–57, 112, 113, 154, 157, 167, 170, 193n.65; and Wilson, 107, 111, 117, 141, 145, 149–53, 154, 162, 166, 167, 172, 173, 200n.42, 208; vs. Zapata, 56, 57, 112, 118, 157, 167, 170; and Zimmerman Telegram, 166. *See also* Constitutionalists; Plan of Guadalupe
Carrizal, Mex., 150, 151, 163, 165, 200n.57
Casa del Obrero Mundial, 135, 153; Carranza appeal to, 112–13; Carranza vs. 155, 156–57; Comité Revolucionario of, 157; of Mexico City, 155; in Monterrey, 132, 197n.42
Casas Grandes, Mex., 26, 27
Celaya, Mex., 113, 114
Champion, Manuela, 75
Champion family, 75
Chao, Manuel, 55, 114
Chaplin, Ralph, 169
Chicago (Ill.), labor strife in, 3. *See also* Haymarket
Chicago Daily Socialist, 34
Chicago Mexican Liberal Defense League, 42
Chicanos, 175, 208
Chihuahua, state of, 14, 26–29, 48, 152
Child labor, PLM vs., 10
Christian Base Communities, 176
Cisneros, E., 187n.14
Citrus trees, Hidalgo Co., 72
Ciudad Chihuahua, Mex., 47, 163
Ciudad Victoria, Mex., 144
Cleyre, Voltairine de, 40–42, 45, 93
Clifford, John, 196n.27
Cline, Charlie, 57, 79, 84, 100, 127, 128
Cline, Howard F., 205
Closner, John, 66, 75, 108
Club Liberal de Cananea, 11
Coahuila, state of, 12, 48, 152
Cockcroft, James D., 179n.26, 205
Coeur d'Alene, Ida., 138
Colonia Dublán, Mex., 163
Colorado, state of, 81, 138

Columbus (N.M.), Villa raid on, 140, 141, 155, 159, 205
Communism: anarchism and, 31; anarchist, 20, 37, 176 (*see also* Kropotkin, Peter); and the Bible, 176; as Marxism final step, 7. *See also* Marxism; Socialism
Compadrazgo, 64, 71
Compadre (term), 186n.33
Company stores, 138
Compañía Humboldt, 193n.53
Conquest of Bread, The (Kropotkin), 20, 29
Conscientization, 175, 204n.9
Constitucional, El, 119
Constitution, 1857 Mexican, 4, 6, 164
Constitutionalists, Mexican, 48–50, 51–52, 71; dissension among, 55–57; general amnesty from, 110; Texas raid of, 119–20; Villa defection from, 170. *See also* Blanco, Lucio; Carranza, Venustiano; González, Pablo; Obregón, Alvaro; Ricaut, Alfredo; Rodríguez, Maurillio; Treviño, Jacinto; Villa, Pancho
Cookson, William, 128
Copper, Mexica. *See* Cananea Consolidated Copper Company
Córcega, W., 84
Corn, of south Texas, 71–72
Corpus Cristi, Tex., 109
Corruption, in Constitutionalist army, 118
Cortina, Juan Nepomuceno, 98, 100, 108, 191n.93
Cota Osuna, Edmundo F., 201n.62
Cotton: of south Texas, 71, 109; of Tamaulipas, 72
Creel, Enrique, 111, 193n.53
Cronaca Sovversiva, 183n.79
Crops, south Texas, 71–72
Cross, Juan, 115
Cruz, Atilano, 73
Cruz, Esmerejüldo, 96
Cruz Ruíz (Constitutionalist officer), 147
Cuauhtémoc, 80
Cuba, *Regeneración* circulation in, 60
Cueto, Manuel, 188n.18
Cuevas, Antonio, 146–47
Cummings, W. W., 196n.27
Cusihuiriachic, Mex., 163
Czolgosz, Leon, 7

Daily Tribune, Los Angeles, 130
Darrow, Clarence, 36, 37
Dayal, Har, 184n.41
Debs, Eugene V., 9, 31; and IWW, 17; and *L.A. Times* disaster, 36, 37; on Mexican situation, 41; and 1912 election, 44; PLM and, 16–17, 34–35, 60, 131; R.F.M. and, 30; and Turner exposés, 16

Deemer (Texas storekeeper), 145. *See also* Boquillas, Tex.
Defensor del Pueblo, El, 15
Defensores de la Patria, 152
Delacroix, Ferdinand, 21
De la Rosa, Luis, 74, 81, 82, 94, 105, 110, 117, 125, 142–46, 161, 174, 186n.30; arrest of, 150, 164; and Austin murders, 88–89, 96; *El Demócrata* and, 119; Nafarrate and, 123; at Norias, 90; as PSD commander, 131; raids of, 88–91 (*see also* De la Rosa, Luis—and Tandy's Station raid); recruiting of, 147, 148; Ricaut capture of, 146; as "social bandit," 208; and Tandy's Station raid, 100, 101–104, 120, 121, 166
De Léon, Francisco, 148
De los Santos, Isabel, 147, 148
Democracy, anarchism vs., 6
Demócrata, El: confiscation of issues of, 109; editorial shakeup at, 121; origin of, 119
De P. Mariel, Francisco, 118, 121
Deportation, of U.S. "undesirables," 167
Diabetes, R.F.M. and, 169, 203n.62
Díaz, Mercedes, 65
Díaz, Porfirio, 3, 54, 65, 80, 125, 133, 171, 172, 173, 206; and *American Magazine*, 16; defeat of, 33, 46, 47, 170; foreigners accommodated by, 156, 165; opposition to, 4–6, 10, 13–15; PLM vs., 34; press suppressed by, 12; vs. *Regeneración*, 9; retirement promised by, 24; U.S. popularity of, 15; Villa vs., 170; Yaqui Indians vs., 82
Díaz Soto y Gama, Antonio, 50, 168, 169, 170
Dillard, Abraham, 75
Dillard, George, 75, 106
Discrimination, against Mexican Americans, 63, 70, 73, 79–80, 98
Dissent, repression of U.S., 154, 167
Dodds, S. S., 94–96, 166
Doerries, Reinhard, 198n.8
Domínguez Tijerina, Alfonso, 132–33, 197n.43
Donna, Tex., 65, 109
Dresden (German steamer), 54
Durango, Mex., 57

Eastman, Max, 159
Ebano, El (Mex.), 113, 114, 155
Ebenezer, Tex., 98
Eckardt, Heinrich von, 142
Edelstein, Morris, 103
Edendale (Calif.), Flores Magóns in, 128–29, 134, 140
Editorial Maucci, 5
Education, Mexican: PSD and, 83; PLM goals for, 10
Elephant Butte, N.M., 70

Ellul, Jacques, 176
El Paso, Tex.: Huertista strength in, 115; PLM in, 12, 14; PSD recruiting in, 133
Embargo, U.S. arms, 51, 54, 117, 167, 201n.66
Engelking, L. J., 87
Era Nuova, L', 60
Escuelas Modernas. *See* Modern Schools
"Espinas, Las," 132–33, 140
Espionage Act of 1917, U.S., 167
Evolución Social, 127
Evolution and Revolution (Reclus), 20
Expropriation, as R.F.M. goal, 58

Falfurrias, Tex., 74
Fall, Albert Bacon, 199n.11, 208
Fanelli, Giuseppe, 20
Fenón Moraida (Texas clergyman), 161, 201n.2
Ferguson, James E., 86, 97, 104, 107, 110, 121
Fernández, Amador, 75
Ferrer, Francisco, 21–22, 38; in *Regeneración* poster, 127. *See also* Modern Schools
Ferrigno, A. L., 187n.14
Ferrua, Piero, 180n.46
Fierros, Esteban, 144–47; recruiting of, 148
Figueroa, Anselmo, 15, 137, 180n.47, 181n.74
First International, disruption of, 20
Fletcher, Henry P., 167
Flooding, of Rio Grande, 72
Flores, Manuel, 187n.14
Flores, Tejano Feliciano, 104
Flores Magón, Enríque, 3, 4, 5, 7–8, 10, 13, 20, 72, 170, 206; arrest of, 33, 134; in Edendale, 128–29; imprisonment of, 8, 46, 137; in *Mother Earth*, 138–40, 159, 198n.68; threat of, 174; and Turner, 48; U.S. government vs., 134–35, 137–40, 197n.47; wounding of, 14, 26, 180n.46, 181n.9
Flores Magón, Jesús, 3; imprisonment of, 7; as Madero functionary, 33, 47; and *Regeneración*, 5
Flores Magón, Ricardo, 4–10, 12, 20, 72, 79, 180n.46; arrest of, 33, 36, 134; birth of, 3; border raiders cheered by, 126; and Carranza, 47, 52, 57, 197n.47; and Casa "defection," 113; charisma of, 5–6; Church opposed by, 5–6; cowardice imputed to, 39; credo of, 169; death of, 39, 169–70, 203n.62, 206; and Debs, 157; in Edendale, 128–29; imprisonment of, 4, 7, 8, 12, 14, 15, 38, 44, 46, 50, 137, 167–68, 174; intellectual tilt of, 7; L.A. trial of, 44; legacy of, 205–206, 209; Liberation Theology echoes

INDEX

of, 176; and Madero, 24, 25–31; Mexican pension refused by, 168; Moncaleano defense of, 135, 197n.54; Moncaleano dispute with, 135–37, 197n.56; and national pride, 155; as 1908 U.S. presidential campaign element, 16; and Obregón, 168, 170; philosophy of, 58, 84 (*see also* Flores Magón, Ricardo—credo of); and Pizaña, 88, 100, 126, 189n.46; as playwright, 129; PSD rejected by, 100, 126–27, 159; and *Regeneración*, 5, 7 (see also *Regeneración*); and [Juan] Sarabia, 33; sexual orientation of, 38–39; sterility of, 38–39; vs. Texas Rangers, 126; threat of, 174; and Turner, 48; U.S. government vs., 134–35, 137–40, 197n.47; and U.S. occupation of Mexico, 52; Villarreal condemned by, 38. *See also* Floresmagonistas; PLM (Mexican Liberal Party); *Regeneración*

Floresmagonistas, 9, 12; in Cananea, 11; *modus operandi* of, 8–9. *See also* PLM (Mexican Liberal Party)

Flynn, Elizabeth Gurley, 135

Focos, Floresmagonista/PLM, 9, 12, 14, 126, 179n.43

Follett, W. W., 72

Fort Bliss, Huerta imprisoned at, 115

Fox, J. M., 86, 87, 91, 207

Franklin, Benjamin, 138

Freedom (bulletin), 31

Free love, 38, 41

Freire, Paulo, 204n.9

Frémont, John C., 39

French Revolution, 93, 176

Fresnos Pump Canal, PSD raid on, 94

Frias Luis, 200n.58

Frick, Henry Clay, 7

Frost, Richard H., 202n.24

Funston, Frederick, 56, 86, 88, 92, 93, 105, 109, 110; Bielaski and, 145; civilian lawmen under, 97; Obregón and, 144, 145; after Ojo de Agua raid, 106; and Parker, 148; Veracruz occupied by, 51

Furlong Detective Agency, 9, 179n.26, 180n.51

Gaceta, La, 162

Gante, L. *See* Cárdenas Martínez, León

García, Cosmo, 73

Garcia, Jesús, 187n.46

Garra, Juan F., 133

Garrett, Alonso, 146

Garza, Agustín S., 80–83, 131, 132, 133, 164, 187n.14, 196n.31

Garza, Amado, 74

Garza, Antonio, 133

General strikes: by Casa, 155, 156; in France, 22

Germans, and south Texas violence, 96–97

Germany: and Huerta, 111, 112, 114; Kroptkin vs. WWI, 60; and Mexico, 111–12, 116–17, 141, 142–43, 152, 166, 173, 198n.8. *See also* Zimmermann Telegram

Gerson, Percival, T., 134

Ghosts (Ibsen), 20

Gillett, James, 35

Glasscock, D. W., 107–108, 121

Glenn Springs, Tex., 145, 149, 152, 200n.55

Godparents, Mexican/Anglo. See *Compadrazgo*

Goldman, Emma, 9, 28, 29, 36, 41, 134; arrest of, 135; and free love, 38; on Madero, 46; PLM assisted by, 60, 137, 140, 160; and Preparedness, 160; in San Diego, 43. See also *Mother Earth*

Gómez, Félix U., 150

Gómez-Quiñones, Juan, 208, 209

Gompers, Samuel, 9, 29, 180n.51; Carranza stroking of, 202n.22; Gutiérrez de Lara "conversion" of, 16; and *L.A. Times* disaster, 36, 37; and Mexican-American Joint Commission, 157; Mexico outreach of, 156, 157, 202n.16; R.F.M. and, 33–34. *See also* AFL (American Federation of Labor); PAFL (Pan American Federation of Labor)

González, A., 187n.14

González, Abraham, 47, 49

González, Benito, 133

González, Pablo, 48, 49, 53, 55, 118, 131, 132, 143, 149, 155, 163; Carranza and, 131; as Tampico defender, 113; and Zapata assassination, 168

González Ramírez, Manuel, 206

Gray, George, 157

Green, James R., 202n.20

Greene, William C., 10–12

Gregory, T. W., 161, 167, 189n.59, 202n.28

Gruening, Ernest, 206

"Grupo Juvenil Libertario, El," 137

Grupos: Floresmagonista, 9; PLM, 179n.43

Guadalupe, Mex., 27

Guadalupe-Hidalgo, Treaty of, 63

Guerra, Deodoro, 82–83, 188n.20

Guerra, Modesto, 83

Guerrero, Mex., 26, 142

Guerrero, Praxedis, 13–14, 18, 26, 73, 180n.46, 181nn.7,9; and Cárdenas, 127–28; death of, 26, 33, 45; and Rangel, 184n.42; in *Regeneración* poster, 21

Gutiérrez de Lara, Lázaro, 11, 12, 16, 29, 48, 134, 197n.50; in Chihuahua, 27; defection of, 27, 33; as Turner interpreter, 15

Haiti, U.S. and, 151
Harlingen, Tex., 65, 87, 88, 94
Harriman, Job, 14–15, 36, 37, 38, 130
Harris, Charles, 196n.32, 199n.12, 208
Harrison, Carter H., 3
Hart, John, 209
Haskell, Burnette G., 30–31
Haymarket, 3–4, 34, 40, 44, 107, 129, 160
Haywood, William, 17
Hearst, William R., 159
Hedda Gabler (Ibsen), 20
Henequen, Mexican, 15
Henninger, L. I., 103
Hernández, Julian, 133
Hernández, Pedro, 132, 197n.38
Herrero, Rodolfo, 168
Hidalgo (Mexican priest), 80
Hidalgo, Tex., 162
Hidalgo County, Tex.: changes in, 63–78; intermarriage in, 64; Mexicans of, 71, 109–10, 193n.46; plight of, 108. *See also* Donna; McAllen; Mercedes; Mission; Raymondville
Hill, Joe, 32
Hill, Lon C., 64, 108, 189n.45
Himno Nacional, 155
Hinojosa, Adela, 74
Hinojosa, Calixto, 74
Hinojosa, Hilario, 133
Hinojosa, Lucinda, 74
Hobsbawm, Eric, 208
Hondo, Tex., 131
Hook, T. Wesley, 161, 162, 201n.2
Hooks, T. J., 65
Horcasitas, Mex., 164
Horton Plaza (San Diego), 43
House of Tiles (Mexico City), 155
Huerta, Victoriano, 46–54, 80, 142, 171; ascension of, 71; Carranza vs., 48–50, 52–54, 57, 151; and Casa, 112; in exile, 111, 114; and land reform, 57; and Madero murder, 184n.10; vs. Orozco, 47; power seized by, 48, 165; resignation of, 54; "return" of, 115; Villa vs., 163, 170
Huitrón, Jacinto, 197n.54
Hulen, E. B., 87
Hunt, Lynn, 190n.70
Hutchings, Henry, 87, 89, 92, 108, 122, 180n.46

IBC (International Boundary Commission), 71
Ibsen, Henrik, 20, 21
Impotence, and sterility contrasted, 39
Indians: Canadian, 27; Mexican, 27, 56 (see also Yaqui Indians); PSD and U.S., 81
Industrial Workers of the World. *See* IWW
Inflation, in Carranza Mexico, 155, 156

Institutionalized Revolutionary Party (PRI), 171
Intermarriage, Mexican/Anglo, 64, 71, 75
International Anarchist Congress, 52
International Association of Bridge and Structural Iron Workers, 36, 182n.58
International Boundary Commission (IBC), 71
International Committees of the Mexican Liberal Party Junta, 31
International Workmen's Association (IWA), 30–31
Irrigation, of Rio Grande valley, 63–72
Ishii, Kikujiro, 173
IWA (International Workmen's Association), 30–31
IWW (Industrial Workers of the World), 43, 180n.47; and Baja California, 32, 173; founding of, 17; and PLM, 22, 27, 57, 84, 126, 135, 137, 173; publications of, 60; U.S. government vs., 167. *See also* Cline, Charlie; Rangel, Jesús; *Rebelde, El*

Jacales, reprisal burning of, 109
Japan, Mexico and, 152, 166, 173
Japanese: in Pizaña raiding party, 106; in PSD, 81, 143, 147, 198–99n.11, 204n.5; in Revolutionary Congress, 84
Jefferson, Thomas, 138
Jiménez, Mex., 12, 200n.55
Johnson, Jesse, 191n.99
Johnson, Richard J., 120
Joll, James, 175
Jones, Mary Harris ("Mother"), 37–38
Juárez, Benito, 4, 24, 57, 80
Juárez, Mex., 26, 27–28, 33, 47
Juárez family (of Los Indios, Tex.), 110
Justice, U.S. Department of, 126, 195n.5
Justicia, 174; essence of, 24–25

Katz, Friedrich, 198nn.8,11, 203n.48, 209
Kaufman, J. D., 134
Kaweah Colony, 31
King Ranch, 64, 76; De la Rosa vs., 89–90 (*See also* Norias, Tex.); counter-PSD precautions at, 98
Kingsville, Tex., 161
Kleberg, Caesar, 108, 121
Kleberg, Robert, 76
Kleberg family, 64, 65
Kleiber, John, 103
Knight, Alan, 209
Kotsch, Georgiana, 134
Kropotkin, Peter, 13, 18, 20, 29, 32, 58, 84, 171, 175; Owen and, 31; in *Regeneración* poster, 21, 22; as R.F.M. cynosure, 170; R.F.M. defended by, 40; on secret socie-

INDEX

ties, 22–23; sexual mores of, 38; and WWI, 60
Krumm-Heller, Arnoldo, 155, 201n.8
Kunimoto, Iyo I., 198n.11

Labor, Mexican: Carranza vs., 154–55, 156–57, 159, 164; PLM goals for, 10. *See also* Child labor; Strikes; Trade unions
La Jarrita, Mex., 145, 146, 147
Lampazos, Mex., 143
Land and Liberty, 52, 57
Land reform, Mexican, 57
Lane, Franklin, K., 157, 202n.36
Langham, Thomas, 209
Langhorne, George, 145
Lansing, Robert, 110, 116–17, 151, 153; Ishii and, 173
Lara, Blas, 128
Laredo, Tex., 8, 80, 85
Larralde, Carlos, 189n.46
La Toluca, Tex., 119–20
Lenin, N., 9, 23
León, Mex., 113, 114
Levenstein, Harvey A., 202n.16
Liberal Laws of Reform, 57
Liberal movement, Mexican, 4, 5, 7, 8. *See also* Floresmagonistas; PLM (Mexican Liberal Party); Program of the PLM
Liberation Theology, 175–77
Liberty cap, 93, 190n.70
Liberty on the Barricades (Delacroix), 21
Limón, José, 207, 210n.9
Lippi, F. F., 83, 84
Lira, Vicente, 148
López, Eugenio, 121, 122
López, Frank, 206
Lorenzo, Anselmo, 20, 22; in *Regeneración* poster, 127
Los Angeles, Calif.: "Brown Scare" in, 204n.6; R.F.M. welcomed to, 17; Socialists of, 14–15, 30 (*see also* Harriman, Job; Murray, John; Turner, John Kenneth)
Los Angeles Times, bombing of, 35–36, 37, 43, 44, 160
Los Indios, Tex., 110
Lott, Uriah, 64, 65
Louisiana, state of, 138
Ludlow, 138
Lutz, Harold, 188–89n.43
"Luz y Vida," 129, 137
Lyford, Tex., 87, 188n.38
Lynching, of Mexicans, 87

Llano Grande grant, 75

McAlister, Paul, 108–109
McAllen (Texas pioneer), 65

McAllen, Tex., 65, 82–83, 162
McCain, Eugene, 103
McGuire (Texas vigilante), 87, 88
McKinley, William, 7
MacLachlan, Collin, 209
McManigal, Ortie, 182n.58
McNamara brothers, 36, 37, 160, 182n.58, 206. *See also Los Angeles Times*, bombing of
McNeil Island, Wash., 44, 46, 50, 73, 137
Madero, Francisco, 9, 24–31, 41, 45, 54, 57, 80, 125, 135, 170, 205, 206; corruption surrounding, 46; imprisonment of, 25; murder of, 48, 151, 184n.10; Orozco and, 47, 111; and PLM, 33, 37–38; problems of, 46–48; R.F.M. and, 24–31; and Turner, 47–48; U.S. conception of, 49; victory of, 28, 37. *See also* Plan of San Luis Potosí
Magón. *See* Flores Magón
Magón, María. *See* Brousse de Talavera, María
Malatesta, Errico, 20, 40, 41, 60, 175; Kropotkin and, 60; sexual mores of, 38
Malato, Charles, 20, 22
Manifestos, PLM, 29–30, 34, 36–37
Mann, W. A., 146
Marseillaise, La, 155
Martínez, Edmundo, 202n.22
Martínez, George, 110
Martínez, Rafael, 119, 121
Marx, Karl, 6, 20
Marxism: and anarchism contrasted, 6–7; Liberation Theology and, 176
Matamoros (Tamaulipas), Mex., 57; antigringo press of, 190n.78; evacuation of, 149; free land near, 110; González pressure on, 53; as refugee point, 85, 86; siege of, 117; Treviño mission in, 119
Maximillian, emperor of Mexico, 80
Mendoza, Marcos, 196n.30
Mercedes, Tex., 65, 75, 92, 119
Mexicali, Mex., 27
Mexican-American Joint Commission, 157, 162–73, 202nn.36,38, 207, 208
Mexican Claims Commission, 207, 208, 210n.11
Mexican Liberal Party. *See* PLM
Mexican Revolt, The (Owen), 42
Mexican Revolution: Carranza "conclusion" of, 164; mandate of, 156; modern historians' assessment of, 209
Mexicans, Mexicans vs., 98–100
Mexico: Americans' holdings in, 156; anti-U.S. agitation in, 79, 89–90, 94, 106, 116, 190n.78 (see also *Demócrata, El*; Nafarrate, Emiliano P.); army privileges in, 4; under Díaz, 4–6; emigrants to U.S. from, 85; Ger-

man community of, 111; German investment in, 193n.53; labor unrest in, 10–12 (*see also* Cananea, Mex.); PLM in, 12 (*see also* Cananea, Mex.; Jiménez, Mex.); reform elements in, 24–26; *Regeneración* circulation in, 60; religious wars in, 5 (*see also* Roman Catholic Church, Mexican); U.S. invasion of, 51, 52. *See also* Cananea; Carranza, Venustiano; Carrizal; Chihuahua, state of; Coahuila, state of; Díaz, Porfirio; Ebano, El; González, Pablo; Huerta, Victoriano; Juárez, Benito; Juárez, Mex.; La Jarrita; Madero, Francisco; Matamoros (Tamaulipas); Mexico City; Monterrey; Nafarrate, Emiliano P.; Obregón, Alvaro; Orozco, Pascual; Ramos, Basilio; Ricaut, Alfredo; San Luis Potosí; Tampico; United States, and Mexico; Veracruz; Villa, Pancho; Zapata, Emiliano

Mexico City, Mex., 33, 155; R.F.M. burial in, 171; Zapata shrine in, 179n.41

Meyer, Michael C., 184n.10

Minck, Carlos, 128, 129

Mines, of Colorado, 138

Minimum wage, PLM for, 10

Minor, Robert, 158

Miranda, José, 204n.12

Mis exploraciones en América (Reclus), 181n.69

Mission, Tex., 75, 161

Moctezuma, 80

Modern Schools, 21–22, 84, 127; *Regeneración* and, 41

Monahan, Mike, 87

Moncaleano, Bianca, 135, 137

Moncaleano, Juan Francisco, 135–37, 197n.54, 201n.62; death of, 197n.56

Montejano, David, 208

Montemayor, José, 133

Monterrey, Mex.: Casa in, 132, 197n.42; anti-U.S. sentiment in, 152, 190n.78; De la Rosa designs on, 164; González pressure on, 53

Mooney, Tom, 160, 206

Mooney Case, The (Frost), 202n.24

Morelos, state of, 46

Morenci, Ariz., 13

Morin, José, 160–61

Morones, Luis, 156

Mosley, Jesse, 143, 198n.10

Most, Johann, 28

Mother Earth, 29, 60; Enrique Flores Magón in, 138–40, 159, 198n.68; U.S. suppression of, 135

Mott, John, 157

Mujer Moderna, 18

Muñoz, Adolfo, 87

Murguia, Francisco, 163–64, 168

Murillo, Gerardo, 156

Murray, John, 15, 130, 157; as informer, 180n.51, 202n.17

Nafarrate, Emiliano P., 83, 117–24, 131, 143, 144, 145, 149, 194n.76

Nagazaqui, J. N., 84

National Revolutionary Party (PNR), 171

Nechaev, Sergei, 9

Newman, A. D., 148

New Mexico, state of, 81. *See also* Columbus, N.M.

New Republic of Lower California, 32

New York Call, 29, 34, 158

Nicaragua, U.S. and, 151

Norias, Tex., 65, 90–93, 104

Norman Guidera, Lucile (Lucía), 38

Nuevo Laredo, Mex., 80, 122

Obregón, Alvaro, 48, 49, 54, 55, 112, 122, 155, 157, 163, 205; assassination of, 171; vs. Carranza, 168; vs. Huerta, 53; R.F.M. and, 168, 170; and Scott/Funston meeting, 144, 145; and Villa, 113, 114, 168, 170

Oil, Mexican, 107, 113, 120, 171. *See also* Tampico, Mex.

Ojinaga, Mex., 47

Ojo de Agua, Tex., 75, 94, 106

Oklahoma, state of, 18

O'Laughlin, Cal, 153

Onestini, María, 192n.21

Orizaba, Mex., 113

Orozco, Pascual, 26, 112, 115; Huerta and, 49, 114; at Juárez, 27; Madero and, 47, 111; murder of, 115; rebellion of, 47

Osgood, E. L., 196n.27

Osuna, Gregorio, 145, 146, 149

Otis, Harrison G., 35–36, 159

Owen, William C., 30–31, 39, 40, 46, 52, 59, 134; and Bakunin Institute, 57, 184n.41; and free love, 38; from L.A. to Hayward, 57; return to England of, 137; R.F.M. obituary by, 185n.51. See also *Land and Liberty*; *Regeneración*, Owen and

Pacific Press, 130

Pact of Torreón, 55

PAFL (Pan American Federation of Labor), 156, 157

Page, Walter Hines, 166

Paine, Tom, 138

Palofax, Mex., 143

Palomas, Mex., 14

Panama, U.S. and, 151

Pan American Federation of Labor (PAFL), 156, 157

Pani, Alberto, 157

Paris Commune, Mexico and, 41–42

INDEX

Parker, James, 148, 149, 162
Parral, Mex., 144, 150
Party of the Mexican Revolution (PRM), 171
Paulet, P. C., 129, 131
Peláez, Manuel, 113, 118
Peons: vs. Carranza, 56; plight of, 85; suffrage for, 116
Pershing, John J., 142, 144, 149, 151; recall of, 166; vs. Villa, 162, 163, 202n.38
Pesquiera, Roberto, 121
Pezzatt, Norberto, 146–47
Pierce, Frank C., 191n.99
Pinchon, Edgcumb, 134
Pinkerton detective agency, 179n.26
Pino Suárez, José, 48
Pío Araujo, Antonio de, 32, 46, 181n.74
Pizaña, Aniceto, 8, 72–73, 74, 82, 87, 91, 117, 121, 125, 142, 166, 174, 186n.30, 189nn.43, 45, 46, 58; arrest of, 131, 150; *El Demócrata* and, 119; imprisonment of, 132; as moderate, 81; Nafarrate and, 123; at Ojo de Agua, 106; and PSD, 88, 94–97, 100; and R.F.M., 88, 100, 126, 189n.46; as "social bandit," 208; at Tandy's Station, 104; U.S. vs., 110
Pizaña, Beatriz, 73
Pizaña, Cela, 73
Pizaña, Guadalupe, 73, 87, 88, 189n.43
Pizaña, Manuela, 73, 87, 88, 189nn.43,46
Pizaña, Praxedis, 73
Pizaña, Ramón, 88, 189n.43
Plan of Ayala, 50, 82, 207
Plan of Guadalupe, 48, 52, 54, 82, 117, 207; social welfare codicils to, 56–57, 184n.40
Plan of San Diego (PSD), 63, 79–100, 107, 205, 208; American radicals and, 158–59, 202n.20; Anglo reaction to, 85; birth of, 81; Carranza and, 90, 120–25, 131–33, 140, 144, 145, 149, 151, 154, 162, 166, 173, 196nn.32,33, 197n.37, 208; in Carranza-controlled press, 119; Constitutionalist support for, 113, 118, 121, 132, 164, 197n.38 (*see also* Plan of San Diego [PSD], Carranza and); death of, 172; *El Demócrata* and, 119; followers of, 125–40 (*see also* De la Rosa, Luis; Nafarrate, Emiliano P.; Pizaña, Aniceto; Ramos, Basilio); "Mexican-ness" of, 156; Mexican support for, 132–33; nature of, 81–82, 172; and PLM, 84, 126–27, 140, 147, 167, 174, 209; as remembered, 206–207, 209; resurgence of, 143–50, 153, 167, 199n.12; revisions to, 83, 84; R.F.M. rejection of, 100, 126–27, 159; significance of, 173, 175; U.S. and, 110, 127, 140, 141, 193n.49; U.S. blacks in, 204n.7; violence initiated by, 87, 88–89, 92–100, 105, 188nn.37, 38 (*see also* De la Rosa, Luis; Pizaña, Aniceto). *See also* De la Rosa, Luis; Nafarrate, Emiliano P.; Pizaña, Aniceto; Ramos, Basilio
Plan of San Luis Potosí, 25, 27, 82, 207
PLM (Mexican Liberal Party), 10, 125; American radicals' support of, 14–18; anarchist press vs., 39–40, 183n.79; vs. Antireelectionist Party, 25–26; in Brownsville, 72; at Cananea, 11, 179n.35; Carranza vs., 174; contributions of, 174; Debs rejection of, 157; grass-roots support of, 42–43; infiltration of, 180n.51; internationalist makeup of, 27; and IWW, 22, 27, 57, 84, 126, 135, 137, 173; Los Angeles trial of, 44; Madero persecution of, 29; manifestos of, 73, 175; Mexican activities of, 12–14 (*see also* Cananea); Moncaleano criticism of, 135–37; 1906 platform of, 205; press manipulation by, 119; propaganda of, 107 (*see also Regeneración*); and PSD, 84, 126–27, 140, 147, 167, 174, 209; and Rangel/Cline defense, 57; reformist program of, 82; as remembered, 209; repression of, 175; in San Diego, Tex., 80; in Tijuana, 32–33; U.S. government vs., 126–31, 133–35, 167, 197n.47; during WWI, 57–58 (*see also Regeneración*). *See also* Arriaga, Camilo; Flores Magón, Enríque; Flores Magón, Ricardo; Guerrero, Praxedis; "Grupo Juvenil Libertario, El"; Gutiérrez de Lara, Lázaro; "Luz y Vida"; Pío Araujo, Antonio de; Rangel, Jesús; *Regeneración*; Sarabia, Juan; Villarreal, Antonio
Pluma Roja, 135
PNR (National Revolutionary Party), 171
Poncé, Victoriano, 161
Poster(s): anarchism personified in *Regeneración*, 18–23, 40, 46, 60, 127; PSD, 107
Powers, Stephen, 76
Prat, José, 127, 196n.11
Prensa, La, 195n.3
Preparedness parades, 160
Presente, El, 195n.3
Press: anarchist, 60, 129, 135, 159 (*see also Regeneración*); anti-gringo Mexican, 190n.78 (*see also Demócrata, El*); Constitutionalist, 119 (*see also Demócrata, El*); of south Texas, 190n.66; suppression of U.S., 134–35, 167 (*see also Regeneración*, U.S. government vs.); U.S. Socialist, 60, 159; U.S. Spanish-language, 79
PRI (Institutionalized Revolutionary Party), 171
Priestley, Herbert I., 206
PRM (Party of the Mexican Revolution), 171
Program of the Mexican Liberal Party (PLM), 10

Proletariado Militante, El (Lorenzo), 181n.67
Property, Proudhon on, 23
Proudhon, Pierre-Joseph, 23
PSD. *See* Plan of San Diego
Puebla, Mex., 56
Pueblo, El (Lorenzo), 181n.67
Puerto Mexico, Mex., 51
Puntos Rojos (Guerrero), 13

Querétaro, Mex., 146, 165

Raat, Dirk, 179n.22, 209
Rabb, Frank, 108
Racism, PSD vs. U.S., 81, 83
Railroad, to south Texas, 64–65, 66. *See also* Saint Louis, Brownsville & Mexico Railroad
Ramos, Basilio, 80–83, 85, 114, 115, 131, 187nn.14,17,18, 188n.20; Nafarrate and, 123
Ranching, in Rio Grande valley, 64, 75
Rancho del Castillo, Tex., 73
Rangel, Jesús, 57, 79, 84, 100, 126, 128, 184n.42
Rangering. *See* Texas Rangers, brutality of
Ransom, H. L., 86, 103, 180n.46, 207; murders by, 104, 105, 191–92n.13
Raymondville, Tex., 87, 188n.38
Rebel, The, 202
Rebelde, El, 129, 130, 137
Reclus, Elisée, 20–21, 40, 41, 181n.69
Redención, 135
"Red Scare," WWI, 167
Reed, John, 116
Refugees, U.S.-based Mexican, 16
Regeneración, 7, 50, 107, 181n.9; and Cananea, 12; Carranza vs., 126; circulation of, 58–62, 128, 129–30, 185nn.49,51, 186n.29, 187n.47, 196n.26; contributions of, 174; defined, 179n.8; financial problems of, 159, 160, 167; first issue of, 5; L.A. headquarters of, 129; last issue of, 167; and Mexican self-perception, 156; Owen and, 30–31, 40, 46, 57, 59, 134, 137; Pío Araujo and, 46; Pizaña and, 88; popularity of, 10; as poster element, 21; protest coupons in, 128, 137, 196n.14; PSD influenced by, 84; and Rangel/Cline case, 79–80; *The Rebel* and, 202n.20; rebirth of, 9, 18, 100 (see also *Revolución*); Sanftleben and, 28; silencing of, 7, 8, 9, 58, 78, 167; in south Texas, 72–75, 77–78; [Ethel] Turner and, 28; in U.S., 9–10, 12; U.S. government vs., 33, 127, 128–31, 134–35, 160, 168, 197n.47 (see also *Regeneración*, silencing of); vs. U.S. Mexican intervention, 50, 52; Voltairine de Cleyre and, 41, 42. See also *Revolución*
Reitman, Ben, 43–45

Religion. *See* Liberation Theology; Roman Catholic Church, Mexican
Rendón, Victor, 152–53
Revindicación, 135
Revolt, 135
Revolución, 18
Reyes, Bernardo, 13
Reynosa, Mex., 86
Ricaut, Alfredo, 118, 121, 122, 123, 125, 132, 164; and Mann, 146; vs. PSD, 145–46, 148, 149, 150
Rice, of Tamaulipas, 72
Richmond, Douglas, 184n.40, 208
Rincones, Manuel, 90–91
Rintelen von Kleist, Franz, 111–12, 142
Rio Blanco, 138
Rio Bravo. *See* Rio Grande
Rio Grande, 63, 185n.2; illegal ferries across, 97; pumping station on, 66; U.S. troops entrenched along, 105
Rio Grande valley: evacuation of, 109–10; violence in (*see* Plan of San Diego [PSD], violence initiated by; Texas Rangers). *See also* Cameron County, Tex.; Hidalgo County, Tex.
Rio Hondo, Tex., 110
Rippy, J. Fred, 206
RIP-RIP. *See* Martínez, Rafael
Rivas, Cenovio, 98
Rivera, Librado, 167, 170, 181n.74, 203n.53; Mexican pension to, 168
Riveras, Nieves, 133
Rivolta, La, 130
Robelo, Ricardo, 114, 115
Robertson, Sam, 65, 108
Rocha, Rodolfo, 189n.46, 208
Rodríguez, Benito, 148
Rodríguez, Consuelo, 74
Rodríguez, Emilia, 74, 188n.18
Rodríguez, Juan Nepomuceno, 100
Rodríguez, Maurillio, 131, 132, 143, 145, 146, 147, 196n.31, 197n.34, 198-99n.11; arrest of, 144; Carranza and, 197n.34; imprisonment of, 131
Rodríguez, Pilar, 187–88n.18
Rogers, J. B., 110, 162, 186n.29, 189n.59, 207
Roman Catholic Church, Mexican, 4, 5; Guerrero vs., 13; PLM vs., 10, 36; Zapatistas and, 112
Romo, Ricardo, 204n.6
Roosevelt, Theodore, 11, 16
Ross, Howard Alsworth, 205
Ross, T., 199n.33
Rudolf, Tex., 65
Russell, Francis, 209n.5

INDEX

Russian Revolution, 167; anarchism and, 175
Rynning, Thomas, 11, 17

Sacco, Nicola, 206, 210n.5
Sadler, Louis, 196n.32, 199n.12, 208
Saenz, A. A., 80, 81, 187n.14
Saenz, Florencio, 75, 119–20
Saint Louis, Brownsville & Mexico Railroad—De la Rosa raid on, 101–103, 104, 117, 120, 121
Saint Louis, Mo., 9, 180n.51
Salinas, Ramón, 72
San Andrés, Mex., 26
San Antonio, Tex., 9, 115, 161, 195n.3
San Benito, Tex., 73, 98, 108, 148
San Benito Land and Irrigation Company, 65
Sanders, J. J., 86, 161, 207; vs. Hook, 161–62
San Diego, Calif., 32, 43
San Diego, Tex., 63, 80–81. *See also* Plan of San Diego (PSD)
Sandos, James A., 186n.29, 187n.17, 191n.93, 192n.21, 193n.66, 200n.34, 203n.48, 208, 210n.11; dissertation of, 210n.17
Sanftleben, Alfred, 28
Sanger, Margaret, 134
San Ignacio, Tex., 147, 148, 149
San José, Tex., 98
San Luis Potosí, Mex., 5–6. *See also* Plan of San Luis Potosí
Santa Isabel, Mex., 163
Santo Domingo, U.S. and, 151
Santos, Porfirio, 187n.14
Sarabia, Elizabeth. *See* Trowbridge, Elizabeth
Sarabia, Juan, 8, 10, 12, 14, 22, 180n.44; as Madero emissary, 33
Sarabia, Manuel (cousin of Juan Sarabia), 14, 47, 130; and *El Defensor del Pueblo*, 15; kidnapping of, 12, 15; marriage of, 16
Sarabia, Tomas (brother of Manuel Sarabia), 180n.44
Sarajevo (Bosnia), assassination at, 52
Satevo, Mex., 163
Schultz, Albert, 77
Schultz, Beda Franksen, 77, 88, 89
Schultz, Ruth, 77, 89
Scott, Hugh L., 144, 145, 150
Scrip, in Carranza Mexico, 155
Scrivner, John D., 87, 88, 189n.43
Sebastian, Tex., 77, 88–89
Sedition Act of 1918, U.S., 167
Shatz, Marshall, 183n.74
Shoaf, George, 34, 36, 37
Silliman, John R., 193n.50, 197n.37
Slavery, Díaz and, 15–16
Smuggling, across U.S.–Mexico border, 86
Snow, Sinclair, 180n.51

Socialism: and anarchism contrasted, 6; Owen rejection of, 34
Socialist League, 31
Socialists, U.S.: of Los Angeles, 14–15, 130–31, 134 (*see also* Harriman, Job; Murray, John; Trowbridge, Elizabeth; Turner, Ethel Duffy; Turner, John Kenneth); and PLM, 35 (*see also* Debs, Eugene V.); political offices of, 44. See also *Appeal to Reason*; Debs, Eugene V.
Soils, of Rio Grande valley, 63–64
Solidaridad Obrera, 127
Solidarity, 181n.1
Solis, Gregorio, 200n.55
Solis, Gumersindo, 75
Solis, Lazaro, 75
Solis, Simon, 146
Sommerfeld, Felix A., 111
Sonora, state of, 48
Soza, Concepción, 74
Soza, Ismael, 74
Soza, Manuela, 74
Spanish-American War, 79
Spanish Civil War, 175
Spanish Conquest, 80
Spears, Sam, 109
Special Rangers, 107, 108
Spengler, Louis A., 196n.27
Stallforth, Alberto, 111
Stallforth, Federico, 111
State, U.S. Department of, 51, 110
Steffens, Lincoln, 159
Sterling, William Warren, 191n.13
Stowe, Harriet Beecher, 16
Strike(s): at Cananea Copper, 11–12; Carranza banning of, 154, 157; Chicago police vs., 3. *See also* General strikes
Submarines, WWI German, 166
Sugarcane: of south Texas, 71; of Tamaulipas, 72
Syndicats, 22

Taft, William Howard, 16, 49, 52, 172, 173; border reinforced by, 29, 145; in Pizaña verse, 73; *Regeneración* readers' appeal to, 42–43; and Rynning, 17; tilt of, 50
Talavera, María. *See* Brousse de Talavera, María
Tamaulipas, state of, 71, 72. *See also* Matamoros; Nuevo Laredo; Reynoso
Tampico, Mex., 113–14, 133; U.S. "insulted" at, 51
Tandy's Station (Tex.), De la Rosa attack on, 101–103, 104, 117, 120, 121
Tannenbaum, Frank, 206
Tarrida del Marmol, Fernando, 20, 22, 40, 41, 181n.67

Taylor, Joe, 87, 188n.43
Tecate, Mex., 27
Telegram, Zimmermann. *See* Zimmermann Telegram
Temps Nouveaux, Les, 39
Terasawa, Fuku [taro; -matsu], 143, 144, 198–99n.11
Terrazas, Luis, 111
Terrorism: anarchism and, 7; Nechaev and, 9
Texas, state of: anti-U.S. agitation in, 106; emigrants to Mexico from, 94, 109–10; Mexican designs on, 79, 80 (*see also* Plan of San Diego [PSD]); Mexicans of, 18, 63, 72–78; radicalist ferment in, 62 (*see also* Plan of San Diego [PSD]; *Regeneración*, in south Texas); *Regeneración* circulation in, 60, 128; Spanish-language press of, 79. *See also* Boquillas; Brownsville; Cameron County; De la Rosa, Luis; El Paso; Ferguson, James E.; Glenn Springs; Harlingen; Hidalgo County; Laredo; McAllen; Mercedes; Mission; Norias; Ojo de Agua; Pizaña, Aniceto; Plan of San Diego (PSD); Rio Grande; Rio Grande valley; San Antonio; San Benito; San Diego, Tex.; San Ignacio; Sebastian; Tandy's Station; Texas Rangers
Texas and Pacific Railroad, 128
Texas Rangers, 86–87, 89–94, 98, 100, 105; brutality of, 89, 91–92, 109, 110, 115, 160, 161, 162, 201n.2, 207 (*see also* Fox, J. M.; Ransom, H. L.; Sanders, J. J.); official investigation of, 192n.13; after Tandy's Station raid, 103–104; Wilson pre-emption of, 202n.30. *See also* Special Rangers; Wallis, Henry
Thompson, Frank G., 134
Tiempo, El, 79, 82
Tierra y Libertad (newspaper), 129
Tierra y Libertad (R. Flores Magón), 129
Tijuana (Mex.), PLM seizure of, 27, 32, 39, 57, 173. *See also* New Republic of Lower California
Tompkins, Frank, 144, 150
Torreón, Mex., 52, 163, 164
Toyah, Tex., 128, 196n.13
Trade unions: forces opposed to U.S., 35; French (see *Syndicats*); Mexican, 155; *See also* AFL (American Federation of Labor)
Trading with the Enemy law of 1917, U.S., 167
Treason, U.S. dissent labeled, 205
Treviño, Jacinto B., 48, 114, 118, 132, 152, 153, 163, 197n.42, 201n.66; in Brownsville, 119; Murguía denunciation of, 164, 203n.40
Trippet, Oscar, 137, 138
Trowbridge, Elizabeth, 15, 16, 47, 130, 157

Tucson, Ariz., 15
Turner, Ethel Duffy, 15, 17, 26, 28, 29, 129, 130, 157, 180n.46
Turner, John Kenneth, 15–16, 17, 30, 34, 47–48; as arms smuggler, 27; Carranza endorsed by, 158; in Mexico, 15, 197n.50
Typhus, U.S. border precautions against, 86

Ubaqui, Inctlaca, 84
Uncle Tom's Cabin (Stowe), 16
Unión Liberal Humanidad, 11
Unions. *See* Trade unions
United States: Mexican lands appropriated by, 79; and Mexico, 49–54, 56, 63, 79, 110, 120, 156, 172; as WWI armorer, 111. *See also* Funston, Frederick; Lansing, Robert; Taft, William Howard; Texas, state of; Wilson, Woodrow
Urbina, Tomás, 114

Valle Nacional, 138
Vann, W. T., 97, 189n.55, 190n.85, 192n.13; after Tandy's Station raid, 103–104
Vanzetti, Bartolomeo, 206, 210n.5
Vargas family, 110
Vásquez Gómez, Francisco, 25
Vásquez Gómez brothers, 206
Veeni, P., 84
Vegetation, of Rio Grande valley, 63–64
Veracruz, Mex., 155; U.S. occupation of, 51–54, 56, 152
Via Libre (Lorenzo), 181n.67
Vigilantes: of San Diego, Calif., 43; Texas, 77, 87, 109 (*see also* Special Rangers)
Villa, Pancho (Doroteo Arango), 26, 48, 53, 149, 162, 202n.38; assassination of, 170; Casa rejection of, 112; Columbus, N.M., raid of, 140, 141, 155, 159, 205; in defeat, 193n.65; fading reputation of, 119; Huerta vs., 112; land reforms of, 57; Murguía vs., 163–64; Obregón and, 113, 114, 168, 170; vs. Orozco, 49; pasturing of, 168; Pershing pursuit of, 142, 144, 149–50, 152; R.F.M. vs., 52; and Sommerfeld, 111; vs. Tampico, 114; vs. Treviño, 163; U.S. and, 51, 52 (*see also* Villa, Pancho—Pershing pursuit of)
Villarreal (Constitutionalist officer), 146, 147
Villarreal, Andres, 82–83
Villarreal, Antonio, 12, 14, 18, 22, 133, 181n.7; defection of, 29, 33; R.F.M. savaged by, 38
Villarreal, Calixto, 133
Villarreal, Manuela, 75
Villarreal, Santos, 133
Villarreal González, Andrea, 18
Voluntad, 135
Vorwaerts, 183n.79

Wagner, May, 89
Walcker, J. Z., 83, 84
Wallis, Henry, 102–103, 105, 191n.9
Warner, David, 94
Warren, Fred, 16
Wayland, Julius, 44–45
Webb, Tex., 146, 148, 149
Webb, Walter, P., 210n.11
Webb County, Tex., 66, 69–70
Wells, James B. ("Jim"), 64, 65, 72, 74–77, 90, 98, 108, 119
Welshman, the (PLM activist), 27, 32
Weslaco, Tex., 75
Western Federation of Miners (WFM), 9, 12, 17
West Virginia, state of, 138
WFM (Western Federation of Miners), 9, 12, 17
Wilson, Woodrow, 44, 122, 173, 189n.59, 201n.2, 205; and Carranza, 107, 111, 117, 141, 145, 149–53, 154, 162, 166, 172, 173, 200n.42, 208; and Carrizal crisis, 165; Glasscock committee appeal to, 108; and Gompers, 156, 157; and Huerta, 49–52, 56, 114, 115; and Mexican-American Joint Commission, 157, 162–63; and Mexican border crisis, 71, 86, 110, 141–42, 145, 150–53, 159; and Mexican land reform, 58; *Regeneración* criticism of, 197n.47; and Texas Ranger outrages, 161; and U.S. arms embargo, 50–51; and Zimmermann Telegram, 166
Wobblies. *See* WWI (Industrial Workers of the World)
Wohlstand fur Alle, 183n.79

Woman Rebel, 135
Women: as anarchists, 129; in 1911 L.A. election, 182n.61; PLM and equality of, 36; in *Regeneración* poster, 19–20, 21; Anglo reprisals against Mexican, 98
"Workers International Defense League," 134
World War I: anarchists and, 60; German strategy in, 111; outbreak of, 52; Owen monitoring of, 57; U.S. entry into, 167, 205; U.S. radicals and, 160
Wright, Howard P., 161

Xochimilco, Mex., 56

Yaqui Indians, 82, 158; Díaz subjection of, 15–16
Yates (Cameron Co. judge), 107
Yoshida, Shunji, 143–44, 198n.11
Ypiranga (German steamer), 51
Yucatan, 138

Zamora, José, 73–74
Zapata, Emiliano, 13, 47, 112, 113; and Aguascalientes convention, 55; assassination of, 168; vs. Carranza, 56, 57, 112, 118, 157, 167, 170; Casa rejection of, 112; vs. Madero, 170; posthumous symbolism of, 170; PSD endorsement of, 84; radicalism of, 50; rebellion of, 46; R.F.M. and, 57; shrine to, 179n.41; Wilson and, 51. *See also* Plan of Ayala
Zaragosa, Ygnacio, 133
Zimmermann, Arthur, 166
Zimmermann Telegram, 167, 173, 203n.48, 205

WHITMAN COLLEGE LIBRARY

DATE DUE

GAYLORD PRINTED IN U.S.A.